THE WORLD OF EL CID

Manchester Medieval Sources Series

series advisers Rosemary Horrox and Janet L. Nelson

This series aims to meet a growing need amongst students and teachers of medieval history for translations of key sources that are directly usable in students' own work. It provides texts central to medieval studies courses and focuses upon the diverse cultural and social as well as political conditions that affected the functioning of all levels of medieval society. The basic premise of the series is that translations must be accompanied by sufficient introductory and explanatory material, and each volume, therefore, includes a comprehensive guide to the sources' interpretation, including discussion of critical linguistic problems and an assessment of the most recent research on the topics being covered.

already published in the series

J. A. Boyle *Genghis Khan: history of the world conqueror*

Trevor Dean *The towns of Italy in the later Middle Ages*

John Edwards *The Jews in Western Europe, 1400–1600*

Paul Fouracre and Richard A. Gerberding *Late Merovingian France*

P. J. P. Goldberg *Women in England, c. 1275–1525*

Janet Hamilton and Bernard Hamilton *Christian dualist heresies in the Byzantine world*
c. 650–c. 1450

Rosemary Horrox *The Black Death*

Graham A. Loud and Thomas Wiedemann *The history of the tyrants of Sicily by 'Hugo Falcandus', 1153–69*

R. N. Swanson *Catholic England: faith, religion and observance before the Reformation*

Elizabeth van Houts *The Normans in Europe*

Jennifer Ward *Women of the English nobility and gentry, 1066–1500*

forthcoming titles in the series will include

Mark Bailey *English manorial records, c. 1180–1520.*

Ross Balzaretti *North Italian histories, AD 800–1100*

Brenda Bolton *Innocent III*

Alison McHardy *The early reign of Richard II*

Edward Powell and Anthony Musson *Crime, law and society in late medieval England*

Ian Robinson *The Pontificate of Gregory VII*

THE WORLD OF EL CID

CHRONICLES OF THE SPANISH RECONQUEST

selected sources translated and annotated by
Simon Barton *and* Richard Fletcher

Manchester University Press
Manchester and New York

Published by Manchester University Press
Oxford Road, Manchester M13 9NR, UK
and Room 400, 175 Fifth Avenue, New York, NY 10010, USA
www.manchesteruniversitypress.co.uk

Distributed exclusively in the USA by
Palgrave, 175 Fifth Avenue, New York NY 10010, USA

Distributed exclusively in Canada by
UBC Press, University of British Columbia, 2029 West Mall,
Vancouver, BC, Canada V6T 1Z2

British Library Cataloguing-in-Publication Data
A catalogue record for this book is available from the British Library

Library of Congress Cataloging-in-Publication Data
A catalog record for this book is available from the Library of Congress

ISBN: 0 7190 5226 2 paperback

ISBN 13: 978 0 7190 5226 2

First published 2000 by Manchester University Press

First digital, on-demand edition produced by Lightning Source 2007

CONTENTS

LIST OF FIGURES

FOREWORD

Long relatively neglected by anglophone historians, the multiple histories of medieval Spain, thoroughly distinctive, post-Roman yet not wholly Latin-Christian, are now beginning to take their rightful places alongside other parts of Europe in the history of the Middle Ages. This welcome development has been due in large part to one of the authors of the present volume, Richard Fletcher, and has latterly been strongly assisted by the other, Simon Barton. Both with expert knowledge, on the historical as on the literary and Hispanist front, of the texts translated and commented upon here, these two scholars have joined forces to make available all the main narrative sources of eleventh-and twelfth-century Spain. This crucially important period, of cultural and social formation and flowering, of political conflict and crystallisation, has until now been fairly impenetrable for non-specialists. Visitors to León and Toledo, Burgos, Zaragoza and Valencia gain a vivid yet imprecise sense of the world of El Cid, negotiating his way between al-Andalus and the Christian north, and of successive Alfonsos ducking and weaving and battling their way to the creation of the medieval kingdoms of Castile and Aragon. Richard Fletcher and Simon Barton now make it possible for those without Latin to read the key texts, to understand their authors' backgrounds and purposes, to appreciate their specific literary and historical contexts, and to analyse the structures of power they reveal. Above all, since, as Marc Bloch wrote, 'it is men that history seeks to grasp', these two fine historians acquaint us with the characters (and they include a few women too) who throng the chroniclers' pages. We gain a familiarity, at once vivid and precise, with the nobles and ecclesiastics, kings and royal kin, whose journeyings and campaigns we follow, and whose religious and material concerns emerge so clearly in these pages. This is exactly the kind of historical material that Manchester Medieval Sources aim to make accessible, and with this splendid volume alongside John Edwards' earlier one, it is a particular delight to have Spain now deservedly well represented in the series.

Janet L. Nelson
King's College London.

PREFACE

The study of the medieval history of Spain in the English-speaking world has taken enormous strides over the last generation or so. In the mid-1960s, when the elder of these two collaborators embarked upon research for a doctorate, there were scarcely any reputable scholarly works to be had; by the year 2000 the list of them is ample and steadily growing. But the publication of surveys and monographs, of articles and editions, has not been matched – at least as regards the central medieval period between the tenth and thirteenth centuries – by comparable publication of extended translations from the original sources. It is in an attempt to take some modest steps towards redressing this imbalance that we have translated the four texts contained within this book. Together they constitute the principal narrative sources for Leonese–Castilian history in the century and a half between *c.* 1000 and *c.* 1150.

We have worked from the following editions:

1 *Historia Silense,* eds J. Pérez de Urbel and A. González Ruiz-Zorrilla (Madrid, 1959).
2 *Chronicon Regum Legionensium* by Bishop Pelayo of Oviedo, under the title *Crónica del Obispo Don Pelayo,* ed. B. Sánchez Alonso (Madrid, 1924).
3 *Historia Roderici vel Gesta Roderici Campidocti,* ed. E. Falque Rey, in *Chronica Hispana saeculi XII,* Corpus Christianorum, Continuatio Mediaevalis, vol. 71 (Turnhout, 1990), pp. 47–98.
4 *Chronica Adefonsi Imperatoris,* ed. A. Maya Sánchez, in the same volume of *Chronica Hispana saeculi XII,* pp. 149-248; together with the associated verses on the Almería campaign of 1147 edited in the same volume by J. Gil at pp. 255-67.

The introductions to these editions furnish details of the surviving manuscripts, previous editions and so forth. No English translation of any of these texts has been published before in its entirety. Brief extracts from 1, 3 and 4 have been translated in Colin Smith's *Christians and Moors in Spain,* vol. I (Warminster, 1988). Modern Spanish translations have been published as follows:

1 (a) M. Gómez-Moreno, *Introducción a la Historia Silense* (Madrid, 1921), pp. lxiii–cxxxvi.
   (b) J. E. Casariego, *Crónicas de los Reinos de Asturias y León* (Madrid, 1985), pp. 110–58.
2 Casariego, as above, pp. 172–81.
3 E. Falque Rey, 'Traducción de la *"Historia Roderici"*', *Boletín de la Institución Fernán González* 62 (1983), pp. 343–75.
4 M. Pérez González, *Crónica del Emperador Alfonso VII* (León, 1997).

We divided responsibility for the introductions, translations and notes between us, to Richard Fletcher falling the *Historia Silense* and the *Historia Roderici* and to Simon Barton the *Chronicon Regum Legionensium* and the *Chronica Adefonsi Imperatoris*. Each of us submitted his draft work to the other for criticism, on the understanding that absolute candour was required of the critic, absolute humility in the criticised. In the resultant shuffling of papers, the muted buzzings and pingings of faxes and emails, extending over some two years or more, we hope that we have improved upon our first hesitant drafts. To our surprise and pleasure we found that harmonious co-operation was never once threatened by even the suspicion of a cross word so much as meditated, let alone uttered. Of the ancillary portions of the work, to which we applied the same routines, Richard Fletcher drafted the general introduction, Simon Barton the bibliography, map and genealogical table.

We are indebted to many colleagues and friends to whom we have turned, and never in vain, for advice, help or information. Specifically we wish to put on record our gratitude to Martin Brett, Roger Collins, Emma Falque, Christopher Holdsworth, John Keegan, Peter Linehan, Raymond McCluskey, Marcelo Martínez Pastor, Maurilio Pérez González, Bernard Reilly, María José de Vega Alonso, Geoff West, John Williams, John Wreglesworth and Roger Wright. A special word of thanks is due to Jinty Nelson, the series adviser, both for her enthusiastic encouragement of our project and for her constructive critique of our efforts; also to Louise Edwards and Vanessa Graham and their colleagues at Manchester University Press in watching over the progress of this book from its outset to its completion.

The dedication is the expression of a different sort of debt. Barrie Dobson has been a colleague, mentor and friend of us both over many years. In dedicating this book to him in the year of his retirement we register our gratitude.

Simon Barton
Richard Fletcher

LIST OF ABBREVIATIONS

AHDE	*Anuario de Historia del Derecho Español*
AHN	Archivo Histórico Nacional, Madrid
BN	Biblioteca Nacional, Madrid
BRAH	*Boletín de la Real Academia de la Historia*
CAI	*Chronica Adefonsi Imperatoris*
CCCM	*Corpus Christianorum, Continuatio Mediaevalis* (Turnhout)
CD Fernando I	*Colección diplomática de Fernando I (1037–1065)*, ed. P. Blanco Lozano (León, 1987).
CHE	*Cuadernos de Historia de España*
ES	E. Flórez, M. Risco *et al.*, *España Sagrada*, 51 vols (Madrid, 1747–1879).
HC	*Historia Compostellana*, ed. E. Falque Rey, *CCCM* 70 (Turnhout, 1988).
HR	*Historia Roderici*
HS	*Historia Silense*
JL	*Regesta Pontificum Romanorum ad annum 1198*, ed. P. Jaffé, revised S. Loewenfeld, *et al.*, 2 vols (Leipzig, 1885).
JMH	*Journal of Medieval History*
PA	*Poem of Almería*
PL	*Patrologia cursus completus. Series Latina*, ed. J.-P. Migne, 217 vols (Paris, 1844–64).
RMP	R. Menéndez Pidal, *La España del Cid*, 2 vols (7th edn., Madrid, 1969).

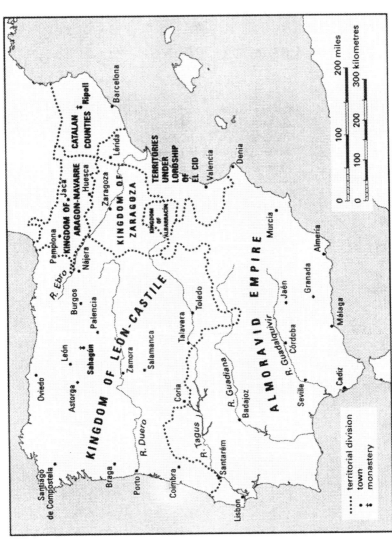

1 The Iberian peninsula at the death of El Cid, 1099

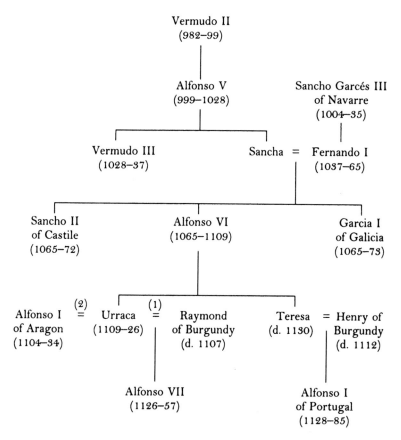

2 Genealogical table of the Leonese–Castilian royal house

To Barrie Dobson

GENERAL INTRODUCTION

The Visigothic monarchy of Spain which flourished in the seventh and eighth centuries was the most sophisticated of the misleadingly so-called barbarian successor states which replaced the Roman Empire in western Europe. It was sophisticated in its grasp of the institutional inheritance from Rome, in its nurturing of the wealth of the rich provinces of the Iberian peninsula and in its encouragement of a lively Christian literary and artistic culture. Later generations would look back nostalgically to the revered figures of the seventh-century golden age: godly lawgiving kings like Sisebut and Wamba, towering giants of Christian learning like St Isidore of Seville and St Julian of Toledo, the devout prelates who attended the long series of ecclesiastical councils of Toledo and elaborated the splendid liturgy of the Visigothic Church. This cultural achievement was shattered and dispersed by the Islamic conquest of Spain in the early years of the eighth century.

'Islamic conquest' is shorthand. The conquerors were led by Arab Muslims, but their rank-and-file were Berbers from north-west Africa, recently subdued with great difficulty by the Arabs and as yet, little touched by Islamic teaching. The Christians who were vanquished did not regard the conquerors as the adherents of a new religious faith but as heretics, deviants from Christian orthodoxy. That the Visigothic state could be destroyed as the result of a single defeat in pitched battle may be seen as paradoxical tribute to the very effectiveness of its monarchy. But Christian Spanish society continued to function, albeit under more-or-less severe dislocation in the course of the eighth century, under the new masters. It was only very gradually that a distinctively Islamic society came into being in what the Arabs called al-Andalus, by which they meant that large part of the Iberian peninsula under Islamic rule. The Berbers became more Islamicised. Some indigenous Christians started to drift across the religious divide and embrace the faith of Islam. Others abandoned their homeland and departed to make new lives for themselves under Christian rulers elsewhere.

Some of these refugees sought asylum in distant places beyond the Pyrenees. Others remained within the peninsula, finding refuge on its northern fringes. Up in the north-west, from the Basque country of the western Pyrenees along the Cantabrian coast to Galicia and the Atlantic, the Arab hold had been uncertain, even reluctant. The area was ecologically unappealing to them: distant, mountainous, cold, wet, a waste land where camels ailed and no dates grew; it was not worth the striving for. The rulers of al-Andalus accordingly withdrew their northern frontier to the line of the River Duero, which they fortified with a network of strongpoints. To the north of that line there grew up in circumstances of some obscurity a Christian mini-principality, initially clustered about the royal residence at Oviedo in the Asturias, later expanding to the east and west, and then spilling southwards over the Cantabrian mountains into the valleys of the northern affluents of the Duero and finding a new focus and centre, early in the tenth century, at the town of León. It is with the activities of the kings of León that three out of the four narratives in this volume are principally concerned.

León was not the only Christian principality in early medieval Spain. In the western Pyrenees a kingdom of Pamplona, later to be known as Navarre, emerged in desperately obscure circumstances in the ninth century. An eastern subdivision of Navarre, taking its name from the River Aragón in whose headwaters it had its nucleus, would be con-stituted a separate kingdom in the eleventh century. Further to the east, in Catalonia, the Frankish aristocracies of southern Gaul set up frontier lordships, collectively known as the 'Spanish March' (or 'Frontier'), in a kaleidoscope of eastern Pyrenean counties – of Urgell, Conflent, Cerdanya, Besalú, Empúries, Girona and Osona (to name only the most important) which, bit by bit, would be amalgamated into a single county of Barcelona. The authors of the works translated here were not much concerned with Navarre or Aragon or the Catalan counties. A partial exception must be made for one of them, the anonymous author of the *Historia Roderici*, whose hero, Rodrigo Díaz (better remembered as *El Cid*), spent much of his turbulent career fighting in eastern Spain and had dealings with both the kings of Aragon and the counts of Barcelona.

Rodrigo was a native of Castilla, or Castile. This region was the south-eastern frontier province of the kingdom of León, taking its name from the *castella*, the castles which defended it from Andalusi raids. Restive under Leonese control, the counts achieved a *de facto* independence in the course of the tenth century, and Castile was constituted a kingdom in the eleventh. The confusing shifts of relation-ship between the kingdoms of León and Castile need no further comment here: we hope that a tortuous path is adequately signposted in our notes. What needs emphasis here is that the ruling élites of León consistently thought of themselves as the primary political authorities in Christian Spain, heirs to the unitary monarchy wielded by the kings of the Visigoths back in the seventh century.

The Muslim rulers of al-Andalus – *amirs* until 929 when they took the spiritual title of *caliph* or 'successor' (to the Prophet) – had laboriously constructed an impressive centralised state, governed from Córdoba, which was at the peak of its power and renown in the tenth century. If, in retrospect, the Caliphate of Córdoba looks a little less stable than some of its historians have claimed, this was not visible to contemporaries. It loomed over the kingdom of León much as Constantinople at the same epoch loomed over the principality of Kiev. Relations between the two ill-matched neighbours were not invariably hostile but could easily become so. This happened during the last twenty years of the tenth century. The Caliph of the day had been effectively sidelined by his first minister, the *vizir* known to Christian chroniclers as Almanzor, from his honorific title *al-Manṣūr*, 'the Victorious'. Between 981 and his death in 1002, Almanzor struck repeatedly at the principalities of the Christian north in a series of campaigns which left a scarred memory in the collective consciousness of their inhabitants: their impact can be felt in Bishop Pelayo's *Chronicle of the Kings of León* and in the *Historia Silense*. Shortly afterwards, however, the terms of Leonese–Andalusi relations were entirely reversed. For reasons which are not wholly understood, the Caliphate of Córdoba lapsed into civil war and fragmented. By 1031 it had been replaced by a score of petty principalities, typically based upon a city and its surrounding territory, known to historians as the *Taifa* states (from an Arabic word meaning 'party' or 'faction') or simply the *Taifas*. The kings of León, notably Fernando I (1037–65) and his son Alfonso VI (1065–1109) became skilful in exploiting and manipulating the factious rulers of the Taifas. They operated what Angus MacKay has called 'a protection racket', offering their services as military 'protectors' in return for payment, normally in gold but sometimes in other forms such, for example, as the mortal remains of St Isidore, whose relics were 'translated' from Seville to León in 1063 as related at length in the *Historia Silense*. These payments of tribute were known as *parias*. There were opportunities here too for the royal henchmen, the nobilities of León and Castile, to profit by playing the same system, and indeed for freelance operators to break away from royal service and to run their own rackets. The most famous of these men was Rodrigo Díaz, *El Cid*, whose astonishing exploits were narrated by the anonymous author of the *Historia Roderici.*

Christian rulers in eleventh-century Spain in general preferred tribute and plunder to gains in land. Some historians have claimed that they were, and had been since the eighth century, imbued with the zeal for *Reconquista*, 'reconquest', the all-consuming imperative of repossessing the homeland for Christian Spaniards. The claim has played a significant part in the Spanish national mythology. The truth would seem to be rather less straightforward. It is reasonably clear that from at least the latter part of the ninth century Asturo-Leonese ruling circles cherished ideas of continuity with the Visigothic past and, at any rate, from time to time dreamed of a restored Christian order which would supersede the alien Islamic presence. It is also indisputable that slow territorial expansion did take place: by the eleventh century the southern frontier of the kingdom of León lay along – very roughly speaking – the valley of the Duero; the no man's land separating Muslim and Christian had shifted to the south. But it would be imprudent to connect expansion with ideology alone. There were less exalted impulses at work. One of these was demographic. The mountainous north was probably densely populated in the early medieval period – in Catalonia, where records have survived in great abundance, it is demonstrable that the Pyrenean valleys were far more thickly settled a thousand years ago than they are today. The pressure of humans upon resources was a powerful stimulus to expansion, as was farming practice. Pastoralism played an important part in the Leonese economy. Surviving documents from the tenth and eleventh centuries reveal big herds of cattle, sheep and goats, and sizeable stud-farms for the stockmen and their lords. Ample pastures were needed. So too were armed men to patrol them and to garrison the strongpoints where a refuge could be found when Almanzor's cavalry was sighted. Eleventh-century León was an expanding kingdom, a frontier society imbued with a militant code of conduct; but that is not quite the same as being wholly animated by an ideal of reconquest.

Of course, some territorial adventures had a special resonance. In 1085 Alfonso VI captured Toledo. The diplomatic background to this was the king's ever-closer involvement, as protector, in the affairs of the unstable Taifa principality of Toledo. Eventually it made more sense to take over the principality than to go on trying to shore up a feckless ruler. But Toledo was no ordinary city: capital of the

Visigothic monarchy, seat of the Primate of the Spanish Church, where Isidore and Julian had sat in council and where the visible monuments of that golden age were a constant reminder of past glory – the gain of Toledo was the most resounding blow for Christendom yet struck in the century which was to close with the even more resounding capture of Antioch and Jerusalem by the armies of the First Crusade. And it was not only in Christian ears that it resounded. The remaining Taifa rulers were scared out of their wits. In their panic they sought help from Morocco and in doing so, signed their own death warrant.

In the middle years of the eleventh century a movement of what today would be styled Islamic fundamentalism had taken root in Morocco. The Almoravids were a sect of austere, unflinching Islamic rigour. Their armies crossed the Straits in 1086 to answer the appeal of their co-religionists and did indeed inflict a heavy defeat upon Alfonso VI at Sagrajas, near Badajoz, and went on to threaten his possession of Toledo. But they were also shocked by what they saw as the religious backslidings of their Taifa hosts. Shortly afterwards the Almoravid leaders turned upon the Taifa rulers and deposed them one by one. By 1095 all the Taifa states of southern and central Spain – the exceptions were Zaragoza and Albarracín in the north-east – had been taken over by the Almoravids. Al-Andalus was once more united, as in the great days of the Caliphate of Córdoba.

The early twelfth century was a time of peril for the Leonese, as the Almoravids kept up their pressure upon Toledo and the Tagus valley. Alfonso VI's empire seemed about to crumble, as the Aragonese seized eastern Castile and the county of Portugal began the drift towards independent statehood which would be realised a generation later when its count assumed the title of king. The author of the *Historia Silense* was a troubled man who wrote for an anxious generation, and the early chapters of Book II of the *Chronicle of the Emperor Alfonso* are witness to the strains of life in Toledo under siege. Clerical contemporaries blamed the sins of the people, of course, for provoking the wrath of God into visiting another Almanzor-like scourge upon them. They also had it in for their ruler, Queen Urraca (1109–26), daughter of the son-less Alfonso VI, who has had a bad press from nearly every historian of her reign until quite recently; a woman who in fact – and like some other twelfth-century queens – did her best in exceptionally difficult circumstances and nursed her kingdom through the worst testing it had had to face for over a century.

It is easier for us than it was for contemporaries to see that the Almoravids were, or at any rate rapidly became, paper tigers. The Almoravid empire was a mushroom-in-the-night Berber creation which quickly lost its impetus, after a pattern which Ibn Khaldūn would delineate two centuries later. The leadership quickly shed its idealism, and in Spain became just a corrupt colonial regime. Within a generation Almoravid rule there began to unravel, the process assisted by widespread revolts which were encouraged by opportunistic Christian rulers. Once more, al-Andalus started to fragment into its component parts, the so-called Second Taifas.

This was the background to the exploits of Urraca's son Alfonso VII (1126–57), the first two-thirds of whose reign were vividly recorded by the author of the *Chronicle the Emperor Alfonso*. Briefly, after establishing his authority within his realm, Alfonso followed in the footsteps of his grandfather and embarked upon a mixture of tribute-taking and territorial expansion which culminated, for our author, in his conquest of the Mediterranean port of Almería in 1147. But there was a novel ingredient in the wars of Alfonso VII. The Almería campaign was contemporaneous with the Second Crusade and perceived as a crusade by, among others, the author of the *Poem of Almería*. Little by little, an ideological edge which would have seemed foreign to Alfonso VI or the Cid had sharpened the encounter between Christian and Muslim in Spain. At the time of writing the emperor's chronicler did not know that Almería would fall back into Muslim hands a mere ten years later, recaptured by yet another sect of Moroccan fundamentalists, the Almohads (who make, indeed, some brief appearances in his pages). But that story lies beyond our scope.

The century that elapsed between the latter years of Fernando I and the death of his great-grandson Alfonso VII saw far-reaching changes in the Leonese kingdom: unprecedented territorial expansion; unprecedented peril. It also saw entirely novel developments in León's relationship with the world of western Christendom beyond the Pyrenees. Though never entirely insulated from the rest of Europe – the tomb of St James at Compostela being alone sufficient to ensure a regular stream of foreign visitors – the kingdom of León had had little contact with the extra-Pyrenean world in the ninth and tenth centuries. From the middle years of the eleventh century, immigrants, especially from France, began to make their way to Spain in considerable numbers – royal brides and their households, Cluniac monks, secular clergy, architects and craftsmen, aristocratic adventurers, farmers, businessmen, artisans and mercenary soldiers. At the same time, the reforming popes of the Hildebrandine age were turning their attention upon Spain for the first time and finding much about its Christian observance which did not fit with their notions of seemly standard-isation. They used the incoming French clergy, alongside their own legates, as agents of change. A good example is Bernard de Sédirac, native of the Agenais in south-western France, monk of Cluny, abbot of the Leonese monastery of Sahagún (a dependency of Cluny) and as archbishop of Toledo from 1086 until 1124 the most influential figure in the modernising of the Church in Spain. The reformers changed much that native Spaniards had cherished: they swept away Spain's ancient liturgy; they forced Spaniards to learn to write with a new script – and the change from 'Visigothic' script to that called *francesa* (i.e. 'French' writing) is one with some implications for the dating of two of the works here translated; they introduced a new canon law. They may have introduced many other new books as well. It is likely, though unprovable, that Einhard's *Life of Charlemagne*, so significant an influence upon the author of the *Historia Silense*, found its way to Spain at this epoch.

These cultural changes were stressful. It may not be wholly implausible to associate with these stresses the remarkable upsurge in historio-graphical activity during this age. The Leonese tradition of historical writing was feeble. A chronicle attributed to the Asturian king Alfonso III (866–910), surviving in several different versions, provided an outline of the doings of the kings from the accession of Wamba in 672 to that of Alfonso III himself in 866 (thus grafting the Asturo-Leonese monarchy onto the stock of the Visigothic). A continuation of this was composed, perhaps by the royal notary and subsequent bishop of Astorga (1035–41), Sampiro, which carried the same story down to the death of Ramiro III in 985 (possibly to that of Vermudo II in 999). And that, apart from a few jejune king-lists and annals, is all that we have from the leading Christian kingdom in Spain from a period of some four centuries. If the dates that will be proposed for the four works translated here are found persuasive, these varied histories were all composed within little more than a single generation: the (arguably) earliest, the *Historia Silense*, not before 1109; the (almost certainly) latest, the *Chronicle of the Emperor Alfonso*, in about 1150. Neither are these four the only historical works from this period. To them we should add the *Historia Compostellana*, the first part of the anonymous *Chronicle of Sahagún*, and perhaps the early

Portuguese annals. (There are in addition works concerning Iberian affairs written by foreigners, for example the English *De Expugnatione Lyxbonensi* and Caffaro of Genoa's *De Captione Almerie et Tortuose.*) It is further to be remarked that the four works translated here differ markedly from one another. And while Pelayo's *Chronicle* is in the same genre as the *Chronicle of Alfonso III* and the *Chronicle* of Sampiro, and may indeed have been conceived as a continuation of the latter, the others strike out in different literary directions. Even when most indebted to literary models, as in the case of the *Historia Silense*, they are not slavish imitations but, albeit in a modest way, genuinely original and experimentative. Furthermore, they had no immediate successors. Leonese narrative history remained absolutely mute from *c.* 1150 until the composition of Lucas of Tuy's *Chronicon Mundi* nearly a century later. The works translated here, varied as they are, stand together as witnesses to a distinct and creative phase of medieval Spanish historical writing.

Further Reading

This introduction is intended as the most basic form of orientation for the newcomer to medieval Spain. For more detail, recourse may be had to the following, listed in order of ascent from the simple to the more complicated.

R. Fletcher, 'The Early Middle Ages' in R. Carr (ed.), *Spain: a History* (Oxford, 2000), 48–68.

S. Barton, 'Spain in the Eleventh Century' in D. Luscombe and J. Riley-Smith (eds), *The New Cambridge Medieval History IV* (Cambridge, forthcoming).

A. MacKay, *Spain in the Middle Ages: from Frontier to Empire 1000–1500* (London, 1977).

D. W. Lomax, *The Reconquest of Spain* (London, 1978).

B. F. Reilly, *The Contest of Christian and Muslim Spain 1031–1157* (Oxford, 1992).

I: *HISTORIA SILENSE*

Introduction to the *Historia Silense*

This is a deeply problematic text. *Historia Silense* (henceforward *HS*) is the misleading name given to a composite historical miscellany whose main claim upon the attention of historians has been that it includes our principal narrative account of the Leonese monarchy between 1037 and 1072. Its interest extends well beyond this, as will emerge in due course. The work owes the title by which it is conventionally known to a supposed origin at the Castilian monastery of Silos. This attribution was defended tenaciously by the work's most recent editor, the late Dom Justo Pérez de Urbel, himself a monk of Silos for almost seventy years of a long life and one of her most loyal sons.[1] There are, however, few things to be said in its favour, but plentiful indications of an origin elsewhere. To lay my cards on the table at the outset, I shall suggest – as others have done before – that there is a strong probability that the work was composed by a member of the religious community of San Isidoro in the city of León, at a date certainly after 1109 and probably before 1118.

All those who have studied it are agreed that the text of the *HS* as it has come down to us is desperately corrupt. The earliest surviving manuscript (Madrid, Biblioteca Nacional 1181) is of the latter half of the fifteenth century and appears to be at least two removes from a presumed original. A glance at the notes to the translation which follows will show how frequently, if reluctantly, the translator has had to resort to emendation of the Latin text in an attempt to make sense of it. The principal editions of the work are not flawless, which further complicates the translator's task. It has also to be said that the author's literary tastes and pretensions, of which more below, constitute a further obstacle to ease of understanding.

1 *Historia Silense. Edición crítica e introducción*, eds J. Pérez de Urbel and A. González Ruiz-Zorrilla (Madrid, 1959) at pp. 68–77. The introduction which follows shares its theme with an earlier paper: see Fletcher, 'A Twelfth-century View of the Spanish Past' published in *The Medieval State. Essays presented to James Campbell*, edited by J. R. Maddicott and D. M. Palliser (London, 2000) pp. 147–61: although there is a considerable degree of overlap between the two pieces they are intended to complement, rather than to duplicate, one another.

Fortunately for us, the author made his intentions unambiguously plain in chapter 7. He proposed 'to write of the deeds of the lord Alfonso, the orthodox emperor of Spain', that is, Alfonso VI (1065–1109). Unfortunately he never completed his task, thus denying to historians a *Gesta Adefonsi* to set alongside other eleventh-century royal biographies such as Wipo's *Gesta Chuonradi*, the anonymous *Vita Ædwardi Regis* or the *Gesta Guillelmi* of William of Poitiers. The *HS* is no more than the lengthy preamble to a work which was apparently never written.

Because the *HS* is too long to be translated for this volume in its entirety, it is appropriate to begin by briefly sketching the outline of the entire work, so that the reader can grasp the overall structure. In doing so I follow Pérez de Urbel's somewhat puzzling chapter-numbering. Chapters 1–6 contain introductory materials on the Visigothic monarchy of Spain, embedded in which lies the enunciation of themes which will be sounded more strongly later on. In chapter 7 (as we have seen) the writer stated his intention of commemorating Alfonso VI; he also offered some cryptic information about himself, with which we shall have to wrestle presently. Chapters 8–13 furnish a guarded narrative of the strife between Alfonso and his brothers Sancho II of Castile and García of Galicia which occupied the years 1065–72 and close with a forward look to the death and burial of García in 1090. The author closed chapter 13 with an announcement of the need to 'unravel the kingdom's origin'. This 'unravelling', which takes up about two-thirds of the entire work, is accomplished by the insertion into the text of three blocks of narrative (which are omitted from the present translation). These are:

1   The *Chronicle of Alfonso III*, a narrative of the deeds of the Christian rulers from the Visigothic king Wittiza (d. 710) to the Asturian king Ordoño I (d. 866), composed under the inspiration of the latter's son Alfonso III (866–910), perhaps even by him.[2] This occupies chapters 14–38 inclusive of the *HS*. The text is differentiated from other recensions of the *Chronicle* by numerous small verbal variants and interpolations whose character is such as to identify the editorial hand of the author of the *HS* (as we shall see in due course).

---

2 An English translation of this work is to be found in K. B. Wolf, *Conquerors and Chroniclers of Early Medieval Spain* (Translated Texts for Historians, vol, 9: Liverpool, 1990), pp. 159–77.

2   A *Continuation* of the preceding work which narrates the deeds of
    Alfonso III and his sons García (910–913/14) and Ordoño II
    (913/14–924). This runs from chapter 39 of the *HS* to chapter 47,
    where it breaks off in the middle of a sentence. There is no
    consensus as to whether this was the composition of the author of
    the *HS* or an editorial insertion by him: a knotty problem which
    is not relevant to our concerns here.[3]

3   The *Chronicle of Sampiro*, a narrative of the reigns of the kings of
    Asturias and León from the accession of Alfonso III in 866 down
    to the reign of Alfonso V (999–1027), attributed to Sampiro,
    notary, courtier and towards the end of a long life, briefly bishop
    of Astorga (1034–6). In Pérez de Urbel's edition of the *HS*
    Sampiro's narrative is, confusingly, given a separate enumeration
    of chapters (1–30), matching the chapter divisions proposed by
    the same scholar in the edition of Sampiro which he had published
    seven years earlier.[4] There are discrepancies between texts 2 and 3
    in their treatment of the years between 866 and 924. Furthermore,
    there are no interpolations into Sampiro's text characteristic of
    the authorial tastes and habits of the writer of the *HS*. These two
    considerations have led to the suggestion that Sampiro's work
    either came late to the knowledge of the author of the *HS* or was
    inserted into his text by a later hand: another knotty problem. I
    am not persuaded that the final chapter (30) of Sampiro was
    wholly and exclusively the work of that chronicler and believe
    that its text shows traces of the editorial attention of the author
    of the *HS*. Accordingly, that chapter *is* included in the present
    translation, re-numbered as chapter 30*.

In the wake of these three inserted narratives the author resumed his
own account in or after chapter 30* with a chapter numbered 69 by
Pérez de Urbel (it is not clear why). Chapters 69–79 narrate the
history of the Leonese kings between 956 and 1037, with a diversion
on the early history of Navarre in chapter 74. The final section of the
work, chapters 80–106, offers a fairly detailed account of the reign of
King Fernando I (1037–65), the father of Alfonso VI. Into this narrative is inserted at chapters 96–102 the text of the *Translatio Sancti*

---

3 Inconclusively discussed by C. Sánchez-Albornoz, 'El anónimo continuador de
   Alfonso III' in his *Investigaciones sobre historiografía hispana medieval (siglos VIII al
   XII)* (Buenos Aires, 1967), pp. 217–23.

4 J. Pérez de Urbel, *Sampiro: su crónica y la monarquía leonesa en el siglo X* (Madrid,
   1952): the cronicle is edited at pp. 275–346.

Isidori, an account of the movement of Isidore's relics from Seville to
León in 1063, with some distinguishing editorial changes.[5] It is
possible that the author also drew, for much of chapters 105 and 106,
upon a contemporary account of Fernando's last days which has not
survived independently. The *HS* closes with the obsequies of Fernando I on 2 January 1066. The author could now have turned to the
deeds of his son Alfonso VI. If ever he did so, the text has not come
down to us. But I suspect that, for reasons about which we can only
speculate, he never committed his *Gesta Adefonsi* to writing.

The author did his work after 1109, the year of Alfonso's death, because
he tells us in chapter 7 that 'the whole length of his fragile life has
been run'. In chapter 13 he informs us that Cardinal Rainerius 'who
later became pope' was in León as papal legate and holding a church
council there at the time of the death of Alfonso's brother García in
1090. Rainerius became pope as Paschal II in 1099 and died in
January 1118. There is no hint in the *HS* that he was anything but
still alive. This does not prove that composition occurred before 1118,
but it certainly suggests it. All recent commentators accept this
dating more or less cautiously.

Two misreadings might suggest that the lost autograph of the *HS*
was written in Visigothic script, and this too would point to an early
date in the twelfth century. In chapter 8 the word *perlabor* was misread
as *profabor* and in chapter 13 *dolore* was read as *dolose*. Abbreviations
and letter-forms in Visigothic script were such that copyists unfamiliar
with it frequently misread *per-* as *pro-* and confused *l* with *f*, *r* with *s*
(the latter with especial frequency). It would be unwise to make too
much of this point, given the manifold corruptions of the text, but it
might be allowed a little weight.[6]

We offer, accordingly, as a working hypothesis that the author was
writing between 1109 and 1118. Where did he do his work ? In a
tantalising sentence in chapter 7 he tells us: 'I, then, submitted my
neck to the yoke of Christ from the very flower of youth and received
the monastic habit at the monastery called *domus seminis*.' Much
ingenuity has been squandered in attempts to identify this mysterious
domus seminis, literally 'the house of (the) seed'. Identification with the
Castilian monastery of Silos appears to descend only from a marginal

5 See F. Santos Coco (ed.), *Historia Silense* (Madrid, 1921), pp. 93–9.

6 See further the introduction to the *Historia Roderici*. The point did not escape
Pérez de Urbel, *Historia Silense*, p. 91.

note reading 'Santo Domingo de Silos' inserted beside the words *domus seminis* in a lost manuscript, now known as the Fresdelval MS, allegedly copied *c.* 1500. This manuscript was used by the antiquary Francisco de Berganza for the earliest printed edition of the *HS* in his *Antigüedades de España* published in 1721. Three copies of the Fresdelval MS have come down to us, of which the earliest dates from *c.* 1600: it contains the attribution to Silos. In other words, one sixteenth-century reader – between the putative dates of Fresdelval and of its earliest derivative – thought that *domus seminis* was Silos. This is very shaky testimony; neither is it strengthened by all the special pleadings of Pérez de Urbel. To this may be added other points that have struck most critical readers of the work: that the author never mentioned Silos; that he displayed little interest in Castile (as against León); and that at one juncture (ch. 92) he showed himself ignorant of Castilian topography. In the light of these considerations nearly all scholars now judge it well-nigh impossible to sustain the case for a Castilian origin for our text.

A much more promising approach lies in the suggestion that the words *domus seminis*, or the single word *seminis*, arose from a copyist's misreading or the mistaken expansion of an abbreviation. Two possibilities have been canvassed. One is that *domus seminis* is a mis-copying of the words *domnis sanctis*, perhaps originally abbreviated as *dms scis*. This would point towards the monastery of Sahagún, some fifty kilometres to the south-west of the city of León, whose dual dedication to Sts Facundus and Primitivus led to its being frequently referred to in its abundant documentation as the monastery *domnis sanctis*, literally 'at the lord saints', more loosely 'of the holy patron saints'.[7] In support of this identification there may be adduced, first, that Sahagún was thrice mentioned in the *HS* (in chs 41, 71 and 104); second, that given that Alfonso VI was buried there it would make sense to locate his biographer there too; and third, that Sahagún's library and intellectual traditions were sufficient to furnish resources,

7 The case for a Sahagún provenance has been developed at greater length by J. M. Canal Sánchez-Pagín, '¿Crónica Silense o Crónica Domnis Sanctis?' *CHE* 63/64 (1980), pp. 94–103. Cautious support for it was shown by R. McCluskey, 'Malleable Accounts: Views of the Past in Twelfth-century Iberia' in *The Perception of the Past in Twelfth-century Europe*, ed. P. Magdalino (London, 1992), pp. 211–25 (at p. 214, n. 13): even more guarded is P. Linehan, *History and the Historians of Medieval Spain* (Oxford, 1993), p. 223. For an example of the phraseology from the very period when our author was at work see R. Escalona, *Historia del Real Monasterio de Sahagún* (Madrid, 1782), escritura cxlv, p. 510: 'loco quo dicitur Domnis Sanctis'.

context and perhaps stimulus to our unknown author. As against these points, it has to be said that indications of specific and strong Sahagún loyalties are lacking in our text. For example, although Archbishop Bernard of Toledo was mentioned in chapter 13, the author failed to draw attention to his earlier abbacy at Sahagún between 1080 and 1085; neither did he allude to Alfonso VI's burial at Sahagún when referring in chapter 7 to the king's death. Sahagún is a much stronger candidate than Silos: but there is one yet stronger.

A more economical and a more convincing emendation of the single word *seminis* was proposed in 1961 by the distinguished codicologist and palaeographer Professor Manuel Díaz y Díaz.[8] The word *seminis* is most plausibly explained as a mistaken expansion of the abbreviated words *sci ihnis, sancti Iohannis*, 'of St John'. This makes sound palaeographical sense: the letters *c* and *e* were frequently confused by copyists, and the rapid single downstrokes of the pen, known as minims, employed to render the letters *h, i, j, l, m, n, t, u* and *v* were (and are) a notorious source of muddle. One monastic 'house of St John' immediately suggests itself, and that is the community in the city of León whose dedication was to St John the Baptist.[9] This was a royal foundation, established by King Sancho I of León in or about 966, and enjoying thenceforward a close and warm relationship with the royal family. It was founded as a double house for both monks and nuns, the monks under the patronage of St John and the nuns under that of the Leonese child-martyr Pelayo. Properly, therefore, 'the house of St John and St Pelayo', it could in practice be referred to as either 'the house of St John' or 'the house of St Pelayo'.[10] Damaged by the destructive raids of Almanzor in the late tenth century, the house was restored by King Alfonso V (999–1028). Lavishly patronised by the latter's daughter Sancha and her husband King Fernando I (1037–65), the community received its most spectacular piece of royal largesse in 1063 when king and queen presented it with the relics of St Isidore,

8 M. C. Díaz y Díaz, 'Isidoro en la edad media hispana', first published in the collection *Isidoriana* (León, 1961), pp. 345–87, repr. in his *De Isidoro al siglo XII. Ocho estudios sobre la vida literaria peninsular* (Barcelona, 1976), pp. 141–201 (at p. 190 n. 139). The writer observed that he had already suggested this emendation on a number of occasions ('ya me pronuncié en varias ocasiones') which I take to refer to unpublished lectures.

9 See R. McCluskey, 'The early history of San Isidoro de León (X–XII c.)', *Nottingham Medieval Studies* 38 (1994), pp. 35–59.

10 See, for example, *Colección Documental del Archivo de la Catedral de León (775–1230)*, vol. III (986–1031) ed. J. M. Ruíz Asencio (León, 1987), no. 711, from the year 1013.

lately translated from Seville, an occasion described at length in the
HS. The arrival of Isidore's relics began the process by which his
patronage slowly replaced that of St John the Baptist. It is necessary
to stress that this was a gradual process. The dual patronage of both
St John and St Isidore for the masculine half of the establishment can
be found in later documents such as a diploma issued by Alfonso VI in
1099.[11] It is not implausible that a writer active between 1109 and
1118, especially if he were an elderly man of conservative temper,
should refer to the community as 'the house of St John'. It is even
possible, if we press the sense of that puzzling sentence in chapter 7 to
the limits, that the author was trying to tell us that he had received
the monastic habit there *before* the arrival of Isidore's relics in 1063.

But this is to run ahead of the argument. Are there other indications
in the text of the *HS* of a connection with this distinguished royal
foundation in the city of León? Yes, and three of them are particularly
telling. One of these lies in a minor editorial change which the author
of the *HS* made when reproducing the text of the *Translatio Sancti
Isidori*. Early on in the *Translatio*, Bishop Alvito of León was referred
to as *Legionensis urbis episcopus*, 'bishop of the city of León'. But the
author of the *HS* (ch. 96) changed the phrase to *huiuscemodi regie urbis
episcopus*, 'bishop of this royal city'. León was often referred to as 'the
royal city' in the documentation of the eleventh and twelfth centuries;
and the community of San Isidoro – as we may for convenience now
call it – lay within its walls. One could hardly ask for a clearer pointer
to a place of composition within the city of León.[12] Second, when
referring in chapter 103 to the rebuilding and embellishment of the
church of San Isidoro by Fernando I and Queen Sancha, the writer
named it as *hanc ecclesiam*, 'this church', thus localising himself and his
primary audience within the community of San Isidoro. Third, in
chapter 12 the author stated that he was aware of the wisdom and
goodness of Alfonso VI's elder sister Urraca 'more by experience than
by report'. Now the Infanta Urraca, who died in 1101, was closely

11 Printed in M. E. Martín López, *Patrimonio cultural de San Isidoro de León I/1: Documentos de los siglos X–XIII. Colección Diplomática* (León, 1995), no. 9, pp. 31–2. For the correct date of this diploma, 17 January 1099, see B. F. Reilly, *The Kingdom of León–Castilla under King Alfonso VI 1065–1109* (Princeton, 1988) p. 292, n. 44.

12 G. West has uttered a caution in 'La "Traslación del Cuerpo de San Isidoro" como fuente de la Historia llamada Silense', *Hispania Sacra* 27 (1974) pp. 365–71 (at p. 366, n. 8): I have explained elsewhere why I consider this unnecessary; see Fletcher, 'A Twelfth-century View', p. 150, n. 7.

associated with the community of San Isidoro. In particular, she set
herself the task of continuing and completing the architectural and
artistic ensemble initiated by her parents Fernando and Sancha. Her
epitaph at San Isidoro gratefully commemorated her patronage and
referred to her 'many gifts' to the house. One among these survives
at San Isidoro to this day, the magnificent 'Chalice of Doña Urraca'.
San Isidoro was the best possible place to observe at first hand, by
experience rather than report, the wisdom and goodness of the
princess.[13]

Now, these features of the HS do not of course prove that it was
composed at the monastery of San Isidoro de León: but this looks
likelier than an origin at Sahagún, let alone Silos. There are plenty of
other pointers in the same direction. The author mourned the passing
of Vermudo III (who was buried at San Isidoro) and perhaps quoted
from a Latin poem which commemorated him (chs 78, 79). He
displayed warm partiality for Queen Sancha (ch. 75), San Isidoro's
royal patron. He knew about the plans of Fernando and Sancha for a
royal mausoleum at San Isidoro (ch. 94). He had access to the
Translatio Sancti Isidori (chs 96–102), which must have been composed
in and for San Isidoro in or shortly after 1063. He displayed a detailed
knowledge of Fernando I's deathbed at San Isidoro (chs 105, 106). He
had access to the semi-official chronicles of the Asturian and Leonese
monarchy, which would surely have been preserved (though we
cannot prove this) in the library of a royal foundation such as San
Isidoro. The whole focus, or tendency, of the work, its 'sense of
subject', is Leonese.[14] The author had heard stories about the snowstorm which saved the city from Almanzor (ch. 71). He knew the precise date of Fernando I's coronation in León (ch. 80). He was aware
that Fernando had held a council in León to announce the partition of
his kingdom (ch. 103). He reported the circumstances of ex-king
García's death and burial in 1090 (ch. 13).

Wherever the libraries to which he had access, our author was a
learned man. His work contains quotations from or verbal remini-

13 On Urraca's patronage see S. H. Caldwell, 'Urraca of Zamora and San Isidoro de
León: fulfilment of a legacy', Woman's Art Journal 7 (1986), pp. 19–25. Her chalice
is illustrated in The Art of Medieval Spain AD 500–1200 (Metropolitan Museum of
Art, New York, 1993), catalogue no. 118.

14 A point rightly emphasised by earlier scholars, for example M. Gómez-Moreno,
Introducción a la Historia Silense (Madrid, 1921) and C. Sánchez-Albornoz, 'Sobre el
autor de la llamada Historia Silense' in his Investigaciones sobre historiografía, pp.
224–34.

scences of the Bible, Ovid, Virgil, Gregory the Great and Isidore. He
knew Julian of Toledo's *Historia Wambae* ('History of [King] Wamba'),
though he surprisingly misattributed it to Isidore (ch. 5). He knew
that very rare work, the *Vitas Sanctorum Patrum Emeritensium* ('The
Lives of the Holy Fathers of Mérida': ch. 4), a copy of which had been
in the royal library in the early years of the tenth century.[15] Two
authors above all others he knew and loved: Sallust and Einhard.
Phrases from Sallust's *Bellum Catilinae* and *Bellum Iugurthinum* ('The
Catiline War' and 'The Jugurthine War') and Einhard's *Vita Karoli*
('Life of Charlemagne') are liberally scattered throughout his work,
not invariably appositely, nor indeed always intelligibly. Their
presence in those chapters (14–38) dependent on the *Chronicle of
Alfonso III* serves to identify his editorial hand; and suggests it,
though less forcibly, in the chapters (39–47) which appear to depend
on the *Continuation*. Their absence from those chapters (1–30*)
dependent on Sampiro raises doubts as to whether this interpolation
is owed to our author or to some other hand (above p. 11).

We may well imagine that if our author had completed the task he
had set himself his *Vita Adefonsi* would have owed much to Einhard's
Vita Karoli. It is legitimate to suppose that it would have displayed no
little literary art – observe how cunningly the author passed over and
isolated the less savoury parts of Alfonso's career in chapters 8–13 –
and there is a hint in chapter 9 that he had it in mind to provide a big
set-piece devoted to the king's most famous conquest, of Toledo in
1085. It is surely reasonable to suppose that what the author had in
prospect was a celebratory, panegyric *Vita* whose tone would chime
with the chorus of praise for Alfonso from all those of his contemporaries whose voices may still be heard.[16]

The preoccupations he revealed, the themes he enunciated, in what
survives of his work, offer further hints as to how he would have set
or framed his image of Alfonso VI – themes and preoccupations which
are matched in the contemporary iconography of the *urbs regia* of

15 The 'Lives of the Fathers of Mérida' has been translated into English by A. T. Fear,
    Lives of the Visigothic Fathers, Translated Texts for Historians, vol. 26 (Liverpool,
    1997), pp. 45–105. The presence of the work in the library of Alfonso III was
    referred to in that king's letter to the clergy of Tours in 906 whose authenticity I
    have attempted to defend in Fletcher, *Saint James's Catapult. The Life and Times of
    Diego Gelmírez of Santiago de Compostela* (Oxford, 1984), appendix C, pp. 317–23.

16 A good example is Pelayo of Oviedo, whose encomium is translated elsewhere in
    this volume: see pp. 84–9. For a dissentient modern voice see the Note at the end
    of this introduction.

León and in particular of San Isidoro.[17] He was interested in
legitimacy and orthodoxy. He encouraged his readers to look back to
the Visigothic monarchy after it had abandoned Arianism in 589 as
the model of a good state. This is the point of the introductory chapters
1–6. Its kings were godly kings like Sisebut and Wamba. It was
doctrinally orthodox, unlike the monarchies of the Vandals and Sueves,
unlike even the emperor Constantine. It was distinguished for its
learning, a trait given special prominence by our bookish author in
the opening sentence of his work. Cherished by divine providence, its
kings were everywhere victorious until their sway extended from the
Rhône to Morocco. Divine providence would also act to punish
wicked kings like Wittiza by unleashing the 'barbarians' upon them –
our author's preferred term for Muslims. But this was not the end.
The heirs of the Visigoths learned the lesson, were cleansed by punishment and were allowed to rebuild their kingdom, what the author
called in one of his additions to the Chronicle of Alfonso III (ch. 15) the
Hispanie regnum, 'the kingdom of Spain'. The author made it plain that
he regarded his own monarchy, the kingdom of León, as the continuation of the Visigothic monarchy, the only legitimate Hispanie regnum.
Fernando I and Alfonso VI were cast in the mould of Sisebut or
Wamba. They did God's work in rescuing captive Christian churches
from the 'sacrilegious hands' (ch. 85) of the barbarians. Divine approval
of their campaigns of conquest was made manifest in the assistance
rendered by St James 'the knight of Christ' (ch. 88). Like the Visigothic kings after 589 they were orthodox (chs 7, 31): and here the
writer sounded a topical note, for it was Alfonso VI who had in the
1070s spurred on the difficult change from the so-called Mozarabic
liturgy, which pope Gregory VII had suspected of doctrinal deviance,
to the orthodox Roman rite.[18] Like the Visigothic kings, too, they set
a high value on good learning: in a passage lifted entire from Einhard
the author lauded the care bestowed by Fernando I on his children's
education (ch. 81).

17 See a number of acute studies by J. W. Williams: 'San Isidoro in León: Evidence for
a New History', The Art Bulletin 55 (1973), pp. 170–184; 'Generationes Abrahae:
Reconquest Iconography in León', Gesta 16 (1977), pp. 3–14; 'León: the Iconography of the Capital' in Cultures of Power. Lordship, Status and Process in Twelfth-
century Europe, ed. T. N. Bisson (Philadelphia, 1995), pp. 231–58.

18 For Alfonso's role in these liturgical changes see Reilly, Alfonso VI, ch. 6 and references there cited. Pope Gregory's reference to 'the tongues of heretics' occurs in a
letter to the king dated 19 March 1074: Gregorii VII Registrum, ed. E. Caspar
(Berlin, 1920–3; repr. 1955) i, 64 (= JL 4840).

The kingdom, then, was legitimated by its past, its ancestry. So too was its ruling dynasty. Possibly unaware that the Visigothic monarchy had been elective, not hereditary, the author could allude in chapter 15 – in another of his additions to the *Chronicle of Alfonso III* – to the *stirps regalis Gotorum*, 'the royal stock of the Goths', from which his hero Alfonso VI was descended. In chapter 31 he announced his intention to 'weave the genealogy' of the king. He had already shown in chapter 26 how Alfonso I (739–57) was descended from the Visigothic king Reccared (significant as the first orthodox Catholic ruler, who had formally abjured Arianism in 589). Thereafter the blood of the royal *stirps* continued in the legitimate male line of the Asturian and Leonese kings until the death of Vermudo III of León in 1037. On his death its sole carrier was his sister the Infanta Sancha. Her marriage to Fernando I (ch. 75) was therefore of critical importance to our author, for it enabled the son of that marriage, Alfonso VI, to be 'sprung from the famous stock of the Goths' as he put it in chapter 8.

The extensive kingdom of the Visigoths had something imperial about it. King Reccared could issue 'imperial commands' in chapter 3. So could his successor Fernando I, who presided over a 'royal empire' (ch. 83) and could issue 'imperial orders' (ch. 95) to a barbarian ruler. Alfonso VI, who intermittently employed the imperial title in his solemn diplomas from the year 1077 onwards, could be described as 'our emperor' in chapter 74 and as 'the orthodox emperor' in chapter 7. Here too there was some topicality of reference. Pope Gregory VII had rashly asserted lordship over the *regnum Hispanie* in the 1070s. Although the claim had not been pressed, it was one to be guarded against. Emperors do not have suzerains over them. The writer's discreet sounding of the imperial theme could be interpreted as a rebuttal of papal claims.[19]

And of other claimants too ? For there were those within Spain who might presume to claim the imperial title. The author's attitude to the other Christian principalities of Spain was dismissive. The 'kingdom of the Cantabrians' (ch. 74: i.e. Navarre) was an upstart realm which could be referred to as a mere 'province' (ch. 76). Its ruling dynasty was 'noble' rather than royal. The kingdom of Aragon was no more than a 'little fragment' of Navarre – a fragment of a province! Three

---

19 For all that concerns Alfonso's pretensions and Gregory's claims see Reilly, *Alfonso VI*, ch. 6 and H. E. J. Cowdrey, *Pope Gregory VII 1073–1085* (Oxford, 1998), pp. 468–80.

times in two chapters (75–6) the writer pointed out that its first king
Ramiro was of illegitimate birth; and he told a mocking story of his
ignominious flight from a battlefield. The implication is that the
kingdom and its rulers lacked legitimacy and dignity. Here we have
another contemporary reference for the primary audience to pick up.
If we are correct about the date of composition, these dismissive
comments were penned at a time when Ramiro's grandson, Alfonso I
el Batallador (1104–34) was attempting to establish his rule as king-
consort, husband of Alfonso VI's daughter and successor Queen
Urraca (1109–26), over the kingdom of León. Furthermore, in the
documents he issued in those years between 1109 and 1118, Alfonso I
styled himself *imperator*, 'emperor', with fair consistency. Alfonso was
not well liked in the city of León, whose bishop he had expelled in
1111 and whose rural hinterland – not impossibly including estates
belonging to San Isidoro – he had laid waste in fighting with the
partisans of his wife. When Lucas of Tuy, canon of San Isidoro, came
to compile his *Liber de Miraculis Sancti Isidori* ('Book of Miracles of St
Isidore') in the early thirteenth century he demonised Alfonso *el
Batallador* as a despoiler of San Isidoro.[20]

The author was also dismissive of the French. In the past they had
aided heretics (ch. 4) and rebels against the Visigothic monarchy (ch.
5). The claims made by the French that Charlemagne had conquered
lands in Spain were baseless. On the contrary, he had been bribed
with gold 'just like the French' and gone off home leaving the peoples
of 'warlike Spain' to fend for themselves (ch. 18). This was an allusion
to the recent past which would again have had resonance for his
audience. When the Almoravid invaders of 1086 had inflicted defeat
on Alfonso VI at Sagrajas and threatened his possession of Toledo, he
had appealed for help to the French compatriots of his queen,
Constance of Burgundy. But the French army which had come to
Spain in 1087 had accomplished nothing and dispersed, leaving
Alfonso VI to face the Almoravids on his own. At the time of writing
the Almoravid threat to Toledo – with all its special significance as
the ancient capital of the Visigothic kings – continued extremely

20 For the troubled reign of Queen Urraca see B. F. Reilly, *The Kingdom of León–
Castilla under Queen Urraca 1109–1126* (Princeton, 1982); for Alfonso of Aragon's
imperial style, see the documents assembled in *Colección Diplomática de Alfonso I de
Aragón y Pamplona (1104–1134)*, ed. J. A. Lema Pueyo (San Sebastián, 1990); for his
posthumous reputation see Archivo de San Isidoro de León, MS LXI ff. 30v–35r (=
Liber de Miraculis Sancti Isidori, chs 25–7).

grave. The French were doing nothing to help the *Hispanie regnum* in its hour of peril. To add insult to injury, they were helping the despised Aragonese to enlarge their illegitimate kingdom by territorial conquests in the valley of the Ebro which culminated in the conquest of Zaragoza in 1118.[21]

The author of the *HS* wrote at a time when the *Hispanie regnum* was being tested anew, as it had been under the attacks of Almanzor (chs 30*, 69–71), or as when, long ago, God had permitted the barbarians to overrun the Visigothic kingdom (ch. 1). He wrote to comfort and instruct an unhappy present by holding up a reassuring past. The kingdom would come through present tribulations as it had done in the past. Its enemies would be 'buried in hell' like Almanzor (ch. 71). God-cherished kings would once more 'extend the kingdom of the Spaniards by waging wars against the barbarians' (ch. 8). They would restore a Christian dominion which had formerly existed in 'cities over whose churches bishops had once upon a time presided' (ch. 85), like Toledo, 'the mirror of Christians of all Spain' (ch. 9). Therein lay the whole duty of a rightful ruler of the *Hispanie regnum*. The *HS* is in its individual way a mirror for the princes of an individual realm. I wonder whether the author had any particular prince or princess in mind. Even as he wrote it, Queen Urraca's son Alfonso (born 1105), later to be Alfonso VII, was of educable age: but his turbulent childhood was spent in an aristocratic household in Galicia. A more likely possibility is Alfonso's beloved elder sister the Infanta Sancha, born in 1095. She was most likely brought up in the city of León; as an adult she was an active and generous patron of San Isidoro; and on her death in 1159 she was buried there and after her death she was warmly remembered there. The important part she played in the counsels of her brother throughout his reign (1126–57) was emphasised by the contemporary author of the *Chronica Adefonsi Imperatoris* and is amply attested by the surviving documentation.[22] It is a nice conceit, and a possibility not to be ruled out, that through the agency of Doña Sancha the author of the *Historia Silense* touched the mind of Alfonso VII and helped to shape the tone and style of his reign.

---

21 Amply surveyed by C. Stalls, *Possessing the Land. Aragon's Expansion into Islam's Ebro Frontier under Alfonso the Battler 1104–1134* (Leiden, 1995).

22 *Chronica Adefonsi Imperatoris*, i, ch. 12 (see below, p. 169); B. F. Reilly, *The Kingdom of León-Castilla under King Alfonso VII, 1126–1157* (Philadelphia, 1998) pp. 139–41; L. García Calles, *Doña Sancha, Hermana del Emperador* (León and Barcelona, 1972) is full but insufficiently critical.

Note: A rival interpretation

A colleague in Spanish medieval studies, Dr John Wreglesworth, has proposed that the *Historia Silense* is a rounded and finished work and that its anonymous author intended to be obliquely critical of Alfonso VI. Such a radically original interpretation of the *Silense* deserves to be presented at length: it is to be hoped that Dr Wreglesworth will elaborate his argument in print. The purpose of this Note, whose text has been approved by Dr Wreglesworth and which is published with his consent, is simply to alert the reader to this alternative interpretation of a puzzling work which has not yet yielded up all its secrets.

The case rests upon the translation of a passage in chapter 7 which differs from that proposed in this book. The key words are as follows:

> *Ubi diversis sententiis sanctorum patrum catholicorum regum, sacris indicentibus libris, mecum ipse diu spatiando revolvens.*

I have rendered this passage thus:

> There for a long time I ruminated in my own mind upon various opinions of the holy fathers proclaimed in the holy books of Catholic kings ...

– a translation which rests upon a separation of the phrase *sanctorum patrum* ('of the holy fathers') from the phrase *catholicorum regum* ('of Catholic kings'). But each of these four words is in the genitive plural case. It is therefore perfectly proper to link *catholicorum* to *sanctorum patrum* and to find an entirely different significance for the word *regum* ('of kings') by linking its sense to the phrase *sacris indicentibus libris*. Dr Wreglesworth would accordingly translate the crucial words in this manner:

> There I gave lengthy consideration to the judgements of the holy Catholic fathers on the sacred Books of Kings.

(In this reading he is at one with the two translators of the text into Spanish, Gómez-Moreno and Casariego.) The author's allusion, therefore, was to the books of Kings in the Old Testament; and herein lies the clue to what Dr Wreglesworth has called his 'coded criticism' of Alfonso VI (and I quote from his doctoral thesis, *The Chronicle of Alfonso III and its significance for the Historiography of the Asturian Kingdom 718–910 AD* (Leeds D.Phil., 1995), p. 112).

Isidore, who would certainly have qualified as a 'holy Catholic father' in the opinion of the author of the *Silense*, had commented upon King

Solomon that he had started out well but had later by his backsliding forfeited God's favour. There were suggestive parallels, for those who had eyes to see, between Solomon and Alfonso VI. Solomon had failed to keep his covenant with God by taking foreign wives and concubines, among them the daughter of Pharaoh, and by slipping into idolatrous worship under their influence. God paid Solomon back by raising up enemies against him. Alfonso VI married five foreign wives and his mistress Zaida had been a Muslim, the daughter-in-law of the ruler of Seville, the most imposing among the amirs of the Taifa principalities of al-Andalus. (She became a convert to Christianity in the course of her attachment to Alfonso.) His religious policies were actively forwarded by the longest-lived of his foreign queens, Constance of Burgundy. Though they might have pleased Pope Gregory VII (and benefited immigrant ecclesiastical adventurers from France), they were regarded by conservative churchmen in Spain as unwelcome innovations. The misfortunes which befell the king and his kingdom – the Almoravid invasion, the death in battle of the heir to the throne Sancho, the civil war which followed hard upon the old king's demise and which was still raging at the (probable) time of the composition of the *Silense* – could most plausibly be interpreted as divine punishment for royal backsliding.

Alfonso VI's father Fernando, however – like Solomon's father King David – was a godfearing ruler who manifested all the virtues of a devout king. His choice of marriage-partner was thoroughly satisfactory and his piety was at once lavish and reassuringly conservative. He was duly rewarded by God with victory, prosperity and the saintly patronage of Isidore and the apostle St James. Fernando I was the true hero of the *Historia Silense*, which was artfully designed to celebrate him. Alongside and in contrast, the life and deeds of his flawed son Alfonso VI were there in suggestion and in allegory for those who were able to read the code.

Such in briefest summary is Dr Wreglesworth's alternative reading of the *Historia Silense*. I have to confess, as is implicit in my translation of the passage quoted above, that I am not quite persuaded by it. Others, however, may be. At all events, in this strikingly new perspective upon a notoriously difficult text we have something which deserves to be pondered sympathetically.

Historia Silense

CHAPTER 1

Once upon a time Hispania blossomed abundantly with every kind of
liberal teaching and in her those thirsting to drink at wisdom's spring
everywhere bestowed care on the study of letters. But then, overwhelmed by the strength of the barbarians,[1] study and teaching
completely died away. In these constraining circumstances, writers
were lacking and *the deeds* of the Spaniards *were passed over in silence.*[2] But
if you wisely ponder why such a disaster should have happened to
Spain, assuredly there comes to mind that *all the paths of the Lord are
mercy and truth.*[3] For He allots some, inexorably ensnared by their
various sins, to the eternal torments; others He invites to the flowery
meadows of the heavenly homeland as rewards for a good life. Some
indeed, answerable in part on both counts, He summons to eternal life
when they have been purged by the cleansing of a transitory fire. This
too must not be omitted, that He strikes very many bodily, so that in
future this punishment shall not be for a remedy, and thus it is for
those who are in no way corrected the affliction of the aforesaid
scourges may be the beginnings of torments to come. Whence the
Psalmist says, *Let them cover themselves with their own confusion, as with
a mantle,*[4] which double garment they put on figuratively who are
condemned to both temporal and everlasting torment.

CHAPTER 2

Kings accordingly, as we have learned from ancient report, *first distinguished themselves with the title of sovereignty in the world.*[5] But *when
little by little sloth insinuated itself in place of industry, pride in place of
equity, lust and greed in place of moderation,*[6] wantonly abandoning to
oblivion the true God and His commands, they started to worship the
created rather than the Creator. And they upon whom above all living
beings the Creator of all things had bountifully bestowed clear and

---

1 'Barbarians' is the term most commonly employed by the author to denote the
  Muslim inhabitants of Spain.
2 Einhard, *Vita Karoli*, preface.
3 Psalm xxv.10.
4 Psalm cix.29.
5 Sallust, *Bellum Catilinae* (henceforward *Bell. Cat.*) ii, 1.
6 Sallust, *Bell. Cat.* ii, 5.

elevated vision to aspire to the celestial things, lost in a fourfold mist, bowed themselves in wicked worship of demons, false idols of wood and stone and metal. We must pass over the details of place and deed in the bringing to good order[7] of those who were renewed by the spring of holy baptism. For if, as we believe, Christ having taken on our humanity preached one baptism and one faith, the Roman Emperor Constantine[8] must indeed be censured in the matter of the faith: who indeed, an Augustus of great eminence, was first cleansed in the font of holy baptism by Pope Sylvester[9] of holy memory after signs and wonders had been seen. From this it is plainly to be understood that the signs were displayed *not for the faithful but for infidels,*[10] whence the Truth Himself thus spoke, *Except ye see signs and wonders ye will not believe.*[11] However, the aforesaid emperor was led astray towards the end of his life by a counterfeiter of the Catholic faith named Eusebius, bishop of the church of Nicomedia,[12] by whom he was rebaptised and thus ran headlong, lamentably, into the Arian heresy. Persisting in this error, he departed this life an infidel. This is clearly proclaimed in the chronicle which Christ's servant Isidore, bishop of the church of Seville,[13] composed in a comprehensive history from the beginning of the world down to the time of the Roman emperor Heraclius and Sisebut the most pious ruler of the Spaniards.[14] A very great proportion of those who followed him perished by the same madness, even though not in a similar way. What indeed am I to say of the leaders of the Vandals and Sueves, among whom very few Catholics are to be found ?[15]

7 Emending *mordendos* to *inordinandos.*

8 Constantine I, Roman emperor 306–37.

9 Sylvester I, Pope, 314–35. The legend that he baptised Constantine first made its appearance in the fifth century, and was widely known from the ninth century onwards owing to the forged 'Donation of Constantine'.

10 This seems to be a reminiscence of Pope Gregory the Great, *Homiliae in Evangelia,* x (=*PL* 76, col. 1110).

11 John iv.48.

12 Eusebius, bishop of Nicomedia and subsequently of Constantinople (d. *c.* 342), baptised Constantine on his deathbed in 337 and led the dominant Arian faction at the court of his son the Emperor Constantius II (337–61).

13 Isidore, bishop of Seville *c.* 600–36, scholar and ecclesiastical statesman. His *Chronicle* was completed in 615 or 616.

14 Heraclius, Roman (Byzantine) emperor 610–41; Sisebut, Visigothic king of Spain 612–20.

15 The Vandals and Sueves were Germanic peoples who set up successor-states in the wreckage of the western Roman Empire in the fifth century, respectively in north Africa and western Spain. The Vandals were Arian Christians who vigorously persecuted the Catholic clergy. The Sueves were intermittently and less fanatically Arian.

Chapter 3

The kings of the Goths also, by land and sea victorious, subdued the nations round about to their dominion:[16] but raging with a twofold madness against the limbs[17] of Christ they expelled the orthodox worshippers and in the height of their damnation embraced the teachings of the Arians. Let us recall to mind one of these rulers, by name Leovigild, for the greatness of his evil-doing.[18] This Leovigild, indeed, burning with zeal for the Arians, because his son Hermenigild refused to join that detestable cult, first subjected him to various tortures, then put him in chains and finally ordered him to be killed. *After Leovigild's death king Reccared, following not his faithless father but the footsteps of his martyred brother,* imbued with the teaching of the venerable bishop Leander of Seville, was made a preacher of the truth and uprooted altogether the madness of the Arians.[19] Pope Gregory writes [of this] in the *Book of Dialogues* which he diligently composed about the lives and miracles of the holy fathers.[20] Thus it came about that his successors as kings of the Goths, obedient to his imperial commands, devoutly observed the Catholic faith in peace and war.

Chapter 4

Their perversity proclaims however, among other things, that the fury of the Franks was striving to overturn sacred cult.[21] For *there were*

16 The Visigoths, another Germanic people, invaded Spain in 456 and had consolidated their hold over it by about 480. The Visigothic monarchy ruled Spain until the Arab–Berber conquest of 711–20.

17 Emending *menia* to *membra* (as found in some MSS).

18 On Leovigild (569–86), perhaps the greatest of the Visigothic kings, and his son Hermenigild, see Roger Collins, *Early Medieval Spain. Unity in Diversity 400–1000* (2nd edn., London, 1995) pp. 41–53.

19 King Reccared (586–601) announced his personal conversion from Arianism to Catholicism in 587 and the transition was formally ratified by the leaders of the Spanish church at an ecclesiastical council held at Toledo in 589 (III Toledo), a defining moment in Spanish historical mythology: but see the cautions of Peter Linehan, *History and the Historians of Medieval Spain* (Oxford, 1993) ch. 2. Leander, bishop of Seville *c.* 580–600, was the elder brother of Isidore.

20 The reference is to Gregory the Great's *Dialogorum Liber* and the quotation in the text is from iii, 31.7 (A. de Vogüé (ed.), *Grégoire le Grand, Dialogues,* Sources Chrétiennes, vol. 260 (Paris, 1979), vol. II, p. 388).

21 This is the first of several chapters which contain unflattering references to the Franks: see the discussion of this feature of the *Historia* in the introduction. This opening sentence has caused difficulty to other editors and translators; the text may be corrupt.

two counts of King Reccared, of whom one was named *Granista* and the other *Vildigerius. They were noble by birth and of great wealth, but of unsound morals and judgement.*[22] A bishop named Athalogus, assuredly an adherent of the Arians, had led them astray into heresy. At the prompting of the Devil this man incited a great revolt against the Catholic faith at the famous city of Narbonne. These two counts, obedient to the instructions of this same Athalogus, *brought a very numerous company of Franks* into the province of Narbonne, thinking indeed to uphold *the Arian faction* with the support of so many soldiers *and if possible to deprive the most serene king Reccared of his kingdom.* Meanwhile, raging hither and thither, shedding the blood of Christ's servants, *they did much damage.* When Reccared heard of this he gave orders to Claudius, the very powerful duke of the city of Mérida, that he should hasten to avenge this innocent blood. So this Claudius, immediately obedient to the king's command, attacked the Franks with great force. In fierce fighting he put *nearly sixty thousand* of them to the sword. Finally the Franks, thrown into confusion by divine chastisement for as long as they reviled the Catholic faith with haughty mien, lost both lives together. Those of them who contrived to escape the hands of the enemy took to flight: *the Goths pursued them as far as the frontiers of their kingdom.*

CHAPTER 5

Nevertheless, in the time of the most glorious King Wamba the fierceness of the Franks is known to have been cast down.[23] For it happened that a certain Paul, to whom King Wamba had delegated the dukedom of the province of Narbonne, was so puffed up with pride and the desire for power that he *placed a crown on his head and was hailed*[24] as king. Strengthened by the aid of the Franks he rose in rebellion at Nîmes. Stung by this insult the Spanish king hastened to Nîmes as fast as he could with a picked force of cavalry with whom he was on campaign. The Franks *were routed and put to flight.*[25] Wamba

22 Much of this chapter derives from two seventh-century works, the *Vitas Sanctorum Patrum Emeritensium* (*Lives of the Holy Fathers of Mérida*) and Isidore of Seville's *Historia Gothorum* (*History of the Goths*): see the English translations respectively by A. T. Fear, *Lives of the Visigothic Fathers*, pp. 99–100, and K. B. Wolf, *Conquerors and Chroniclers of early medieval Spain* (Liverpool, 1990). p. 104.

23 The reign of Wamba (672–80) furnished the author with another opportunity to insert material hostile to the Franks.

24 Einhard, *Vita Karoli*, ch. 30.

25 Sallust, *Bellum Iugurthinum* (henceforward *Bell. Iug.*) xcix, 3.

besieged and captured the city and levelled a part of it to the ground. The province of Narbonne thus brought back to his authority, he returned rejoicing to Toledo, carrying Paul captive with him. These things are written in the book of the blessed Isidore which is among the other fourteen which he diligently composed about the deeds of the Vandals, the Sueves and the Goths.[26]

CHAPTER 6

The Spanish kings governed in a Catholic manner from the Rhône, the greatest river of the Gauls, as far as the sea which divides Europe from Africa; six provinces, that is to say, of Narbonne, Tarragona, Betica, Lusitania, Carthago and Galicia. Furthermore they subjected the province of Tingitana, in the furthest bounds of Africa, to their lordship.[27] Then at length divine providence, descrying that Wittiza king of the Goths[28] had for long been skulking among the Christians like a wolf among the sheep, lest all the flock should again be defiled by this age-old *swinish wallowing*[29] allowed barbarian peoples to take possession of Spain – just as in the time of Noah the Flood [covered] the earth – few of the Christians being spared.

CHAPTER 7

It disgusts me, to be candid, to dwell on the ruin of my homeland and the wicked doings of its kings, and *the while I have proceeded at too great length; the subject itself summons me to return to what I had begun.*[30] I, then, submitted my neck to the yoke of Christ from the very flower of youth and received the monastic habit at the monastery called Domus

---

26 A surprising misattribution by our learned author. Isidore died in 636; Paul's rebellion against Wamba took place in 673. The work to which our author refers is the *Historia Wambae* (*History of Wamba*) by Julian, bishop of Toledo (680–90), composed shortly after the events it describes.

27 See Roger Collins, *Early Medieval Spain*, map 1, for the Roman provinces of Spain inherited by the Visigoths. Tingitana, more accurately Mauretania Tingitana, was the town of Tingis (Tangier) with a modest hinterland, the shrunken remains of a much larger Roman province which between the first and the third centuries had extended further down the Atlantic coast of present-day Morocco and inland as far as the town of Volubilis (near today's Meknes).

28 King Wittiza (692/4–710) features as a scapegoat in the semi-historical accounts of the Arab–Berber conquest which were current in the Christian kingdoms of northern Spain from the ninth century onwards.

29 II Peter ii.22.

30 Sallust, *Bell. Cat.* v, 9; *Bell. Iug.* iv, 9.

Seminis.[31] There for a long time I ruminated in my own mind upon various opinions of the holy fathers proclaimed in the holy books of Catholic kings, and *decided to write of the deeds* of the lord Alfonso, the orthodox emperor of Spain,[32] *and, separately, the life of the same:*[33] in the first place because his more noble deeds seem worthy to be remembered; second because, now that the whole length of his fragile life[34] has been run, he seems the most worthy of respect among all the kings who govern Christ's church in a Catholic manner. But before I embark on the beginning of this discourse I must dwell a little on the many difficulties and threatening obstacles which he overcame in coming to the throne.

CHAPTER 8

Alfonso, then, sprung from the famous stock of the Goths,[35] was *of great strength in both judgement and arms* to a degree rarely found among mortal men; for we see *that the one stems from* the fear of death, *and the other from the bravery* of strength.[36] To him in extending the kingdom of the Spaniards,[37] in waging wars against the barbarians, what spirit was given! I go forward upon[38] my journey, so far as the diligence of

31 For the various conjectures as to the identity of this community, see the introduction.

32 Alfonso VI, King of León 1065–72, King of León, Castile and Galicia 1072–1109. For a suggestion as to why the author should have laid stress upon Alfonso's orthodoxy, see the introduction. From 1077 onwards Alfonso was intermittently styled *imperator Hispanie* ('Emperor of Spain') in official documents.

33 Einhard, *Vita Karoli*, preface; Sallust, *Bell. Cat.* iv, 2.

34 Emending *vitam fragili* to *vitae fragilis.*

35 The author, who may have been unaware that the Visigothic monarchy was elective, not hereditary, believed that there had existed 'a royal dynasty of the Goths' (*Gotorum regalis stirps*, ch. 15) from which Alfonso VI was descended through his mother Queen Sancha, the wife of Fernando I. In ch. 31 (not here translated) he stated his intention 'to weave the genealogy' of Alfonso VI (*genealogiam texere*), and the first two-thirds of the text as it has come down to us is given over to this end.

36 Sallust, *Bell. Cat.* v, 1; *Bell. Iug.* vii, 5. The sense is not wholly clear, perhaps because the author misquoted or misunderstood his source.

37 This is the first of two occurrences of the term *regnum Hispanorum* in the *Silense*, the other one being in ch. 13: he also uses, once, the phrase *Hispanie regnum* ('kingdom of Spain') in ch. 15 which is one of his additions to the *Chronicle of Alfonso III*. For a brief discussion of its implications, see the introduction.

38 Emending the non-existent word *profabor* to *perlabor*. If the original text had been written in Visigothic script (see introduction) a misreading of *perlabor* for *profabor* by a copyist who was ignorant of that script would be intelligible.

my capabilities shall allow, in listing one by one the provinces reclaimed from their unholy hands and returned to the faith of Christ. After King Fernando of good memory breathed his last he was survived by his children: Sancho, the eldest; the aforesaid Alfonso; and the youngest, García; there were in addition their two sisters Urraca and Elvira.[39] Although while yet alive their father had divided the kingdom equally among them,[40] nevertheless for eight[41] entire years they waged internecine war without result. No small number of soldiers perished in two major battles.[42] So intense was the brothers' strife! but who does not know that so it has been among mortals from the beginning, except he who has given himself over to other concerns and does not wish to bestow care on the discipline of reading in order to study the deeds of kings.[43] For there never was a lasting peace for the inhabitants in the kingdom. Indeed, the Spanish kings are reputed to be of such bellicosity that when any prince of their line has reached manhood and taken up arms for the first time, he prepares to contend by force, against his brothers or if they are still alive his parents, so that he alone may exercise royal authority.

39 King Fernando and Queen Sancha were married in (probably) 1032. For the sequence of their children's births (Urraca, Sancho, Elvira, Alfonso, García) see ch. 81 below, also the order in which they witnessed *CD Fernando I*, no. 66. Precise dates of birth are not known, but all had been born by 21 April 1043 when all five were mentioned in a document issued by their father: *CD Fernando I*, no. 21. The Sahagún chronicler tells us that Alfonso VI was aged 72 when he died on 1 July 1109 which would indicate a date of birth in the second half of 1036 or the first half of 1037.

40 The decision to divide the kingdom was formally taken at a great council held, it would seem, early in 1064 (though presumably long meditated beforehand): see below, ch. 103. The division was far from 'equal', Alfonso being favoured at the expense of both his brothers, especially the elder, Sancho.

41 Between Fernando I's death on 29 December 1065 and the murder of Sancho II on 7 October 1072 there elapsed rather less than seven years. For a possible explanation of the chronicler's 'eight' see Reilly, *Alfonso VI*, p. 21.

42 That is, Llantadilla in July 1068 and Golpejera in January 1072. The first was not a 'major battle' but a modest skirmish; possibly the second too.

43 In translating this puzzling sentence I have taken a hint from Gómez-Moreno's rendering (p. lxviii) and have also emended the punctuation in such a fashion that the words *scrutare etenim regum gesta* are detached from the following sentence and added to the end of this one.

CHAPTER 9

Now Sancho his brother compelled this Alfonso, deprived of his native kingdom, to go to Toledo.[44] But we believe that this came about by the provident disposition of God. For when, driven by necessity, an exile from his homeland, he was forced to keep barbarian company – saving his faith – for a span of nine months,[45] he was hugely esteemed by those very same Saracens as a great king.[46] Looked upon as the greatest friend by the band of Moors, he was even conducted here and there throughout Toledo, enabling him to master it for himself. He lodged in his own mind, pondering the matter *more deeply than anyone might have believed*,[47] at which places and with which siege engines that city, once the mirror of Christians of all Spain, might be wrested from the hands of the pagans. I shall show in what follows how it was captured by him in hard fighting.[48]

CHAPTER 10

Meanwhile King Sancho assembled an army and laid siege to Zamora, which long ago used to be called Numantia.[49] The Zamorans, however, remained unmoved by this development. Fortified by the assistance of King Alfonso and not minded to put up with the repulse of their lord, the Zamorans despatched a knight of great courage and killed King

44 Toledo, formerly capital city of the Visigothic kings (see ch. 5 above), was now the seat of one of the Taifa rulers who had succeeded to the authority of the Caliphate of Córdoba when it fragmented earlier in the century. Al-Ma'mūn – rendered by our author as Halmemon in ch. 11 – governed Toledo from 1044 to 1075. At this juncture he was at the height of his power, having conquered the neighbouring Taifa state of Valencia in 1065. The ease with which a Christian princely exile like Alfonso could find asylum in a Muslim state is noteworthy.

45 That is, from January to October 1072.

46 As pointed out earlier (see note 1 above), the writer's preferred name for Muslims is 'barbarians'. In this single short chapter, presumably to avoid verbal repetition, he referred to them additionally as 'Saracens', 'Moors' and 'pagans'. 'Moors' is the designation he used most frequently after 'barbarians'. He used the term 'pagan' sparingly. This is the only occurrence of the word 'Saracen' in any part of the work attributable to the anonymous author: in chs 99 and 100 it is borrowed from the *Translatio Sancti Isidori* (see above, pp. 11–12, n. 5).

47 Sallust, *Bell. Cat.* v, 3; *Bell. Iug.* xi, 7.

48 There is a hint here that the author planned a literary set-piece devoted to Alfonso's conquest of Toledo in 1085.

49 Numantia, the Iberian town besieged, taken and destroyed by Scipio Aemilianus in 133 BC, lies about 8 km north of the Castilian city of Soria. Subsequently the identity of the site was forgotten and much later on Numantia was erroneously identified with Zamora, on the River Duero south of León, about 300 km west of Soria.

Sancho by treachery while he was besieging them.[50] The king was transfixed with a spear by him, unexpectedly, from behind, and *shed his life
together with his blood.*[51] After the king's death *you might plainly discern
how so much courage,*[52] so much rejoicing, were turned to as much despair,
as much sorrow, in so great and noble an army. Every soldier encamped
about the city, when assailed by the dreadful news, was driven frantic
and took to flight, abandoning nearly all of his possessions. Finally
they all sought out their homeland, though not in the disciplined manner
in which the army had been used to conduct itself when protected by
arms and vigilance, but in scattered bands travelling by day and night.

CHAPTER 11

However, a squadron of the bravest knights of Castile, *mindful of their
birth and of their deeds of old while under arms,*[53] carried off the lifeless
body of their lord with such honour as they could. They laid him in
his tomb with the trappings of a royal funeral, with great honour as
was fitting, at the monastery of Oña.[54] The news of so great an out-
rage afterwards came to the ears of King Alfonso in Toledo. Taking
his leave of Halmemon, the aforesaid barbarian king of Toledo, he told
him that he would return to his native land at once so that he might

50 All that one may reliably conclude about Sancho II's murder on 7 October 1072 is
   that foul play was involved. In Castilian circles rumours circulated that Alfonso VI
   – the beneficiary of it – had been implicated in his brother's killing. Later elabor-
   ations, in a Latin poem commemorating Sancho's death (composed *c.* 1160?) and in
   a vernacular epic (composed *c.* 1220?), would also involve the Infanta Urraca, their
   elder sister. The truth will never be known. Naturally, the author of the *Silense*
   would be reluctant to criticise either Alfonso or Urraca. He was careful not to
   define the nature of Alfonso's 'assistance' (*presidium*). In a diploma dated 17
   November 1072 Alfonso claimed that his recovery of the throne had been achieved
   without bloodshed: J. M. Ruiz Asencio (ed.), *Colección documental del archivo de la
   catedral de León (775–1230)*, vol. IV (1032–1109) (León, 1990), no. 1182. Modern
   discussion may be found in C. Smith, *The Making of the 'Poema de Mio Cid'*
   (Cambridge, 1983), pp. 30–37; Reilly, *Alfonso VI*, pp. 65–8; R. Fletcher, *The Quest
   for El Cid* (London, 1989), pp. 116–18.

51 Virgil, *Aeneid*, ii, 532.

52 Sallust, *Bell. Cat.* lxi, 1.

53 Sallust, *Bell. Cat.* lx, 3,7.

54 The monastery of Oña, near the headwaters of the River Ebro in the north of Old
   Castile, had been founded in 1011 by Count Sancho of Castile, a double house for
   men and women under the direction of his daughter, Abbess Tigridia. The
   founder's namesake and son-in-law, Sancho *el Mayor* ('the Great') of Navarre, was
   buried there on his death in 1035. The decision by his son Fernando I to establish
   a royal mausoleum at San Isidoro de León (see below, ch. 94) frustrated Oña's
   ambitions to become the burial place of the kings and queens of León–Castile.

assist his people. Furthermore, because Alfonso said nothing whatsoever to him about the death of his brother, the barbarian at first felt pity
for this noble man who was about to suffer.[55] He advised him not to fall
again into hostile hands. He [al-Ma'mūn] informed him [Alfonso] that
his brother's good luck and courage were still pretty well-known to
him[56] by experience. At length – for that people glows with innate
cunning – the Moor enquired privately of him, though he was unwilling, about his brother's death. But in this doubtful pass both were
hurt by one wound. Alfonso, by avoiding the barbarian's snares,
declined to reveal matters to him as they really stood. Indeed, his
[Alfonso's] nature, greedy for power, used to alarm Halmemon greatly.[57]

CHAPTER 12

The king of Toledo debated these matters with himself for a long
time. It is said that he contemplated the imprisonment of our king.
When King Alfonso discovered this by means of an informer, because
he was prudent in counsel as well as very mighty in arms, he boldly
returned to the city of Zamora protected by his knights. There,
occupying himself with the secure government of the kingdom, he
summoned his sister Urraca to him and other very prominent men.
Secret discussions were held. This Urraca indeed had loved Alfonso
from childhood more than the other brothers with the warmest sisterly
love; and since she was the elder, she chose for herself[58] and took on
the place of a mother. She was outstanding in both wisdom and goodness,
which indeed we have learned more by experience than by report.[59]
Spurning carnal ties and the perishable garments of a husband,
outwardly in secular guise but inwardly under monastic discipline,
she clove to Christ as her true spouse, and throughout the term of her
life she persisted in her cherished practice of embellishing holy altars
and priestly vestments with gold and silver and precious stones.[60]

55 Emending iacture to iacturi.

56 Emending illum to illi.

57 Sallust, Bell. Iug. vi.3. The general sense of the second half of this chapter is plain
enough, though as it stands the text makes less than complete sense. Other
translators seem to have been baffled too. see Gómez-Moreno, p lxx and
Casariego, pp. 117–18.

58 Emending allebat to allegebat.

59 For the implications of this phrase see the introduction.

60 For the Infanta Urraca's artistic patronage see S. H. Caldwell, 'Urraca of Zamora
and San Isidoro de León: fulfilment of a legacy', Woman's Art Journal 7 (1986), 19–

CHAPTER 13

So Alfonso took her advice, troubled as he was at this juncture lest the kingdom should again be threatened either by his own illness[61] or by his brother's death. He captured his younger brother García and immediately[62] put him in chains.[63] Every royal honour was shown to him save only the liberty of ruling. Alfonso also had it in mind that in the fullness of time, all being well, García should succeed him on the throne. But imperious nature, who fixed for mankind the inescapable frontier of death, intervened. Much later on, worn down by fever, [García] died in captivity.[64] Both his sisters, Urraca and Elvira, attended his funeral *in royal fashion*.[65] At that time Rainerius, legate of the Roman church, who later became pope, happened to be presiding over a synodal council at León together with Archbishop Bernard of Toledo and the other bishops and abbots of his province.[66] Offering Mass to God for the repose of his soul, they committed his body to the tomb in the company of his forebears in the same city. Thus was Alfonso strengthened in his hold over his father's kingdom. Before we come to the narrative of his wars and conquest of cities, of how he governed the kingdom of the Spaniards,[67] of how greatly he enlarged it from so small [a nucleus], we must go back to an earlier date and unravel the kingdom's origin.

---

25 and above all J. W. Williams, 'León: the Iconography of the Capital' in T. N. Bisson (ed.), *Cultures of Power. Lordship, Status and Process in Twelfth-century Europe* (Philadelphia, 1995), pp. 231–58.

61 Emending *dolose* to *dolore*.

62 Emending *preto* to *presto*.

63 According to a usually reliable source García was captured on 13 February 1073: *Chronicon Compostellanum*, in *ES* 20, p. 610. He was imprisoned at Luna, in the mountains to the north-west of León.

64 According to the source cited in the previous note, García died on 22 March 1090.

65 Sallust, *Bell. Iug.* xi, 2.

66 Rainerius, cardinal-priest of San Clemente since 1078, legate in southern France and Spain 1090, elected Pope 1099 and took the name Paschal II, died 21 January 1118. On the council of León see Reilly, *Alfonso VI*, pp. 217–19. Bernard, native of south-western France and monk of Cluny, came to Spain *c.* 1079, Abbot of Sahagún 1080–85, Archbishop of Toledo 1086–1124.

67 The second (and last) occurrence of the phrase *regnum Hispanorum*: see above, ch. 8, n. 37.

In order to 'unravel the kingdom's origin' the author went right back to the
reign of the Visigothic king Wittiza. To traverse the period from the late
seventh century to the late tenth he leant principally upon the *Chronicle of
Alfonso III* and the *Chronicle of Sampiro*, as explained in the introduction. The
present translation resumes with a chapter numbered 30 in Pérez de Urbel's
edition because he believed it to be the thirtieth and final chapter of Sampiro's
work. It is not wholly clear that this is so, and for that reason the chapter is
here numbered 30*. The chapter presents various problems and I suspect
that our unknown Leonese author of the Silense had a hand in shaping it.[68]
Whether this is so or not, I detect at any rate his preoccupations in the last
sentence concerning the marriage of Fernando I. For this reason alone it
seemed appropriate to include the chapter in its entirety.

CHAPTER 30*

On the death of Ramiro [III], Vermudo [II] the son of Ordoño [III]
entered León and acquired the kingdom peacefully.[69] He was a man of
more-than-average statesmanship. He confirmed the laws established
by King Wamba; he ordered canon law to be observed; he loved *mercy
and judgement*,[70] he sought to reject evil and to choose good. But in the
days of his reign, on account of the sins of the Christian people, there
grew a huge multitude of the Saracens.[71] Their king – who chose a
false name for himself, Almanzor[72] – was like none who has gone
before nor will be again. He formed an alliance with the Saracens across
the sea, and at the head of the whole people of the Ishmaelites he
invaded the frontiers of the Christians and began to lay waste many of
their kingdoms and to put [many] to the sword. These are the kingdoms of the Franks, the kingdom of Pamplona and the kingdom of
León.[73] He laid waste cities and castles, indeed, and depopulated all

68 Linehan, *History and the Historians*, p. 158, n. 110, draws attention to some of the
problems and possibilities.

69 The writer's assessment of Vermudo II (982–99) is notably more sympathetic than
the very hostile account penned by Pelayo of Oviedo: see pp. 74–9.

70 Psalm ci.1; Hosea xii.6. On Vermudo's legal activities see Collins, *Early Medieval
Spain*, pp. 240–1.

71 If this sentence is indeed the work of our author, this is an additional use of the
term 'Saracen': see above, ch. 9, n. 46.

72 Almanzor (al-Manṣūr) was not a given name but a *laqab* or honorific name
meaning 'the Victorious'.

73 By 'the kingdoms of the Franks' the author presumably meant the Catalan counties
of north-eastern Spain which notionally formed part of the kingdom of West
Francia (France), itself still (until 987) under the rule of the Carolingian dynasty.
Barcelona was sacked by Almanzor in 985.

the land, until he reached the coastal regions of western Spain[74] and destroyed the city of Galicia in which the body of the blessed apostle James is buried. He had intended indeed to go to the tomb of the apostle in order to destroy it; *but he drew back in terror.*[75] He pulled down churches, monasteries, palaces and destroyed them by fire. [This took place] in the Era 1035 [= AD 997]. *The heavenly king, remembering his mercy, wrought vengeance on his enemies: that very people of the Hagarenes began to fall away by the sword and sudden death, and day by day to come closer to annihilation.*[76] But King Vermudo, assisted by the Lord, began to restore that same place of St James for the better. And in the second year after that campaign he died a natural death in the region of El Bierzo, rendering up his spirit in confession of the Lord. He reigned seventeen years. On his death his son Alfonso [V] being three years of age, succeeded to the kingdom in the Era 1037 [= AD 999]. From this descent Fernando, the son of Sancho the Cantabrian king, took his wife and sprang forth as the king-to-be who would make it his task to expel the barbarians in the future.[77]

CHAPTER 69

However, in the time of Sancho, son of the aforesaid King Ramiro, on account of the wickedness of some of those who had governed – for some had cast friends out of the kingdom, some [like the father of this Sancho] had torn out the eyes of kinsmen – by God's leave the Moors were again allowed dominion over the Spains – just as pagan peoples had lorded it over the Israelites for their manifold sins.[78]

---

74 Removing the full stop between *occidentalis* and *Ispanie*.

75 The same phrase occurs in Sampiro ch. 29.

76 This sentence occurs almost exactly word for word in Pelayo's account of Vermudo II: see p. 79. It also contains a reminiscence of Luke i.54 (the Magnificat).

77 For Fernando's marriage see below ch. 75. The language here used of the king's mission might prompt reflection on the prophetic strain in Leonese historiography, possibly not unconnected with the remarkable popularity in early medieval Christian Spain of the *Commentary on the Apocalypse* attributed to the eighth-century monk Beatus of Liébana. San Isidoro de León possessed a very handsome copy of this work donated by Fernando I and Queen Sancha in 1047 (now in the Biblioteca Nacional in Madrid).

78 The author backtracks again. The kings referred to here are Ramiro II (930–51) and his son Sancho I (956–8, 959–66). Ramiro blinded his half-brother and three cousins in order to render them unfit for the throne. Sancho was restored to power in 959 with the aid of the Muslim Caliph of Córdoba 'Abd al-Raḥmān III, to whom he paid tribute.

CHAPTER 70

Accordingly, in the Era 1004 [= AD 966], on the death of King Sancho, Almanzor, the greatest of all the barbarians, boldly invaded the bounds of the kingdom of the Christians.[79] Sure enough after Sancho's death, as tends to happen in such circumstances, the counts who administered the regions, some calling to mind a royal authority[80] endured beyond what was just, others putting fortifications in order with the aim of ruling without restraint, refused obedience to the still tender-aged Ramiro, the son of King Sancho. So when the barbarian heard of this discord among the Christians he forded the River Duero which then marked the frontier between Christians and barbarians.[81] *In doing this there assisted*[82] the barbarian both the size of the payment with which he had bound to his service no small numbers of Christian soldiers, and his justice in giving judgements which, as we have learnt from a father's report,[83] he always held dear above all other people, even (if it is fitting to say so) the Christians. For example, if while in winter quarters there were to occur any mutiny, punishment would be applied more severely upon barbarian than upon Christian. So, laying waste with fire and sword all that lay within the province, he boldly made camp beside the River Esla in order to attack the city of León; rightly estimating that nothing would later stand in his way if only he might enter the royal city of the Leonese.

79 His chronology is at fault here: Almanzor did not come to uncontested power in al-Andalus until 981.

80 The Latin words are *regnum imperium*, literally 'kingdom-empire'. Although the phrase has found defenders as a correct reading, it seems likely that it is a copyist's error for *regium imperium*, 'royal empire' or (as suggested here) 'royal authority', a phrase which the author used again in ch. 83. Other translators have been like-minded, Gómez-Moreno rendering it 'una autoridad real', Casariego 'una potestad regia'.

81 The narrative seems to run on naturally with the sentence beginning 'So, laying waste ...' a few lines below. Perhaps the two sentences in between have been interpolated at some later stage.

82 Einhard, *Vita Karoli* ch. 9.

83 On a strictly literal reading these words could be interpreted as indicating that the writer's father had been among the Christian soldiers who took service with Almanzor, though this is surely all but impossible on chronological grounds. However, the phrase might plausibly suggest that tales from that period had been handed down to the author's own day. Some of the episodes of chs 70 and 71 have the feel of story-telling about them: for instance, Almanzor's good justice, his golden helmet, his manner of showing displeasure and the snowstorm which saved León. These are not sufficient to encourage speculation about some lost epic poem which could have been the author's source, though some enquirers have viewed this question more indulgently.

CHAPTER 71

When he heard this the young Ramiro, whom his mother Queen
Teresa was still looking after at León, went forth armed to meet the
enemy accompanied by certain counts. Battle was joined, and Ramiro
drove them back to their tents with huge slaughter. But when the
barbarian saw that his men were exposing themselves in cowardly
flight he sprang from his seat to counter this. For it is said that
Almanzor used to show this sign of displeasure to his troops when
they were fighting poorly: taking off the golden helmet which he
habitually wore on his head he would sit upon the ground with
dishonour. When the barbarian soldiers saw him bareheaded, exhort-
ing one another to action, they surrounded our men on all sides with
much noise. The tables were turned: pursuing our people from behind,
they would have poured headlong through the gates of the city had
not a massive snowstorm interrupted the conflict.[84] His plans for that
year unaccomplished owing to the approach of winter, the barbarian
returned to his own land. Divine displeasure, however, allowed him
such licence in the future that for twelve successive years he assaulted
the frontiers of the Christians in as many campaigns.[85] He took León
and other cities, destroyed the churches of St James and of the holy
martyrs Facundus and Primitivus, as I have said above, together with
many others which it is long to enumerate.[86] He profaned whatever
was sacred with his reckless audacity; and at the end he made the
whole kingdom submit to him and pay tribute. During that same
terrible time in Spain all holy worship *perished, all the glory* of the
Christians *fell away, the accumulated treasures* of the churches *were
dispersed.*[87] At last divine piety, having compassion on such wreckage,
saw fit to lift this scourge from the necks of the Christians. Indeed, in
the thirteenth year of his reign,[88] after many dreadful defeats of the

84 This is not a literal translation: the text does not make sense as it stands; yet the
   general drift is clear. So too Gómez-Moreno, p. cxi and Casariego, p. 140.

85 Almanzor's campaigns against the Christians lasted for over twenty years in all
   until cut short by his death. Fourteen years elapsed between the sack of León in
   988 and Almanzor's death in 1002.

86 The 'church of the holy martyrs Facundus and Primitivus' is the monastery of
   Sahagún (San' Fagun'), about 50 km south-east of León, founded in the early years
   of the tenth century by King Alfonso III. It was sacked by Almanzor in the same
   year as was León, 988; Santiago de Compostela was sacked in 997. If 'as I have said
   above' be taken as referring to Sahagún, it has not previously been mentioned; if to
   Santiago, see above, ch. 30* (with implications for the authorship of that chapter).

87 Einhard, *Vita Karoli* ch.13.

88 See above, n. 85.

Christians, Almanzor was snatched away by the Devil (who had taken possession of him during his lifetime) at the great city of Medinaceli and buried in Hell.[89]

CHAPTER 72

The people indeed of the Goths,[90] freed by God's mercy from such a yoke, little by little recovered strength. For Ordoño, the son of King Fruela, who had reigned for a short time, left a son who survived him named Vermudo.[91] This Vermudo indeed, when he had taken up the direction of the kingdom in the marches of Galicia, was neither hasty nor idle in his duties: from the very beginning of his reign he began to do battle with the Moors with earnest effort.

CHAPTER 73

He fathered Alfonso,[92] a man well-endowed with *bowels of mercy*[93] towards the churches and Christ's poor, and a very vigorous enemy of the barbarians and their cities. In his zeal for the true law of God, in the course of his pursuit with the greatest hatred of the superstitious sect of the barbarians, it is said that he held some of the Moors fast bound by weaponry and hunger at the castle of Viseu.[94] During that campaign he was clad only in a linen shirt owing to the great heat: while he was passing near the city walls on horseback he was struck with an arrow fired from a tower by a certain barbarian who was a skilful archer; he died of the wound, rendering up his soul, as we believe, to God. He left children, Vermudo and a daughter Sancha.[95]

---

89 Almanzor died on 11 August 1002. 'Great city' is a rendering of *maxima civitas*, but both the English and the Latin phrases give a misleading impression. Medinaceli was not a densely-populated town but a military strongpoint and administrative depot which controlled the so-called Middle March in the sparsely settled borderlands of the northern frontier of al-Andalus. See R. Collins, *Spain. An Oxford Archaeological Guide* (Oxford, 1998), pp. 183–4.

90 The author refers, significantly, to the Leonese of the tenth century as the *gens Gotorum*.

91 We return to Vermudo II (see ch. 30* above), son of Ordoño III (951–56). The latter was not the son of Fruela but of Ramiro II.

92 Alfonso V (999–1028).

93 Phil. ii.1; Col. iii.12.

94 In central Portugal, about 110 km north-east of Coimbra.

95 Alfonso's death occurred in July or August 1028. Vermudo III reigned as king of León 1028–37. Sancha married Fernando I (below ch. 75).

CHAPTER 74

For the rest, having demonstrated the maternal descent of Alfonso
our emperor, in order that the noble pedigree of his father may also be
made clear, our tale must turn back for a little while. Accordingly, we
know that the kingdom of the Cantabrians was in part overturned by
Moorish occupation; in part, however, it remained intact by means of
fortification and through the difficulty of gaining entry to its lands.
For whenever the dreaded enemy penetrated further than usual,
leaving the plain behind, he would be making his way to towns and
castles situated in the valleys between the mountains. Then the
Cantabrians, well able to put up with cold and exertion, given the
[nature of the] place and the circumstances, taking up their lighter
arms, would take to *the hills and the hidden forest places.*[96] By creeping
unexpectedly upon the enemy camps,[97] while they were there,[98] and by
attacking them, they often threw them into confusion. *Neither could
such action ever be avenged* by the enemy;[99] for the Cantabrians, agile
and lightly armed, would immediately disperse themselves as soon as
occasion demanded. Thus the fierceness of the Moors which to others
was dreadful was to the Cantabrians a [subject for] mockery. But
García, who was descended from the noble stock of Duke Pedro of the
Cantabrians, after he was proclaimed king, encountered the barbarians frequently in battle and vehemently repulsed their attacks, so
that they should not rage furiously after their usual manner against
the Christians' frontiers.[100] On his death his son Sancho succeeded to
his father's kingdom. God, seeing him to be a devout vindicator of the
Christian faith with the strength of his army, both showered him with
prosperous achievements and made his progeny to grow with multiple

96 Einhard, *Vita Karoli* ch. 9 (in which Einhard was describing the same region in his
    account of the Roncesvalles campaign).

97 Sallust, *Bell. Iug.* lviii, 1.

98 Emending *adderant* to *aderant.*

99 Einhard, *Vita Karoli* ch. 9.

100 The reference seems to be to King García Sánchez II (994–1004), the father of
    Sancho *el Mayor* ('the Great') of Navarre. Certain MSS have a date at the end of
    this sentence which has been the cause of some confusion: Era MVIII (= 970 AD).
    This was the date of the death of King García Sánchez I (933–70), but by being
    taken by many historians as the date of the death of his grandson García Sánchez
    II, the accession of *his* son was pushed back to 970, thus giving him an impossibly
    long reign of sixty-five years. Sancho the Great of Navarre became king in 1004,
    absorbed the county of Castile in 1028 and much of the kingdom of León in 1030,
    and died in 1035. For the history of the kingdom of Pamplona-Navarre in the
    tenth and eleventh centuries see R. Collins, *The Basques* (Oxford, 1986), chs 4 and
    5, with a helpful genealogy on p. 164.

generation. For from the very pinnacles of the Pyrenees as far as the fortress of Nájera[101] he snatched from the power of the pagans as much land as was contained within those bounds. He caused the way of St James to run without the hindrance of deviation, which for fear of the barbarians the pilgrims had trodden by the roundabout route of Alava.[102]

CHAPTER 75

He deserved to enjoy long and happily the company of his sons, among whom the father generously divided the kingdom during his lifetime. He placed the firstborn, García, over the people of Pamplona; warlike Castile received Fernando as her governor on the father's order; and to Ramiro, whom he had fathered from a concubine, he gave Aragon, a little fragment of his realm, so that he should not appear to inherit a kingdom like his brothers, *as being inferior on his mother's side*.[103] Meanwhile Fernando took to wife the very noble young woman Sancha, the daughter of Alfonso the Galician king, her brother Vermudo presiding over the regal nuptials of his sister.[104] Prince Vermudo indeed ruled as king upon the death of his father from the bounds of the Galicians as far as the River Pisuerga which marks off the kingdom of the Cantabrians.[105]

CHAPTER 76

King Sancho, *full of days*[106] and in a benign old age, departed this life in the Era 1073 [= AD 1035] *while* his son García *was on a journey to*

101 In the Rioja, about 40 km to the west of Logroño.

102 For a sketch-map of the pilgrim road to Compostela through the kingdom of Navarre see Collins, *Basques*, p. 212.

103 Sallust, *Bell. Iug.* xi, 3. The sons of Sancho the Great ruled as follows: García (Navarre) 1035–54; Fernando (Castile) 1035–65 (adding León 1037–65); Ramiro (Aragon) 1035–63. The author makes no mention of a fourth son, Gonzalo, for whom a principality was constituted in the Pyrenean counties of Sobrarbe and Ribagorza, to the east of Aragon, 1035–44.

104 Fernando's marriage to Sancha, of critical significance for the writer because it enabled his hero Alfonso VI to be 'sprung from the famous stock of the Goths' (above, ch. 8), took place in (probably) 1032. The description of Alfonso V as 'the Galician king' was also applied to him by a contemporary chronicler writing in Angoulême: Adémar of Chabannes, *Chronique*, ed. J. Chavanon (Paris, 1897), iii, 70 (pp. 194–5).

105 The Pisuerga rises not far from the head-waters of the Ebro and runs southward until its confluence with the Duero a little to the south-west of Valladolid.

106 Jeremiah vi. 11.

Rome in fulfilment of a vow.[107] Fernando had him interred with great
honour, as was fitting for such a father, at the monastery of Oña.[108]
When García returned from Rome, having fulfilled his vows to God,
and already, having been told of his father's death, was approaching
the province of Pamplona, he heard that his brother Ramiro – the one
born of a concubine – was concerting treacheries against him
concerning the kingdom. Ramiro indeed, in order to wreak this crime,
had entered into alliance with some of the neighbouring Moorish
kings, those that is of Zaragoza, Huesca and Tudela.[109] Relying more
on their assistance than on his own efforts, they made camp together
beside the town of Tafalla.[110] Shamefully, he threatened his brother
with war. King García's *spirit could not put up with this contumacy which
seemed* to dishonour him.[111] He assembled a force of the bravest
soldiers of the Pamplonans and at once launched an attack on the
enemy encampments. The greater part of them were cut down like
cattle; those that remained abandoned tents and possessions and,
weaponless, took to flight. But as for Ramiro – the illegitimate one –
that would have been his last day had he not sought places of safety,
having lost his boots, on a horse guided only by a halter.[112]

CHAPTER 77

Meanwhile, from the bond of unity and affection, black discord arose
between Fernando and his kinsman, which from the beginning was
the seedbed of all evils and the unexpected disturber of things good.
For what wonder is it if, there being a pretext, [discord] exercised its
powers here ? While the various impulses of humankind are growing
stronger it obtrudes itself by unbalancing even the sweet-tempered.
Seeing that it even separated that immortal creature, no less, from the
angelic concord, it is matter for no surprise if it stirred up death-deal-

107 Einhard, *Vita Karoli* ch. 2.
108 See above, ch. 11 and n. 54.
109 Alliances of this sort, which spanned religious and cultural frontiers, were not
    uncommon in eleventh-century Spain. For two examples from 1069 and 1073 see
    the texts printed with illuminating commentary by J. M. Lacarra, 'Dos tratados de
    paz y alianza entre Sancho el de Peñalén y Moctadir de Zaragoza (1069 y 1073)'
    in *Homenaje a Johannes Vincke*, I (Madrid, 1962), 121–34, reprinted in his *Coloniza-
    ción, parias, repoblación y otros estudios* (Zaragoza, 1981), pp. 77–94.
110 About 30 km south of Pamplona.
111 Einhard, *Vita Karoli* ch. 11.
112 I.e. without saddle or bridle. The point is that Ramiro's flight, barefoot as well as
    bareback, was undignified as well as cowardly. For the author's attitude to the
    Aragonese, see the introduction.

ing wars among mortals, even among those wise after their earthly fashion.[113] In truth, in this conflict each seemed to have his justification according to human reason. For after the death of Alfonso prince of the Galicians, Sancho of the Cantabrians took advantage of the tender age of Vermudo and had brought under his rule a part of the latter's kingdom, namely from the River Pisuerga as far as the Cea.[114] Vermudo indeed, now of adult age when King Sancho breathed his last, determined to gain his father's kingdom for himself.

CHAPTER 78

In reaction to this Fernando, to whom Alfonso's daughter had been joined in marriage, considered it unjust and almost contrary to any reason that he should be deprived of this land. The two therefore contended together and a great quarrel arose between them. But because they were unequal in military strength, so that Fernando was in no position to withstand Vermudo's attack, he earnestly requested the help of his brother García in campaigning against the enemy. Grief always seizes me, writing of the death of such a king, when I consider his excellent rule. For Vermudo, that noble youth become king, was not a slave to childish diversions and wanton desires as that age tends to be: but from the very outset of his youthful reign he began to govern the churches of Christ and defend them from evil men and to act (like a devout father) as the comforter of the monasteries. There can be no doubt that once Vermudo had been taken from this world he would be a stone fixed in the building of the heavenly Jerusalem. As it is written, *Pile her in heaps*, and the stones are brought together for the celestial building: and again, *The righteous perisheth, and no man layeth it to heart.*[115]

---

113 This is another passage in which the general sense is plain while difficulties of comprehension in detail remain.

114 The River Cea rises in the mountains to the north-east of León and flows southward past Sahagún to its confluence with the River Esla near Benavente due south of León; roughly parallel to the Pisuerga (above, n. 105) but significantly further to the west. In other words, Sancho had appropriated an extensive – and agriculturally rich – tract of the kingdom of León, that region known as the Tierra de Campos.

115 Jeremiah 1.26; Isaiah lvii.1.

CHAPTER 79

So Fernando and his brother gathered together a force of very brave soldiers and made haste to engage the enemy. Vermudo with his following crossed the marches of the Cantabrians and went on his way armed for the encounter. And then across the valley of Tamarón the two opposing armies with their bright weapons regarded one another.[116] Vermudo, ardent and undaunted, at first urged on his famous horse Pelayuelo with his spurs and, desirous to strike the enemy, galloped lance in hand against the densest squadron.[117] But dastardly death, whom no mortal can escape, laid hold on him. As fierce García and Fernando pressed upon [him] ever more strenuously, he was struck down in the very act of charging and fell lifeless to the ground. Seven among his warriors fell bitterly beside him. His body was carried for burial among the other kings at León.

CHAPTER 80

Afterwards Fernando, Vermudo being now dead, coming from the borders of Galicia, besieged León and all the kingdom passed under his control.[118] In the Era 1076, on the tenth of the Kalends of July [= 22 June 1038] the lord Fernando was consecrated in the church of St Mary at León and anointed king by Servando of venerable memory, Catholic bishop of the same church.[119] After he took up the sceptres of the realm's governance with his wife Sancha *it is incredible to relate in*

---

116 Tamarón is about 16 km west of Burgos. The battle took place on 4 September 1037.

117 Some of the phrases used here have rhythms suggestive of the endings of Latin hexameters, e.g. *fulgentibus armis, calcaribus urget, stricta asta incurrit.* This feature, and a few other literary touches such as the reference to the king's horse by name, have suggested to some enquirers that the author might have been drawing upon some lost work lamenting the death of King Vermudo III in Latin verse.

118 It is assumed that after his victory at Tamarón in September Fernando I made a circuit round the city of León before approaching it 'from the borders of Galicia'. One might compare William the Conqueror's approach to London in the autumn of 1066 after his victory at Hastings.

119 For this and other royal inauguration rituals see Linehan, *History and the Historians*, ch. 5. In an apparently original diploma dated the day before the ceremony the scribe Ansur could put into the king's mouth the words 'when I entered León and accepted ordination' (*quando ego rex domno Fredinando in Legione introibi et ordinacione acepi*): see *CD Fernando I*, no. 8. The ceremony was referred to as an *ordinatio* in the king's own prayer book, commissioned by Queen Sancha in 1055 and produced most probably in León or Sahagún: it is now in the Biblioteca Universitaria of Santiago de Compostela.

how short a time[120] the fear of him overshadowed the provinces of the barbarians throughout Hispania. These he would from the outset the more swiftly have laid waste had he not first, to calm the disturbances of his kingdom, prudently taken care to punish the rebel souls of certain noblemen.[121] In this context the extent of his kingdom excited the ambition of his brother García, leading him from brotherly unanimity to the very summit of envy. King Fernando therefore, obstructed by such circumstances, for a full sixteen years accomplished nothing in campaigning against the outsiders beyond his borders.

CHAPTER 81

Meanwhile Queen Sancha conceived and bore a son, who was called Sancho; then she gave birth to a daughter, Elvira; again she conceived and bore a son, whom it pleased both parents to call Alfonso; finally she gave birth to the youngest, García. The parents bore Urraca, a girl of the utmost nobility in comeliness and behaviour, before they attained the fullness of the kingdom.[122] King Fernando took pains so *to educate his sons and daughters that, first, they should be instructed in the liberal disciplines to which he himself had given study. Then, when they were of the right age, he had his sons learn to ride after the manner* of the Spaniards, *to practise the use of weapons and to hunt. Lest his daughters should languish in idleness he ordered them to be taught every womanly skill.*[123] So the government of King Fernando's realm, once it was strengthened by free customs and by troops, *seemed tolerably flourishing and powerful* [but] *as is generally the case in human affairs from its very prosperity there arose envy*[124] between him and his brother García. Notwithstanding Fernando showed himself in all things mild and devout, unwilling to sever himself *from his inherent good nature and customary piety*, he had determined in his heart to endure *the rivalry and envy* of his brother come what may, *lest he might be provoked to anger by him.*[125] He thought that he might always subdue his brother's jealousy by means of his own fame.

120 Sallust, *Bell. Cat.* vii, 3.

121 This discreet hint at disturbances is occasionally amplified by references in Fernando's surviving diplomas to rebellions and confiscations, e.g. *CD Fernando I*, no. 59.

122 See above, n. 39. Observe the writer's flattering tribute to the Infanta Urraca, patroness of San Isidoro de León.

123 Einhard, *Vita Karoli* ch. 19.

124 Sallust, *Bell. Cat.* vi, 3.

125 Einhard, *Vita Karoli* chs 18, 20.

CHAPTER 82

Accordingly, while García lay ill at Nájera, King Fernando, moved by brotherly affection, hastened to pay him a visit. When he had come to him, García took counsel about making the king captive, and an ambush was prepared for him. But in the event it was in vain: apprehensive of such an outcome, Fernando promptly departed to his own land. It so fell out that Fernando in his turn fell ill and King García, as if to make up for so great a crime, humbly approached because of Fernando's illness. It seems to me that García came more to assuage the frustrated crime than to comfort his brother in his illness. Indeed García wished that *he alone might possess the kingdom,*[126] that his brother might be not merely impeded by illness but completely removed from this world: for thus do work the covetous minds of kings. When King Fernando learnt of this he was moved to anger: he ordered him to be put[127] in chains at Cea. García cunningly escaped a few days later and returned to his own land with a few soldiers whom he had secretly gathered together.

CHAPTER 83

Afterwards García, hostile and fierce, began openly to seek out occasions of war and, thirsting for his brother's blood, to lay waste his marches wherever he could. When he heard this King Fernando assembled an enormous army from the borders of Galicia and made ready to avenge the injury [done to] the kingdom. Meanwhile he sent fitting envoys to King García, [requesting him] to leave his marches and embrace peace, so that he should not choose the strife of death-bearing swords with him: for they were brothers, and it was fitting that each of them should dwell peaceably in his own kingdom. He also stated that he could not maintain a multitude of so many soldiers. But King García, ferocious and rash, in contempt of his brother's restraint, heard the envoys out and ordered them to be expelled from his camp. And immediately adding threats, he said that when their lord had been defeated he would carry them off like cattle into his own country together with their conquered companions. For García trusted in his own might, because at that time he was reputed an outstanding soldier, above any knight in all the royal empire.[128] For indeed in

126 Sallust, *Bell. Iug.* viii, 1.
127 Emending *ponere* to *poneri.*
128 Emending *excepto* to *ex toto* (as found in one MS).

every battle he had been accustomed *to perform at once the duties of a valiant soldier and of a good general.*[129] He had also brought with him a very great contingent of Moors whom he had engaged for warfare in the impending campaign.[130]

CHAPTER 84

And so a day and a place was agreed upon between them for the ill-fated conflict. King García had already pitched camp in the middle of the valley of Atapuerca, when King Fernando's troops took possession by night of the hillside which rose above.[131] These troops indeed, for the most part attached to the affinity of King Vermudo, when they learnt of the fervent wish of their lord to take his brother alive rather than dead – at the prompting, as I believe, of Queen Sancha – resolved each and all to avenge the blood which was common to them. At daybreak, when Titan first emerged from the waves,[132] the lines of battle were drawn up, a great clamour went up on both sides, hostile javelins were hurled from a distance, the common fate was dealt out by death-dealing blades. The troop of very brave soldiers whom I touched upon a little earlier loosed their reins and charged downhill at great speed brandishing their spears. Cutting through the middle of the enemy line they fell upon King García, transfixed him and hurled his lifeless body from his horse onto the ground. In that fight two of García's warriors were killed with him. The Moors who had taken part in the battle tried to take to flight, but the greater part of them were taken prisoner. King García's body was taken for burial to the church of Sta María de Nájera which he himself had devoutly raised from its foundations and had splendidly embellished with silver and gold and silken textiles.[133]

CHAPTER 85

King Fernando, after the death of his brother and his brother-in-law, saw that the entire kingdom was subject to his authority without

129 Sallust, *Bell. Cat.* lx, 4.

130 See above ch. 76 and n. 109. The peace-treaties of 1069 and 1073 there referred to stipulated mutual military aid.

131 Atapuerca is about 15 km to the east of Burgos. The battle was fought on 15 September 1054.

132 Pérez de Urbel (p. 187, n. 203) detected an echo of Lucan and/or Manilius here.

133 García had founded the monastery of Nájera in 1052. It was affiliated to Cluny by Alfonso VI in 1079.

challenge. Now secure in his native land, he ordained that the remaining time be given over to campaigning against the barbarians and strengthening the churches of Christ. Accordingly, when winter was past and the summer had begun and owing to the abundance of foodstuffs the army could campaign, the king left the Tierra de Campos and set off for Portugal, over the greater part of which, from the provinces of Lusitania and Betica, the barbarians held sway, belching forth profanities. *Indeed* King Fernando, *throughout his whole life*, kept this resolve firmly in his mind, *never to abandon what he had undertaken nor to lay down a task once begun before he had completed it to the best of his ability.*[134] Because of this trait, dread of him, like the sight of a snake, had terrified the hearts of the barbarians. So he gathered together all his paid troops[135] and first attacked the town of Seia and its surrounding castles.[136] Some barbarians were slaughtered, others at his command he humbled in slavery to himself and his men. It would be tedious to note down one by one the settlements and the many castles of the barbarians laid waste by the ever-victorious King Fernando. Accordingly I have sought to record [only] the names of the principal cities over the churches of which once upon a time bishops presided, which stoutly fighting he dragged from their sacrilegious hands.

CHAPTER 86

After the conquest of the town of Seia he made haste to invest the city of Viseu, with this in mind that the barbarians of that city should make due recompense for the death of his father-in-law Alfonso:[137] the time to avenge their crimes had come round [?].[138] For there was in

---

134 Einhard, *Vita Karoli* chs 5, 20.

135 Emending *stipendiis* to *stipendiariis*. The author probably had in mind those vassals whose service was rewarded by a money payment rather than by a landed fief: see S. Barton, *The Aristocracy in Twelfth-century León and Castile* (Cambridge, 1997), pp. 83, 91, 109–10 and references there cited.

136 Seia is in central Portugal, on the western slopes of the Serra da Estrêla, about 30 km south of Viseu. The author's chronology of Fernando's Portuguese campaigns is vague. If he is correct in placing the capture of Seia before that of Lamego and Viseu, the campaign perhaps took place in the summer of 1057.

137 See above, ch. 73. The author has reversed the order of these triumphs: Lamego fell to Fernando on 29 November 1057, Viseu on 25 July (St James's day) 1058. These dates are derived from the Portuguese annals edited by P. David in his *Etudes historiques sur la Galice et le Portugal du VIe au XIIe siècle* (Paris, 1947), p. 296.

138 This seems to be the general sense: the text is corrupt.

that city a company of very skilled archers. If ever men were to scale the walls in order to assault, unless they strengthened their shields with boards or some stronger protection, the force of the arrow was such as to pierce each shield and a threefold coat of mail. Having reconnoitred all the city's entrances and pitched camp, the king *ordered* picked soldiers accompanied by slingers *to approach* the city of Viseu *and lay siege to the gates.*[139] Then battle was joined, and after some days of fierce fighting he conquered it. Inside the town he found the archer who had killed King Alfonso: he ordered both his hands to be struck off. The other Moors were booty for his soldiers. *Speedily striking camp*[140] Fernando set out for the city of Lamego and when he got there invested it with his army.[141] He endeavoured with a great effort to break down the wall. Although it seemed impregnable owing to the difficulty of the terrain, he *set up towers and siege-engines of various kinds*[142] and conquered it in a short space of time. He subjected the conquered city to his own laws. Some of the Moors of Lamego were put to the sword, others were despatched in chain-gangs for building works on churches.

CHAPTER 87

King Fernando always used to see to it with special care that the better part of the spoils of his victories should be distributed among the churches and Christ's poor to the praise of that highest Creator who gave him victory. He also captured the castle of San Justo on the River Alva, and Tarouca with several other fortifications in the vicinity, which were rendered threatening by the inhospitable landscape.[143] *He levelled them to the ground*[144] so that the barbarians

---

139 Sallust, *Bell. Iug.* xci, 4.

140 Sallust, *Bell. Cat.* lvii, 3.

141 Lamego is situated a little to the south of the River Douro (Duero) about 80 km inland from the Atlantic coast.

142 Sallust, *Bell. Iug.* xxi, 3.

143 Tarouca is about 8 km south of Lamego. I have not identified the castle of San Justo: the River Alva (so, correctly, one MS: others, *Malva*) on which it stood runs from the Serra da Estrêla to its confluence with the River Mondego about 17 km north-west of Coimbra.

144 The phrase used here, *ad solum usque destruxit,* exactly matches the wording used of Charlemagne's dismantling of the walls of Pamplona in the *Annales Regni Francorum s.a.* 778, suggesting that this text (or parts of it) as well as Einhard's *Vita Karoli* was available to the author.

would not be able to place garrisons in them against the Christians.[145] After these triumphs, in order that Coimbra, the biggest city of those parts and the capital of the region, might be restored to Christian cult, the king solicitously sought out the shrine of St James the Apostle, whose body is said to have been borne to Spain by the divine visitation of our Redeemer. He prayed for three days there that this campaign might yield happy and prosperous results, pleading that the apostle would be an intercessor for him with the divine majesty. So, having worshipped at that venerable place, King Fernando, armoured with divine help, boldly made his way to Coimbra and settled down in his camp to besiege it. I have thought it worth recording, so that it might be clear to all, how his very fervent prayer was answered by God.

CHAPTER 88

For there was in the perfected devotions of King Fernando the firm promise of our Saviour when he says, 'Amen, I tell you that *whatsoever ye shall ask of the Father in my name, He may give it you.*'[146] For in this he was imploring that that city might be wrested from the rites of the pagans and restored to the faith of the Christians. Earnestly in the name of Jesus – which means Saviour – he prayed to God the Father for his safety. But because Fernando was still enmeshed in corruptible flesh and knew that he was not close to divine grace by the merit of his life, he sought the assistance of the apostle to intercede as a most privileged courtier of his most holy Master. King Fernando therefore fought at Coimbra with the material sword; James, the knight of Christ,[147] ceased not to implore his Master to bring about the king's victory. At length the blessed apostle of Compostela made known after this fashion that victory had been granted from heaven to the most serene King Fernando.

---

145 The passage which follows from here until the end of ch. 89 has been translated into English by C. Smith, *Christians and Moors in Spain*, vol. I: *711–1150* (Warminster, 1988), text no. 16, pp. 80–4.

146 John, xv.16.

147 Assuming that the author was writing *c.* 1115 (see introduction) this is the earliest known reference to St James under this title.

CHAPTER 89

There had come from Jerusalem a certain Greek pilgrim,[148] poor as I believe both in spirit and in worldly wealth, who settled himself for a long time at the entrance to the church of St James and gave himself over day and night to prayers and vigils. As he little by little acquired facility in our language he heard the local people, as they frequently entered the sacred edifice for their intercessions, importuning the ears of the apostle under the name of 'the good knight'. He said to himself that not only was [St James] no knight, but that he had never even got astride a horse! When nightfall came and daylight was extinguished in the normal way, and the pilgrim was spending his night in prayer, suddenly he was seized by terror. The apostle James appeared to him, holding as it were keys in his hand, and with a cheerful expression said to him, 'Yesterday, mocking the devout intercessions of the people praying, you believed that I had never been a very valiant knight!' As he said this, there was led up to the church's portals a most magnificent horse of great size, whose snow-white brightness filled all the church with light through the open door. The apostle mounted the horse and, displaying the keys to the pilgrim, informed him that the city of Coimbra would surrender to King Fernando on the following morning at about the third hour of the day. The stars went down, and when on the Lord's day the sun first lit up the bright globe, the Greek, amazed at such a vision, *calls together all*[149] the clergy and all the leading men of the town and, ignorant as he was of the [king's] name and campaign, he recounted the incident to them just as it had happened and announced that on that very day King Fernando would enter Coimbra. His hearers, taking note of the day, sent messengers with all speed to the encampments of the undefeated king. Eagerly pursuing their journey, they proclaimed[150] that whether [or not] this vision proceeded from God it should be made known to this world to the praise of the name of His servant. The messengers hastened on their way and reached Coimbra. There they discovered that on the third hour of that very day which the apostle James had indicated at Compostela the king had

---

148 This may seem very odd, but it can be matched by a Greek bishop and his attendant – *Andreas episcopus de Grecia, Gregorius discipulus illius* – who feature in a document drawn up at Oviedo in 1012: *Colección de Documentos de la Catedral de Oviedo*, ed. S. García Larragueta (Oviedo, 1962) no. 41 (at p. 140).

149 Sallust, *Bell. Cat.* xvii, 2.

150 Emending *percipiant* to *praecipiunt.*

taken possession of the city.[151] He had, indeed, for some time confined the inhabitants of Coimbra within their ramparts. Positioning battering-rams round the circumference, he had managed to breach the city wall in part. The barbarians, seeing this, *sent envoys with supplications to the king, asking only life for themselves and their children.*[152] They surrendered to the king the city and all its contents, except for [their] provisions for the journey and a very small[153] sum of money.

CHAPTER 90

Thus was the frenzy of the Moors driven out of Portugal. King Fernando compelled them all to cross the River Mondego which separates the province from Galicia.[154] Over those cities which he recovered from the law of the pagans he set a certain Sisnando, famous in counsel.[155] This man had once been carried off from Portugal a captive by Benahabet king of the province of Betica along with other spoils.[156] Performing many distinguished services Sisnando had achieved such renown among the barbarians by his industry that he was valued more highly by the barbarian king than all [others] in his whole kingdom *as a man indeed whose advice and whose efforts were never useless.*[157] When indeed, having left Benahabet, Sisnando entered the service of King Fernando, owing to his aforesaid experiences, he was invaluable to us, and to the barbarians the mightiest terror, until his

151 Coimbra surrendered to Fernando I on 9 July 1064.

152 Sallust, *Bell. Iug.* xlvi, 2.

153 Emending *per parium* to *perparvum* and supplying *et.*

154 A most surprising error. It was the River Miño (Port. = Minho) which then separated Galicia from Portugal – as it still does – as is clear from a number of references in, for example, the near-contemporary *Historia Compostellana*. Alternatively, is 'Galicia' a mistake for 'Lusitania'? Yet this would still present problems, for it was the Duero and not the Mondego which separated the (Roman) provinces of Galicia (Gallaecia) and Lusitania. Whatever the error, and whether it arose from a simple slip of the authorial pen or from a copyist's lapse of concentration, it had entered the manuscript tradition no later than 1174 when it is found in the *Crónica Najerense,* here dependent on the *Historia Silense: Crónica Najerense,* ed. A. Ubieto Arteta (Valencia, 1966) iii, 22 (p. 100). For the date see D. W. Lomax, 'La fecha de la Crónica Najerense', *Anuario de Estudios Medievales* 9 (1974–9), 405–6.

155 For Sisnando's career see E. García Gómez and R. Menéndez Pidal, 'El conde mozárabe Sisnando Davídez y la política de Alfonso VI con los Taifas', *Al-Andalus* 12 (1947), 27–41.

156 'Benhabet' is the author's rendering of Ibn 'Abbād, the *kunya* or family name of the ruling dynasty of Seville: Sisnando's captor had been al-Mu'taḍid (1041–69).

157 Sallust, *Bell. Iug.* vii, 6.

dying day. King Fernando, in return for his victory over the enemy, worshipped at the shrine of the blessed apostle with gifts and joyfully returned to the city of León. Then, holding a general council of his great men, he ordered a campaign against the barbarians who, assailing from the eastwards regions, from the province of Carthaginensis and the kingdom of Zaragoza, were laying hold of the strongpoints and numerous castles along the River Duero. For by reason of this proximity they were unavoidable enemies, mounting lightning raids for slaves on the frontiers of Castile.

CHAPTER 91

So when the campaigning season came round again, King Fernando reassembled his army and attacked them. After quickly taking the castle of Gormaz, he came to Vadorrey.[158] He subjected that town to his lordship and then boldly approached the city of Berlanga which other castles situated round about protected.[159] But the Moors of that city were struck by great terror that they might become enemy booty. So before the king might lay hold on them they spent several days pulling down the wall in different places and made ready to flee, leaving a throng of women and children behind. After this victory Fernando fell upon the town of Aguilera, triumphed over the castle of Santiuste, and took by combat the fortress of Santamera. Then approaching the castle of Huérmeces del Cerro, he levelled it to the ground. For the safety of the oxen ploughing the fields he also dismantled all the watch-towers which the barbarians had built after their custom on the slopes of Mount Parrantagón and the strongpoints erected throughout the valley of Bordecorex.

CHAPTER 92

When he had made the frontiers of the Cantabrians safe from the threat of the barbarians spewing out of the province of Celtiberia and the kingdom of Toledo, King Fernando gathered together from his whole kingdom very strong forces of soldiers and slingers, intending to conquer the province of Carthaginensis. Having traversed the

---

158 The stupendous tenth-century fortress of Gormaz guards a crossing of the Duero some 33 km south-west of Soria: see Collins, *Archaeological Guide*, pp. 136–8. The other places mentioned in this chapter are in the same general area, the south-eastern zone of Old Castile round Soria, Almazán and Sigüenza.

159 Emending *protegebat* to *protegebant*.

peaks of the mountain of *Honia* very rapidly,[160] just as a starving lion
when he gazes upon the proferred herd of cattle on the open plains,[161]
so the thirsty Spanish king fell upon the lands of the Moors. He drew
up his army opposite the town of Talamanca and pitched camp.[162] He
laid hold of many barbarian *settlements, very rich* in flocks and herds
and other good things; *he laid waste the countryside; he captured and
burnt many castles and towns, inadequately fortified or without a garrison*; he
slaughtered Moors; he ordered women and children and *all their goods
to be the booty of his soldiers.*[163] Then reaching the city of Complutum
which is now called Alcalá he laid waste with fire and sword its
neighbouring farmland and surrounded its defences with [his]
encampments.[164] When the barbarians of Complutum, pinned within
their defences, *see the wall shaken by the battering rams and all their
possessions threatened* from outside,[165] in their necessity they sent
messengers to Halmemon, king of Toledo,[166] [pleading] that he should
look to his safety and that of his kingdom, either by driving back such
an enemy in battle or by buying him off with gifts. He should know
that unless he acts very swiftly both he and the kingdom of Toledo
will soon be lost.

CHAPTER 93

The barbarian, however, heeding the wiser advice, had gathered
together an immense amount of gold and silver coin and of precious
textiles. Under safe conduct he made his way very humbly to the king's
presence and steadfastly[167] besought his excellency to accept gifts and

160 There is a difficulty here. Either *mons Honia* is an unidentified mountain in the
    region which was the focus of attention in the last chapter; or it is Oña, in the far
    north of Old Castile (above, note 54). The trouble with the latter identification is
    that it makes no geographical sense: no king in his right mind would go from
    León to Talamanca and Alcalá by way of Oña. This apparent unfamiliarity with
    the geography of Castile is but one of several indications that our author is
    unlikely to have been an inmate of the Castilian monastery of Silos: see the
    discussion of authorship in the introduction. (Professor Janet Nelson has
    suggested to me that Fernando might have gone out of his way to visit the tombs
    of his ancestors at Oña: see below, ch. 94 and references.)
161 Pérez de Urbel *et al.* (p. 196, n. 229) caught a Virgilian echo here.
162 Talamanca de Jarama, about 40 km north of Madrid.
163 Sallust, *Bell. Iug.* liv, 6.
164 Alcalá de Henares, about 30 km east of Madrid.
165 Sallust, *Bell. Iug.* lxxvi, 6.
166 See above, n. 44.
167 Emending *obnoxius* to *obnixius.*

desist from laying waste his marches. He said furthermore that both he and his kingdom were commended to Fernando's lordship. Now indeed King Fernando, *though he thought that* the barbarian king *spoke insincerely, and though he himself was entertaining designs of a far different nature, nevertheless for the time being*[168] accepted the treasure and called off his campaign against the province of Carthaginensis. Laden with much booty he returned to the Tierra de Campos.

CHAPTER 94[169]

Meanwhile Queen Sancha, seeking an audience with the lord king, persuaded him that a church should be built in León as a royal mausoleum where the bodies of the kings might he *rightly and splendidly*[170] entombed. For King Fernando had [formerly] ordered that his body should be delivered to the tomb either at Oña, a place which he always held dear, or in the church of San Pedro de Arlanza.[171] Queen Sancha on the other hand, given that her father of worthy memory Prince Alfonso and her brother the most serene king Vermudo rested in Christ in the cemetery of the kings at León, exerted all her influence to bring it about that both she and her husband should lie alongside them after death. And so the king yielded to the request of his most faithful wife. Masons were commissioned, who strenuously devoted themselves to such a very worthy task.

CHAPTER 95

Thus King Fernando had ordered everything aright within his frontiers. When the first opportunity arose he summoned his army again and set off to campaign against the provinces of Betica and Lusitania.

168 Sallust, *Bell. Iug.* xi, 1.

169 This chapter has been translated in Williams, 'León: the Iconography' (above, n. 60), p. 234. See also R. McCluskey, 'The early history of San Isidoro de León (X–XII c.)', *Nottingham Medieval Studies* 38 (1994), pp. 35–59.

170 Sallust, *Bell. Iug.* xi, 2.

171 For Oña see above, n. 54. Arlanza, about 40 km south of Burgos, claimed to have been founded by the celebrated early Count of Castile, Fernán González, in the middle years of the tenth century. In a diploma granted to Arlanza in 1039, apparently reliable, Fernando promised to be buried there; and the promise was renewed in 1046: *CD Fernando I,* nos. 12, 32. (It may be significant that though the diploma ran in the name of king and queen together, the undertaking concerning burial was given in the name of the king alone: Queen Sancha was consistently loyal to her Leonese connections.) Fernando was a very generous benefactor whose most imposing gift consisted of the relics of Sts Vincent, Sabina and Christeta, translated from deserted Avila to Arlanza in 1062.

When he had laid waste the fields of the barbarians and burned many
of their villages, Benhabet King of Seville came to meet him with
great gifts.[172] He implored him *for the sake of friendship and for*[173] the
honour of the kingdom to desist from attacking him and his land.
King Fernando indeed, merciful as was his wont to human sufferings,
while he was softened by the prayers of the elderly barbarian,
summoned all the suitable men *from their winter quarters*[174] and debated
with their counsel what answer he should give to the supplications of
the king of the Moors. Then the matter was decided by judgement of
the council. [Fernando] received gifts and gave orders that the body
of the martyr-saint Justa, who formerly at Seville made her way to
Christ with a martyr's crown, should be given back to him so that he
might translate her to the city of León.[175] The barbarian immediately
assented to Fernando's imperial orders and pledged himself to give
him the body of the most blessed virgin.

CHAPTER 96[176]

This undertaking having been accepted, when he had returned from
that campaign King Fernando summoned to him at León the
venerable Bishop Alvito of this royal city and Ordoño the reverend
bishop of Astorga and also Count Muño, and sent them with an escort
of knights to Seville to collect the body of the aforesaid virgin.[177] On
arriving there they reported the king's orders to Benhabet, who
replied to them: 'I know well' he said, 'that what you ask I have
promised to your lord. But neither I nor any of my people can show
you the body which you seek. Search for it yourselves: and when you
have found it take it up and depart in peace.' We little understood

172 For 'Benahabet' see above, n. 156.

173 Sallust, *Bell. Iug.* lxxi, 5.

174 Sallust, *Bell. Iug.* lxii, 4.

175 St Justa was allegedly martyred at Seville in the year 287.

176 As explained in the introduction, chs 96–102 inclusive follow closely the anonymous *Translatio Sancti Isidori*, but with characteristic editorial changes and
additions.

177 Alvito was bishop of León from 1057 to 1063, Ordoño of neighbouring Astorga
from 1062 to 1065. It seems very probable that both men had served in the royal
chancery of King Fernando I before their advancement to the episcopate: see *CD
Fernando I*, nos 20, 29, 31, 34, 35, 39. Their respective sees were well rewarded for
their services in translating the relics of Isidore. Count Muño Muñoz was also
handsomely rewarded, and he thanked the king by giving him 'a very fine hawk':
CD Fernando I, no. 68. For some comments upon the significance of the phrase
'this royal city', see the introduction.

whether the barbarian spoke this truthfully to our embassy, or by way of concealment: *but frequently human desires are as inconstant as they are importunate.*[178] Hearing this the distinguished bishop Alvito counselled his companions and said: 'We must understand, brothers, that we shall return in vain unless divine mercy come to assist the toil of our journey. It seems fitting, best beloved, that we should seek the help of the Lord, to whom nothing is impossible, and engage in three days of fasting and prayer, so that the divine majesty may deign to reveal the treasure of the holy body which is hidden from us.'

CHAPTER 97

The bishop's exhortation that they should spend those three days in prayers was pleasing to all. On the third day, when the sun had traversed the heavens and gone to his repose and the fourth night was approaching, the venerable bishop Alvito, ever wakeful, was still engaged in prayer. He had sat down briefly to rest his weary limbs as he recited to himself one – I know not which – of the psalms and, on account of the great length of his vigils, was overcome by sleep. There appeared to him a man of grizzled and venerable appearance clad in episcopal robes, who addressed him as follows: 'I know that you have come with your companions to this place to take with you from here in translation the body of the most blessed virgin Justa. However, it is not God's will that this city should be left grieving by the departure of this virgin. But His mighty love will not suffer you to depart empty-handed. It is my body that has been given to you, which you may take up and return in triumph to your own.' When the reverend man asked who it was who was giving him these orders, he replied: 'I am Isidore, Doctor of the Spains and bishop of this very city.' Having said this he vanished from the beholder's sight.

CHAPTER 98

Waking, the bishop fell to rejoicing over the vision and giving praise to God more earnestly, imploring that if this vision were from God it might be vouchsafed more fully a second and a third time. Praying thus, he fell asleep again and Lo! the same man in the same apparel [appeared], speaking to him in words not dissimilar to [those uttered on] the previous occasion, and again disappeared. Waking once more, the bishop implored more eagerly of God a third repetition of the

178 Sallust, *Bell. Iug.* cxiii, 1.

vision. While he the more strenuously[179] was praying, for the third
time he fell asleep. Then the aforesaid man appeared to him as on the
first and second occasions and repeated for the third time what he had
said beforehand. He struck the ground three times with the staff
which he held in his hand to show the place where the holy treasure
lay concealed, saying, 'Here, here, here you will find my body. And
lest you think that you are being tricked by an apparition, this will be
a sign to you of the truth of my words. Soon after my body will have
been brought up to the earth's surface you will be attacked by a grave
illness of the body, to which you will succumb; and having shaken off
this mortal flesh you will come to us with the crown of righteousness.'
He made an end of speaking and the vision was taken away.

CHAPTER 99

The bishop woke from sleep assured about so great a vision, more
joyful still about the summons to him. Daybreak had come, and he
exhorted his companions, saying: 'Most beloved, we must worship the
divine omnipotence of the highest Father with humbled minds, who
deigns to go before us[180] with his grace and does not suffer the recompense of our labour to be in vain. We are forbidden by divine
command to take from here the relics of the blessed virgin Justa, dear
to God; but we may take with us gifts no lesser when we shall bear off
the body of the most blessed Isidore, who in this city was vested in
the robe of pontifical authority and who graced all Spain with his
word and his work.' And having said this he told them in order about
the series of visions. They heard it and offered heartiest thanks to
God. They went together to the king of the Saracens and related all
these things to him in order. The barbarian was greatly alarmed.
Though he was an infidel, he wondered at the power of the Lord and
said to them: 'And if I give Isidore to you, with whom shall I remain
here?' However, not daring to resist men of such authority, he gave
permission to search for the relics of the confessor. I speak wondrous
things, related to me, however, by those who were present. While the
search was taking place for the tomb of the blessed body, the tip of the
staff with which the holy confessor by his threefold knock had
indicated his resting-place was found. When it was uncovered, so
powerful a fragrance was emitted that it drenched the hairs of the

179 Emending *obnoxius* to *obnixius*.
180 Emending *precedente* to *precedere*.

head and beard of all who stood by as if with a mist of nectar[181] or the dew of balsam. The blessed body was enclosed in a wooden coffin made of juniper. No sooner had it been opened than sickness attacked the venerable man Bishop Alvito and on the seventh day later he underwent penance and, as true faith believes, surrendered his soul into the hands of the angels.[182]

CHAPTER 100

Taking up the relics of the blessed Isidore and the body of the bishop of León, Bishop Ordoño of Astorga and his escort made haste to retrace their steps to King Fernando. The aforesaid king of the Saracens Benahabet draped a hanging woven with marvellous craftsmanship over the sarcophagus of the blessed confessor,[183] and heaving great sighs from deep within his chest, said 'Lo! O Isidore, man worthy of veneration, so you depart from here! But you yourself have known how this matter is mine as well as thine!'[184] These things were remembered by those who have sworn that they heard them when they were present. So the envoys set out with so great a gift bestowed from heaven, and went back to their own land. Upon their return the most glorious King Fernando laid on a splendid welcome. Although he mourned the death of the bishop of León, nevertheless he organised a magnificent reception for the arrival of the most blessed confessor Isidore. He re-interred the holy body in the basilica of St John the Baptist which the same most serene king had recently built at León, as I have mentioned earlier. The venerable bishop Alvito was buried in the [cathedral] church of St Mary over which with God's aid he had presided.

CHAPTER 101

Thus, four hundred years after his death,[185] the body of the blessed confessor of Christ Isidore was translated from the city of Seville and buried with fitting honour in the city of León. Having gathered together the noblemen, the bishops and the abbots of his entire kingdom, the king had the aforesaid church consecrated in honour of

181 Emending *nectaroque* to *nectareaque*.

182 Later Leonese tradition commemorated his death on 3 September 1063.

183 It is just possible that this textile is the same which (or a part of which) still lines the saint's reliquary in its resting place in the Real Colegiata de San Isidoro de León.

184 The sense of this sentence is not clear.

185 To be precise, 427: Isidore died on 6 April 636.

the confessor on the 22nd day of December in the year of the Lord's Incarnation 1052.[186] On that festive occasion the most glorious king is said to have been assiduous in humility, with such great devoutness, out of reverence for the holy bishop, that when the time came for the feast he laid aside his royal pride and, in place of the servants, with his own hands served the elaborate dishes to some of those men of religion. Queen Sancha also, with her sons and daughters, humbly waited upon the remainder of the company in every respect after the manner of servants.

CHAPTER 102

In that place where the relics of the blessed body are venerated by the faithful people our Lord has deigned to show forth so many and so great miracles to the honour and glory of his name, that if any skilled person were to commit them to writing he would fill no small number of books.[187] But my only purpose is to write of the deeds of kings: it is not my intention for the present to relate how many and how frequent miracles have been wrought upon the bodies of those diverse sufferers who sought his intercession, through the merits of that confessor, by the divine Maker. To Him be glory for ever and ever: Amen.

CHAPTER 103

After the arrival of the body of Isidore the bountiful bishop, the most serene prince Fernando [occupied himself] *in the protection, the enlargement and the embellishment of his kingdom.*[188] Holding sway at León he held a general council of his magnates. He chose to partition his kingdom among his sons in order that after his death they might – should this be possible – live at peace among themselves.[189] Accordingly he set Alfonso, whom before all his children he held dear, over the Tierra de Campos, and subjected to his authority all the kingdom of the Leonese. He appointed his first-born son Sancho king over Castile. And he put[190] the younger, García, in charge of Galicia. Upon

186 An extraordinary error. The translation of Isidore's relics formally took place on 21 December 1063: see *CD Fernando I*, no. 66.
187 Lucas, canon of San Isidoro and later bishop of the Galician see of Tuy, composed such a work early in the thirteenth century, the *Liber Miraculorum Sancti Isidori* (*The Book of Miracles of Saint Isidore*). The text remains unpublished.
188 Einhard, *Vita Karoli* ch. 18.
189 See above ch. 8 and n. 40; also Reilly, *Alfonso VI*, pp. 14–22.
190 Emending *pertulit* to *pretulit.*

his daughters he bestowed all the monasteries of his whole kingdom, in which they might live to their lives' end without the bond of a husband.[191] *He observed the Christian religion, to which he had been devoted since his childhood, with the greatest piety.*[192] He embellished this church which he had newly built and had consecrated in honour of the holy bishop Isidore with gold and silver of the utmost beauty and precious stones and silken hangings.[193] *He would tirelessly attend church morning and evening, also for the late-night hours and at the time of the sacrifice* [of mass],[194] and he rejoiced exceedingly to join with the voices of the clergy in praise of God.

CHAPTER 104

He cared for the church of San Salvador at Oviedo *above other sacred and venerable places* and endowed it with much gold and silver.[195] Furthermore he strove to adorn the church of the blessed apostle James with varied gifts.[196] What more [need I say]? Throughout the whole course of his life the devout and most excellent prince Fernando held nothing more dear, than that the leading churches of his kingdom should *be strengthened* by his gifts *in their ancient dignity* and

191 This sentence has given rise to much discussion. It must not be accepted at its face value: there were scores of religious communities scattered throughout the dominions of Fernando I which were under the ownership or patronage of persons or families unconnected with the royal dynasty. Understanding of the text is assisted if the words 'of his whole kingdom' (*totius regni sui*) are interpreted as 'under his entire control'. The princesses were to manage and be sustained by the resources of certain prominent nunneries or double-monasteries under the patronage of the crown. The resultant lordship was known as the *infantaticum* (Spanish *infantado*). Arrangements of this nature are traceable in Castile and León between the late tenth and the mid-twelfth centuries. It was a device for ensuring livelihood with honour and power to the unmarried ladies of the royal family. Comparable arrangements were to be found in Germany and England at the same period. See most recently P. Stafford, 'Queens, Nunneries and Reforming Churchmen: Gender, Religious Status and Reform in Tenth- and Eleventh-Century England', *Past and Present* 163 (1999), pp. 3–35, especially p. 17. Further research on the institution of the *infantado* is needed. For the present, reference may be made to L. García Calles, *Doña Sancha*, pp. 105–23.

192 Einhard, *Vita Karoli* ch. 26.

193 See Williams, 'León: the Iconography', also the splendid illustrations in *The Art of Medieval Spain* in the section 'Romanesque Spain', pp. 167–328. The phrase 'this church' is yet another pointer to the authorship of an inmate of San Isidoro de León.

194 Einhard, *Vita Karoli* ch. 26.

195 Einhard, *Vita Karoli* ch. 27. San Salvador was the cathedral church of Oviedo.

196 The church of St James (Santiago) at Compostela, not formally the seat of a bishop until 1095, though in practice the seat of the bishops of Iria from at latest the middle years of the tenth century.

that *they should be not only through his agency secure and at peace but also by
his efforts well-endowed and beautiful.*[197] He loved poor pilgrims and
took great trouble in caring for them. Indeed, wherever he discovered
Christian monks, or clergy, or women vowed to God, living in
poverty, having compassion for their need, it was his custom either to
come in person to comfort them or to send money frequently. Thus it
came about that, coming in his mercy to inspect the monks of
Sahagún, satisfied with the monastic routine, he would humbly take
his meal with them at the hour appointed for eating.[198] As was the
custom, vessels for the blessing of the wine had been set out upon the
abbot's table, at which the king was also sitting. Somebody handed a
glass goblet full of wine to the lord king. On the abbot's command
that he should drink of the wine for a blessing, the king took it
clumsily, and it fell onto the table, and because it was delicate it was
shattered into little pieces.[199] The king was overcome by dismay and
felt very guilty. He summoned peremptorily to him one of his
retainers, who were standing by, and ordered him to bring him as
quickly as possible the golden vessel from which he himself was
accustomed to drink. It was brought without delay and placed upright
upon the table. Then he addressed the brothers thus: 'See, my lords, I
restore this vessel to the blessed martyrs in place of the broken one.'
Furthermore he ordered that one thousand gold coins should be given
annually during his lifetime from his own resources to the monks of
Cluny to unloose the fetters of his sins.[200]

CHAPTER 105

When these things had thus been well ordered, he set out with his
armed forces to lay waste the fields and destroy the settlements of the
Moors of the Celtiberian province. He remained there for a long time,
laying waste with fire and sword [those settlements] which were
without fortifications. He came to the city of Valencia[201] which he

197 Einhard, *Vita Karoli* ch. 27.

198 This episode set at the monastery of Sahagún has been pressed into service by
those who attribute the authorship of the *Silense* to a monk of Sahagún.

199 Emending *frustratim* to *frustatim.*

200 This, Fernando's most resplendent piece of munificence, has been very fully studied
by C. J. Bishko, 'Fernando I y los orígenes de la alianza castellana–leonesa con
Cluny', *CHE* 47–8 (1968), 31–135 and 49–50 (1969), 50–116. There is an English
translation in his volume of collected essays, *Studies in Medieval Spanish Frontier
History* (London, 1980), no. II.

201 On the Mediterranean coast of Spain.

would have conquered within a short space of time had he not been struck down with illness and bedridden. *Having accepted the surrender of all the cities and castles*[202] of the Celtiberian province, sick in body he was carried to León in the month of December [where] he prayed at the shrine of St Isidore the confessor of Christ. He entered the city on Saturday 24 December.[203] As was his custom he adored the bodies of the saints on bended knees, imploring that, if already the fearful hour of death should seem to threaten him, his soul might be presented without hurt, free from the power of darkness, before the court of Christ his redeemer, through their intercession and that of the angelic choirs. Then, in the festal night of the Lord's Nativity, when the clergy were singing the early morning mass of the Nativity appointed for that festival, the lord king was present with them. With what strength he could summon he joyfully joined in singing the last response of matins, *Advenit nobis*, which at that time they sang in the Toledan manner, the succentors responding *Erudimini omnes qui iudicatis terram*;[204] which seemed then not unsuitable for the most serene King Fernando who while it was given him to live both governed his kingdom in a Catholic manner and himself in an entirely devout one, restraining unchastity as with a bridle.

CHAPTER 106

When the clear day of the Nativity of the Son of God lightened the whole world, the lord king began to feel the strength ebb from his limbs. He asked for Mass to be sung and after receiving the body and blood of Christ he was led by hand to his bed. At daybreak on the following day, knowing what was to come, he summoned to him the bishops and abbots and religious men, and that they might fortify his passing he was carried to the church, together with them, clad in his royal apparel with his crown upon his head. Then he knelt before the altar of St John and the bodies of the saints – the blessed Isidore

---

202 Einhard, *Vita Karoli* ch. 9.

203 For what follows, see Charles J. Bishko, 'The Liturgical Context of Fernando I's last days according to the so-called *Historia Silense*', *Hispania Sacra* 17–18 (1964–5) 47–59, reprinted in his second volume of collected essays, *Spanish and Portuguese Monastic History 600–1300* (London, 1984), no. VII. Professor Bishko has suggested that the author was drawing upon a written account of the king's deathbed, composed presumably at San Isidoro.

204 'Be instructed, ye judges of the earth', from Psalm ii.10. These responses formed part of the liturgy for Christmas Day according to the so-called Mozarabic Rite ('the Toledan manner') which was abandoned in favour of the Roman liturgy in 1080.

confessor of the Lord and St Vincent the martyr for Christ[205] – and in
a loud voice addressed the Lord: 'Thine is the power, thine the
kingdom, O Lord. Thou art above all kings. All realms both heavenly
and earthly bow to thy governance. Behold, I therefore render back to
thee the kingdom which I received as thy gift, and which I have ruled
for as long as it freely pleased thy will. Only, I pray thee, receive my
soul in peace, snatched from the whirlpool of this world.' When he
had spoken these words he took off the royal cloak with which his
body was attired and removed the gem-encrusted crown with which
his head was adorned and, tearfully prostrating himself on the floor of
the church, he earnestly implored God for the forgiveness of his sins.
Then he underwent [the sacrament of] penance at the hands of the
bishops. He was robed in a hair shirt in place of his royal garments
and scattered with ashes instead of a golden diadem. God granted him
two days to live in this state of penance. On the following day, which
was Tuesday, at the sixth hour of the day on which the feast of St
John the Evangelist is celebrated, he rendered his soul to heaven
between the hands of the bishops. Thus, in a good old age, full of
days, he departed in peace in the Era 1103 [= AD 1065]. His body
was buried in the church of St Isidore the mighty bishop, which he
himself had built from its foundations in León, in the twenty-seventh
year of his reign, with six months and twelve days.[206]

205 When St Vincent's relics were translated to Arlanza in 1062 (above ch. 94 and n.
   170), a portion of them were given to San Isidoro de León.
206 As Bishko has shown, the correct date of Fernando's death was Thursday 29
   December 1065 (not Tuesday 27 December); he has also plausibly demonstrated
   how the error arose: above, n. 203. The calculation in the closing phrase is the time-
   span from coronation to burial: 22 June 1038 plus twenty-seven years, six months
   and twelve days gives us 2 January 1066 as the date of the king's interment.

II: BISHOP PELAYO OF OVIEDO, *CHRONICON REGUM LEGIONENSIUM*

Introduction to the *Chronicon Regum Legionensium* of Bishop Pelayo of Oviedo

The *Chronicon Regum Legionensium*, or Chronicle of the Kings of León, attributed to Bishop Pelayo of Oviedo (1101–30 and 1142–3), is a brief history of the Leonese monarchy from the accession of Vermudo II in 982 to the death of Alfonso VI in 1109.[1] The *Chronicon* forms part of a compilation of historical works, the *Liber Chronicorum*, which was put together in the *scriptorium* of Oviedo cathedral some time before 1132, and which itself belongs within the voluminous collection of writings that was assembled under Bishop Pelayo's supervision, today known as the *Corpus Pelagianum*.[2] Although some elements of the *Corpus*, such as the *Chronicon* itself, are original compositions, many others are either heavily interpolated copies of earlier works and documents, or else outright forgeries. If Pelayo is well known today, it is less for his accomplishments as a scholar than for his wholesale falsification of the historical record, an activity which has earned him the soubriquet of *el Fabulador*, 'the Fabulist'.[3]

Nothing is known of Pelayo's background. From the inclusion of a genealogy in the *Liber Testamentorum*, the cathedral cartulary commissioned by the bishop *c.* 1120, it has been conjectured that he may have been related to the founding families of the monasteries of Coria and Lapedo in the western Asturias.[4] Pelayo may also have had Leonese connections. In 1136 he granted to the canons of Oviedo the

---

1 B. Sánchez Alonso (ed.), *Crónica del obispo Don Pelayo* (Madrid, 1924) is the most recent edition. There has been a partial translation into Spanish by J. E. Casariego, *Crónicas de los reinos de Asturias y de León* (León, 1985), 172–81.

2 For a guide to the contents of the *Corpus*, see the *Inventario General de Manuscritos de la Biblioteca Nacional*, IV (Madrid, 1958), no. 1513, pp. 401–4; F. J. Fernández Conde, *El Libro de los Testamentos de la catedral de Oviedo* (Rome, 1971), pp. 50–69.

3 For an introduction to the life and works of Bishop Pelayo, see Fernández Conde, *Libro de los Testamentos*, pp. 35–80; M. G. Martínez, 'Regesta de Don Pelayo, obispo de Oviedo', *Boletín del Instituto de Estudios Asturianos* 18 (1964), 211–48.

4 Fernández Conde, *Libro de los Testamentos*, p. 37.

properties he owned at Villamoros and Trobajuelo near León;[5] that he admired and was well-acquainted with the city of León is clear to see from his description of the final days of Alfonso VI in the *Chronicon*, and from the lines he penned as part of the treatise he composed on the origins of the cities of León, Oviedo, Toledo and Zaragoza in 1142.[6] It is possible that Pelayo served successively as deacon and archdeacon of the cathedral chapter of Oviedo before being elected bishop of the see.[7] According to the prologue to the *Corpus Pelagianum*, he was then consecrated into the see of Oviedo on 29 December 1098, which has led some historians to speculate that he served as auxiliary to Bishop Martín until the latter's death on 1 March 1101.[8] However, there is no documentary evidence to support this. Pelayo ruled the see of Oviedo for the best part of three decades, until in February 1130, at the Council of Carrión, he and his fellow prelates Diego of León and Muño of Salamanca, were deposed by the papal legate Cardinal Humbert, apparently for having challenged the validity of Alfonso VII's marriage to Berengaria of Barcelona on the grounds of consanguinity.[9] After the death of his successor Alfonso, in January 1142, Pelayo returned briefly to administer the affairs of the see until the early summer of 1143.[10] He died on 28 January 1153.[11]

During his thirty years in office, Pelayo was a political figure of some importance. He attended most of the major councils of the kingdom that were held during the early decades of the twelfth century and was a regular visitor to the court of Queen Urraca. His stalwart

5 S. García Larragueta (ed.), *Colección*, no. 151.

6 M. Risco, *ES* 38 (Madrid, 1793), pp. 373–5.

7 If he may be identified as the same *Pelagius diaconus* and *archidiaconus* who confirmed two Oviedo charters of 1096 and 1097: Fernández Conde, *Libro de los Testamentos*, p. 37, n. 9.

8 Risco, *ES* 38, pp. 99 and 371. Cf. Fernández Conde, *Libro de los Testamentos*, p. 37 and n. 11 and B. F. Reilly, *The Kingdom of León–Castilla under Queen Urraca, 1109–1126* (Princeton, 1982), p. 32, n. 66.

9 On the background to Pelayo's deposition, which was carried out by the papal legate Cardinal Humbert, apparently in league with Alfonso VII and Archbishop Diego Gelmírez of Santiago de Compostela, see B. F. Reilly, 'On getting to be a bishop in León–Castile: the "Emperor" Alfonso VII and the Post-Gregorian Church', *Studies in Medieval and Renaissance History* 1 (1978), 37–68, at pp. 48–51.

10 He is cited as bishop of Oviedo in a number of private documents of March and April 1142 and March 1143: see Reilly, *Alfonso VII*, p. 33, n. 50. By June 1143, however, the archdeacon Froila Garcés had assumed the administration of the see: García Larragueta (ed.), *Colección*, no. 155. The new incumbent of the see, Bishop Martín, was elected at the council of Valladolid in September 1143.

11 Fernández Conde, *Libro de los Testamentos*, p. 44.

support, both moral and monetary, for Urraca's cause during her struggles with her estranged husband, Alfonso I of Aragon (1104–34), and with her son, the future Alfonso VII, in 1110–17 earned Pelayo the queen's gratitude.[12] He also played a part in bringing about the reconciliation between Urraca and her son Alfonso at the council held in Sahagún in 1116.[13] However, Pelayo's star appears to have waned after the accession of Alfonso VII in 1126. The bishop appears only rarely in the records of the new king's court and he was never the recipient of royal largess. What is more, it was probably Pelayo's opposition to Alfonso's proposed marriage with Berengaria in 1127 that led to the bishop's eventual removal from office three years later, by which time the king and his advisors, anxious to consolidate the authority of the crown, may have regarded the independent-minded Pelayo as a positive threat to the good order of the realm.[14]

At a local level, Pelayo was to all apppearances a busy and conscientious prelate: he supervised a programme of building works in the cathedral of San Salvador; he reorganised the administration of the cathedral chapter and the archdiaconate of the diocese; he conducted property transactions on behalf of the see; and he travelled widely within his diocese, consecrating churches and abbots, and settling lawsuits.[15] What is more, he worked hard to promote Oviedo as a centre of pilgrimage to rival that of Santiago de Compostela.[16] Even after his removal from office he continued to look after the wellbeing of the church of Oviedo, as is vouchsafed by his grant of two Leonese properties to the cathedral refectory in February 1136.[17]

Throughout his career Bishop Pelayo proved to be a ferocious defender of the rights and privileges of his see. This defence was based upon three strategic principles which were to condition and underpin his subsequent scholarly activity. First, he sought to protect

12 Details in Fernández Conde, *Libro de los Testamentos*, pp. 44–50. Urraca made grants to Oviedo in 1112, 1118 and 1120: García Larragueta (ed.), *Colección*, nos 131, 140 and 142. On the first of these, which has been interpolated, see Reilly, *Urraca*, p. 79, n. 107.

13 *HC*, pp. 197–8.

14 Reilly, 'On getting to be a bishop', 49–50.

15 Details in Fernández Conde, *Libro de los Testamentos*, pp. 69–72.

16 See S. Suárez Beltrán, 'Los orígenes y la expansión del culto a las reliquias de San Salvador de Oviedo', in *Las peregrinaciones a Santiago de Compostela y San Salvador de Oviedo en la Edad Media*, ed. J. I. Ruíz de la Peña Solar (Oviedo, 1993), 37–55, at pp. 46–51.

17 See above, n. 5.

and consolidate the seigneurial rights of the church of Oviedo within its own diocese. The lawsuits the bishop fought with Count Fernando Díaz and Countess Enderquina Muñoz and with the abbot of Corias in 1104 bear ample witness to Pelayo's resolution in this regard.[18] Second, Pelayo was determined to ensure that the borders of his diocese were respected, and to this end he became embroiled in lengthy but inconclusive jurisdictional disputes with his episcopal neighbours: to the east with the diocese of Burgos over their respective claims to the territory of Asturias de Santillana; to the west with the see of Lugo over ownership over a group of parishes.[19] Last, and most important of all, Pelayo waged a vigorous campaign to maintain the independence of his see from the metropolitans of Toledo and Braga, both of which sought to make Oviedo their suffragan.

Bishop Pelayo held office at a time of considerable upheaval for the church in western Iberia.[20] The territorial expansion of the kingdom of León in the late eleventh century had been accompanied by a far-reaching programme of ecclesiastical reform designed to ensure the integration of the western Spanish churches into the wider community of western Christendom. The changes introduced by the reforming popes and their legates, as well as by the incoming French clerics who were appointed to most of the top ecclesiastical positions, were many and varied: they included the suppression of local ecclesiastical customs (notably the so-called Mozarabic liturgy), the introduction of a new-fangled canon law, and even the imposition of a new form of writing. What is more, they introduced a system of metropolitan and territorial diocesan organisation designed to replace the one that had been destroyed by the Muslim conquest nearly four centuries earlier. In an ideal world, the reformers would have preferred to have restored the administrative framework of the Visigothic church *in toto*. But political realities on the ground made it impossible to turn the clock back. Although the majority of dioceses had formerly existed in the Visigothic period, there were a handful which could boast no such pedigree, among them those of Oviedo and León, both of which had come into being because of their role as royal centres of government in the fledgling Asturian–Leonese kingdom. The accommodation of these 'new' sees into the administrative framework

18 Fernández Conde, *Libro de los Testamentos*, p. 38.
19 Fernández Conde, *Libro de los Testamentos*, pp. 73–8.
20 For what follows, see R. A. Fletcher, *The Episcopate in the Kingdom of León in the twelfth century* (Oxford, 1978), pp. 21–6, 135ff.

of the Church was to require a complicated process of restructuring and redefinition of diocesan boundaries which in turn gave rise to numerous jurisdictional disputes. Matters were further complicated by the re-establishment of the metropolitans of Toledo in 1086 and Braga in 1091, to which that of Santiago de Compostela was added in 1120. The three archbishoprics wasted little time in seeking to enforce their authority over their suffragan sees and were keen to extend their provinces further. Thus, Oviedo, along with León and Palencia, was declared a suffragan of the ecclesiastical province of Toledo by Pope Urban II in 1099, but after an appeal to Rome was granted a privilege of exemption by Paschal II in 1105.[21] The battle was won, but not the war. Some time between 1109 and 1113 Braga launched its own unsuccessful attempt to make Oviedo and León its suffragans, and in 1121 Toledo successfully persuaded Pope Calixtus II to strip both sees of their privilege of exemption.[22] Although León soon managed to get this ruling overturned, almost another forty years would elapse before Oviedo would regain its cherished independence.

Pelayo's work as an author and as a patron of learning took place against this backdrop of fiercely competitive ecclesiastical politics. By the early twelfth century, Oviedo, although it could claim to be the cradle of the self-proclaimed revived Visigothic monarchy in Asturias, had become something of a backwater. The diocese was eyed greedily by the predatory metropolitans of Toledo and Braga. Power and influence lay elsewhere. Compared with the ambitious and energetic Diego Gelmírez, the newly elevated archbishop of Santiago de Compostela, who could count upon a network of friends and allies in high places – both at home and abroad – to support his cause, Bishop Pelayo's horizons appear to have been more circumscribed.[23] By the end of his career one not only gets the impression that his presence was seldom in demand at the royal court, but also that he lacked the international connections and the financial wherewithal which might have enabled him to fight a successful rearguard campaign at the papal court to retain the privilege of exemption for his see. In these straitened circumstances, it was hardly surprising that Pelayo should have turned to his cathedral *scriptorium* to provide him with the ammunition he needed if the rights of his church were to be successfully defended.

---

21 *JL*, nos 6039, 6931.

22 C. Erdmann (ed.), *Papsturkunden in Portugal* (Göttingen, 1927), no. 12, pp. 164–5; *JL*, no. 6934.

23 Fletcher, *Saint James's Catapult*, pp. 195ff.

Bishop Pelayo was far from being the only Iberian churchman prepared to forge documents in order to exalt his church and buttress the rights and privileges – real or imagined – of his see.[24] What set Pelayo apart from his contemporaries, however, was the sheer scale and ambition of this activity. Pelayo of Oviedo, it has been said, was the 'prince of falsifiers', who elevated the activity to a virtual art-form.[25] The interpolations and outright forgeries carried out by Pelayo or, at any rate, under his supervision, were so many and so varied that they cannot be listed here in full. Among the most egregious inventions, however, were the various adulterated texts which sought to establish that far from being a 'new' see, the church of Oviedo was in fact descended from that of Lugo de Asturias, supposedly founded in the era of the Vandal invasions of the fourth century; a collection of forged charters which purported to uphold Oviedo's territorial claims in jurisdictional disputes with the sees of Burgos and Lugo; and a number of documents which even claimed that Oviedo had itself once enjoyed metropolitan status.[26] Among the latter texts were a forged *epistola* of Pope John VIII granting metropolitan status to Oviedo, and the spurious *acta* of the councils supposedly held in Oviedo in 821 and 872, which not only listed Lugo and Braga as suffragans of Oviedo, but went so far as to state that after the Islamic conquest, in punishment for sin, God had transferred all the rights and privileges of the church of Toledo, as well as its splendid collection of relics, to Oviedo.[27] To enhance the prestige of his see yet further, Pelayo composed a separate account of the Pilgrimage of the *Arca Santa* (the celebrated reliquary housed in the cathedral of San Salvador) from Jerusalem to Oviedo via Toledo, which was subsequently copied into the *Liber Testamentorum*, and interpolated into the *Chronicle of Sebastian* that is

24 McCluskey, 'Malleable accounts', p. 219. On the efforts of the twelfth-century church of Palencia to strengthen its claim to metropolitan status, for example, see A. D. Deyermond, *Epic Poetry and the Clergy: Studies on the 'Mocedades de Rodrigo'* (London, 1969), pp. 97ff; Linehan, *History and the Historians*, pp. 177–9.

25 The phrase was coined by P. A. Linehan, 'Religion, nationalism and national identity in medieval Spain and Portugal', in *Religion and National Identity*, ed. S. Mews, *Studies in Church History* 18 (Oxford, 1982), 161–99, at p. 162.

26 For a detailed study of the Pelagian forgeries, see Fernández Conde, *Libro de los Testamentos, passim.* See also L. Vázquez de Parga, *La División de Wamba* (Madrid, 1943); D. Mansilla, 'La supuesta metropolí de Oviedo', *Hispania Sacra* 8 (1955), 259–74.

27 García Larragueta (ed.), *Colección*, nos 4 and 9; Pérez de Urbel, *Sampiro*, pp. 289–302.

included in the *Liber Chronicorum*.[28] Pelayo was nothing if not ambitious. By recreating such a glorious and ancient past for his cathedral church, the bishop sought not simply to protect his see from the unwelcome attentions of the archbishops of Braga and Toledo, and to strengthen its claim to metropolitan status, but to reinforce Oviedo's credentials as a major centre of veneration and pilgrimage. In short, Bishop Pelayo hoped that the collection of holy relics housed within the cathedral of San Salvador would do for the see of Oviedo what the body of St James had done for Santiago de Compostela.

Pelayo's *Chronicon* is one of the very few original works contained within the celebrated *Corpus Pelagianum*. It survives in some two dozen manuscripts, the earliest of them dating from the late twelfth century.[29] Intended as a continuation of the work of Sampiro, which was copied, extensively interpolated and finally truncated by the *scriptorium* of Oviedo cathedral, the *Chronicon* is, in many respects, a strange and sadly laconic text. Pelayo's Latin is unsophisticated and workmanlike. His writing altogether lacks the verve and the rhetorical flourishes which are so characteristic of his contemporary the author of the *Historia Silense*; and although, to judge by the contents of the *Corpus*, the bishop of Oviedo was presumably an exceedingly well-read man, his *Chronicon* displays none of the conspicuous erudition that is such a hallmark of the *Silense* and the *Chronica Adefonsi Imperatoris*. Indeed, the handful of phrases which appear to have been copied from the *Chronicle of Sampiro* are the only clear indication we have that Pelayo undertook any preparatory reading at all.[30] The *Chronicon* gives every impression of having been put together with some haste.

When did Pelayo compose his history? The preface to the *Liber Chronicorum*, dated 1132, which lists the bishop's work amongst its contents, provides us with a clear *terminus ante quem*.[31] There is a

28 On the supposed origins and contents of the *Arca Santa*, see García Larragueta (ed.), *Colección*, no. 217; L. Vázquez de Parga, J. M. Lacarra and J. Uría Ríu, *Las peregrinaciones a Santiago de Compostela*, 3 vols (Madrid, 1948–49), II, pp. 479ff.

29 For a full discussion of the manuscript tradition, see Sánchez Alonso (ed.), *Crónica*, pp. 17–33; Pérez de Urbel, *Sampiro*, pp.165–96.

30 For all that, the Preface to the *Liber Chronicorum* assures us that Pelayo had based his *Chronicon* 'sicut a maioribus et predecessoribus suis inquisiuit et audiuit': Pérez de Urbel, *Sampiro*, p. 480. On the use that Pelayo made of the *Chronicle of Sampiro*, see Sánchez Alonso (ed.), *Crónica*, pp. 43–4; Pérez de Urbel, *Sampiro*, pp. 43ff.

31 Pérez de Urbel, *Sampiro*, pp. 479–80.

further clue in the text of the *Chronicon* itself, where reference is made to the marriage of the Infanta Sancha Alfonso, daughter of Alfonso VI, to Count Rodrigo González. We know that the latter was not elevated to the countship until 1121 and that his marriage to the infanta had certainly taken place by July 1122.[32] Elsewhere, the fact that Alfonso VII is referred to as *rex* might be taken to indicate that the *Chronicon* must have been composed after March 1126 when Alfonso's mother Urraca died. But this argument is not conclusive, for Alfonso VII had assumed regal status in 1111, well before his mother's death. Accordingly, we can only narrow down the date of composition of the *Chronicon* to some time between 1121 and 1132.

The *Chronicon* is a work of limited scope and ambition. Pelayo provides a brief sketch of events between 982 and 1109, but his focus is often narrowly ecclesiastical, some of the events he narrates are clearly legendary, and he evinces precious little interest in the political and military deeds of the Leonese kings. Moreover, his narrative tends towards the superficial.[33] Thus, while roughly half of his work is given over to a damning account of the reign of Vermudo II, which was designed to supersede the positive portrayal provided by Sampiro's *Chronicle*, his coverage of that of Alfonso V covers barely a dozen lines of printed text; and his description of the notable feats of arms of Fernando I and Alfonso VI amounts to little more than a bald list of the towns they conquered. Yet, for all its weaknesses as a narrative work of history, the *Chronicon* is not without interest. Pelayo's admiring account of the reign of Alfonso VI, 'the father and defender of all the Spanish churches', short though it is, is the only surviving contemporary account to cover the reign in its entirety. The highly critical portrayal of Vermudo II, whom Pelayo blamed for his extra-marital affairs and the consequent invasion of the Leonese kingdom by al-Manṣūr (Almanzor) in the late tenth century, as well as for the rough justice meted out to Pelayo's predecessor, Bishop Godesteo of Oviedo, may be highly tendentious stuff, but it tells us much about the attitudes and interests of Pelayo himself.[34] In particular, Pelayo's account of the imprisonment of Bishop Godesteo, as well as his entirely fictional description of the testing of Bishop Adaúlfo of Santiago de Compostela, were clearly designed as a warning to other

32 Barton, *Aristocracy*, p. 292.

33 See the crushing verdict of B. Sánchez Alonso, *Historia de la historiografía española* (Madrid, 1947), p. 117.

34 On the reasons for Pelayo's negative portrayal of Vermudo II, see Pérez de Urbel, *Sampiro*, pp. 46–52.

'tyrant kings' to respect the Church and its leaders. The bishop displays in abundance the providential sense of history common to most writers of this period: thus, according to Pelayo, it was on account of the sins of Vermudo II that God was provoked to inflict a long drought on Spain, to allow the attacks on the Leonese kingdom by Almanzor, and even to inflict the king with gout. Similarly, the miracle Pelayo claimed to have witnessed in the church of San Isidoro in León was said to have been nothing less than a portent of 'the sorrows and tribulations that befell Spain' after the death of Alfonso VI: a clear reference to the wars of Queen Urraca's reign. Elsewhere, Pelayo's detailed account of the descendants of Vermudo II and of the matrimonial strategy of Alfonso VI reveals a keen interest in genealogy which can be glimpsed elsewhere in the *Corpus Pelagianum*.[35] And needless to say, Pelayo was never slow to spot an opportunity to enhance the reputation of his see, as can be seen from his account of the translation of the holy remains of St Pelagius from León to Oviedo, and those of St Froilán to nearby Valle César in the Asturian mountains, as well as from his detailed description of the royal pantheon that was established in the church of St Mary in Oviedo.

Brief and idiosyncratic though it may seem to the modern eye, Pelayo's *Chronicon* was widely used and copied by later historians. The author of the *Chronica Adefonsi Imperatoris*, for one, drew a limited amount of material from the *Chronicon* and from the Pelagian version of the Chronicle of Sampiro, and many of Pelayo's writings (and inventions) were extensively incorporated into the late twelfth-century compilatory work known as the *Crónica Najerense*, and into the thirteenth-century 'general histories' of Lucas of Tuy and Rodrigo Jiménez de Rada, and from them into Alfonso X's vernacular *Estoria de Espanna*.[36] Modern scholars have been far more critical of Pelayo's work as a historian.[37] But that is perhaps to misunderstand the man and the

35 See Fernández Conde, *Libro de los Testamentos*, p. 60 and n. 102; M. Calleja Puerta, 'Una genealogía leonesa del siglo XII: la descendencia de Vermudo II en la obra cronística de Pelayo de Oviedo', in *La nobleza peninsular en la Edad Media* (León, 1999), 527–39. Pelayo's outline of the genealogy of the Leonese royal house was not without error, however: see below, *Chronicon*, nn. 28, 30, 32, 34.

36 See F. J. Fernández Conde, 'La obra del obispo ovetense D. Pelayo en la historiografía española', *Boletín del Instituto de Estudios Asturianos* 25 (1971), 249–91, at pp. 250–55.

37 See above, n. 33; Fernández Conde, 'La obra', 256–90. A notable exception to the rule was A. Blázquez y Delgado Aguilera, 'Elogio de Don Pelayo, obispo de Oviedo y historiador de España', *Memorias de la Real Academia de la Historia* 12 (1910), 439–92.

sense of purpose that underlay his scholarly activity. The very brevity of Pelayo's *Chronicon* suggests that in the wider scheme of things reconstructing the past *per se* was never central to the bishop's concerns. The priority for Pelayo was always to defend the interests of Oviedo and in doing so, to provide his see with the glorious history that he felt it deserved.

Bishop Pelayo of Oviedo, *Chronicon Regum Legionensium* (Chronicle of the Kings of León)

VERMUDO II

On the death of Ramiro [III], Vermudo [II] the son of Ordoño [III] entered León and acquired the kingdom peacefully.[1] That king was foolish and a tyrant in everything he did.[2] Without any reason, he imprisoned Bishop Godesteo of Oviedo[3] in the castle which is called Peña Reina[4] on the borders of Galicia, and for three years he kept him in chains. During that time the Saviour of the world gave such a drought on earth, that no man could either plough or sow, which caused great famine in all of Spain. Then some God-fearing men said to the king: 'Lord King, some of God's servants have seen a vision, and have told us that you sinned before God when you imprisoned the bishop of Oviedo, and that it will not rain nor will famine leave your kingdom until you release the bishop and send him away in peace'. When he had heard this, the king sent messengers to Bishop Jimeno of Astorga, to whom he had entrusted the church of Oviedo,[5] and he ordered that the bishop of Oviedo be freed, and he restored him to his church.

1 This phrase, which also appears in the text of the *Historia Silense*, was in all likelihood drawn from the *Chronicle of Sampiro*: see the introduction to this text, n. 30; cf. the introduction to the *HS*, p. 11, and ch. 30* and preceding comments. Ramiro III, king of León (966–85) had been ousted from the throne towards the end of his reign by his cousin Vermudo II (982–99), son of King Ordoño III (951–56), and died shortly afterwards.

2 Pelayo's extremely hostile portrayal of Vermudo II should be compared with the more sympathetic assessment in the *HS*, ch. 30*, most but not necessarily all of which was probably penned by Bishop Sampiro. On the reasons for Pelayo's hostility towards the Leonese monarch, see the introduction to this text: pp. 72–3.

3 Godesteo, bishop of Oviedo (992–1012).

4 Peña Reina has not been identified.

5 Jimeno, bishop of Astorga (992–1028), administered the affairs of the diocese of Oviedo between 996 and 999: A. Quintana Prieto, *El obispado de Astorga en los siglos IX y X* (Astorga, 1968), pp. 495–9.

From that day, therefore, Lord Jesus gave rain over the face of the earth, the earth gave forth its fruit, and famine was expelled from his kingdom.

Then that tyrant king did a worse thing. Three servants of the church of St James the Apostle, whose names were Zadón, Cadón and Ensión, falsely accused their lord, Bishop Adaúlfo, of the very worst of crimes before him. And since Vermudo was foolish, he readily lent his ears to those very false accusations and believed them. He swiftly sent messengers to command the bishop of Santiago that on Palm Sunday, after the consecration of chrism, he should leave Compostela and go to Oviedo on the day of the Lord's Supper,[6] where he himself was. In the meantime, the king ordered several wild bulls to be brought to him and he chose a very fierce one, which he ordered to be kept until the bishop arrived. So the bishop came to Oviedo on the appointed day. The king's soldiers told him that he should go first to the king before he entered the church. But he, supported by God, said: 'First I shall go to the King of Kings and Our Saviour, and afterwards I shall come to your tyrant king'. He entered the church of Our Saviour and put on the sacred pontifical robes, and when he had celebrated Mass he left the church dressed in this way and came to the place where the bull was, in front of the portals of the king's palace, where nearly all the Asturians had gathered to witness the spectacle. Then the king ordered the bull to be set loose and it ran very swiftly and surrendered its horns into the hand of the bishop. Turning back, it killed many scoffers, and afterwards returned to the woods from whence it had come. Then the bishop returned to the church, threw down the horns that he was holding in front of the altar of Our Saviour and excommunicated Cadón, Ensión and Zadón. And he prayed and said that of their seed right up until the end of the world some would be lepers and others blind, some lame and others crippled, because of the false crime they had laid upon him. And he cursed the king and said that this crime had openly arisen in his seed whilst all of them were living. Then the bishop, having laid aside his sacred vestments, did not want to see that tyrant ever again, but stayed there in that same see for four days. On the second day after Easter he left Oviedo with his followers and came to the church of Santa Eulalia in the valley of Pravia,[7] and there he remained. He was struck down by sickness in

6 Maundy Thursday.

7 Pravia had been one of the chief royal centres of the eighth-century Asturian kingdom prior to the foundation of Oviedo, 20 kilometres to the south-east.

that place, and took the body and blood of the Lord, and on the Wednesday at daybreak he entrusted his spirit to the Lord. Then those who had come with him immediately made a coffin in which they wished to carry him to the church where he had been bishop. But Our King in heaven made him so hard to move, that the hands of a thousand men were unable to move him even a little. Then, having deliberated together, they buried him in a very fine stone tomb in the shrine which is on the north side of the aforementioned church of the Virgin Eulalia. Then each of them returned to his own home.[8]

Then that most abominable prince did another wicked deed. There were two noble sisters, by one of whom he fathered the Infante Ordoño, and by the other the Infanta Elvira. The Infante Ordoño fathered many children by the Infanta Fronilde Peláez: their names are Alfonso Ordóñez, Pelayo Ordóñez, Vermudo Ordóñez, Sancho Ordóñez and Jimena Ordóñez.[9] By Count Muño Rodríguez, Jimena bore Count Rodrigo Muñoz, who was later slain at the battle of Sagrajas.[10] The same prince [Vermudo] also fathered the Infanta Cristina by a country girl named Velasquita, who was the daughter of Mantello and Bellalla from Mieres near Monte Copián.[11] Cristina bore many sons and daughters by the son of the Infante Ramiro, the Infante Ordoño,[12] who

8 Little credence need be attached to Pelayo's account of the testing of Bishop Adaúlfo of Santiago-Iria; it is a standard twelfth-century topos: Linehan, *History and the Historians*, pp. 118–19; E. Falque Rey (trans.), *Historia Compostelana* (Madrid, 1994), p. 71, n. 50. The *Historia Compostellana*, which places these events in the reign of Ordoño I of Asturias (850–66), states that the bishop was falsely accused of sodomy: *HC*, pp. 9–10; cf. E. Flórez (ed.), *Chronicon Iriense, ES* 20 (Madrid, 1765), 598–608, at p. 602. According to the later account of Rodrigo Jiménez de Rada, which embroiders Pelayo's version of events yet further, Bishop Adaúlfo's reported crime was to have entered into negotiations with the Muslims with the promise that he would embrace Islam and deliver Galicia into their hands: Rodrigo Jiménez de Rada, *Historia de rebus Hispanie sive Historia Gothica*, ed. J. Fernández Valverde, CCCM 72 (Turnhout, 1987), p. 161.

9 Fronilde Peláez was the daughter of Count Pelayo Rodríguez. On 18 September 1042 Fronilde, her husband Ordoño, and their children Vermudo, Sancho, Fernando and Jimena endowed the monastery of Santa María de León, which they had founded, and placed it under the authority of the bishop of that city: Ruiz Asencio (ed.), *Colección documental*, vol. IV, no. 1002.

10 See below, n. 74.

11 Mieres lies about 15 kilometres south-east of Oviedo. On Velasquita, see below n. 16.

12 The Infanta Cristina accompanied her mother Velasquita to Asturias after her mother's divorce from Vermudo II *c.* 989. On the death of her husband, Ordoño Ramírez, who was probably the son of Ramiro III, Cristina may have entered the nunnery of San Pelayo de Oviedo: see A. Sánchez Candeira, 'La reina Velasquita de León y su descendencia', *Hispania* 10 (1950), 449–505, at pp. 480–6.

was blind, namely Alfonso Ordóñez, Sancha Ordóñez and Countess Eldonza, who was the wife of Pelayo Froilaz,[13] who was a deacon, and he fathered by her Count Pedro Peláez, Ordoño Peláez, Pelayo Peláez, Muño Peláez, and the mother of Count Suero and his brothers,[14] and Countess Teresa of Carrión who built the church of San Zoilo.[15] The aforesaid prince [Vermudo] also had two legitimate wives. One was named Velasquita, whom he divorced while she was living;[16] the other woman whom he took as his wife was called Elvira,[17] by whom he fathered two children, Alfonso[18] and Teresa. After the death of her father, Teresa was given away in marriage by her brother Alfonso to a certain pagan king of Toledo for the sake of peace, although she was herself unwilling. But as she was a Christian, she said to the pagan king: 'Do not touch me, for you are a pagan. If you do touch me the Angel of the Lord will slay you'. Then the king laughed at her and slept with her once, and just as she had predicted, he was immediately struck down by the Angel of the Lord. As he felt death approaching, he summoned his chamberlains and his councillors and ordered them to load up camels with gold, silver, gems and precious garments, and to take her back to León with all these gifts. She stayed in that place in a nun's habit for a long time, and afterwards she died in Oviedo and was buried in the monastery of San Pelayo.[19]

13 On Count Pelayo Froilaz, his wife Countess Eldonza Ordóñez and their offspring, see A. C. Floriano Cumbreño (ed.), *Colección diplomática del monasterio de Belmonte* (Oviedo, 1960), pp. 301–3.

14 On Count Suero Vermúdez, and his brothers Alfonso and Gutierre, the sons of Vermudo Ovéquiz and Jimena Peláez, see below *CAI*, i.2 and n. 13. It has been speculated that by tracing Suero Vermúdez's lineage back to the alleged extramarital union between Vermudo II and the 'country girl' Velasquita, Bishop Pelayo may have been seeking to besmirch the reputation of the Asturian count: Calleja Puerta, 'Una genealogía leonesa', 527–39.

15 Teresa Peláez was married to Count Gómez Díaz of Carrión. The monastery of San Zoilo de Carrión was granted by the countess to the Order of Cluny on 1 August 1076: J. A. Pérez Celada (ed.), *Documentación del monasterio de San Zoilo de Carrión* (Burgos, 1986), no. 7.

16 Velasquita had married Vermudo II by October 981 and was probably repudiated in 989. The Velasquita mentioned here and the concubine referred to above were almost certainly one and the same person: see Sánchez Candeira, 'La reina Velasquita', 449–505.

17 Elvira Garcés was the daughter of Count García Fernández of Castile (970–95). Her marriage to Vermudo II took place *c.* 991.

18 The future Alfonso V, king of León (999–1028).

19 Pelayo's account of the supposed marriage of the Infanta Teresa Vermúdez to a Muslim ruler of Toledo passed into a number of later chronicles. Not all historians have been equally convinced, however: see J. M. Fernández del Pozo, 'Alfonso V, rey de León', in *León y su historia: miscelánea histórica 5* (León, 1984), 9–262, at pp. 36–8.

On account of the sins of Prince Vermudo and the people, the king of
the Hagarenes, whose name was Almanzor,[20] together with his son
Adamelch[21] and some exiled Christian counts,[22] prepared to come and
destroy and lay waste the kingdom of León. When the citizens of
León and Astorga heard and realised that this blow was about to fall
upon them, they gathered up the bones of the kings who were buried
in León and Astorga, together with the body of Saint Pelagius the
Martyr, and they went to Asturias and they buried them with great
honour in the church of Saint Mary in Oviedo. They placed the body
of Saint Pelagius on the altar of the Blessed John the Baptist. Some of
the citizens of León carried the body of Bishop Saint Froilán to Valle
César in the Pyrenean mountains[23] and placed it on the altar of Saint
John the Baptist.[24] Then the aforesaid king of the Saracens came with
a big army as he had planned and destroyed León, Astorga and
Valencia de Don Juan, and he devastated the surrounding area.[25] He
did not enter Asturias, Galicia and the Bierzo, and he was unable to
capture certain castles, namely Luna, Alba, and Gordón.[26] They buried
the bodies of the kings of whom we have already spoken, outside and
in front of the tombs of the previous kings. In the first coffin, which is
in the middle, they laid to rest the bodies of King Alfonso [III][27] and

20 Muḥammad b. Abī 'Āmir, known by his honorific title al-Manṣūr (whence Almanzor),
   'the Victorious', was the effective ruler of al-Andalus between 981–1002. On his
   career, see H. Kennedy, Muslim Spain and Portugal: a political history of al-Andalus
   (London, 1996), pp.109–22. On Hagarenes, see p. 175 n. 76.

21 'Abd al-Malik, al-Muẓaffar held the reins of power in al-Andalus between 1002 and
   1008: Kennedy, Muslim Spain and Portugal, pp. 122–4.

22 On the support lent by Christian magnates to Almanzor, see J. M. Ruiz Asencio,
   'Rebeliones leonesas contra Vermudo II', Archivos Leoneses 23 (1969), 215–41.

23 Manuel Risco identified Valle Cesar as Valdecésar in the mountains of León, where
   on 9 January 916 King Ordoño II of León (914–24) granted property to Abbot
   Servando so that he might found a monastery on the site. Risco further observed
   that by Pirineos montes Bishop Pelayo was referring to the Cantabrian chain in
   general, and to the Leonese mountains in particular: M. Risco, ES 34 (Madrid,
   1784), pp. 191–93. This is confirmed by a spurious document attributed to King
   Alfonso II 'the Chaste', produced under Pelayo's supervision, which sets out the
   limits of the see of Oviedo and refers to totas scilicet Asturias per Pireneos montes
   usque Sumrostrum et usque Transmera et usque ad litus maris: Fernández Conde, Libro
   de los Testamentos, p. 379.

24 The repetition of the phrase et posuerunt eum super altare Sancti Iohannis Babtiste is
   probably due to a copyist's blunder.

25 The campaign took place in 986.

26 The castles of Luna, Alba and Gordón lay in the mountainous districts to the north
   of the territory of León.

27 Alfonso III, king of Asturias–León (866–910).

his wife Queen Jimena. In the second coffin, which is on the right-hand side, they placed the bodies of King Ordoño [II], the son of Alfonso [III] and Jimena, together with his wives Mummadonna and Sancha.[28] In the third coffin they buried the bodies of King Ramiro [II],[29] the son of Ordoño [II] and Mummadonna, with their sons King Ordoño [III] and his wife Elvira,[30] and King Sancho [I] and his wife Teresa.[31] And in the second coffin to the left they laid to rest the bodies of King Fruela [II], the son of Alfonso and Jimena, together with his wife Queen Mummadonna.[32] And next to them they buried in a third coffin Queen Elvira, called the Chaste, the daughter of Ramiro [II] and Teresa.[33] And in the fourth coffin, which is high up, they buried Queen Teresa, the wife of the aforesaid King Ramiro [II].[34] At the head and at the side of the tomb of King Alfonso the Chaste[35] they buried the bones of the sons and daughters of these kings in the Era 1035 [= AD 997].

But *the heavenly king, with His customary piety, remembering His mercy, wrought vengeance on His enemies: that very people of the Hagarenes began to fall away* ceaselessly *by sudden death and by the sword, and day by day to come closer to annihilation.*[36] The Lord struck down King Vermudo with gout because of all the sins that he had committed, so that he was unable from that time forward to climb into any carriage, but whilst he lived was carried from place to place on the shoulders of humble men. He ended his life in the Bierzo and was buried in Villabuena,[37] and after several years he was translated to León. He reigned for 17 years.

28 Ordoño II was married three times: first to Elvira Menéndez, then to Aragonta, and finally to Sancha Sánchez, daughter of Sancho Garcés I of Navarre (905–25).

29 Ramiro II (931–51), was the son of Ordoño II and Elvira Menéndez.

30 Pelayo is mistaken. Ordoño III married Urraca Fernández, daughter of Fernán González, count of Castile (931–70).

31 Sancho I 'the Fat' (956–66) married Teresa Ansúrez, daughter of the Castilian magnate Asur Fernández.

32 Fruela II (924–5) was in fact married twice: first to Nunilo and then to Urraca.

33 Elvira, daughter of King Ramiro II and his second wife, Urraca Sánchez, served as abbess of the convent of San Salvador in León. Between 967 and 975 she exercised the regency for her nephew Ramiro III.

34 Pelayo is again in error. Ramiro II was married first to the Galician Adosinda Gutiérrez and then to Urraca Sánchez, daughter of Sancho Garcés I of Navarre.

35 Alfonso II 'the Chaste', king of Asturias (791–842).

36 Here, Pelayo again appears to be drawing upon the testimony of the *Chronicle of Sampiro*: see above, n. 1.

37 Villabuena lies in the heart of the Bierzo on the borders of León and Galicia.

ALFONSO V

On his death his son Alfonso, being five years of age, succeeded to the kingdom in the Era 1037 [= AD 999].[38] He was raised in Galicia by Count Menendo González and his wife Countess Mayor, and they gave him their daughter Elvira in marriage,[39] by whom he fathered two sons, Vermudo[40] and Sancha.

At this time King Fernando, the son of King Sancho the Fat,[41] married Sancha, the daughter of King Alfonso.[42] Then King Alfonso came to León and held a council there with all his bishops, counts and magnates. He resettled the city of León which had been laid waste by King Almanzor of the Hagarenes and he bestowed upon León precepts and laws which are to be preserved until the end of this world, and they are written at the end of the History of the Kings of the Goths and of the Aragonese.[43] He reigned for 26 years[44] and was killed by an arrow at the town of Viseu in Portugal.[45] He was buried in León with his wife Elvira.

38 Yet another apparent borrowing from Sampiro. For details of the reign, see Fernández del Pozo, 'Alfonso V', 9–262.

39 The marriage of Alfonso V and Elvira Menéndez took place c. 1017; the queen died on 2 December 1022. In 1023 Alfonso V remarried, this time to Urraca Sánchez, daughter of Sancho III Garcés 'the Great' of Navarre (1004–35).

40 The future Vermudo III, king of León (1028–37).

41 *Fredenandus Rex, filius Sancii Grassi Regis.* Pelayo is referring to Sancho Garcés III of Navarre, on whom see above, *HS*, ch. 74 and n. 100. *Grassi* may well be the result of a copyist's mistranscription of *Garsiae.*

42 The marriage of Fernando and the Infanta Sancha Alfonso took place in 1032.

43 The council of León was held under the auspices of Alfonso V in July 1017. The decrees promulgated at that meeting, the *Fuero de León*, to which Pelayo refers, were later copied into the *Liber Testamentorum*, the cartulary commissioned by the bishop c.1120, and later into the *Corpus Pelagianum*: J. M. Pérez Prendes, 'La potestad legislativa en el reino de León. Notas sobre el Fuero de León, el Concilio de Coyanza y las Cortes de León de 1188', in *El reino de León en la alta Edad Media.* I: *Cortes, Concilios y Fueros* (León, 1988), 497–545. The phrase *et sunt scripte in finem Hystorie Regum Gothorum, siue et Arragonensium,* which appears in the thirteenth-century manuscript of Pelayo's *Chronicon* (BN MS 1513), upon which Sánchez Alonso largely based his edition, but not in the earlier copies (BN MSS 1358, 2805), seems to be a later interpolation. The reference to the *Hystorie Regum Gothorum, siue et Arragonensium* echoes the Preface to the *Liber Chronicorum,* where it is stated that Bishop Pelayo *de Gotis et Arragonensibus regibus prout potuit plenissime scripsit:* Pérez de Urbel, *Sampiro,* p. 480. Manuel Risco suggested that *arragonensibus* may simply have been a misrendering of *legionensibus:* M. Risco, *ES* 38 (Madrid, 1793), p.133.

44 In fact, for 29 years. The king was killed in July or August 1028: Fernández del Pozo, 'Alfonso V', 160–1.

45 See above, *HS,* ch. 73.

VERMUDO III

On his death, his son Vermudo [III] succeeded to his father's kingdom.[46] Then King Fernando, having gathered a great army, fought with his brother-in-law King Vermudo in the Tamarón valley, and King Vermudo was killed there and was buried in León, in the Era 1060 [= AD 1022].[47] He reigned for 10 years.

FERNANDO I

After these things had happened, King Fernando came and besieged León, and after a few days he captured it and entered with a very great number of soldiers. He accepted the crown there and was made king in the kingdom of León and Castile.[48] Then he confirmed the laws that his father-in-law King Alfonso had given to León and added others which are to be preserved.[49]

This king was a good and God-fearing man, and he fathered by the aforesaid Queen Sancha five children: Urraca, Sancho, Alfonso, García and Elvira.[50]

He then made a great slaughter of the Saracens and each and every year he received from their kings the appointed tribute.[51] Waging war

---

46 Some twenty charters of Vermudo III have been edited by L. Núñez Contreras, 'Colección diplomática de Vermudo III, rey de León', *Historia. Instituciones. Documentos* 4 (1977), 381–514.

47 The battle of Tamarón in fact took place on 4 September 1037. For a fuller account, see *HS*, chs 77–9.

48 Fernando I was anointed king in León on 22 June 1038: see above, *HS*, ch. 80 and n. 119.

49 This is a reference to the decrees of the Council of Coyanza, held under the auspices of Fernando I in 1055, which, like the *Fuero* of 1017, were subsequently copied (and interpolated) at Bishop Pelayo's behest: A. García Gallo, 'El Concilio de Coyanza: contribución al estudio del Derecho Canónico español en la Alta Edad Media', *AHDE* 20 (1950), 275–633, at pp. 286–302.

50 That is, the Infanta Urraca Fernández (d. 1101), the future Sancho II, king of Castile (1065–72), Alfonso VI, king of León–Castile (1065–1109), García I, king of Galicia (1065–73), and the Infanta Elvira Fernández (d. 1099). Cf. *HS*, ch. 8 and n. 39, and ch. 81.

51 By the end of his reign, Fernando I was receiving regular payments of *parias*, or tribute, from the Muslim rulers of Badajoz, Toledo and Zaragoza, and occasional ones from the rulers of Seville and Valencia, too. If the payment of 5000 gold dinars that Fernando was reportedly promised by al-Muẓaffar of Badajoz was typical, then it is likely that by the time of his death the Leonese–Castilian king was in receipt of an annual income of at least 25,000 gold dinars: Ibn 'Idhārī, *La caída del Califato de Córdoba y los reyes de Taifas (al-Bāyan al-Mugrib)*, trans. F.

he captured Lamego, Viseu, Coimbra, Seia and many other cities and
castles of the Hagarenes.[52] Joining battle at Atapuerca he killed his
brother King García[53] and captured his kingdom in the Era 1095 [=
AD 1057].[54]

He translated the body of the bishop Saint Isidore from the metropol-
itan see of Seville to León, through the agency of the bishops Alvito of
León and Ordoño of Astorga in the Era 1096 [= AD 1058].[55] He
translated the holy martyrs Vincent, Sabina and Cristeta from Avila:
Vincent to León, Sabina to Palencia, and Cristeta to San Pedro de
Arlanza.[56]

He lived in peace and reigned for 18 years, and he died and was buried
in the city of León with his wife Queen Sancha in the Era 1103 [= AD
1065].[57] Before he died, he divided his kingdom among his sons in
this way: he gave Sancho all of Castile as far as the River Pisuerga,
Nájera, and Pamplona, with all the royal rights pertaining to them; he
gave Alfonso León as far as the River Pisuerga, and all the Asturias
de Trasmiera as far as the River Eo, Astorga, Campos, Zamora, Campo
de Toro, and the Bierzo as far as the town of La Uz on Monte

Maíllo Salgado (Salamanca, 1993), p. 198. Fernando I's son and successor Alfonso
VI may have realised an annual income well in excess of 70,000 dinars from his
Muslim tributaries: Reilly, *The Contest*, p. 58.

52 These, and the other campaigns waged by Fernando I, are related in greater detail
in the *HS*, chs 85–93, 95.

53 García Sánchez III, king of Navarre (1035–54).

54 Correcting Sánchez Alonso, who renders the 'x aspado', or 'x with tittle' (which was
employed in Spain to abbreviate the numerals XL, and which is copied faithfully in
several of the manuscripts of the *Chronicon*) simply as X, with the result that thirty
years have disappeared from the date: Sánchez Alonso (ed.), *Crónica*, p. 74. The
battle of Atapuerca, near Burgos, in fact took place on 15 September 1054. On the
background to the campaign, see *HS*, chs 82–4.

55 Sánchez Alonso again mistranscribes the date. The formal translation of the relics
of St Isidore in fact took place on 21 December 1063. A far fuller account is given
by the *HS*, chs 96–102, following the anonymous *Translatio Sancti Isidori*.

56 The mortal remains of Sts Vincent, Sabina and Arteta were initially donated to the
cathedral church of Palencia. Then, in 1062, having had second thoughts about the
matter, Fernando I shared them out between the monastery of San Juan Bautista in
León and the Castilian abbey of San Pedro de Arlanza near Burgos, and
compensated the church of Palencia for its loss: *CD Fernando I*, nos 62 and 72.

57 Fernando I died on 29 December 1065 having reigned on the throne of León for 28
years. A far fuller account of the final days of the king is provided by the *HS*, ch.
106. Queen Sancha died on 7 November 1067.

Cebrero; he gave García all of Galicia, together with the whole of Portugal.[58]

SANCHO II

After this King Sancho began to fight against his brother King Alfonso in order to take his kingdom. They agreed a day and appointed a place at Llantadilla[59] so that they might fight each other, and whoever should be victorious would receive his brother's kingdom. They came on the appointed day and fought each other, and King Alfonso was defeated there, and he returned to León. Again they engaged in their quarrel at Golpejera, and King Alfonso was captured there in that battle and put in chains and taken to Burgos.[60] Then he went into exile with King Alimemone[61] of Toledo and he remained in exile with him until the death of his brother King Sancho. Then King Sancho seized the kingdom of his brother King Alfonso and crowned himself in León.[62] He was a very handsome man and a valiant soldier. He travelled throughout the Asturias, Galicia and Portugal.[63] He reigned for six years and was killed by treachery by a soldier named Vellito Ariulfo outside the walls of Zamora which he had besieged.[64] He was buried in Castile in the monastery of San Salvador de Oña.[65]

---

58 The River Eo marked the border between Galicia and Asturias de Oviedo. Cebrero, on the pilgrim-road to Compostela, was the principal mountain pass linking the Bierzo and Galicia. On Fernando I's decision to divide his kingdom, see above HS, ch. 8 and n. 40 and ch. 103; cf. Reilly, Alfonso VI, pp. 14–22. A slightly later source, composed after 1126, records that in addition Sancho was allotted the parias from the taifa of Zaragoza, Alfonso those from Toledo, and García those from Badajoz: E. Flórez (ed.), Chronicon Compostellanum, ES 20 (Madrid, 1765), 608–13, at p. 609.

59 The clash at Llantadilla, near the Pisuerga, about 50 kilometres due west of Burgos, is said to have taken place on 19 July 1068: E. Flórez (ed.), Annales Complutenses, ES 23 (Madrid, 1767), 310–14, at p. 313.

60 The battle of Golpejera, about 30 kilometres west of the Pisuerga, appears to have been fought in January 1072: Reilly, Alfonso VI, pp. 49–50 and n. 58.

61 Al-Ma'mūn, ruler of Toledo (1044–75). Cf. HS, chs 9, 11–12 and n. 44.

62 Pelayo's statement that King Sancho crowned himself in León may have stemmed from the unwillingness of Bishop Pedro of León to perform the task: Reilly, Alfonso VI, pp. 50, 63.

63 Sancho II invaded the Galician and Portuguese territories of his brother García some time in the spring of 1072 and forced the latter to seek asylum in Seville: Flórez (ed.), Chronicon Compostellanum, p. 609; cf. Reilly, Alfonso VI, pp. 32–3.

64 See HS, ch. 10 and n. 50.

65 HS, ch. 11 and n. 54.

ALFONSO VI

When he had heard this, King Alfonso came quickly and took the
kingdom of his brother King Sancho and his own kingdom which he
had lost. After a few days he resolved to seize the kingdom of his
brother García, and by a cunning trick King García was captured
without a fight and was kept in chains for twenty years and more.
And there in captivity he [García] wanted to let his blood, and after
he had bled himself he fell onto his bed and died and was buried in
León.[66] May he rest in peace. In this way the aforesaid king seized his
brothers' kingdoms.

Then King Alfonso swiftly sent messengers to Rome to Pope Hilde-
brand, known as Gregory VII, and he did this because he wanted to
have the Roman rite in all his kingdom. So the Pope sent Cardinal
Richard, abbot of Marseilles, to Spain, and he held a council in the city
of Burgos, and confirmed the Roman rite in all the kingdom of King
Alfonso in the Era 1114 [= AD 1076].[67]

Since the aforesaid king had many armies of soldiers, he traversed all
the towns and castles of the Saracens, and whilst he lived he received
from them the appointed tribute every year.[68] He laid waste,
devastated and plundered many of their towns, and he besieged and
captured many towns of the Saracens and many castles as well. He
captured Toledo, Talavera, Santa Olalla, Maqueda, Alamín, Argenza,
Madrid, Olmos, Canales, Calatalifa, Talamanca, Uceda, Guadalajara,
Hita, Ribas, Caracuel, Mora, Alarcón, Albendea, Consuegra, Uclés,
Masatrigo, Cuenca, Almodóvar, Aledo and Valencia;[69] and on the other

66 Cf. *HS*, ch. 13 and commentary thereon.
67 Alfonso VI's decision to replace the so-called Mozarabic liturgy with the Roman
    rite, in response to papal pressure to enforce liturgical standardisation throughout
    the Latin West, provoked a long and bruising dispute which was not resolved until
    the council of Burgos, held in 1080: see the collected studies in B. F. Reilly (ed.),
    *Santiago, Saint-Denis, and Saint Peter: The Reception of the Roman Liturgy in León–
    Castile in 1080* (New York, 1985); Reilly, *Alfonso VI*, pp. 95–115.
68 'Abd Allāh, the ruler of the Taifa of Granada, for example, undertook to pay Alfonso
    VI 10,000 gold mithqals per annum. For an illuminating account of the negotiations
    that led to the agreement, see 'Abd Allāh, *The Tibyān. Memoirs of 'Abd Allāh b.
    Buluggīn, last Zirid amir of Granada*, trans. A. T. Tibi (Leiden, 1986), pp. 89–90.
69 The conquest of Toledo in 1085 enabled Alfonso VI to capture most of the towns
    in the Tagus valley that had previously owed allegiance to the ruling family of
    Toledo. The Taifa kingdom of Valencia, which had formerly been incorporated
    within the Toledan domains, was annexed in March 1086, and the erstwhile ruler
    of Toledo, al-Qādir, who also retained a lordship around Cuenca, was installed as
    its ruler. Aledo, 45 kilometres south-west of Murcia, was captured in 1086.

side Coria, Lisbon, Cintra and Santarém.[70] He also settled all of Extremadura, the castles and towns of Salamanca, Avila, Coca, Arévalo, Olmedo, Medina [del Campo], Segovia, Iscar and Cuéllar.[71] After this, he reached such a pitch of elation because of such good fortune that at the instigation of King Abenabet[72] some foreigners called Almoravids[73] were summoned from Africa to Spain, with whom he fought many battles, and whilst he lived he suffered many attacks by them. In the Era 1124 [= AD 1086] was the battle on the field of Sagrajas with King Yusuf.[74]

This Alfonso was the father and defender of all the Spanish churches, and he did this because he was a Catholic in all respects. He was so terrifying to evil doers that they never dared to show themselves in his sight. All the magnates, both the nobles and those not of noble

However, the Almoravid advance after 1090 led to the evacuation of all the territories south of the Tagus: J. González, *Repoblación de Castilla la Nueva*, 2 vols (Madrid, 1975–6), I, pp. 81–99.

70 Coria, which guarded the access route to the trans-Duero from the territory of Badajoz, was conquered by Alfonso VI's forces in 1079. The strongholds of Lisbon, Cintra and Santarém, in central Portugal, were ceded to the Leonese monarch in 1093 by the ruler of the Taifa of Badajoz, al-Mutawakkil, in return for a military alliance against the Almoravids (on whom see below n. 73). However, Badajoz fell to the Almoravids the following year, and Lisbon and the other towns soon followed suit.

71 The resettlement of the trans-Duero was a gradual process which began with the repopulation of Sepúlveda, just to the north of the Guadarrama mountains, in 1076. By the early twelfth century an entire defensive frontier system, stretching from Salamanca to Soria, had been established; a string of strategically situated fortress towns designed both to bear the brunt of Muslim attacks and to act as a springboard for future campaigns of conquest. The best guide to the process is L. M. Villar García, *La Extremadura castellano–leonesa: guerreros, clérigos y campesinos (711–1252)* (Valladolid, 1986), pp. 91ff.

72 *Abenabet* is a rendering of Ibn 'Abbād, the family name of the ruling dynasty of Seville. Pelayo is referring to Al-Mu'tamid, ruler of Seville (1069–91): cf. *HS*, ch. 90.

73 The Almoravid movement is said to have had its origins in the teaching of a Malikite scholar and misssionary, Ibn Yāsīn, among the tribes of the Senegal and upper Niger rivers. Ibn Yasin's followers, the *al-Murābiṭūn*, from which 'Almoravid' derives, aspired to live a life of religious purity and were committed to extending the frontiers of Islam by *jihād*, or holy war. The Almoravid ruling dynasty held sway over much of north-west Africa between c. 1055 and 1147, and brought al-Andalus under its control between 1090 and 1110: for details, see Kennedy, *Muslim Spain and Portugal*, pp. 154–88.

74 Yūsuf b. Tāshufīn, emir of the Almoravids (1087–1106), on whom see Kennedy, *Muslim Spain and Portugal*, pp. 159–72. The battle of Sagrajas, or Zalaca, near Badajoz, was fought on 23 October 1086 and resulted in a crushing victory for the Almoravids.

birth, the rich and poor, who were in his kingdom, did not dare to quarrel with one another, nor to carry out any wrong deed. There was such peace in the days in which he reigned that a woman alone, carrying gold or silver in her hands through all the land of Spain, whether inhabited or uninhabited, through the mountains or fields, would not encounter anyone who would touch her, or do any wrong to her. Merchants and pilgrims crossing his kingdom had nothing to fear, for there was no one who would have dared to take away even a pennyworth of their goods.[75] On top of this, lest any moments of his life were lacking in good works, he had built all the bridges that there are from Logroño to Santiago.[76]

When the time of his death was very near, he took to his bed and was ill for a whole year and seven months. Although he was ill he rode a little every day by order of his doctors, so that he might have some relaxation for his body. But eight days before he passed away from this life, God worked a great wonder in the church of Bishop Saint Isidore in the city of León. On the feast day of the nativity of Saint John the Baptist,[77] at the sixth hour of the day, water began to flow through the stones which are in front of the altar of Saint Isidore, where the priest stands when he celebrates Mass; not through the cracks between the stones, but through the middle of the stones. This was seen by all the citizens, both by the nobles and by those not of noble birth, together with the bishops Pelayo of Oviedo and Pedro of León.[78] And this happened for three days on Thursday, Friday and Saturday. Then on the fourth day, which was Sunday, the afore-mentioned bishops put on their episcopal robes, and all the clergy likewise put on their holy vestments, and carrying candles in their hands they went in a procession from the church of Saint Mary to the altar of Saint Isidore, accompanied by all the citizens – men and women – and they entered the church of Bishop Saint Isidore tearfully shouting and praising the miracles of Our Saviour. When the bishop

---

75 This was a common topos in earlier-medieval historical writing: see T. Reuter, 'Die Unsicherheit auf den Strassen im europäischen Früh- und Hochmittelalter: Täter, Opfer und ihre mittelalterlichen und modernen Betrachter', in *Träger und Instrumentarien des Friedens im Hohen und Späten Mittelalter*, ed. J. Fried, Vorträge und Forschungen XLIII (Sigmaringen, 1996), 169–202, esp. pp. 174–5, n. 16. I am grateful to Professor Janet Nelson for bringing this article to my attention.

76 That is, on the pilgrim-road to Compostela. On Alfonso VI's support for the infrastructure of the pilgrimage, see Vázquez de Parga, Lacarra and Uría Ríu (eds), *Las peregrinaciones*, II, pp. 20–2.

77 24 June.

78 Pedro, bishop of León (1087?–1111?).

of Oviedo had completed the sermon, and Mass had finished, the bishops went to the place where the water was and drank from it, and so did many other men. They placed the water that remained in a glass vessel and there it remained for a long time in witness. This sign presaged none other than the sorrows and tribulations that befell Spain after the death of the aforesaid king; that is why the stones wept and the water flowed forth.

This man had five legitimate wives: the first was Ines;[79] the second was Queen Constance,[80] by whom he fathered Queen Urraca,[81] the wife of Count Raymond,[82] who fathered Sancha[83] and King Alfonso [VII];[84] the third was Berta, who was of Tuscan descent,[85] the fourth was Elizabeth,[86] by whom he begat Sancha, the wife of Count Rodrigo,[87] and Elvira who married Duke Roger [II] of Sicily;[88] the fifth was Beatrice,[89] who returned to her own country after his death. He also had two concubines, although they were most noble: the first was Jimena Muñoz,[90] by whom he fathered Elvira, the wife

79 Inés, daughter of Duke William VIII of Aquitaine, was married to Alfonso VI in 1074. The marriage was dissolved three years later, probably because of the queen's failure to provide Alfonso with a male heir. On the purposes of the marriage alliance, see Reilly, *Alfonso VI*, pp. 79–82.

80 Constance, sister of Duke Eudes I of Burgundy, was married to Alfonso in 1079, and died late in 1093.

81 Urraca, queen of León–Castile (1109–26).

82 Raymond, cousin of Eudes I of Burgundy, was probably betrothed to Urraca in 1087. He ruled the county of Galicia from about 1090 until his death in 1107. For details of his career, see Reilly, *Alfonso VI*, pp. 194–5, 217, 247–54, 333–4, 341.

83 On the Infanta Sancha Raimúndez, see García Calles, *Doña Sancha*.

84 Alfonso VII, king of León–Castile (1126–57).

85 Alfonso married the Italian Berta in 1094; she died in January 1100 without having borne the king any children.

86 The family background of this Elizabeth is obscure, but Bernard Reilly has suggested that the new queen 'was drawn from some cadet line of the house of Burgundy': Reilly, *Alfonso VI*, pp. 296–7. She was married to Alfonso in 1100 and died in 1107.

87 The Infanta Sancha Alfonso and Count Rodrigo González de Lara were married some time before July 1122. The infanta had died by 10 May 1125 by which time she had already borne the count three daughters: Barton, *Aristocracy*, p. 292, n. 4.

88 The marriage between the Infanta Elvira Alfonso and Duke Roger II of Sicily took place some time after 1118.

89 Beatrice was another French noblewoman, but her family origins are unknown. She had married Alfonso VI by May 1108: Reilly, *Alfonso VI*, pp. 345–6.

90 Jimena Muñoz was the daughter of a magnate of the Bierzo, Count Muño González. Alfonso VI's liaison with Jimena may have taken place in 1081 or the following year according to Reilly, *Alfonso VI*, p. 193. Cf. J. M. Canal Sánchez-

of Count Raymond [IV] of Toulouse,[91] who was the father by her of
Alfonso Jordan,[92] and Teresa, the wife of Count Henry,[93] who was the
father by her of Urraca, Elvira and Afonso;[94] the second was Zaida,
the daughter of King Abenabeth of Seville, who was baptized and
named Elizabeth,[95] by whom he fathered Sancho who died at the
battle of Uclés.[96]

This glorious king lived for 79 years, and reigned for 43 years and six
months. He died in Toledo on the first of July in the Era 1147 [= AD
1109], early on Thursday morning, whereupon all the citizens wept
and shouted: 'O shepherd why have you deserted your sheep? Now
the Saracens and evil men will fall upon the flock which has been
entrusted to you and your kingdom'. Then the counts, knights (both
the nobles and those not of noble birth),[97] and citizens tore out their
hair and rent their clothes, the women scratched their faces, and they

---

Pagín, 'Jimena Muñoz, amiga de Alfonso VI', *Anuario de Estudios Medievales* 21
(1991), 11–40; J. de Salazar y Acha, 'Contribución al estudio del reinado de Alfonso
VI de Castilla: algunas aclaraciones sobre su política matrimonial', *Anales de la Real
Academia Matritense de Heráldica y Genealogía* 2 (1992–93), 299–343, at pp. 310–16.

91 The Infanta Elvira Alfonso had married Raymond of Toulouse by 1094. On the
latter's death in 1105 she returned to the peninsula and by July 1117 had married
a Leonese nobleman, Fernando Fernández, from whom she later separated. She
was still alive in 1157. Details in J. M. Canal Sánchez-Pagín, 'La Infanta Doña Elvira,
hija de Alfonso VI y de Gimena Muñoz, a la luz de los diplomas', *Archivos Leoneses* 33
(1979), 271–87; Barton, *Aristocracy*, p. 236, n. 3; Reilly, *Alfonso VII*, pp. 142–3.

92 On Alfonso Jordan, so-called because he was reputedly baptised in the river of that
name, see below *CAI*, i, 2, n. 14.

93 Count Henry (d. 1112), the nephew of Duke Eudes I of Burgundy, may have joined
the court of Alfonso VI in 1087. His marriage to the Infanta Teresa Alfonso (d.
1130) and the grant to the couple of the county of Portugal in 1096 appears to have
been engineered by Alfonso VI as a means of driving a wedge between Henry and his
cousin Count Raymond, both of whom had the previous year plotted to partition the
kingdom on the king's death: for details, see Reilly, *Alfonso VI*, pp. 251–5.

94 The future Afonso Henriques, king of Portugal (1128–85). His sister Urraca was
married to the Galician magnate Vermudo Pérez in 1122: Barton, *Aristocracy*, pp.
308–10.

95 The relationship between Alfonso VI and Zaida, who was in fact the daughter-in-
law of al-Mu'tamid of Seville, probably began in late 1091 or early 1092. In March
1106 the couple married, thereby legitimising their son Sancho, born in 1093:
Reilly, *Alfonso VI*, pp. 234–5, 338–40. On Abenabeth, see above, n. 72.

96 Uclés lies just south of the Tagus, about 100 kilometres east of Toledo. The battle
took place on 29 May 1108.

97 *milites, nobiles et innobiles.* The distinction being made here is between the
infanzones, who enjoyed noble rank by hereditary right, and the *caballeros villanos*,
whose privileged status was determined exclusively by their military function:
Barton, *Aristocracy*, pp. 33–5.

sprinkled ashes and with great moaning and heaviness of heart they shouted to the heavens. After 20 days they bore him into the region of Cea[98] and all the bishops and archbishops, representatives of the ecclesiastical as well as the secular order, buried the aforesaid king in the church of the saints Facundus and Primitivus[99] with praise and hymns. May he rest in peace. Amen.

98 Cea lies about 50 kilometres south-east of León.
99 That is, the monastery of Sahagún, about 50 kilometres south-east of León, which enjoyed close ties with the Leonese royal family, and to which Alfonso VI made at least seventeen generous benefactions during his reign. On the origins of the abbey, see above, HS, ch. 71, n. 86.

III: *HISTORIA RODERICI*

Introduction to the *Historia Roderici*

The anonymous Latin work known to historians of Spain as the *Historia Roderici* or 'History of Rodrigo' (henceforward *HR*) has a claim to be regarded as one of the earliest biographies of a layman who was not a king, like Charlemagne, nor a saint, like Gerald of Aurillac, to have been composed in medieval Christendom. The Rodrigo whom it commemorates was an eleventh-century Castilian nobleman who enjoyed a strikingly successful career as a military adventurer. He is better known to posterity as El Cid.

Rodrigo was born near Burgos *c.* 1045. As a young man who showed promise as a soldier he was attached to the household of King Sancho II of Castile (1065–72). After Sancho's murder he transferred to the service of his brother, Alfonso VI (1065–1109). In the mid-1070s he married Jimena, reputedly a member of an aristocratic family from Asturias. After several years of profitable service to the king, Rodrigo fell from favour, partly by undertaking an unauthorised military campaign, partly owing to the calumnies of enemies he had made at the royal court. In 1081 he was sent into exile by the king, a not infrequent occurrence in the career of a warrior-aristocrat of that epoch. During the following five years Rodrigo took service as a mercenary captain with the Muslim dynasty of the Banū Hūd, rulers of the Taifa principality of Zaragoza in the valley of the River Ebro. Reinstated in Alfonso's favour when the king was desperate for troops after the Almoravid invasion and the defeat at Sagrajas in 1086, Rodrigo remained in his service for the ensuing three years. A further breach with the king occurred in 1089. For the remainder of his life Rodrigo acted as an independent commander in the eastern parts of Spain. Skilful exploitation by diplomacy and force of the fractious Taifa principalities enabled him to become a tribute-taker on a princely scale. His greatest prize was secured in 1094 when he captured Valencia, the main city of the Spanish Levante. For the last five years of his life Rodrigo defended his vulnerable principality. He died in Valencia, peacefully, in July 1099.[1]

---

1 A fuller treatment of Rodrigo's career is to be found in Fletcher, *The Quest for El Cid*, chs 8–11.

Rodrigo's truly remarkable career was made possible by the distinctive circumstances of his age: the instability of the Taifa principalities; the acceptability of tribute-taking as the primary mode of Christian–Islamic relationship in Spain; the ease of crossing cultural frontiers; the absence of any ideology of crusade; the availability of mercenary knights. Roughly comparable circumstances made possible the approximations to his career that we can see in other frontier zones of contemporary Christendom; for example, among the Normans who adventured in southern Italy and Sicily and in the Byzantine Empire. Yet his fame was more than that of a particularly talented and fortunate *condottiere* in the coastlands of the Spanish Levante. His Muslim enemies respected and admired him even as they hated him; his death was noted by a French chronicler writing hundreds of miles from Valencia, in Poitou. Rodrigo had become a hero in his own lifetime. This heroic aspect would be developed obscurely after his death until it yielded the portrait, or vision, that we find in Spain's greatest medieval epic, the *Poema de Mio Cid,* composed perhaps in the last quarter of the twelfth century, certainly in existence by 1207. A legendary Cid had been launched upon the world, to be further elaborated and celebrated as the centuries passed in chronicle, ballad, drama, painting, sculpture and film.

The *Historia Roderici* is our principal source for his historical – as opposed to his legendary – career. It can now be consulted in the excellent edition by Emma Falque Rey.[2] The author focused attention on Rodrigo's chief claim to fame, his warlike exploits, but his coverage of them was uneven, as is immediately apparent when we break the text down into its component blocks as follows.

1   Chs 1–6 provide a brief narrative of the first thirty-odd years of Rodrigo's life, until his marriage: the author evidently knew little about his subject's early career.

2   Chs 7–24 narrate in considerably more detail the events leading up to Rodrigo's exile in 1081 and the years spent in Zaragoza between 1081 and 1086.

3   Chs 25–7 furnish a very sketchy account of Rodrigo's return to

---

2 *Chronica Hispana saeculi XII* eds E. Falque, J. Gil and A. Maya [= Corpus Christianorum, Continuatio Mediaevalis vol. lxxi] (Turnhout, 1990) at pp. 47–98. Dr Falque's introduction (pp. 1–46) contains details of manuscripts and previous editions (pp. 25–37). The only complete translation into a modern language we also owe to Dr Falque: 'Traducción de la "Historia Roderici'", *Boletín de la Institución Fernán González* 62 (1983), pp. 339–75.

Alfonso VI's favour and to his Castilian homeland in the years
1086–8. Ch. 27 seems to register a break in the flow of the text.

4   Chs 28–63 constitute a detailed narrative of Rodrigo's doings in
     eastern Spain between 1089 and 1094, culminating in the con-
     quest of Valencia and its defence in the battle of Cuarte.

5   Chs 64–75 chronicle selectively Rodrigo's activities as prince of
     Valencia from 1094 until his death in 1099.

6   Chs 76–7 form an epilogue in which Rodrigo's widow Jimena
     evacuated Valencia in 1102 and took her husband's body back to
     Castile for re-interment at the monastery of Cardeña.

The most notable feature to emerge from this analysis of the
structure of the *HR* is the degree to which the author's attention was
upon the *non-Castilian* doings of his hero: the geographical slant of the
text is towards the Ebro valley and the Levante, away from Rodrigo's
native Castile. The author displayed a particularly informed knowledge
of the Mediterranean coastal regions. Certain passages (for example,
in ch. 36) contain such abundant detail of dates and of places that one
may not unreasonably suspect the testimony of an eye-witness.

The author wrote in a plain, spare, unadorned Latin. There are several
reminiscences of biblical phraseology.[3] Knowledge of Latin and of the
text of the Bible render it likely, though not certain, that the writer
was a cleric. There are indications of a concern with documents: see
ch. 1, n. 2 and ch. 7, n. 18. In three places (chs 35, 38, 39) documents
were copied verbatim into the text, and one may suspect their
background presence elsewhere (e.g. in chs 23, 25, 26, 73). Notarial
connections on the part of the author are not to be ruled out.

Generally favourable to the hero of his work, the author was at one
point – and only one point – critical of him. This occurs in ch. 50,
where he sharply condemned Rodrigo's devastation of the Rioja in
1092. This has suggested to some that the author could have been a
native of that region. An origin in the Rioja, along the upper waters of
the Ebro, might help to explain author's eastern-facing gaze.

When did he write? The penultimate chapter furnishes *termini* both
post and *ante quem.* Composition must post-date the latest event
mentioned in the text, the evacuation of Valencia in 1102; and since
the author mentions that the city was still in Muslim hands at the

3 More than I realised when I published *The Quest for El Cid* in 1989 (see p. 94).
They have been noted by E. Falque.

time of writing, it must pre-date the conquest of Valencia by James I of
Aragon in 1238. (The earliest surviving manuscript was copied c. 1230,
possibly in the Rioja. Dr Falque judges it to be at least two removes
from a lost original.) Various attempts have been made to pinpoint the
time of composition between these terminal dates of 1102 and 1238.

An early date of composition was expounded and defended by the
eminent Spanish authority on Cidian matters, Ramón Menéndez Pidal
(1869–1968), in successive editions of his celebrated work La España
del Cid, first published in 1929.[4] Noting that the author of the HR
drew attention (ch. 76) to the continuing Muslim possession of the
city of Valencia, why, asked Menéndez Pidal, did he not allude to the
Christian conquest of Zaragoza in 1118? Plainly, he argued, because it
had not yet occurred at the time of writing. Pressing this line of
argument even further, he found similar significance in the author's
omission of any reference to the Almoravid take-over of Zaragoza in
July 1110. He concluded that the HR was composed within at most
eleven years of Rodrigo's death.

Menéndez Pidal's scholarly authority was such as to persuade most
readers of the accuracy of his dating for a generation or so after the
first publication of La España del Cid. However, in the second half of
the twentieth century many scholars have voiced reservations and
proposed alternatives. The most influential protagonist of a date of
composition about the middle of the twelfth century was the Aragonese historian Antonio Ubieto Arteta. Ubieto believed that he could pin
it down to the years between 1144 and 1147 because of verbal usages
in references to the Almoravids, the manner of rendering the title of
the king of Aragon and a mistake made by the author in referring to
one of the rulers of the Taifa states.[5] Ubieto's arguments, on close
examination not well founded, have been oddly influential. Though
few have shared his bold precision of dating, under his influence an
approximate date for the composition of the HR round the middle years
of the twelfth century has commended itself to many noted historical
and literary scholars in Spain, France, Britain and the United States.[6]

4 I have worked from the last edition revised by the author, the seventh, of 1969. In
the notes to my translation of the HR this is referred to as RMP.

5 A. Ubieto Arteta, 'La "Historia Roderici" y su fecha de redacción', Saitabi 11 (1961)
241–6; reprinted in his El 'Cantar de Mio Cid' y algunos problemas históricos
(Valencia, 1973), pp. 170–7.

6 For example, M. Lacarra, J. Horrent, C. Smith and B. F. Reilly in various
publications scattered between 1964 and 1988. References to the HR in P.
Linehan's History and the Historians of Medieval Spain (Oxford, 1993) are prudently
non-committal in the matter of dating.

An even later date of *c.* 1170 was initially favoured by the distin-
guished Dutch orientalist Reinhardt Dozy in a justly famous essay,
'Le Cid d'après de nouveaux documents' first published in 1849 in his
*Recherches sur l'Histoire et la Littérature de l'Espagne pendant le Moyen
Age.* But in the second (1860) and third (1881) editions of that work
Dozy had changed his mind and opted for the middle years of the
century.

In a book published in 1989 I admitted to finding an earlier dating
more plausible than a later one.[7] The suggestions there tentatively
advanced have not (to my knowledge) been decisively refuted. Accordingly I advance them again here, with some changes of emphasis, and
some amplifications, reflecting continuing ruminations over the last
ten years. I stress at the outset that these are suggestions only. A
precise dating of the *HR* which would command general assent is
unattainable. Readers are encouraged to speculate for themselves.
This reader, at any rate, is struck by four features of the text.

I A PALAEOGRAPHICAL CONSIDERATION

In ch. 23 the earliest and best MS contains the word 'Suggiz' where
the reading should be 'Saggiz', probably a slip for 'Sāggiz' with a
mark of abbreviation indicating 'Sanggiz': it is a patronymic, whose
modern rendering is 'Sánchez' meaning 'son of Sancho'. The (correct)
letter 'a' is replaced by the (incorrect) letter 'u'. It appears to be no
more than a trivial slip of the pen, but there is more to it than meets
the eye.[8] During the later eleventh century and the earlier twelfth the
traditional script employed in Spain, known as 'Visigothic' script, was
gradually being ousted by the script known in Spain as *francesa*,
'French' writing, whose letter-forms were devised in the Frankish
kingdom during the Carolingian renaissance: in all essentials the
letter-forms of *francesa* script, better known outside Spain as Caroline
or Carolingian minuscule, are those that we still use today (as printed,
for example, on this page). The use of Visigothic script in Aragon,
Castile, León – and the Rioja – was rare by about 1125 and to all
intents and purposes obsolete by the 1140s. One point of difference
between Visigothic and *francesa* scripts lay in the rendering of the first
letter of the alphabet in minuscule or lower case. In Visigothic script
the letter 'a' was open at the top and looked remarkably like the letter

7 *The Quest for El Cid,* pp. 93–8.
8 And it did not escape the vigilance of Menéndez Pidal: *RMP,* p. 907.

'u' as written in *francesa*. Where scribal error occurs in which the open-ended 'a' is rendered as 'u' there is a reasonable presumption that the manuscript from which the scribe was copying was in Visigothic script. Anyone who has worked on Spanish manuscripts of this epoch will know this as a very frequent error. It would therefore seem likely that the text of the *HR* from which the scribe of *c.* 1230 copied – or its (original?) exemplar – had been written in Visigothic script. This does not of course prove that the original had been committed to writing before *c.* 1125, but it renders it likely. The obvious objection to this argument is that a *single* slip of this character in a text of this length, offering several possibilities for similar slips on practically every page, is precious little to go on.

II THE AUTHOR'S OMISSIONS

As we have seen, Menéndez Pidal considered that the author's omissions held clues to the dating of the work. The unknown author not only failed to allude to changes in the fortunes of Zaragoza in 1110 and 1118; he failed in addition to register the death of King Alfonso VI in 1109 and that of Rodrigo's widow in (probably) 1116. I have elsewhere stigmatized negative evidence of this type as 'nearly always slippery'.[9] But when all is said and done, I do find that the omission of any reference to the Christian conquest of Zaragoza in 1118 is extremely singular. Zaragoza had played a significant part in Rodrigo's life as the scene of his exile for five years between 1081 and 1086 when he first acquired fame and fortune as a soldier outside his Castilian homeland. Only one other city – Valencia, for obvious reasons a special case – was mentioned more frequently in the text of the *HR*. Rodrigo's ally in later life – and a very important one – had been King Pedro I of Aragon (see chs 64–66 and 70 and relevant notes), and the conqueror of Zaragoza was Pedro's younger brother Alfonso I, *el Batallador*, 'the Battler'. It is surely very odd indeed that this famous Christian conquest of the year 1118, just down the valley of the Ebro from where our author may have written in the Rioja, went unregistered by him – if it had indeed taken place when he composed his text.

9 *The Quest for El Cid*, p. 97.

III THE TREATMENT OF RODRIGO'S FINAL RESTING-PLACE

The re-interment of Rodrigo's body at the Castilian monastery of
Cardeña three years after his death was reported laconically in the
last chapter of the HR. The monks of Cardeña were later on to make
a great deal – in every sense – out of their possession of the bodies not
only of Rodrigo but also of his wife, his son, his servant and his horse.
The author's failure to linger on his hero's last resting-place strengthens
the case for an early date of composition.

IV A POLEMICAL EDGE?

As already indicated, the anonymous author's treatment of Rodrigo
was favourable, with the single exception of the criticism recorded in
ch. 50. He provided Rodrigo with an improbably distinguished ancestry
and improbably dashing youthful exploits. He presented him as
always with right on his side, for instance in his stormy dealings with
Alfonso VI. He exaggerated the size of the enemy armies which
Rodrigo invariably defeated. This protective tone seems to me to take
on a slightly more polemical edge in the later chapters of the work
which deal with the last, Valencian, phase of Rodrigo's career. The
author went out of his way to portray his enemies as men of bad faith
who dishonoured agreements and thereby put themselves culturally
beyond the pale (chs 59, 71, 72 and see also the comments in note 103
on the phrase *mixti conmanebant* which occurs in ch. 54). He laid
unprecedented stress on Rodrigo's Christian devotion (chs 62, 66, 68,
73). He drew attention to his building and embellishment of churches
(chs 67, 72, 73). He was also suggestively reticent about the years 1095
and 1096, those in which Rodrigo consolidated his hold over Valencia
by a series of harsh and rapacious measures of which the most brutal
was the burning alive of the former *qāḍī* Ibn Jaḥḥāf.[10] One has the sense
that the unknown author was concerned to answer critics. If this were
the case, it is surely permissible to surmise that they were near-
contemporary ones; for the passage of time raised Rodrigo above
criticism. Who might the critics have been? We have not the faintest
idea.

The author's purposes remain opaque. Somewhat unusually, the HR is
not prefaced by a dedication (at any rate in the form in which it has
come down to us) and the text yields no clue as to the identity of the

10 *Ibid.*, pp. 180–2.

patron, if any, for whom it was composed. The small number and the brevity of the references to Doña Jimena render it unlikely that the work was commissioned by Rodrigo's widow. It has been shown that the text displays some indebtedness to hagiographical literary convention (which strengthens the case for clerical authorship).[11] And it has rather remote analogies with other secular biographies of this period such as Ralph of Caen's *Gesta Tancredi*. But these possible models or analogues convey us no closer to the author's motives. All that we can say is that his memorial was intended to honour Rodrigo's memory, and in part perhaps to defend him against calumny.

The author's recourse to documents raises questions about how and where he gained access to them. It was Ramón Menéndez Pidal who first launched the notion of an *archivo cidiano*, a 'Cidian archive', and it is entirely credible that in a society which held the written word in high regard – as eleventh-century Spain did – a military commander would accumulate documents as well as treasure and booty.[12] What might have happened to this archive after the evacuation of Valencia in 1102? It has long been surmised that custody might have been entrusted to Rodrigo's nominee to the see of Valencia, Bishop Jerónimo. (It is one of the puzzles of the *HR* that there is no mention of the bishop in it.) That will direct our attention to Salamanca, to which see Jerónimo was translated in 1102 and over which he presided until his death in 1120. It is indeed in the cathedral archive of Salamanca that there survive to this day two diplomas, the one issued by Rodrigo in 1098 and the other by his widow in 1101, recording grants to the cathedral church of Valencia. (These have been claimed as part of the *archivo cidiano*: strictly speaking they belonged to the episcopal rather than the Cidian archive, though this may be a distinction without a difference.) Colin Smith suggested that a cleric of Salamanca was the unknown author of the *HR*; and in one of his last articles he even went so far as to propose the name of Berenguer, bishop of Salamanca from 1135 to 1150.[13] Among the difficulties about such a localisation is the fact that the author chose neither to quote nor to refer to the Salamanca diplomas when he discussed the endowment of the bishopric of Valencia.

11 G. West, 'Hero or Saint? Hagiographic elements in the life of the Cid', *Journal of Hispanic Philology* 7 (1983), pp. 87–105.

12 *RMP*, p. 910.

13 C. Smith, *The Making of the 'Poema de Mio Cid'* (Cambridge, 1983), p. 58; see also his 'A conjecture about the authorship of the *Historia Roderici*', *Journal of Hispanic Research* 2 (1993–4), pp. 175–81.

However he might have gained his access to documentation, the tone
of vividness and immediacy in many passages of the author's work
suggest that he also had access to the witness of persons, or a person,
who had lived through some of the events described.[14] My guess –
and it's only a guess – is that he had spoken to someone who had
listened, scared, to the Almoravid troops as they prowled outside the
walls of Valencia, 'shrieking and shouting with a motley clamour of
voices' (ch. 62) in 1094. Perhaps he had heard those voices himself.
We shall never know.

Historia Roderici

Here begin the deeds of Rodrigo the Campeador.[1]

CHAPTER 1

The flux of years is vast and ceaseless: if the doings of this mutable
world are not fixed in written form, they will without doubt be consigned to oblivion.[2] We have therefore determined to embody and
establish by the light of the written word the descent of that most noble

14 *The Quest for El Cid*, p. 96.

1 This is the title given to the work in the earliest surviving manuscript, Madrid,
Biblioteca de la Real Academia de la Historia, A-189, fol. 75r. There is no
manuscript authority for the title *Historia Roderici* by which the work is generally
known: a more appropriate title might be *Gesta Roderici*, 'The Deeds of Rodrigo';
but the traditional title is retained here to avoid confusion. The division of the text
into chapters has no manuscript authority but was introduced by successive editors
for the reader's convenience. The Spanish term *campeador* renders the author's
campidoctus. This in turn derives from the Late Latin *campi doctus*, meaning 'a
regimental drill instructor'. Never a common word outside Roman military circles,
it seems to have dropped out of use altogether in the west after the dissolution of
the imperial armies in the fifth century. Its re-appearance in eleventh-century
Spain is puzzling. We do not know when the title was first adopted by or applied
to Rodrigo. Its first securely datable appearance, in the form *campeator*, occurs in
Count Berenguer of Barcelona's letter to Rodrigo of 1090 (below, ch. 38). Its second,
in the form *campidoctor*, is in the diploma of 1098 recording Rodrigo's donation of
endowments to the cathedral church of Valencia; and it was used of him again by
his widow in an analogous grant of 1101 (*RMP*, pp. 869, 872). To these formal
usages in letters or legal documents may be added the literary usage of the
unknown author of the *Carmen Campidoctoris* ('Song of the Campeador'), a Latin
panegyric poem on Rodrigo, which may have been composed as early as 1083.

2 This opening sentence has verbal affinities with one among the standard types of
formal opening preamble, technically known as an *arenga*, to be found in many Spanish
legal documents of this period. Its employment in this context might just possibly
suggest that the author had had some experience in the drafting of such documents.

and warlike man, Rodrigo Díaz, and the battles heroically fought by him.

CHAPTER 2

This then seems to be the origin of his stock. Laín Calvo fathered many sons, among them Fernán Laínez and Bermudo Laínez. [Fernán Laínez begat Laín Fernández;][3] Bermudo Laínez begat Rodrigo Bermúdez; Laín Fernández begat Nuño Laínez; Rodrigo Bermúdez begat Fernán Rodríguez; Fernán Rodríguez begat Pedro Fernández and a daughter named Eylo. Nuño Laínez took this Eylo for his wife, and from her he fathered Laín Núñez, who was the father of Diego Laínez. Diego Laínez fathered Rodrigo Díaz the Campeador from the daughter of Rodrigo Alvarez – the brother of Nuño Alvarez who held the castle of Amaya and several other regional provinces. Rodrigo Alvarez held the castle of Luna and the provinces of Mormojón, Moradillo, Cellorigo and Curiel, and many other estates on the *meseta*: his wife was the lady Teresa, the sister of Nuño Laínez of Relias.[4]

3 Editors are agreed that there are gaps or lacunae in the text of the *Historia Roderici* as it has come down to us, and some of them, notably Ramón Menéndez Pidal, have tried to fill them from later sources allegedly dependent on the *Historia*. Some of these attempts are less convincing than others. The readings supplied will be placed within square brackets in this translation, and commented upon if this seems necessary. The phrase supplied here is drawn from the *Liber Regum* of *c.* 1200 and seems unexceptionable: see further *RMP*, p. 921. The author reports Rodrigo's genealogy with more than a hint of doubt ('seems'), which we may well share. Whoever concocted its upper reaches was evidently motivated by a wish to trace Rodrigo's descent from Laín Calvo, one of the semi- or perhaps wholly legendary ninth-century 'judges' of Castile to whom patriotic Castilians looked back as the founding fathers of their principality. Dr E. Falque in her edition of the text has drawn attention to the analogies between this chapter and biblical genealogies such as that in Matthew i.1–16.

4 We are on firmer ground when we reach the generation of Rodrigo's grandparents. They were important people in the Castilian establishment during the reign of Fernando I (1037–65). His paternal grandfather Laín Núñez can be traced in documents between 1045 and 1063: he subscribed royal diplomas issued by the king in 1049, 1056, 1059 and 1063: *CD Fernando I*, nos 38, 49, 52, 63. His maternal grandfather Rodrigo Alvarez, traceable between 1038 and 1066, subscribed royal diplomas in 1038 and 1039 (*ibid.*, nos 8, 11) as well as a number of later and less reliable ones from the same reign. The places held by Rodrigo Alvarez under the king were close to Castile's eastern and southern marches. Nothing at all is known of Rodrigo's unnamed mother. The fact that he was given a name that was current in her family but not in his father's might indicate that he was not the eldest son: see also n. 6 below. Professor Janet Nelson has suggested to me that it might alternatively indicate that Rodrigo's mother's family was of higher status than his father's, directing my attention to the discussion of such marriages – technically known as hypogamous – in R. Le Jan, *Famille et pouvoir dans le monde franc (VIIe–Xe siècle)* (Paris, 1995), at pp. 298–305.

CHAPTER 3

Diego Laínez, father of Rodrigo Díaz the Campeador, with great and
unflagging courage seized from the Navarrese the castle of Ubierna,
and Urbel and La Piedra.[5] He fought the Navarrese too in open battle,
and defeated them. After he had thus triumphed over them, never
again could they prevail against him. On his death his son Rodrigo
Díaz succeeded by the destiny of paternal ruling.[6]

CHAPTER 4

Sancho, King of Castile and lord of Spain,[7] brought Rodrigo Díaz up
in his household and girded him with the belt of knighthood. When
King Sancho went to Zaragoza and fought with the Aragonese king
at Graus, whom he defeated and killed there, he took Rodrigo Díaz
with him: Rodrigo was a part of the army which fought the victorious
battle.[8] After this triumph King Sancho returned to Castile.

5 Little is known of Diego Laínez from other sources. His name features among the
   witnesses to a grant by his wife's uncle Nuño Alvarez to the monastery of Cardeña,
   near Burgos, in 1047. Ubierna, Urbel and La Piedra, all places in northern Castile,
   were among territories ceded by King Fernando I to his brother García III of
   Navarre in 1037–38. Their recovery by Diego Laínez is hard to date, but the
   operations probably belonged to the years after King García's death in 1054.

6 in paternalis iuris sorte, literally 'in the fortune of paternal law', or 'in the allotment
   of paternal right'. Emma Falque translates the phrase simply en la heredad paterna,
   'in the father's property'. But the author's use of this curious phrase suggests
   something a little less straightforward. It is possible that Rodrigo was preferred
   over his sibling(s) in the interests of preserving the integrity of the family
   property. This was a strategy traceable elsewhere in the aristocratic circles of
   western Christendom at this period. For the legal background see A. Otero, 'La
   Mejora', AHDE 33 (1963), pp. 5–131.

7 Sancho, eldest son of Fernando I, received Castile in the division of his father's
   dominions, over which he ruled as Sancho II between 1065 and 1072. The author
   applies these grandiose titles to Sancho with reference to a period two-and-a-half
   years before his father's death, whereas the formal decison to divide the kingdom
   was not taken until 1064: see the Historia Silense chs 8 and 103 and commentary
   thereupon. The title 'lord of Spain' translates dominator Hyspanie. At this period the
   term Hispania usually indicated that part of Spain under Islamic rule, not the whole
   Iberian landmass. The only part of Hispania so defined of which Sancho could
   properly be regarded as the dominator was the neighbouring amirate of Zaragoza
   (see following note).

8 The Graus campaign of 1063 furnishes a good example of the complicated
   diplomatic relationships of eleventh-century Spain. Sancho was sent by his father
   Fernando I to support the Muslim ruler of Zaragoza, al-Muqtadir, against the
   territorial aggrandisement of the Christian Aragonese under their King Ramiro I,
   younger brother of Fernando I and thereby Sancho's uncle. The battle in which
   Ramiro met his death was fought on 8 May 1063.

CHAPTER 5

King Sancho valued Rodrigo Díaz so highly, with great esteem and affection, that he made him commander of his whole military following.⁹ So Rodrigo throve and became a most mighty man of war, and Campeador in the household of King Sancho. In every battle which King Sancho fought with King Alfonso, at Llantada and Golpejera, and defeated him, Rodrigo bore the king's royal standard, and distinguished himself among all the warriors of the king's army, and bettered himself thereby.¹⁰ When King Sancho besieged Zamora¹¹ it happened that Rodrigo Díaz fought alone with fifteen enemy soldiers: seven of them were in chain-mail; one of these he killed, two he wounded and unhorsed, and the remainder he put to flight by his spirited courage. Afterwards he fought with Jimeno Garcés, one of the more distinguished men of Pamplona, and defeated him. He fought with equal success against a certain Saracen at Medinaceli, whom he not only defeated but also killed.

CHAPTER 6

After the death of his lord King Sancho, who had maintained him and loved him well, King Alfonso received him with honour as his vassal and kept him in his entourage with very respectful affection.¹² The king gave him one of his relatives to wife, the lady Jimena, daughter of Count Diego of Oviedo. She bore him sons and daughters.¹³

9 *constituit eum principem*, 'made him commander', echoing Daniel ii.48. On the problems connected with Rodrigo's alleged tenure of the court office of *armiger* or *alférez* see Fletcher, *Quest for El Cid*, pp. 114–15.

10 The strife between the sons of Fernando I in the course of the years 1065–72 has been carefully surveyed in Reilly, *Alfonso VI*, chs 2–4. The encounters referred to in this chapter occurred respectively on 19 July 1068 and early in January 1072.

11 Sancho II met his death while besieging Zamora on 7 October 1072 in mysterious circumstances involving treachery: brief discussions of the possibilities are to be found in Reilly, *Alfonso VI*, pp. 65–8 and Fletcher, *Quest for El Cid*, pp. 116–18; see also *Historia Silense*, ch. 10 and commentary thereon.

12 Alfonso VI ruled over the combined kingdoms of León, Castile and Galicia from 1072 to 1109.

13 The marriage probably took place in 1074 or 1075. Jimena is well-attested in several reliable contemporary documents, but her ancestry is more problematical: it is investigated, somewhat speculatively, in *RMP*, pp. 721–6. It is just possible that she was a great-granddaughter of King Alfonso V (d. 1028). Her father Count Diego is otherwise unknown. The document recording the settlement of property in favour of the bride at the time of her marriage, technically known as a *carta de arras*, or dower charter, has survived: it presents problems as to authenticity and date. It is printed in *RMP*, pp. 837–42 and discussed by Reilly, *Alfonso VI*, p. 83 and

CHAPTER 7

In due course[14] King Alfonso sent him as his ambassador to the king of Seville and the king of Córdoba to collect the tribute due to him.[15] At that time al-Mu'tamid king of Seville and 'Abd Allāh (*Almudafar*) king of Granada[16] were [enemies. And with the king of Granada were] García Ordóñez, and Fortún Sánchez the son-in-law of King García of Pamplona, and Lope Sánchez the brother of Fortún Sánchez, and Diego Pérez, one of the magnates of Castile: each of these men with his following of warriors came to fight against the king of Seville.[17] When Rodrigo Díaz came to al-Mu'tamid he was at once told that the king of Granada with his Christian allies was advancing upon al-

Fletcher, *Quest for El Cid*, pp. 121–3. We know of two daughters and a son who were born to Rodrigo and Jimena. Cristina married a Navarrese magnate named Ramiro, a grandson of King García III of Navarre (1035–54): their son García became King of Navarre in 1134. María married Ramón Berenguer III, Count of Barcelona (1096–1131). The son, Diego, is attested only in the *Liber Regum* of c. 1200: for what it is worth, it records that Diego was killed in the battle of Consuegra in 1097.

14 The Cabra campaign which occupies chs 7–9 probably occurred in 1079. B. Powell, *Epic and Chronicle* (London, 1983) p. 13, is sceptical about the account in the *Historia Roderici*, perhaps unduly so; for a more indulgent treatment see Fletcher, *Quest for El Cid*, pp. 128–30.

15 The author implies that there were two separate amirs – almost invariably referred to as 'kings' in Christian sources – of Seville and Córdoba. But they were one and the same: al-Mu'tamid of Seville (1069–91) had absorbed the Taifa principality of Córdoba a few years before, in 1076.

16 'Abd Allāh, amir of Granada from 1073 until 1090, has left a most remarkable autobiography, translated and extensively annotated by A. T. Tibi, *The Tibyān. Memoirs of 'Abd Allāh b. Buluggīn, last Zirid amir of Granada* (Leiden, 1986). On the use in this chapter of the correct title *Almudafar* – properly al-Muẓaffar – see, in the last-named work, p. 193, n. 32. The immediately following phrase in square brackets, which the sense requires, was plausibly supplied by Menéndez Pidal from the thirteenth-century *Primera Crónica General* (*RMP*, II, p. 921).

17 García Ordóñez, contemporary and rival of Rodrigo Díaz, was among the leading magnates of Alfonso VI's realm: *alférez* to the king in 1074, count of Nájera certainly by 1081, active as a warrior and resettler of conquered lands (for example at Miranda de Ebro, *nutritor* or tutor to Alfonso's son, the *Infante* Sancho, whom he died trying vainly to protect in the disastrous battle of Uclés in 1108; see further Barton, *Aristocracy*, pp. 249–50 and references cited. He married Urraca, daughter of García III of Navarre (or Pamplona). Thus he was a brother-in-law of Fortún Sánchez, another son-in-law of King García as our author correctly states, who had married Urraca's sister Ermesenda. Fortún and his brother Lope were natives of Alava who were prominent in the service of Sancho IV of Navarre, the son of García III. After Sancho's murder in 1076 and Alfonso VI's annexation of the Rioja they seem to have gravitated into the service of the latter. Diego Pérez is otherwise unknown, just possibly the father of Count Froila Díaz on whom see Barton, *Aristocracy*, p. 245.

Mu'tamid and his kingdom. So he sent letters[18] to the king of Granada and to the Christians who were with him, [requesting them] for the love of their lord King Alfonso not to come against the king of Seville nor to enter his kingdom. But they, trusting in the great size of their army,[19] not only refused to listen to his requests but even altogether rejected them. Instead they advanced laying waste all the land as far as the castle known as Cabra.[20]

CHAPTER 8

When Rodrígo Díaz heard and checked the truth of this, he at once went out with his army to confront them. A hard-fought battle took place, lasting from the third hour of the day until the sixth. The army of the king of Granada, both Saracens and Christians, suffered very great carnage and casualties. Eventually, defeated and disordered, all fled from the face of Rodrigo Díaz. There were captured in that battle Count García Ordóñez and Lope Sánchez and Diego Pérez and many others of their fighting men. After his victory Rodrigo kept them captive for three days: then he deprived them of their tents and all their booty and set them free to go their way.

CHAPTER 9

Rodrigo returned in triumph to Seville. Al-Mu'tamid gave him the tribute for the lord King Alfonso, and added over and above this many presents and gifts which he delivered to his king. These tributes and presents were accepted and peace was made between Alfonso and al-Mu'tamid. Rodrigo returned with honour to Castile and to his lord King Alfonso. In return for this success and victory granted him by God, many men both acquaintances and strangers became jealous and accused him before the king of many false and untrue things.

CHAPTER 10

After Rodrigo had returned with honour as aforesaid to Castile, King Alfonso at once ordered him to a land of the Saracens that was in

18 The first of several references in the *Historia Roderici* to written communications, evidently a subject of interest to the author.

19 Dr Falque has caught here an echo of Judith ix.9.

20 Cabra is just to the north of Lucena, about two-thirds of the way from Granada to Córdoba.

rebellion, to lay it waste with his army and amplify and pacify his kingdom. Rodrigo, however, was lying ill in Castile at the time. The Saracens meanwhile invaded and fell upon a castle named Gormaz where they seized no little booty.[21] When this came to the ears of Rodrigo he was consumed with great anger and bitterness and said, 'I shall go after those robbers and with any luck I shall take them.'[22] So he gathered together his army and all his well-armed knights, and pillaged and laid waste the land of the Saracens in the region of Toledo.[23] He rounded up 7000 captives, both men and women, ruthlessly laying hold of all their wealth and possessions, and brought them back home with him.

CHAPTER 11

However, when King Alfonso and the elders of his court heard of this exploit of Rodrigo they were very gravely displeased. The courtiers who were envious of him held it against him and said with one voice to the king, 'Lord King, your Highness must surely know that Rodrigo perpetrated this in order that all of us who live together in Saracen territory to take tribute from it will be killed by the Saracens and die there.'[24] The king was unjustly impressed and angered by this wicked and envious accusation. He expelled Rodrigo from his kingdom.[25]

21 The castle of Gormaz, on the Duero, had been conquered by Fernando I: see *Historia Silense*, ch. 91. A few years after the action described in the present chapter Alfonso VI entrusted it to Rodrigo's care: below, ch. 25. Or did he *re*-entrust it? If the latter, this would explain why Rodrigo felt protectively responsible for Gormaz in this earlier year of 1081. It may be significant that the author assumed that his primary audience did not need an explanation.

22 There seems to be a reminiscence here of 1 Samuel xxx.8.

23 We know nothing of his route. The natural one to take, and that which offered the richest pickings, would have been along the axis Medinaceli–Sigüenza–Guadalajara.

24 The castles of Brihuega, Canales and Zorita, which lay to the south of the Medinaceli–Guadalajara line, had been ceded to Alfonso VI by al-Qādir, amir of Toledo, in 1080. The author of the *Historia Roderici* was either ignorant of, or chose to say nothing about, Alfonso's treaty with al-Qādir, a fragile pact threatened by Rodrigo's maverick reprisal raid. For the context see Reilly, *Alfonso VI*, pp. 127–9 and Fletcher, *Quest for El Cid*, pp. 126–8, 130–32.

25 For a comparable account of Alfonso VI's punishment of those who broke the peace by unauthorised attacks on the Saracens see La *'Vita Dominici Siliensis' de Grimaldo*, ed. V. Valcarcel (Logroño, 1982) ii.26 (pp. 376–8): this was composed between 1088 and 1109.

CHAPTER 12

So Rodrigo, leaving his sorrowing friends behind him, departed from Castile and came to Barcelona.[26] Then he went to Zaragoza, where al-Muqtadir was then reigning. [Rodrigo gave his allegiance to al-Muqtadir of Zaragoza, who received him with great honour and treated him with much respect. While Rodrigo was residing contentedly at Zaragoza, al-Muqtadir fell ill] and died.[27] His realm was divided between his two sons, al-Mu'tamin and al-Hāyib: al-Mu'tamin reigned in Zaragoza, his brother al-Hāyib in Denia.[28] This al-Mu'tamin was very fond of Rodrigo and set him over and exalted him above all his kingdom and all his land, relying upon his counsel in all things.[29] A dreadful and most bitter quarrel broke out between al-Mu'tamin and his brother al-Hāyib, and they agreed a time at which they might do battle together. Now Sancho, king of Aragon and Pamplona, and Berenguer, count of Barcelona, accompanied al-Hāyib as his allies.[30] With al-Mu'tamin was Rodrigo Díaz, who served him faithfully and guarded and protected his kingdom and land. Because of this King Sancho and Count Berenguer were especially hostile to him and on the lookout for him.

CHAPTER 13

When King Sancho heard that Rodrigo Díaz wished to go from Zaragoza to Monzón he swore an oath and said that in no manner

26 This is the point at which the action of the epic *Poema de Mio Cid* begins.
27 The obvious lacuna here was supplied by Menéndez Pidal from the *Primera Crónica General.*
28 For the fullest treatment of the family Afif Turk, *El Reino de Zaragoza en el siglo XI de Cristo (V de la Hégira)* (Madrid, 1978). There are chronological problems arising from this chapter. RMP (p. 270) suggests that Rodrigo's exile began in '1081, agosto?', which seems as good a guess as any. Dr Turk (pp. 119–21) suggests that al-Muqtadir delegated power to his sons on account of illness in Yumada I of 474 AH, i.e. between 7 October and 5 November 1081, but did not die until 475 AH, i.e. between 1 June 1082 and 20 May 1083. In the territorial division of the amirate of Zaragoza the eldest son of al-Muqtadir, Yūsuf al-Mu'tamin received the city of Zaragoza and the western parts of the principality, while the younger, Mundhir al-Hāyib, received the eastern parts comprising Lérida, Tortosa and Denia.
29 This is almost certainly an exaggeration. It is likely that Rodrigo was but one of several Christian mercenary captains in the service of al-Mu'tamin.
30 Sancho Ramírez, king of Aragon 1063–94; Berenguer Ramón II, count of Barcelona 1076–97.

should he dare to do that.[31] When Rodrigo heard of the king's oath his
spirit was moved and with his whole army [he left Zaragoza and went
a day's journey as far as the village of Peralta] where he set up camp
within eyesight of his enemies, the whole army of al-Ḥāyib. On the
next day he entered Monzón under the eyes of King Sancho [by
arrangement with the Saracens of the castle]. But the king did not
dare to come against him. [After this the Cid left Monzón and went
to Tamarite and stayed there for a few days. One day he left the town
with ten knights and encountered nearly a hundred and fifty knights
of King Sancho: and he defeated them all, and captured seven knights
with their horses, and the rest fled. Afterwards these knights asked
Rodrigo to release them, which he did, and also gave back their
horses.][32] Meanwhile al-Mu'tamin and Rodrigo decided to restore
and fortify an old castle called Almenar; and this was done at once.[33]
Soon afterwards the quarrel between al-Mu'tamin and his brother al-
Ḥāyib flared up again, to the point that they began to prepare for war.

CHAPTER 14

Al-Ḥāyib, however, entered into an agreement with Count Berenguer
and the count of Cerdaña, and with the brother of the count of Urgel,
and with the lords of Besalú, Ampurdán, Rosellón and Carcassonne.[34]
Al-Ḥāyib made this arrangement with them, that all of them should
come and join him in laying siege to the castle of Almenar; which they
immediately did. They besieged and attacked it for many days, until
those who were inside the castle lacked for water.

31 Monzón was one of the strongpoints which guarded the northern marches of the
   principality of Zaragoza. For its strategic significance see A. Ubieto Arteta,
   Colección Diplomática de Pedro I de Aragón y Navarra (Zaragoza, 1951), pp. 55–6.
   The Christian rulers of Aragon had long harboured designs on it which were
   finally realised when it fell to King Sancho Ramírez in 1089.
32 Lacunae supplied by Menéndez Pidal from the Primera Crónica General. The first
   phrase ('by arrangement with the Saracens of the castle') seems inoffensive, even
   necessary. The second is a more speculative addition which has the air of a later
   embroidery designed to exalt the Cid's prowess and magnanimity.
33 Almenar and Tamarite were strongpoints a little to the east of Monzón. They fell
   to the Aragonese in 1093 and 1104 respectively.
34 These were modest Catalan lordships scattered to south and north of the eastern
   end of the Pyrenees. For a brief introduction see T. N. Bisson, The Medieval Crown
   of Aragon. A Short History (Oxford, 1986), pp. 19–30 with map at p. 20.

CHAPTER 15

Now Rodrigo was based at that time at the castle of Escarp, between
the two rivers Segre and Cinca, which he had boldly taken earlier on
and made all its inhabitants captive.[35] From there he sent a messenger
to al-Mu'tamin to tell him of the sufferings of and the threat to the
castle of Almenar and to let him know that all those who were in the
castle were worn out and starving[36] and almost at the end of their
tether. Again Rodrigo, gravely anxious, sent other messengers bearing
his letters to al-Mu'tamin, [imploring him] to come and relieve the
castle which he had built. Al-Mu'tamin came at once to Rodrigo and
found him at the castle of Tamarite. There they took counsel together.
Al-Mu'tamin asked Rodrigo to fight against the enemies who were
besieging the castles [sic] of Almenar. But he replied, 'It is better that
you pay al-Ḥāyib money to abstain from attacking the castle than to
offer battle with him, for he has come with a great multitude of
troops.' Al-Mu'tamin willingly agreed to this. So Rodrigo at once sent
a messenger to the aforesaid counts and to al-Ḥāyib, proposing that
they accept money and depart from the castle. But they were unwilling to accede to this proposal and did not cease from attacking the
castle. So the messenger came back to Rodrigo and told him all that
he had heard from them.

CHAPTER 16

Greatly worried, Rodrigo ordered all his soldiers to arm and prepare
themselves bravely for battle. He led his army out to a place where
both sides – the counts and al-Ḥāyib, and Rodrigo Díaz – faced each
other. With a great noise of shouting and weaponry on both sides the
troops advanced and joined battle. The aforesaid counts and al-Ḥāyib
at once turned their backs and fled from the face of Rodrigo in
confusion and defeat. The greatest part of them were killed: a few,
however, escaped. All their goods and booty passed by custom into
the hands of Rodrigo. He led the count of Barcelona and his warriors
captive to the castle of Tamarite, and there in the wake of victory
delivered them into the hands of al-Mu'tamin. After five days he set
them free to depart to their own country.

35 The present-day Granja de Escarpe, some thirty kilometres to the south-west of
   Lérida. Presumably Rodrigo had taken it from al-Ḥāyib.
36 An emendation from the tautological *defessi* to *(fame) defecti* has been accepted by
   most editors: see *RMP*, p. 928 and E. Falque's edition, p. 53.

CHAPTER 17

Rodrigo Díaz returned with al-Mu'tamin to Zaragoza, where he was
received by the citizens with the greatest honour and respect. In those
days al-Mu'tamin raised Rodrigo up above his own son and over his
kingdom and over all his land. He seemed to be as it were the lord of
the whole realm.[37] Al-Mu'tamin showered him with innumerable
presents and many gifts of gold and silver.

CHAPTER 18

After many days had passed it occurred that a certain unworthy man
named Albofalac, who then held the castle of Rueda near Zaragoza,
withdrew himself and the castle from the authority and lordship of
King al-Mu'tamin and rose in rebellion there in the name of al-
Muẓaffar, the uncle of al-Mu'tamin, who had been imprisoned in the
castle by his brother al-Muqtadir.[38] Because of this the aforesaid al-
Muẓaffar besought the Emperor Alfonso with many prayers to come
and help him. In response the Emperor Alfonso sent the Infante
Ramiro and Count Gonzalo and several other magnates with a huge
army to assist him.[39] When they reached him they agreed together
that they should send to the emperor and ask him to come in person:
which was done. He came with his army at once and stayed there for
a few days. And then al-Muẓaffar died. Albofalac, the rebel of the
castle of Rueda, took counsel with the Infante Ramiro about handing
Rueda over to the Emperor Alfonso. Albofalac went from there to the
emperor and addressed him with peaceful words, but deceitfully,
imploring him with many prayers to come to Rueda and take over the
castle. However, before the emperor could go to the castle, Albofalac
allowed the emperor's magnates to enter it, he himself remaining
nearby. When they entered, Albofalac's deceit and treachery were at

37 Compare n. 29 above.

38 The background to the massacre of Rueda on 6 January 1083 is briefly outlined in
Reilly, *Alfonso VI*, p. 165 and Fletcher, *Quest for El Cid*, pp. 137–8. The man
referred to as *Albofalac* is otherwise unknown. Rueda, in the valley of the Jalón
some 33 km west of Zaragoza, was a strongpoint on the important line of communication between the Ebro valley and Calatayud, Medinaceli, Guadalajara and
Toledo.

39 Ramiro was the brother of Sancho IV of Navarre, and brother-in-law of García
Ordóñez and Fortún Sánchez on whom see ch. 7 and n. 17 above. Count Gonzalo
Salvadórez was one of the leading magnates of Castile and a patron of the
monastery of Oña: on him see Barton, *Aristocracy*, pp. 45, 87, 204, 251 and
references cited.

once revealed: for the knights and footsoldiers who garrisoned the
castle pelted the emperor's men with stones and rocks, killing many of
those noblemen [including the Infante Ramiro and Count Gonzalo].
The emperor returned to his camp in great sorrow.

CHAPTER 19

Rodrigo was in Tudela at the time. When he heard of this business he
went to see the emperor. Alfonso received him honourably and
earnestly pressed him to follow him back to Castile. So Rodrigo
followed him. But the emperor still harboured jealous thoughts in his
heart, and evil designs of expelling Rodrigo from his land.[40] Rodrigo
learnt of this and did not want to go on into Castile, so he left the
emperor and returned to Zaragoza, where King al-Mu'tamin welcomed
him fittingly.[41]

CHAPTER 20

After this indeed divine clemency granted a great victory to the
Emperor Alfonso. He doughtily took Toledo, the famous city of
Hispania, which he had for long – for seven years indeed – invested
and attacked. He incorporated it into his empire with its dependent
settlements and territories.[42]

CHAPTER 21

Meanwhile King al-Mu'tamin ordered Rodrigo Díaz to gather his
troops and invade the land of Aragon with him to lay it waste. They
ravaged the land of Aragon and stripped it of its riches and led off
many of its inhabitants captive with them. After five days they
returned victoriously to the castle of Monzón. The Aragonese king

40 Echoing Proverbs xxvi.24 and Ecclesiastes ix.1.
41 The story told in this chapter is implausible. It is surely more likely that Rodrigo's
   motive in visiting the court of Alfonso VI was to exculpate himself from any
   suspicion of responsibility for the treachery at Rueda.
42 This is an odd place, between events which occurred in 1082-3 (ch. 19) and those
   which were to take place in 1084 (chs 21-3), to insert a notice of the fall of Toledo
   in 1085. Perhaps the author wanted to signal the beginning of Alfonso's final siege
   of Toledo, or to indicate that the king would be offstage for a while as the *Historia's*
   action shifted back to the east. Alfonso VI made his triumphal entry into Toledo on
   25 May 1085, which was also, by coincidence, the date of the death, in exile, of
   Pope Gregory VII.

Sancho was indeed present at that time in his land and kingdom but
in no manner did he dare to resist Rodrigo. After this Rodrigo fell
upon the land of al-Mu'tamin's brother al-Ḥāyib, and ravaged it. He
wrought much damage and destruction there, especially in the
mountains of Morella and thereabouts. There was not left in that
region a house which he did not destroy, nor property which he did
not seize. He campaigned too against the castle of Morella, and fought
his way up to the gate of the castle and inflicted great damage on it.
Al-Mu'tamin asked him by means of letters and a messenger to
rebuild the fortress of Olocau, over against Morella. He at once rebuilt
and fortified it and stocked it well with all necessary provisions, and
men and weapons.[43]

CHAPTER 22

When King al-Ḥāyib heard this he went to see the Aragonese king
Sancho and made a great complaint about Rodrigo. They made an
agreement together to help one another to defend their kingdoms and
lands stoutly against Rodrigo, and then to fight bravely with him in
open battle.[44] Both rulers gathered their armies and fixed their joint
camp beside the River Ebro. Rodrigo was near them. King Sancho at
once sent envoys to Rodrigo [telling him] to retire from the spot.
where he was without delay and not to return there afterwards. But
he was in no way prepared to acquiesce in their instructions. Instead
he gave this reply to the messengers: 'If my lord king wishes to pass
by me in peace, I shall willingly permit him [to do so]; and not only
him, but all his men as well. Furthermore, should he wish it, I shall
give him a hundred of my troops to attend upon him and be the
companions of his journey.'[45] The envoys returned to the king and
gave him Rodrigo's message.

CHAPTER 23

However, when King Sancho heard that Rodrigo would not fall in
with his wishes nor retire from the spot where he was, he was
possessed with anger. Together with al-Ḥāyib he set off as fast as he

43 Morella lies about 60 km south-west of Tortosa; Olocau is some 22 km due west of
   Morella.
44 The agreement may have been committed to writing like the two treaties
   illuminatingly studied by J. M. Lacarra, 'Dos tratados de paz y alianza', pp. 77–94.
45 As Dr Falque has pointed out, the last phrase echoes Genesis xxxiii.12, xxxv.3.

could until he had almost reached Rodrigo's encampment. When Rodrigo saw this he swore to resist them to the end, and never to flee their face: constant and brave he remained there. On the following day King Sancho and al-Ḥāyib and their troops armed themselves and advanced their formations against him. Battle was joined. The fight was long. Eventually King Sancho and al-Ḥāyib turned their backs and fled from Rodrigo's face defeated and disordered. Rodrigo pursued them for a long way and captured many of them. Among the prisoners were Bishop Ramón Dalmacio, Count Sancho Sánchez of Pamplona, Count Nuño of Portugal, Gudesteo González, Nuño Suárez of León, Anaya Suárez of Galicia, Calvet, Iñigo Sánchez of Monclús, Jimeno Garcés of Buil, Pepino Aznar and García Aznar his brother, Laín Pérez of Pamplona the nephew of Count Sancho, Fortún Garcés of Aragon, Sancho Garcés of Alquézar, Blasco Garcés the king's *mayordomo*, and also García Díaz of Castile.[46] In addition to these he captured more than 2000 men whom later he allowed to go free to their own land. These men indeed he captured by brave fighting, and sacked all their camp and goods. After this overwhelming victory he returned to Zaragoza with unreckonable booty and those very noble prisoners named above. Al-Mu'tamin and his sons and a great

---

46 This is a most remarkable assemblage of prisoners. They fall, roughly speaking, into three categories. (A) Grandees. The two most imposing names are those of Ramón Dalmacio, Bishop of Roda (de Isábena) from 1076/7 until 1094 (on whom see A. Durán Gudiol, *La Iglesia de Aragón durante los reinados de Sancho Ramírez y Pedro I* (Rome, 1962), pp. 34–6, 56–7, 61) and Count Sancho Sánchez of Pamplona, said to have been the son of a bastard brother of Sancho IV of Navarre (see A. Ubieto Arteta, *Colección Diplomática de Pedro I de Aragón y Navarra* (Zaragoza, 1951), p. 175). (B) Less exalted but still distinguished vassals of the king of Aragon, all of them traceable among the *tenentes* of the crown in the late eleventh or early twelfth centuries with the aid of the invaluable work of reference by A. Ubieto Arteta, *Los 'Tenentes' en Aragón y Navarra en los siglos XI y XII* (Valencia, 1973). Shortage of space precludes lengthy demonstration here; a single example must suffice: Iñigo Sánchez is traceable as the *tenente* of various places between 1082 and 1116, including Calasanz, Estada (with whose re-settlement he was charged after its conquest in 1087) and Monzón, as well as Monclús where he can be traced between 1082 and 1093. (C) Natives of the dominions of Alfonso VI, presumed to have been voluntary or involuntary exiles in the kingdom of Aragon: namely, Count Nuño of Portugal, Gudesteo González, Nuño Suárez of León, Anaya Suárez of Galicia and García Díaz of Castile. How did our author, assumed to have been writing perhaps some thirty or more years later, know the names of prisoners taken in battle in 1084? It is difficult – and perhaps it is not necessary – to resist the obvious and natural answer, that he had a written list of names in front of him. This speculation may gain support from the consideration that it is here, and here alone in the *Historia Roderici*, that we have in the unanimous reading of both MSS 'Ennecus *Suggiz* de Montecluso' (= Iñigo Sánchez de Monclús) a strong suggestion that the author was transcribing a document in Visigothic script which he misread. See further my comments in the introduction.

multitude both of men and women from the city of Zaragoza, rejoicing and exulting with tremendous joy in his victory, came out to meet him at the village of Fuentes, which is distant fifty *stadia* from the city.[47]

CHAPTER 24

Rodrigo Díaz stayed at Zaragoza until the death of al-Mu'tamin. After his death his son al-Musta'īn succeeded him as king. Rodrigo remained with him at Zaragoza in the greatest honour and respect for nine years [*sic*].[48]

CHAPTER 25

After this he returned to his native land of Castile. King Alfonso received him honourably and gladly. Soon afterwards the king gave him the castle of Duáñez with its dependents, and the castle of Gormaz, and Ibio and Campóo and Iguña and Briviesca, and Langa which is in the western parts, together with all their territories and inhabitants.[49]

---

47 Fuentes de Ebro is about 25 km downriver from Zaragoza. The unknown site of the battle must have been somewhere to the east of that. *RMP* (pp. 742–3) presented a case for dating the encounter to 14 August 1084.

48 The death of al-Mu'tamin cannot be fixed more closely than 'approximately, the autumn of 1085' (Turk, *Reino de Zaragoza*, p. 143). Al-Musta'īn governed Zaragoza from 1085 to 1110. All commentators agree that the author's (or copyist's) reading 'nine years' must be a mistake for 'nine months'.

49 It is plausible to suppose that Rodrigo returned to Castile late in 1086 in the wake of Alfonso VI's defeat at the hands of the invading Almoravids at Sagrajas on 23 October. The king was desperate for troops to defend his vulnerable southern frontier. In this vassal's market Rodrigo could negotiate favourable terms for his rehabilitation. There is disagreement over the identification of some of the places mentioned. The author's *Donnas* is usually taken to be Dueñas on the River Pisuerga between Palencia and Valladolid: but this seems implausibly far to the west; might the place not be Duáñez, just to the east of Soria and about 60 km north-east of Gormaz? For Gormaz, see above ch. 10 and n. 21. It is generally agreed that the author's *Campos* should be identified with Campóo. If his *Ibia* be taken as Ibio and his *Egunna* as Iguña, we have in these three district-names three regions in northern Castile adjacent to the landholdings known to have been in Rodrigo's possession at the time of his marriage; as also is Briviesca. *Langa* is assumed to be Langa de Duero, significantly – about 35 km – to the west of Gormaz, itself the most westerly of the Duero holdings. The writer's 'gave' (*dedit*) is ambiguous, perhaps deliberately so. I have suggested an interpretation elsewhere: Fletcher, *Quest for El Cid*, pp. 152–3.

CHAPTER 26

Furthermore, Alfonso pardoned him and gave him this privilege in his
kingdom, written and confirmed under seal, stipulating that all the
land or castles which he might acquire from the Saracens in the land
of the Saracens, should be absolutely his in full ownership, not only
his but also his sons' and his daughters' and all his descendants'.[50]

CHAPTER 27

The wars and rumours of wars in which Rodrigo engaged with his
knights and companions are not all written in this book.[51]

CHAPTER 28

In the Era 1127 (= AD 1089), at that season at which kings were
accustomed to set out with their army to wage war or to subdue land
in revolt against them, King Alfonso departed from the city of Toledo
and set out on campaign with his army.[52] Rodrigo the Campeador,
however, remained then in Castile, handing out payment to his troops.

CHAPTER 29

Having distributed wages and assembled a multitude of his army in
Castile – 7000 fully-armed men – Rodrigo went to the frontier region
adjoining the River Duero, and crossing by the middle ford he ordered
his camp to be made at the place called Fresno. Proceeding from there

50 Some commentators have found this chapter incredible, though what it records
   appears to have analogies with the legal process of *pressura*, the 'taking possession'
   of conquered land, which is well-documented in the early phases of the Christian
   reconquest of Spain from the Muslims. The author might have been summarising
   or quoting from a royal charter. The words 'under seal' translate the Latin *sigillo*.
   It is important to bear in mind that at this date the word *sigillum* in Leonese–
   Castilian usage did not indicate what we normally understand by the word 'seal'
   today and that therefore the verbal usage in this chapter is not, as some have
   claimed, anachronistic: on these matters see R. Fletcher, 'Diplomatic and the Cid
   revisited: the seals and mandates of Alfonso VII', *JMH* 2 (1976), pp. 305–337.

51 As Dr Falque has pointed out, there are reminiscences here of Matthew xxiv.6,
   Mark xiii.7 and John xx.30. Whatever might be thought of the author's curious
   disclaimer in this chapter, its positioning here seems to mark some sort of
   deliberate break in the flow of the text.

52 This is the first of only three occurrences of a year-date in the entire work (the
   others are in chs 62 and 75): it seems to herald a new section; cf. previous note.
   There is also a clear recollection of II Samuel xi.1.

with his army he came to the place called Calamocha. There he encamped and celebrated the feast of Pentecost.[53] Envoys from the king of Albarracín came to him there, requesting a face-to-face meeting. After this meeting had taken place the king of Albarracín became a tributary of King Alfonso and remained at peace with him.[54]

CHAPTER 30

Rodrigo left that region behind and went on into the territory of Valencia. He set up camp in the valley called Torres, which is near Murviedro. Now at that time the count of Barcelona, Berenguer by name, was encamped with all his army near Valencia. He was attacking the city, and was building [the castles of] Cebolla and Liria against it. When Count Berenguer heard that Rodrigo the Campeador was approaching him with hostile intent, he trembled with great fear: for the two were mutual enemies. But Count Berenguer's knights began to boast, and to utter many curses against Rodrigo, and to scorn him with much mockery. They threatened him with many threats of capture and imprisonment and death – which afterwards they were unable to fulfil. This talk came to Rodrigo's ears. However, he was unwilling to fight against the count: for he respected his lord King Alfonso, whose relative the count was. Count Berenguer, shaken with fear, left Valencia in peace and speedily returned to Requena; from there he went to Zaragoza, and at length returned to his own land with his followers.[55]

CHAPTER 31

Rodrigo, however, remained at the place where he had fixed his tents, attacking his enemies on all sides. Moving on from there he approached Valencia, and pitched camp. At that time al-Qādir was

53 Calamocha is some 25 km south of Daroca, roughly midway between Calatayud and Teruel. Pentecost fell on 20 May in 1089. Reilly, *Alfonso VI*, p. 201, places this campaign in 1088.

54 Abū Marwān 'Abd al-Malik b. Hudhayl Ibn Razīn ruled the principality of Albarracín from 1045 to 1103: on him see further J. Bosch Vilá, *Albarracín Musulmán* (Teruel, 1959), pp. 140–70.

55 The places mentioned in this chapter are grouped round Valencia. Murviedro, the ancient Saguntum and the modern Sagunto, is on the Mediterranean coast some 25 km to the north, with Torres about 15 km inland up the valley of the river Palancia. Cebolla is between Valencia and Murviedro, Liria about 25 km to Valencia's north-west and Requena about 60 km due west.

ruling as king of Valencia.[56] He at once sent his envoys with innumerable and very valuable presents to Rodrigo. He became a tributary, and so did the commander of Murviedro. Afterwards Rodrigo the Campeador arose and entered the mountains of Alpuente. He fought fiercely there and mastered and laid waste the country, and remained there for not a few days. Then he left the region and established his camp at Requena, where he stayed for many days.

CHAPTER 32

While he was there he learned that Yūsuf the king of the Ishmaelites[57] and many other Saracen kings of Spain had come with the Moabites[58] to lay siege to the castle of Aledo which was then in the hands of the Christians. Then these aforesaid Saracen kings besieged that castle of Aledo and invested it so closely that those who were inside defending the castle ran seriously short of water.[59] When King Alfonso heard this he sent a letter to Rodrigo ordering him to join him at once to relieve the castle of Aledo and bring help to its defenders by attacking Yūsuf and all the other Saracens who were fiercely besieging it. Rodrigo gave this reply to the king's messengers who delivered this letter to him: 'Let my lord the King come as he promised. According to his command I am ready with good heart and will to succour that castle. When he is pleased that I should set out with him, I request his majesty that he should deign to inform me of his coming.'

CHAPTER 33

Rodrigo the Campeador at once left Requena and went to Játiva. There a messenger from King Alfonso found him, and told him that the king was in Toledo with a very large army – an infinite multitude

---

56 Al-Qādir, formerly of Toledo, had been installed as a puppet ruler of Valencia by Alfonso VI in 1085.

57 *Hysmaelitarum.* The author normally referred to the Muslims of Spain as 'Saracens' (e.g. chs 5, 8, 10, 11, 13 etc.). The adoption of new terminology, Ishmaelites and Moabites – both of them terms borrowed from the Old Testament – signals the appearance of a new group on the scene, namely the Almoravids, the Berber sectarians from Morocco, led by Yūsuf b. Tāshufīn from 1062 to 1106. The author was not absolutely consistent in his verbal usage, sometimes referring to them as 'Saracens' or simply 'barbarians'.

58 *cum gentibus Moabitarum*: see previous note.

59 Aledo lay far to the south-east of Alfonso VI's dominions, between Murcia and Lorca. For some suggestions about the king's decision to instal a garrison there see Fletcher, *Quest for El Cid,* pp. 154–5.

of horsemen and footsoldiers. On hearing this Rodrigo went up to
Onteniente and waited there for tidings of the king's coming. For the
king had ordered Rodrigo by messengers beforehand to wait for him
at Villena, through which place he had stated that he would certainly
pass. Meanwhile Rodrigo remained at Onteniente so that his army
should not lack for provisions, awaiting the king. He sent out scouts
from there to Villena and to the region of Chinchilla, who were under
orders to inform him as soon as they should hear of the king's
approach. While the scouts were thus confidently awaiting the royal
arrival, the king took a different route and reached Hellín.[60] When
Rodrigo heard that the king had already accomplished the journey
and arrived before him, he was deeply dismayed. He set out with his
army for Hellín, and went ahead of his troops in his eagerness to
discover the truth about the king's movements. When he knew for
certain that the king had completed his journey he left his army which
was coming along after him and went on with a few companions as far
as Molina. Yūsuf king of the Saracens, however, and all the other
Ishmaelite kings of Spain and all the other Moabites who were there,
learning of King Alfonso's arrival, left the fortress of Aledo in peace.
They turned in flight at once, terrified by fear of the king even before
his arrival, and fled before his face in confusion. When Rodrigo
reached Molina the king, seeing that he could not possibly pursue the
Saracens, had already set out with his army on the return journey to
Toledo. Rodrigo, greatly sorrowing, returned to his camp which was
at Elche. There he allowed certain of his knights whom he had brought
with him from Castile to return to their homes.[61]

CHAPTER 34

Then the Castilians, jealous of him in all things, accused Rodrigo
before the king. They told Alfonso that Rodrigo was not a faithful
vassal but an evil man and a traitor. They falsely and lyingly claimed
that Rodrigo had been unwilling to go to the assistance of the king, in

---

60 The MSS read *ad fluvium*, 'to the river', which makes no sense in a context
concerning a part of Spain where rivers do not exist during the summer months.
RMP (p. 936) plausibly emended to *ad Felin*, 'to Hellín', following readings in the
Crónica de 1344. From Játiva in the north, a line through Onteniente, Villena and
Hellín forms a sickle-shaped trajectory curving to the south-west, a little inland
from the Mediterranean coastline between Denia and Cartagena.

61 Elche is between Murcia and Alicante. The author here loyally attempts to fudge
the fact that some of Rodrigo's followers were deserting him in the autumn of
1089.

order that the king and all who were with him should be killed by the Saracens. When the king heard this false accusation he was possessed and fired by very great rage. He at once gave orders that that the castles, estates and all the honour which Rodrigo held from him should be confiscated.[62] In addition he ordered [his men] to enter upon Rodrigo's own hereditary lands and, what was still worse, he ordered his wife and children, arrested by trickery, to be cruelly retained in custody. The king also ordered [his men] to take charge of all Rodrigo's goods – gold and silver and everything that could be found of his possessions. Rodrigo considered the matter carefully and fully understood that the king had thus been roused to anger against him by the crafty tales and false accusations of his enemies; that this monstrous injury and unheard-of dishonour had been thus wickedly inflicted on him by their manoeuvres. Forthwith he sent one of his most distinguished knights to the king, to defend him firmly against the unjust charge and the false accusation of treason, and completely to clear his name. On being shown into the lord king's presence, this man spoke as follows: 'O renowned and ever-worshipful king, my lord Rodrigo, your most faithful vassal, has sent me to you to kiss your hands on his behalf and request that you accept in court his defence against and clearance of the charge which his enemies have falsely laid against him in your presence. My lord himself will fight in person in your court against another equal and similar to him; or his champion will fight on his behalf against another equal and similar to him. All those who proclaimed to you that Rodrigo was guilty of any deceit or any treachery towards you in the course of your journey to relieve Aledo such that the Saracens might kill you and your troops, have lied as false and evil men and lack good faith. Rodrigo intended to participate in that campaign. There is no count nor magnate nor knight faithful to assist you among all those who accompanied you to the relief of that castle, of greater fidelity in your aid against those Saracens and against all your enemies, than he, so far as lies within his power.' However the king, strongly enraged against them, would not only not accept his defence, although it was most just – he would not even give it a fair hearing. He did, however, permit Rodrigo's wife and children to return to him.

---

62 The Latin word *honor* had several shades of meaning at this epoch, among them 'landed wealth held by a vassal from a lord in return for service', which is clearly the sense intended here. See J. F. Niermeyer, *Mediae Latinitatis Lexicon Minus* (Leiden, 1976), *s.v. honor* at pp. 495–8.

CHAPTER 35

When Rodrigo saw that the king did not deign to accept his defence, he personally drafted his own pleas of defence and innocence and then sent them to the king in proper written form.[63]

'This is the plea which I Rodrigo submit concerning the accusation with which I am charged before King Alfonso. My lord the king was holding me in such love and honour as beforehand he was wont to hold me. I will fight in his court against one equal and similar to me, or my champion will fight against one equal and similar to him, stating as follows: "I Rodrigo swear to you who wishes to fight with me and who accuses me in connection with that expedition which King Alfonso made to Aledo to fight the Saracens, that the fact that I was not with him sprang from no other cause but this, that I did not know of his route, and could have learned it from no man. This is the very truth of the reason why I was not with him. On that campaign I was guilty of no lie, but obeyed the king's commands transmitted by his messenger[64] and by letter: no mandate of his did I disregard. During that campaign, whatever the king intended to do against the Saracens who were besieging the aforesaid castle, I was guilty of no deceit towards him, no conspiracy, emphatically no treachery, and no evil

---

63 The documents which constitute chapter 35 of the *Historia Roderici* present various difficulties. These cannot be discussed in detail here, but some brief indications of both the problems and possible approaches to solving them are in order. (1) Are these unique documents authentic? We can show that Rodrigo, unsurprisingly for a person of his rank, possessed a good working knowledge of the law: on at least two occasions that we know of, in 1073 and 1075, he was appointed to a panel of judges by Alfonso VI (see *RMP*, pp. 836, 849–53 and references). The documents bristle with technical legal jargon and must have been drafted by someone who had had a legal training. The most recent authority on trial by battle judges that this originally Frankish mode of proof had spread into Spain 'at some indeterminate date before 1000' (R. Bartlett, *Trial by Fire and Water. The Medieval Judicial Ordeal* (Oxford, 1986), ch. 6, 'Trial by Battle', pp. 102–26, quotation from p. 105): several more citations from Spanish documents might be added to those assembled by Bartlett. No less a person than Count Berenguer of Barcelona was found guilty of fratricide after a trial by battle before the court of Alfonso VI in the winter of 1096/7. There is therefore a plausible context for these documents. (2) How did they survive? Given the gravity of the charges and the cultural context of a society which had a high regard for the written word, it is surely reasonable to suppose that a prudent man would keep copies of such documents as these. How, where and by whom they were preserved in the longer term is a good deal more problematic; though I see no inherent difficulty in Menéndez Pidal's postulated *archivo cidiano* which survived Rodrigo's death (see discussion in the introduction). (3) If genuine, what do these documents have to tell us about the Aledo campaign of 1089? The reader is free to speculate.

64 *portarius*, literally 'carrier, porter', Spanish *portero*.

thing for which my body stands dishonoured or deserves to stand dishonoured. No-one among the counts or magnates or knights, whoever were in the army which accompanied the king, had greater fidelity towards the king to assist him to fight the aforesaid Saracens than I, as far as lies within my power. I swear this to you, that whatever I say to you is entirely true. If I lie, may God deliver me into your hands to do your will upon me. If not, may God who judges justly deliver me from a false accusation." A similar oath will be sworn by my champion against the knight who wishes to fight with him over this charge.'

This is the second oath of Rodrigo's plea which he drafted: 'I Rodrigo swear to you, the knight who wishes to fight with me, who accuses me concerning the king's arrival at Aledo, that I had no reliable information about the king's arrival and could by no means discover that he was before me, until I heard reports that he was already on his way back to Toledo. If I had known, when I advanced as far as *Mostellim*,[65] I tell you in truth that unless I had been ill or a captive or dead I would have presented myself before the king at Molina and accompanied him to Aledo and been at his side in any engagement he might have had with the Saracens, in good faith and truly without any evil intent. I swear to you concerning this by God and his saints that I never either thought nor spoke any evil against the king for which my body might stand dishonoured. If in anything touching these matters I lie, may God deliver me into your hands to do your will upon me. If not, may God who judges justly deliver me from a false accusation. Let my champion swear the same and maintain the same against the knight who wishes to fight with him over this charge.'

This is the third oath: 'I Rodrigo swear to you the knight who accuses me concerning the king's arrival at Aledo to fight there with the Saracens who were besieging that castle, that I sent him the letters in good faith and truthfully without any evil intent or without any evil design. I did not send the letters to the end that he should be defeated or made captive by the Saracens his enemies. For when he set out with his army for the aforesaid town he sent his messenger to me at Villena telling me to await his arrival there. This I did according to his order. In truth I swear to you and state that I never thought nor spoke against the king, nor was I guilty of treason nor evil design for which my body might stand dishonoured, or for which I deserve to

65 Unidentified.

lose my land[66] or my money, or for which the king should serve me with such great and unheard-of shame, as he has. Thus I swear to you by God and his saints, for what I swear is the truth. If in anything touching these matters I lie, may God deliver me into your hands to do your will upon me. If not, may the just and pious Judge deliver me from so very false an accusation. Let my champion swear the same and maintain it against the knight who wishes to fight with him over this charge.'

This is the fourth oath: 'I Rodrigo swear to you, the king's knight who wishes to fight with me, by God and his saints, that from the day on which I acknowledged the king as my lord in Toledo, until the day when I discovered how unreasonably and cruelly he had imprisoned my wife and had completely stripped me of all the property[67] which I had in his kingdom, I spoke no evil of him, thought no evil, neither did anything against him for which I might become of ill-repute or for which my body might stand dishonoured. Unjustly and unreasonably he took from me who was blameless my property and imprisoned my wife. He inflicted great and very hurtful shame upon me. I swear to you, the knight who wishes to fight with me, that what I have said above is true, and that if I lie may God deliver me into your hands to do your will upon me. If not, may the truest and most pious Judge free me from so very false an accusation. This and no other let my champion swear and maintain against the knight who wishes to fight with me.'

'This indeed is the plea which I Rodrigo confidently indite and unhesitatingly subscribe. If the king should wish to accept one of these four statements under oath aforewritten, let him choose whichever one he wishes and I shall willingly take the oath. If however he should not so wish, I am ready to fight with a knight of the king who shall be my equal and the equivalent of what I was in the king's eyes when I was in his favour. I acknowledge that thus I should defend myself against the king and emperor, if he accuses me. If however he should wish to disregard me and censure me concerning this plea, and to offer a better and more just procedure than this one touching this accusation, let him have it committed to writing and send it to me, [explaining] how I may defend and clear myself. If I should recognise it to be more equitable and just than mine, I shall acknowledge it willingly, and according to it let me defend and clear myself. If not, I shall fight for my plea, or my champion on my behalf. If the king

66 honorem, cf. n. 62 above.
67 honorem, cf. nn. 62 and 66 above.

should be defeated, let him concede my case. If I should be defeated, let me receive my sentence.'

But the king did not wish to accept this plea submitted by Rodrigo himself, nor his defence and innocence.

CHAPTER 36

After the king returned to Toledo, Rodrigo camped at Elche: there he celebrated Christmas Day. After the feast he departed from there and made his way along the coast until he reached Polop where there was a great cave full of treasure.[68] He laid siege to it and invested it closely; after a few days he overcame its defenders and boldly entered it. He found inside it much gold and silver and silk and innumerable precious stuffs. Loaded thus with the riches he needed from what he had found, he left Polop and moved on until he came to *Portum Tarvani*, and outside the city of Denia, at Ondara, he restored and strengthened a castle.[69] He fasted there for the holy season of Lent and celebrated at the same place the Easter of the Resurrection of Jesus Christ our Lord.[70] While he was there al-Ḥāyib, who at that time was king of that land and reigned over it, sent an embassy to discuss terms of peace with him. When peace had been agreed and firmly established between them the Saracen envoys returned to al-Ḥāyib. Rodrigo left Ondara with his army and moved towards Valencia. King al-Ḥāyib left the region of Lérida and Tortosa and made his way to Murviedro. When al-Qādir, who was then king of Valencia, heard that King al-Ḥāyib had made peace with Rodrigo he was greatly terrified and extremely apprehensive. After taking counsel with his advisers he sent messengers to Rodrigo with very great and innumerable gifts of money. They heaped the many, the innumerable presents which they bore upon Rodrigo, and thus amicably brought about peace between him and the king of Valencia. In the same fashion, from all the castles which were rebelling against the king of Valencia in an attempt to throw off his rule, Rodrigo accepted many and innumerable tributes and gifts. When King al-Ḥāyib heard that al-Qādir king of Valencia had made peace with Rodrigo he was struck with great fear and retreated from Murviedro by night; thus, terrified, he fled from that region.

68 Polop is about 32 km south-west of Denia and lies a little inland some 10 km north of the modern Benidorm.

69 *Portum Tarvani* has not been identified. Ondara is 5 km due west of Denia.

70 In 1090 Lent began on 6 March and Easter Day fell on 21 April.

CHAPTER 37

Rodrigo left the Valencia area and went to Burriana.[71] There he heard
a trustworthy report that al-Ḥāyib of Lérida and Tortosa was
attempting to bring together Sancho king of the Aragonese and
Berenguer count of Barcelona and Ermengol count of Urgel[72] in a
coalition against him, in order to expel him from the kingdom of al-
Ḥāyib. But King Sancho and Count Ermengol would not accede to al-
Ḥāyib's request nor help him against Rodrigo. Meanwhile Rodrigo
remained in Burriana as still as a stone.[73] Soon afterwards he left
Burriana and went up into the mountain region of Morella. There was
great abundance of food there and innumerable plenty of livestock.
Count Berenguer of Barcelona held discussions with al-Ḥāyib – he
had already accepted an enormous sum of money from him – and at
once set out from Barcelona with a huge army. He travelled through
the Zaragoza region and then encamped at Calamocha in the lands of
Albarracín. Then the count, accompanied by a few men, visited al-
Musta'īn, king of Zaragoza, at Daroca, and held discussions with him
there about making peace between them. He took tribute from al-
Musta'īn and they were at peace. At the count's request al-Musta'īn
accompanied him to King Alfonso who was then near Orón.[74] The
count earnestly implored the king to lend him the help of his troops
against Rodrigo. But the king refused his request. So the count with
his commanders – Bernardo, Giraldo Alemán and Dorca – went to
Calamocha with an immense army.[75] A very formidable alliance of
warriors was gathered there against Rodrigo. Rodrigo was lurking at
the time in the mountains, at a place called *Iber*.[76] King al-Musta'īn
sent a messenger to him there, to tell him that the count of Barcelona

---

71 Burriana is about 30 km north of Murviedro, a little to the south of the modern
Castellón de la Plana.

72 Ermengol IV (1065–92)

73 This simile, the only figure of speech in the entire work (used again in ch. 50) is
drawn from Exodus xv.16.

74 Near Miranda de Ebro in the north-east of Castile.

75 These were noted Catalan magnates. I have emended the MS reading *Dorea* to
Dorca. *RMP*, p. 948 suggested that the *dominus Bernaldus* of ch. 40 should be
emended to *Deusdedit Bernaldi* and that he be identified with the 'Bernard' of ch. 37.
On Deudonat Bernat de Claramunt, Guerau Alemany de Cervelló and Dorca de
Castellvell – to give the Catalan name-forms – see S. Sobreques i Vidal, *Els Grans
Comtes de Barcelona* (2nd edn., Barcelona, 1970) pp. 132, 135, 144, 194, 210; P.
Bonnassie, *La Catalogne du milieu du Xe à la fin du XIe siècle: croissance et mutations
d'une société* (Toulouse, 1976), vol. II, pp. 788, 848, 857–8, 867–8; and references cited.

76 On the localisation of this place, a little to the north of Morella, see *RMP*, pp. 757–9.

was all prepared to fight against him. Rodrigo made this cheerful
reply to the messenger: 'To al-Musta'īn, king of Zaragoza, my faithful
friend, I give my hearty thanks since he has disclosed to me the
count's plans and his intention of waging war against me in the near
future. I altogether contemn and despise the count and the multitude
of his warriors. With God's help I shall willingly await him here in
this place. If he comes, I am confident that I shall defeat him.' Count
Berenguer came with his huge army through the mountains to a place
near to where Rodrigo was, and pitched camp not far from him. One
night he sent out scouts, who reported that Rodrigo's camp had a
high mountain rising above it [?... and that] his tents were pitched
below this mountain.[77]

CHAPTER 38

On the next day the count had a letter composed as follows which he
sent by messenger to Rodrigo:[78] 'I Berenguer count of Barcelona with
my knights tell you Rodrigo that we have seen your letter which you
sent to al-Musta'īn and told him to show to us, which scorned and
gravely insulted and moved us to great frenzy. Beforehand you had
done us many injuries, for which we should be hostile to you and
mightily angered; so much the more should we be your enemies and
adversaries for the insult with which by your letter you have scorned
and derided us. You are still in possession of our money, which you
stole from us. God who is mighty will avenge such injuries which you
have shown us. Yet another and worse insult and scorn you have
inflicted on us, when you likened us to our wives. We abstain from
mocking you and your followers with such despicable insults: but we
pray and implore the God of heaven to deliver you into our hands and
power; then we can show you that we are worth more than our wives.
You have told King al-Musta'īn that if we come to do battle with you,
you will come out to meet us more quickly than he could get back to
Monzón; and that if we delay in coming against you, you will meet us
in the way. We earnestly ask of you that you do not already scorn us,
because we have not today come down to you; for we have acted thus

77 One or more words appear to be missing in the second half of this sentence, though
the general sense is clear enough.
78 The most recent defender of the authenticity of the extremely curious letters which
occupy chs 38 and 39 is E. Falque Rey, 'Cartas entre el Conde Berenguer de
Barcelona y Rodrigo Díaz de Vivar', Habis 12 (1981) pp. 123–37: I am grateful to
Dr R. Wright for sending me a photocopy of this article.

because we want to know more of your troops and dispositions. We
see moreover that you trust in your mountainous position and want to
fight us there. We see and understand that your gods are mountains,
ravens,[79] crows, hawks, eagles and nearly every sort of bird: you trust
more in their auguries than in God. But we believe in and worship the
one true God, who will avenge us on you and deliver you into our
hands. Know this for very truth, that tomorrow at dawn, God willing,
you shall see us next you and before you. If you will abandon your
mountain and come out to meet us on the plain, you will indeed be the
Rodrigo whom men call the warrior and the Campeador. If you do not
do this you will be what they call in Castilian *alevoso* [= traitorous]
and in French *bauzador* and *fraudator* [= deceiver].[80] It will profit you
nothing to show that you have the equivalent of our strength. We
shall not withdraw nor depart from you until you have come into my
[*sic*] hands either dead or a captive in chains. Then at length we shall
exult over you just as you yourself have over us. God will avenge his
churches which you have broken into violently and violated.'

CHAPTER 39

This letter was read to Rodrigo and he listened to it. Then he at once
ordered this letter to be written and sent to the count, containing his
reply. 'I Rodrigo, together with my companions, to you Count Berenguer
and your men, greeting. Know that I have heard your letter and
understood everything contained in it. In the course of it you say that
I wrote a letter to al-Musta'in in which I derided and reviled you and
your men. Indeed you have spoken the truth. For I did revile you and
your men and I still do so. Let me tell you why I insulted you. When
you were with al-Musta'in near Calatayud you spoke insultingly in his
presence, saying to him that for fear of you I did not dare to enter that
region. Moreover your men, Ramón de Barbarán and the other knights
who were with him, said the same to King Alfonso in Castile, insult-
ing me in the presence of the Castilians. Further you yourself, as al-
Musta'in who was present witnessed, told King Alfonso that you would

79 The text may be corrupt here. Dr Falque suggests emending *montes et corvi*,
  'mountains and ravens', to *montenses corvi*, 'the mountain ravens' or 'the ravens of
  the mountains'. In the *Poema de Mio Cid* Rodrigo is portrayed as seeking auguries
  in the flight of birds: see lines 11–12, 859, 2615.
80 On the term *alevoso* see J. García González, 'Traición y alevosía en la alta edad
  media', *AHDE* 32 (1962), pp. 323–45. On *bausia* as 'treason' see Bonnassie, *La
  Catalogne*, pp. 777–8; *bauzador* thus signifies 'traitor'.

do battle with me and having defeated me would drive me out of the lands of al-Ḥāyib; and that I should never dare to face you in those lands. But for love of the king you let off doing all this and have not as yet molested me; and because I was his vassal, therefore you have held back from and been unwilling to inflict shame on me. For these insults shown so scornfully to me I reviled and will revile you and your men, and for your womanly courage I likened you and made you equal to your wives. But now you can make no excuse for not doing battle with me – if you dare to fight. If however you refuse to come to me, all men will think the better of me.[81] If you dare to come against me with your army, I am already here with mine and do not fear combat. But make no mistake about what I shall do to your men, the damage I shall inflict upon you. I am aware that you have entered into an agreement with al-Ḥāyib that in return for his money you would expel me and drive me out of his territory. But I think that you are frightened of fulfilling your promise and that you simply do not dare to come and engage me. Do not be shy of advancing against me because I am drawn up in a flatter place than anywhere else round here. I tell you for certain that if you and your men come against me it is not [the terrain] that will betray you. I'll pay you the wages I usually pay you, if you will only dare to advance. If you refuse to, if you daren't fight with me, I shall send letters to the lord King Alfonso and messengers to al-Musta'īn. I shall tell them that what you promised to do with boasting and arrogance, you could not perform for fear of me. I shall make this known not only to these two rulers, but to all the nobility both Christian and Saracen. Already Christians and Saracens alike know that you were made captive by me and that you and your men were ransomed for money. Now I await you on level ground, calm of mind and strong of spirit. If you will attempt to come against me, here you will see a part of your money – not for your profit but rather to your hurt. You have hurled boastful words at me, saying that you would defeat me and possess me as a captive dead or alive: but this lies in the hand of God, not yours. You have most falsely made sport of me in saying that I have acted *aleve*, in the speech of Castile, or *bauzia*, in that of Gaul, an obvious lie uttered by your own mouth. Never have I acted thus. Rather has he who is already renowned for it in such stories as you well know: and what I refer to is widely known to many both Christian and pagan.[82] But it is enough that we have

81 The text is corrupt here but this seems the likely sense.
82 This is an oblique reference to the widespread belief – subsequently proven by ordeal, see above, n. 63 – that Count Berenguer had murdered his brother Ramón in 1082.

contended with words. Let us leave words behind, and as befits brave knights settle this quarrel between us with the noble encounter of weapons. Come, do not delay. You will be paid the wages which I usually deal out to you.'[83]

CHAPTER 40

When Berenguer and all his followers heard this letter, they were one and all filled with mighty rage. They held a council of war and then sent some soldiers under cover of night to climb and take possession unobserved of the high ground which rose above Rodrigo's camp. Their plan was to attack Rodrigo's position from above, to fall upon his tents and capture his lines. So they came by night and scaled the higher ground and held it. Rodrigo was unaware of this manoeuvre. On the next day, at dawn, the count and his armed men surrounded Rodrigo's encampment and fell upon it with much shouting. When Rodrigo saw this he began to grind his teeth,[84] and ordered his troops to don their mail coats at once and form their ranks bravely against the enemy. Rodrigo himself charged fiercely against the count's formation and with this first charge shifted and broke it. But in this skirmish, while fighting valiantly, Rodrigo fell from his horse and was immediately struck and wounded on the ground. But his soldiers did not give up the fight: they battled on courageously until they had defeated and bravely overcome the count and all his army. Many – indeed an innumerable multitude – of the enemy were slain and met their deaths. Finally they took the count himself and led him captive to Rodrigo with nearly five thousand of his men who had been taken prisoner in the battle. Rodrigo ordered that certain of them – Deusdedit Bernard, Giraldo Alemán, Ramón Mir, Ricart Guillem and very many other most noble men – should be held apart under rigorous custody.[85] Thus was accomplished that victory ever to be extolled and remem-

83 It may be significant that in this detailed rebuttal of the count's accusations Rodrigo did not attempt to defend himself against the charge of being a despoiler of churches.

84 Psalm cxii.10; Job xvi.10; Lamentations ii.16.

85 On Deudonat Bernat and Guerau Alemany see above n. 75. There were several prominent Catalan magnates named Ramón Mir at this period. Ricart Guillem has been described as 'a gentrified Barcelona real estate speculator' by S. B. Bensch, *Barcelona and its Rulers 1096–1291* (Cambridge, 1995), p. 107. The remark may not give us the entire man, but it usefully points to the adroitness with which the Catalan aristocracy ploughed the spoils of war into entrepreneurial urban investment.

bered of Rodrigo over Count Berenguer and his army. Rodrigo's troops
sacked Count Berenguer's encampment. They seized all the plunder
they could find there – many vessels of gold and silver, precious
textiles, mules, horses, palfreys, spears, coats of mail, shields and all
objects of worth whatsoever they could find. All of it they faithfully
brought and presented to Rodrigo.

CHAPTER 41

Count Berenguer, realising that he had been chastised and con-
founded by God and made captive at the hands of Rodrigo, humbly
seeking his mercy came before Rodrigo who was seated in his tent
and earnestly craved his indulgence. Rodrigo, however, would not
receive him mercifully nor allow him to be seated at his side in the
tent. He ordered the count to be kept under guard by his troops
outside in the open air. Magnanimously, however, he gave orders that
the count be fed there in abundance. At length he allowed him to
return a free man to his own land. When, after a few days, Rodrigo
recovered his bodily health he negotiated an agreement with the lord
Berenguer and Giraldo Alemán that they should pay him a ransom of
80,000 gold marks of Valencia.[86] All the other captives bound themselves and promised to pay sums – in aggregate, innumerable – for their
ransoms. These were individually fixed at precise amounts according
to Rodrigo's wish. They soon returned to their homes. And then
without delay there flowed back to Rodrigo an enormous quantity of
gold and silver, together with children and relatives and their escorts
as pledges for payment of the ransoms agreed; and they undertook
that everything would without fail be fully paid over in Rodrigo's
presence. When Rodrigo saw this he consulted his followers and,
moved by a spirit of charity, not only did he allow them to depart in
freedom to their own land, but he went so far as to remit all the
ransom. They for their part returned most devoted thanks to his

86 The MSS read *marcas/marcos*, the latter reading hinting at a copyist's
   misinterpretation of the abbreviation of the word *mancusos*, the standard term in
   the Christian north for the gold coin of al-Andalus in the pre-Almoravid period.
   Bonnassie, *La Catalogne*, p. 868, suspects a considerable exaggeration on the
   author's part here. True, it is a very large sum indeed, but not quite impossibly so.
   One must remember that the sum raised was divided between the two individuals,
   perhaps in the proportion of – at a guess – something like 60,000 for Berenguer
   and 20,000 for Giraldo. For purposes of comparison, al-Muqtadir of Zaragoza
   undertook in 1069 to make monthly payments to Sancho IV of Navarre of 1000
   gold *mancusos* of Zaragoza: see the article by Lacarra cited in n. 44 above.

nobility and piety on account of so great mercy, and promising to serve him they returned rejoicing with all their goods and with great honour to their land.

CHAPTER 42

Rodrigo journeyed to the Zaragoza region and stayed there for nearly two months at the place called Sacarca.[87] Leaving there he went to Daroca where he stayed for many days. There was there a great quantity of food and plentiful livestock. There Rodrigo was seriously ill. Then he sent some of his warriors to King al-Musta'in of Zaragoza bearing letters. They found the king at Zaragoza and delivered to him the letters which they carried. They also found Count Berenguer there, seated with al-Musta'in, accompanied by his noble knights. When the count heard that Rodrigo's knights and messengers were present he at once invited them to his presence and respectfully gave them this message to convey to Rodrigo: 'Greet well Rodrigo my friend on my behalf and emphasise to him that I wish to be a true friend and a helper in all his necessities.' The messengers made their way back to Rodrigo, who was by now recovering his health, and delivered the count's message. Rodrigo, however, gave no credence to it and vigorously denied that he wished to be the count's friend and live at peace with him. To him his knights and captains said, 'What is this? What ill has Count Berenguer ever done to you, that you do not wish to be at peace with him ? You have defeated and overcome him, you have held him in your power as a captive, you have ruthlessly despoiled his goods and riches – yet you don't want to live at peace with him! It is not you who are asking him, but *he* who is asking *you* for peace.' At length Rodrigo was persuaded by the advice of his knights and noblemen and promised that he would live at peace with the count. So his messengers went straight back to Zaragoza and told Count Berenguer and his noblemen that Rodrigo would be his friend and live at peace with him. When they heard this the count and his men were overjoyed. Then the count left Zaragoza at once and came to Rodrigo at his camp. Peace and friendship between the two of them was publicly and amicably proclaimed. Then the count placed in Rodrigo's hand and protection that part of Hispania which was subject to his overlordship.[88]

87 Outside Zaragoza.

88 On the term *Hispania* see n. 7 above. Count Berenguer surrendered – at any rate temporarily – his claims to lordship over the Muslim principalities (Tortosa, Albarracín, Valencia etc.) of the Mediterranean seaboard or Spanish Levante.

Afterwards the two together went down to the coast. Rodrigo established his camp at Burriana. Berenguer, leaving Rodrigo, crossed the Ebro and returned to his own land.

CHAPTER 43

Rodrigo stayed at Burriana near Valencia. He celebrated Christmas at Cebolla. Then he laid siege to Liria, a castle near Valencia, and there handed out enormous wages to his troops.

CHAPTER 44

While he was there letters reached him from the queen,[89] King Alfonso's wife, and from his friends. They informed him as a matter of certainty that the king was undertaking a campaign against the Saracens and was determined to bring them to battle. For already the Saracens had taken Granada and all its territories.[90] This indeed was the reason why the king was going out to fight them. In their letters Rodrigo's friends advised him to go as quickly as possible – putting all else aside – with his army to the king and to accompany him in battle against the Saracens, and to merge his own forces with the royal army in bringing help to the king: by doing this he would undoubtedly at once recover the king's love and favour. Rodrigo bowed to his friends' advice. He left the castle of Liria – even though he believed that its defenders were on the point of surrender, so weakened were they by fighting, hunger and thirst – and at once undertook the long journey to the king with all his forces. He found the king at Martos, near Córdoba.

CHAPTER 45

When the king heard that Rodrigo was on his way he immediately went out to meet him and received him in peace with great honour. Together they journeyed towards the city of Granada. The king gave

89 Constance of Burgundy, sister of Duke Eudes of Burgundy and niece of Abbot Hugh of Cluny, had married Alfonso VI in 1079: she died in 1093. Reilly, *Alfonso VI*, p. 228, finds the narrative of chs 44–45 'fantastic ... totally at variance with the known facts'. But given that the king's movements in 1091 are untraceable for the three months between 18 April and 19 July (*ibid.*, pp. 222–3) there is plenty of time for an expedition to al-Andalus.

90 The Almoravids had taken over Granada in September 1090, banishing its ruler 'Abd Allāh into exile in Morocco where he composed his autobiography.

orders for his camp to be made in a mountainous region known as
Libriella.[91] Rodrigo on the other hand fixed his tents on level ground
in front of the royal encampment. He did this to be out of the way of
and to protect the king's camp. But it seriously displeased the king.[92]
Led astray by jealousy the king said to his followers: 'Look at the
insult and shame which Rodrigo inflicts upon us! Today indeed he
tagged along after us as though worn out by the long journey; but
now he usurps precedence over us and fixes camp in front of us.'
Nearly all his courtiers, influenced by jealousy, replied together that
the king had spoken the truth. Because they were in all things envious
of Rodrigo they accused him before the king of acting with over-bold
presumption. The king remained there for six days. King Yūsuf of the
Moabites and Saracens did not dare to wait for King Alfonso and fight
against him, for he was terrified of him. He retreated secretly from the
region, fleeing with his army. When King Alfonso was certain that the
Saracen king Yūsuf had fled from him out of fear and had retired
secretly from the area, he immediately ordered his forces back to Toledo.
On the way back to Toledo King Alfonso came to the castle of Ubeda,
on the River Guadalquivir. Rodrigo ordered his men to pitch camp
next to the river. There the king attacked Rodrigo brusquely with
angry and provocative words. He reproached him indeed for many
and various causes – but untrue ones. So vehemently was Alfonso
moved and inflamed against Rodrigo that he wished and decreed that
he should be put under arrest. When Rodrigo grasped clearly what
was going on he bore patiently all the hurt of the king's words. In the
course of the following night, not without fear, Rodrigo withdrew and
at once returned to his own camp. Many of his troops then left him
and transferred themselves to the king's camp: abandoning their lord
Rodrigo they gave themselves into the service of the king.[93] The king
was stirred up by a number of quarrelsome men not to receive
Rodrigo's exculpation of himself from the accusations launched at
him. Filled with violent anger, Alfonso went back to Toledo with his
army.

91 Unidentified, possibly a corruption of Iliberris, the name of the settlement which
   had preceded relocation to a more defensible site at Granada: evidently not far
   from Granada.

92 The observance of a strict order of precedence in the positioning of tents has been
   a matter of serious military etiquette since at least the Roman period. For a
   modern example, from the British army in Tibet in 1904, of the friction which may
   be caused by failure to observe conventions, see P. French, *Younghusband* (London,
   1994) ch. 14, p. 207. I am grateful to Sir John Keegan for advice on this point.

93 Desertions reminiscent of those of 1089: cf. above ch. 33 and n. 61.

CHAPTER 46

Greatly troubled and distressed, Rodrigo withdrew at once to the
Valencia region: it was a difficult journey. He stayed there for many
days. There was a castle there named Peña Cadiella, which the Saracens
had completely demolished.[94] Rodrigo rebuilt it, surrounding it with a
very strong wall and reconstructing its many solid defensive buildings. At length the castle was effectively fortified. Rodrigo garrisoned
it with a huge number of horsemen and footsoldiers well-equipped
with all sorts of arms, and stocked it with an ample supply of bread
and wine and meat. Then he left the castle and went down towards
Valencia. From there he moved on to Morella where he stayed for a
few days and solemnly observed Christmas Day.

CHAPTER 47

While he was there a man came to him and promsied to give him by
stealth the castle of Borja near Tudela.[95] Rodrigo took counsel and
immediately set off for Borja with his men. There came to him suddenly
a messenger from al-Musta'in king of Zaragoza reporting that he was
being much coerced and molested by the Aragonese king Sancho.
After this messenger left, Rodrigo travelled to Zaragoza secretly by
night with a small following and there discovered that the man who
had promised to give the castle of Borja to him had been telling a lie.
Nevertheless he did not want to go back to his base; he stayed where
he was. When news of this got about the citizens of Zaragoza both
great and small came to him. They besought him with many prayers
to have love and friendship and peace with their king. So it came
about that al-Musta'in and Rodrigo had an interview and established
a very firm peace between themselves.

94 Peña Cadiella is a peak in the Sierra de Benicadell about 55 km west of Denia and
   65 km south of Valencia, not far from Onteniente where Rodrigo had waited in
   vain for the king during the Aledo campaign of 1089 (above, ch. 33).
95 Borja – from which the Borgia family later took its name – lies a little to the south
   of the Ebro between Tudela and Zaragoza. The significance of the Borja episode is
   unclear, though it is evident enough that the unnamed castellan of Borja was intent
   on setting Rodrigo and his ally al-Musta'in at loggerheads. In view of the
   imminent events of 1092 (see ch. 50) it is tempting to speculate about the possible
   role of Rodrigo's Castilian enemies in stirring up trouble for him.

CHAPTER 48

By then Rodrigo had already brought his army to Zaragoza. He crossed the river there and made camp at Fraga.[96] When he heard this the Aragonese King Sancho together with his son King Pedro ordered an immense army to be mustered. When the army had assembled he ordered it to camp at Gurrea.[97] The king and his son then sent peaceful ambassadors to Rodrigo, conveying proposals of love and peace. When he heard what was afoot Rodrigo received them honourably and with pleasure, and in reply to their proposals told them that he wished in all things to be at peace with King Sancho and his son. He at once despatched his own messengers to transmit these words of peace to the king and his son. Finding themselves of one accord, King Sancho and his son and Rodrigo established peace and love among themselves most firmly by an indissoluble bond. At Rodrigo's request King Sancho also made peace with al-Musta'in. Rodrigo acted as mediator and the two entered amicably into pacification. After this King Sancho returned at once to his own land. Rodrigo, however, remained in Zaragoza for not a few days, being treated with the greatest honour at the court of al-Musta'in.

CHAPTER 49

Menéndez Pidal persuaded himself that there had once existed a chapter recounting Alfonso VI's campaign against Valencia in 1092. There is no evidence that this was so. The most recent editor of the text, Dr Emma Falque, does not even deign to consider the possibility. However, to avoid confusion, the numbering of the blank 'chapter' has been retained here (as it was by Dr Falque both in her edition of the Latin text and in her Spanish translation of it). See also chapter 51 below.

CHAPTER 50

At length Rodrigo left Zaragoza with a very great and innumerable army and entered the regions of Calahorra and Nájera, which were in Alfonso's kingdom and subject to his authority. Stoutly fighting, he took both Alberite and Logroño.[98] Most savagely and mercilessly

96 Between Zaragoza and Lérida.
97 Gurrea del Gállego, some 40 km north of Zaragoza.
98 Logroño was (and is) the principal town of the Rioja region; Alberite is its near neighbour to the south. The passage immediately following is difficult to translate. There is no evidence of textual corruption. Rather, as I have observed elsewhere (*Quest for El Cid*, p. 97), 'the author's stylistic discipline breaks down'.

through all those regions did he lay waste with relentless, destructive, irreligious fire. He took huge booty, yet it was saddening even to tears. With harsh and impious devastation did he lay waste and destroy all the land aforesaid. He altogether stripped it of all its goods and wealth and riches, and took these for himself. Then leaving the region behind him he went with an enormous army to the castle called Alfaro, which he bravely attacked and captured.[99] While he was there messengers came to him from García Ordóñez and all his kinsmen.[100] They announced to Rodrigo on behalf of the count and his family that he should wait there for seven days and no longer: if he were to do this, the count and his kinsmen would assuredly come to fight with him. Rodrigo cheerfully replied to the messengers that he would wait seven days for the count and his kinsmen and would willingly fight with them. So Count García Ordóñez summoned all his kinsmen and chief supporters – the great men who held lordships over all the land which stretches from the city called Zamora as far as Pamplona. Having gathered an immense, innumerable army of knights and footsoldiers, the aforesaid count together with that multitude of men made his way to the place called Alberite. Greatly timid and fearful of advancing further and joining battle with Rodrigo, he went back without delay, terrified, to his own land with his army. Rodrigo however waited there as motionless as a stone,[101] cheerful and brave of heart, until the seventh day as agreed. Then it was reliably reported to him that the count and all those who were with him, fearing to fight with him, had withdrawn from the promised conflict and had already dispersed and returned to their homes. They had left Alberite empty, denuded of all troops. At that time Count García, Rodrigo's enemy, was lord by appointment of King Alfonso of Calahorra and of all the region which Rodrigo had laid waste. Because of the count's enmity and because of his insults Rodrigo burnt that land with flame of fire, and laid it waste, and almost destroyed it. When Rodrigo heard, as was related, that for fear of him the count had already gone back to his own country with his followers, and had left Alberite stripped of troops, he left Alfaro with his army and went back to Zaragoza.

In this, the only part of the *Historia* where he was openly critical of his hero, he wrote with a passion which overcame his usual literary bleakness. It is on the strength of this passage that some have supposed that the author was a native of the Rioja.

99 Alfaro is on the Ebro between Calahorra and Tudela.

100 On whom see above, n. 17, and references there cited.

101 See above, ch. 37 and n. 73.

CHAPTER 51

As with chapter 49, so here too Menéndez Pidal believed that an additional chapter had once existed. As in the earlier instance, there is no evidence which might support this view, but the numbering of the chapters is retained for the same reason.

CHAPTER 52

He stayed there for many days with immense honour. He collected and garnered to his own use the yield of all that land which was not subject to the authority of al-Musta'in.

CHAPTER 53

Leaving Zaragoza with his army he began to journey towards Valencia. While he was on the way there a messenger met him and told him that the barbarian Saracen peoples had penetrated to the eastern regions and laid them waste most savagely; that they had even got as far as Valencia, and had already obtained control of it; and what was worse, that those barbarian peoples had already killed all the men of Valencia, betrayed by al-Qādir king of Valencia, and were carrying on with their evil deeds.[102] When Rodrigo heard this he went swiftly to the town of Cebolla and at once laid siege to it. If he had not moved so quickly those barbarian peoples would already have overrun the whole of Hispania as far as Zaragoza and Lérida, and taken complete control of it.

CHAPTER 54

The castle of Cebolla was closely invested on all sides and he soon captured it. He established a settlement there, surrounding and defending it with fortifications and very strong towers. Many people came from the surrounding villages to live in his new settlement. The men of Valencia who had escaped death were subjected to those barbarians

102 Wild rumours were evidently flying about as the Almoravids advanced in the south-east and there must have been plentiful scope for misunderstanding. What had actually happened in Valencia was a coup in the Almoravid interest led by the qāḍī of the city, Ibn Jaḥḥāf. Al-Qādir was not the instigator of violence but its victim; captured by Ibn Jaḥḥāf's partisans he was summarily executed on 28 October 1092. Other editors have been reckless here. Menéndez Pidal drastically emended the sentence; E. Falque chose to omit it altogether. I prefer to leave the text as it stands in the MSS. The Almoravids did not in fact set foot in Valencia until 1102.

who are known as Moabites and lived under their rule and were mixed together with them.[103] In the month of July, at harvest time, Rodrigo encamped beside Valencia. He began to devastate their crops with his horses and to destroy their houses which were outside the walls. When the inhabitants of Valencia saw this they sent envoys to him there, asking and indeed beseeching him to be peaceable towards them and to allow the Moabites to live with them. But he would in no wise allow himself to live at peace with them unless they cut all connections with the Moabites and expelled them from the city altogether. But they were not willing to do this and shut themselves up together in the city.

CHAPTER 55

Rodrigo attacked a certain part of Valencia called Villanueva so vigorously that he took it. He thoroughly ransacked all the money and riches which he found there. Then he attacked and captured another part of the city known as Alcudia. The men who lived in that district submitted and bowed at once to his authority.[104] Rodrigo restored those who had submitted to him to their houses and lands and all their goods, freely and in peace.

CHAPTER 56

The remaining inhabitants of the city of Valencia, apprised of what was going on, were thoroughly scared. They immediately expelled the Moabites from their city, just as Rodrigo had ordered, and surrendered to his authority. He allowed them to go free and in peace to Denia, and to dwell there unmolested.[105]

---

103 By 'Moabites' the author means the Almoravids: see above, n. 57. The last phrase of the sentence, *apud illos mixti conmanebant* – this reading itself the result of a small but plausible emendation, see *RMP*, p. 958 and Falque, p. 84 – is puzzling. The word *mixti* would normally imply some biological, sexual 'mixture'. Did the author want to put the Valencians beyond the pale by the alleged intimacy of their connection with the Almoravids, the better to justify Rodrigo's aggression? One may suspect some such polemical edge to the author's account at several points over the next few chapters. The sentence containing this phrase fits awkwardly into the chapter: was it perhaps an interpolation as a result of second thoughts?

104 These were extra-mural suburbs of Valencia.

105 At first sight thoroughly confused, this chapter makes sense if taken as referring to other extra-mural suburbs: cf. the verbal usage of the previous chapter, where *partem urbis*, 'part of the city', undoubtedly refers to a suburb. The 'Moabites' who were expelled would then become the supporters of the pro-Almoravid Ibn Jaḥḥāf, on whom see above, n. 102.

CHAPTER 57

Shortly before this Yūsuf had sent letters to him strictly forbidding
him to dare to enter the land of Valencia. When he heard this Rodrigo
was mightily angered. Warmed by the flame of his rage he spoke of
Yūsuf in terms of the strongest contempt and mocked him with
jeering words. He sent letters to all the princes and leaders of the
Spains,[106] telling them that for fear of him Yūsuf did not dare to cross
the sea and come to Valencia. When Yūsuf heard this he ordered that
an immense, innumerable army be gathered and prepare to cross the
Straits without delay. Meanwhile Rodrigo spoke words of mildness to
the inhabitants of Valencia, thus: 'Men of Valencia, I freely offer you a
period of truce until the month of August. If Yūsuf should come in the
meantime to your assistance, and should defeat and expel me from
these lands and liberate you from my dominion, serve him and remain
beneath his rule. But if he should not do this, serve me and be mine.'
This message was pleasing to all the men of Valencia. They at once
sent letters to Yūsuf and to all the leaders of Hispania under his
authority in which they asked them to come to Valencia with a huge
army to liberate them from the hand and authority of Rodrigo. If this
were not done before the month of August, they emphasised, they
would undoubtedly have to bow to Rodrigo's power and serve him in
all things. Meanwhile Rodrigo left Valencia free in peace and went
with his army to Peña Cadiella. He ravaged as far as Villena and the
land round about. He took many captives and plunder and quantities of
provisions. He sent everything to Peña Cadiella and stored it there with
the greatest part of his treasure. Then he went straight back to Valencia.

CHAPTER 58

Then, leaving that region behind, he went up into the land round
Albarracín, whose people had defaulted on the payment of tribute to
him. He laid waste all that land and ordered all the provisions which
he found there to be sent to Cebolla. He meanwhile returned to
Cebolla with immense plunder.

CHAPTER 59

When the month of August had gone by the people of Valencia heard
a reliable report that the Moabites were coming to their aid with a

106 *Yspaniarum,* i.e. Muslim Hispania and Christian Hispania.

huge army under the command of Yūsuf, to help to free them from
the lordship of Rodrigo. So they dishonoured the agreement which
they had made with him. In being unfaithful to their agreement they
made themselves in every way rebels against Rodrigo and [became]
his enemies: and he well understood this. So he again laid siege to
Valencia with intense hostility, and pressed the city from every side
with the most aggressive tactics possible. It became known that severe
food shortages were being experienced inside the city.

CHAPTER 60

Meanwhile, however, the army of the Moabites, swiftly on its way to
relieve the siege, approached Valencia. But they did not dare to
commit themselves to battle with Rodrigo. Greatly fearful of him they
dispersed by night and retired to their bases in confusion.

CHAPTER 61

Rodrigo continued to press the siege of Valencia ever more closely for
no little time. At long last he valiantly took it by assault.[107] At once he
subjected it to sack. He found and took possession of vast and innumerable riches: immense, uncountable quantities of gold and silver,
precious jewellery, gems set in fine gold, treasures of various sorts,
silken textiles decorated with precious gold. So vast were the hoards
of riches which he seized in the city that he and his followers were
rendered wealthier than it is possible to say.

CHAPTER 62

Yūsuf king of the Moabites, hearing that Valencia had been captured
and sacked by Rodrigo in this very savage fashion, was powerfully
moved to anger and bitterness. After taking counsel with his followers
he appointed as general to command in Spain a kinsman named
Muḥammad, his sister's son. He sent him with an infinite multitude of
barbarians and Moabites and Ishmaelites drawn from all over Hispania
to besiege Valencia and to bring Rodrigo to him captive and in chains.
They arrived at the place called Cuarte, about four miles from the city
of Valencia, and pitched camp there. [The inhabitants of] all the
region round about constantly went to them with the necessary food

107 Valencia fell on 15 June 1094: RMP, pp. 793–4.

and provisions: some of these victuals they gave to them and some they sold. Their number was nearly 150,000 mounted men and 3000 footsoldiers.[108] When Rodrigo saw that so vast and innumerable a multitude had come to fight against him, he was very apprehensive. This Moabite army lay about Valencia for ten days and as many nights, and remained inactive. Every day indeed they used to go round the city, shrieking and shouting with a motley clamour of voices and filling the air with their bellowing. They often used to fire arrows at the tents and dwellings of Rodrigo and his soldiers, provoking them to immediate combat. But Rodrigo, stout of heart as ever, comforted and strengthened his men in a manly fashion, and constantly prayed devoutly to the Lord Jesus Christ that he would send divine aid to his people. There came a day when the enemy were as usual going round outside the city yelling and shouting and skirmishing, confident in the belief that they would capture it, when Rodrigo, the invincible warrior, trusting with his whole mind in God and His mercy, courageously made a sortie from the city: he was accompanied by his well-armed followers, and they shouted at the enemy and terrified them with threatening words. They fell upon them and a major encounter ensued. By God's clemency Rodrigo defeated all the Moabites. Thus he had victory and triumph over them, granted to him by God. As soon as they were defeated they turned their backs in flight. A multitude of them fell to the sword. Others with their wives and children were led captive to Rodrigo's camp. Our men seized all their tents and equipment, among which they found innumerable treasure of gold and silver and precious textiles. They thoroughly plundered all the wealth they found there. Rodrigo and his men were greatly enriched thereby – with much gold and silver, most precious textiles, horses, palfreys and mules, various sorts of weaponry: they were amply stocked with quantities of provisions and treasures untold. This victory took place in the Era 1132 [= AD 1094].[109]

CHAPTER 63

After this triumph Rodrigo took the castle called Olocau. There he found a great treasure which had belonged to King al-Qādir. He

108 The MS reading CL is quite plain, and the proposal by Menéndez Pidal to read c.L for circa L milia, 'about fifty thousand' is unconvincing. The figure is wildly exaggerated: no Almoravid army could possibly have numbered 150,000.
109 Probably towards the end of October.

divided this in good faith with his men. Then he took another town
called Serra.[110]

CHAPTER 64

Then died Sancho, king of Aragon, of happy memory. He had lived
fifty-two years and afterwards went to Christ in peace. He was buried
with honour in the monastery of San Juan de la Peña.[111] After his
death his son Pedro was raised up as king over the Aragonese kingdom.
All the noblemen of his kingdom were gathered together at one time.
Then they addressed the king as follows: 'Renowned king, we unanimously beseech your majesty to deign to listen to our counsel. We
believe this policy to be sound and useful to you, that you should have
friendship and love with Rodrigo the Campeador. We offer you this
advice with no dissentient voice.' This advice of his aristocracy was
very pleasing to the king and he at once sent envoys to Rodrigo to
negotiate an alliance.[112] The envoys sent to Rodrigo said: 'Our lord
the king of Aragon has sent us to you, that you may join with him and
institute in friendly fashion the firmest possible peace and love; that
you may be of one mind in campaigning against your enemies, and
may render each other every assistance against our common foes.'
This was greatly pleasing to Rodrigo, and he replied to them that he
would willingly do it. King Pedro then travelled down to the coast at
a place called Montornés.[113] Rodrigo left the city of Valencia and went
to Burriana to meet him. In the course of their meeting at the latter
place they decided to have the firmest possible peace between them
and undertook with good and sincere intent to help one another
before all other men against their enemies. After this the king at once
went back to his land and took measures to ensure that his kingdom
should live in accordance with good justice by the sanction of the law.
Rodrigo made his way back to Valencia.

---

110 This is Olocau de Valencia, some 25 km inland from Murviedro/Sagunto (not to
be confused with the Olocau near Morella of ch. 21 above): Serra is nearby.

111 Sancho Ramírez died on 4 June 1094. The monastery of San Juan de la Peña,
about 10 km to the south-west of Jaca, was the mausoleum of the Aragonese royal
family.

112 It makes more sense to suppose that Rodrigo, rather than King Pedro, was the
suppliant: see Fletcher, *Quest for El Cid*, p. 171. The renewal of the alliance
between Rodrigo and the Aragonese first formed in 1092 (above, ch. 48)
presumably occurred shortly after Pedro's accession.

113 The modern Puebla Tornesa, just to the north of Castellón.

CHAPTER 65

Some time later King Pedro came to Valencia with his army to help his ally Rodrigo, who received him with the greatest honour.[114] Having mustered their forces they left Valencia together and set out towards the town of Peña Cadiella. They intended to send foodstuffs there and supply it adequately with provisions. As they approached Játiva they encountered Muḥammad, the nephew of Yūsuf, king of the Moabites and Ishmaelites. He had a huge army of 30,000 well-armed soldiers and was intent on battle. However, that day the Ishmaelites and Moabites did not offer battle with them but throughout the day remained in the mountains thereabouts howling and shouting. King Pedro and Rodrigo boldly sent all the foodstuffs which they could find in the region, together with all the booty they had taken, to the town of Peña Cadiella. Thus they stocked the town most amply with victuals for its defence.

CHAPTER 66

Moving southwards from there, they went down together to the coast and made camp at Bairén. On the next day Muḥammad prepared to engage the king and Rodrigo in battle, with his huge and innumerable forces of Moabites and Ishmaelites and all barbarian peoples. There was in the place a big hill extending in length about forty *stadii.* Here, on the hill, was the Saracen camp.[115] Opposite it was the sea, and on it a great number of Ishmaelite and Moabite ships, from which they harrassed the Christians with bow and arrow. And from the mountain quarter they attacked them with other weapons. When the Christians realised what was happening they were not a little afraid. When Rodrigo saw how frightened they were, he at once mounted his horse and armed himself, and began to ride among his army, greatly cheering

---

114 The author's vagueness as to chronology conceals the fact that he has skipped two years. He reports nothing of his hero's doings during the years 1095 and 1096. The Bairén campaign described in chs 65–6 took place in the spring of 1097. It is referred to in two documents of Pedro I belonging to that year: A. Ubieto Arteta, *Colección Diplomática de Pedro I de Aragón y Navarra* (Zaragoza, 1951), nos 31 (*quando venit rex de Penna Catiella*) and 39 (*eo anno quo devicta est multitudo paganorum a predicto rege*).

115 On the localisation of Bairén, near Gandía, between Denia and Valencia, see *RMP*, pp. 813–15, who also ingeniously explains away the author's slip in asserting that Bairén was 'southwards' of Peña Cadiella. In actual fact it lies to the north-east. The classical *stadium* measured 606 feet and 9 inches, or 202.25 yards: forty *stadii* is therefore about 4.5 miles or 7 km. In the eleventh century the sea came in much closer to the mountains than it does now.

them with these words: 'Listen to me, my dearest and closest companions. You must be strong and powerful in battle. Take a firm grip on yourselves. You must be fearless. Do not quail before the enemy numbers. Today our Lord Jesus Christ will deliver them into our hands and into our power.' At the middle of the day the king and Rodrigo with all the Christian army fell upon them and engaged them in strength. At length by God's clemency they defeated them and turned them in flight. Some were killed by the sword, some fell in the river, and enormous numbers fled into the sea where they were drowned. After the Saracens had been defeated and slaughtered the Christian victors plundered all their goods. They took all the spoil they could – gold and silver, horses and mules, excellent weapons and many rich goods. They glorified God with full-hearted devotion for the victory which He had granted them. After this memorable and ever-to-be-praised triumph King Pedro and Rodrigo returned with their army to Valencia praising God. But they stayed in the city only a few days. They left together for the castle of Montornés which was in the king's territory and was rebelling aginst him. After arriving there they laid siege to it. They besieged and boldly assaulted it and brought it back to its allegiance. Then the king returned rejoicing to his kingdom, and Rodrigo returned to his city of Valencia.

CHAPTER 67

One day Rodrigo left the city to reconnoitre the doings of his enemies. While he was on his journey the alcaide of Játiva, a certain Abū-l-Faṭah, left his city and entered Murviedro. When Rodrigo learnt this he turned after him and pursued him until he managed to shut him up in the town of Almenara.[116] He besieged the town, investing it closely on every side for three months, after which he conquered it. He allowed all the men whom he captured inside it to go free to their own homes. He ordered a church with an altar dedicated to the Blessed Virgin Mary to be built there.

CHAPTER 68

After things had thus fallen out by God's grace, Rodrigo left Almenara with his troops, letting it be known that he was going to return to Valencia: but secretly he intended to besiege and conquer

116 Just to the north of Murviedro.

Murviedro.[117] Meanwhile he prayed to God, his hands upraised to
heaven, saying 'O eternal God, who knows all things before they come
to pass, from whom no secret is hid: Thou knowest, O Lord, that I do
not wish to enter Valencia before I have with the aid of thy power
secured Murviedro by siege and conquest and sack; and if the town by
thy gift will fall under our possession and authority, there I will cause
Mass to be celebrated to Thee and thy praise, O God.' After praying
in this fashion he laid siege to the town of Murviedro, attacking it
with swords, arrows, javelins and all manner of weapons and siege-
engines.[118] Rodrigo pressed hard upon and sternly afflicted [the defenders of the fortress and its inhabitants] and altogether prevented entry
to or exit from the place.[119]

CHAPTER 69

The inhabitants and the defenders of the castle, perceiving themselves
to be under attack and hard-pressed on every side, said among
themselves, 'What shall we poor wretches do? This tyrant Rodrigo
will completely prevent us from carrying on living in the castle. He
will treat us as he lately treated those inhabitants of Valencia and
Almenara who could not resist him. Let us see what we can do. Already
we and our wives and our sons and our daughters are about to die of
hunger. But there is no-one who can deliver us from his hands.' Aware
of this, Rodrigo began to press the siege more strongly and relent-
lessly than before, and the plight of the defenders became very serious.
When they found themselves in such bitter straits they appealed to
Rodrigo as follows: 'Why do you inflict such unbearable ills upon us?
Why kill us with spear and arrow and sword? Soften your heart and
have mercy upon us. Together we implore you to heed the prompt-
ings of pity and give us a few days' truce. In the meantime we shall
send our messengers to the king and our lords,[120] asking them to
come to our aid. Should no one come by the agreed term to free us

117 The narrative of the siege and conquest of Murviedro contained in chs 68–72 has
    been translated by Smith in his *Christians and Moors in Spain*, no. 25, pp. 124–9.
    Murviedro was an immensely strong fortress: for a brief description see Fletcher,
    Quest for El Cid, p. 176 and plate 14.
118 *machinamentis*: this is the only reference to siege-engines in the *Historia*.
119 A line seems to have been omitted from the text here and the bracketed words
    have been supplied.
120 *ad regem et ad dominos nostros*. The implication is that King Alfonso VI is to be
    understood, which would seem to be confirmed by the information of the
    following chapter. Smith's 'to our King and other rulers' is misleading.

from your hands, we shall be yours and will serve you. You should know for very truth that the town of Murviedro is of such name and fame among all peoples that we shall never surrender it quickly to you. Rather than surrender without a term of truce, we should all of us sooner die. Only after every one of us is dead will you be able to have this place.' Rodrigo knew well that this course would avail them nothing, yet he offered them a truce of thirty days.

CHAPTER 70

They sent messengers to King Yūsuf and the Moabites, and to King Alfonso, and to King al-Musta'īn of Zaragoza, and to the king of Albarracín, and to the count of Barcelona,[121] imploring them to come to their relief within thirty days: if they did not do so, when the thirty days were up they would surely surrender the town to Rodrigo and faithfully serve him as their lord thereafter. When King Alfonso saw and heard the envoys from Murviedro he replied to them thus: 'You must believe that I speak the truth when I tell you that I will not come to your aid, because I prefer that Rodrigo should have the town of Murviedro rather than any Saracen king.'[122] When the envoys heard this they returned home disconsolate. To the messengers who had been sent to Zaragoza al-Musta'īn made this reply: 'Go and do what you can to help yourselves. Be brave in resisting him by fighting. Rodrigo is a hard man, a very brave and invincible fighter, such that I do not care to engage with him in battle.' Now shortly beforehand Rodrigo had sent messengers to him, saying: 'Be it known to you, al-Musta'īn, that if you dare to come against me with your army and engage me in battle, you and your noblemen will in no manner escape death or captivity at my hands.' Being mightily afraid of Rodrigo, he did not dare to come. The king of Albarracín addressed the messengers who presented themselves to him in this fashion: 'Do your utmost to have confidence and stand up to him, for I cannot be of assistance to you.' The Moabites replied to the messengers sent to them: 'If our king Yūsuf shall choose to come, we shall all together accompany him and willingly come to your aid. But without him we should never dare to fight against Rodrigo.' The count of Barcelona, who had received a

121 Ramón Berenguer III (1096–1131).
122 That the people of Murviedro should have appealed to Alfonso VI *against* Rodrigo is one of the strongest indications that Rodrigo as self-styled Prince of Valencia was acting as an independent ruler rather than as a vassal of Alfonso VI: see Fletcher, *Quest for El Cid*, p. 179.

vast tribute from them, replied thus to the envoys sent to him: 'Know
that I do not care to fight against Rodrigo. However, I shall come
quickly and surround his castle named Oropesa, and while he is
approaching to attempt battle with me you can send sufficient
foodstuffs into your castle from the other direction.'[123] As he had undertaken, the count soon laid siege to the castle [of Oropesa]. When he
heard this Rodrigo considered it a matter of no importance and
refused to go to its relief. Meanwhile a certain knight addressed the
count while he was besieging the castle, saying, 'Most noble count, I
have heard for a certainty that Rodrigo is coming against you and
intends to fight with you'. When he heard this the count was not
prepared to test the truth of the report, immediately retired from the
siege of the castle and for fear of Rodrigo fled in terror to his own
land.[124]

CHAPTER 71

When the thirty days of truce were up, Rodrigo spoke to the barbarians in the castle of Murviedro: 'Why do you delay in surrendering
the town to me?' They replied to him deceitfully as follows: 'Lord, the
messengers whom we sent out have not yet returned to us: accordingly
we unanimously implore your nobility to extend by a little the term of
truce.' Rodrigo realised that they addressed him treacherously and
deceitfully, and that they had made up this tale just to gain time, so he
said: 'In order to make it plain to all men that I fear no king of yours,
I shall extend the truce by twelve days so that they may have no
pretext for not coming to your aid. When the twelve days have
expired – and I tell you of a truth[125] – if you do not at once surrender
the castle to me, as many of you as I can lay hands on I shall burn
alive or execute after torture.' The appointed day came. Rodrigo
addressed the men in the fortress: 'Why do you continue to delay and

123 Oropesa, about 18 km north of Castellón, was in the hands of the Aragonese at
    this date. The Catalan attack on it may indicate that Aragonese troops were
    assisting Rodrigo in the siege of Murviedro under the terms of the alliance of
    1094.
124 It was presumably in the wake of the Oropesa incident, and in a diplomatic move
    to allay Catalan hostility, that Rodrigo arranged a marriage between his daughter
    María and the count of Barcelona.
125 Luke iv.25. Rodrigo's threats were not idle: in 1095 he had burned alive the
    former qāḍī of Valencia, Ibn Jaḥḥāf. Ibn 'Idhārī's account of this atrocity is to be
    found translated in Charles Melville and Ahmad Ubaydli, Christians and Moors in
    Spain, volume III (Warminster, 1992) at pp. 102–5.

not surrender the castle to me as promised?' They replied: 'Look, your feast of Pentecost is now close. On the day of the feast we shall surrender the castle to you, for our kings are unwilling to come to our aid. You and your men may enter in safety and deal with the place as you wish.' Rodrigo replied to them: 'I shall not enter the castle upon the very day of Pentecost, but I offer you a truce until the feast of St John the Baptist.[126] In the meantime take your wives and children and servants and all your household goods, and go in peace with your possessions wheresoever you wish. Evacuate the castle and leave it to me freely and without trickery. I shall enter the castle, divine clemency being my aid, on the Nativity of St John the Baptist.' The Saracens returned many and grateful thanks for such loving mercy.

CHAPTER 72

On the feast of the Nativity of St John the Baptist Rodrigo sent his soldiers ahead of him to enter the castle with orders to climb up to it and take possession of it. They at once made their entry and taking possession of the castle's topmost point they gave joyful thanks to God. Shortly afterwards Rodrigo himself entered the castle, and devoutly ordered a Mass to be celebrated at once and an offering to be made. He gave orders for the building there of a handsome church in honour of St John. He ordered his soldiers to guard well the gates of the city and all its defensive walls and everything that was in the town and the fortress. In the castle itself, although it had been evacuated, they found many riches. Some of the Saracen inhabitants of Murviedro still remained there. Three days after the taking of the town Rodrigo addressed them as follows: 'Now I tell firmly that you must return into my hands all that you have kept back from my men and that you have taken from the Moabites, against my will and to my loss and shame. If you do not do this, believe me, you will be imprisoned and strongly bound in iron chains.' Those who would not surrender what was sought were on Rodrigo's orders completely stripped of their possessions, chained together and despatched immediately to Valencia.

---

126 In 1098 Pentecost fell on 16 May. The Nativity of John the Baptist is celebrated on 24 June.

CHAPTER 73

After these doings Rodrigo returned to Valencia. In the Saracen building which they call a mosque[127] he built a fine and seemly church in honour of St Mary the Virgin, Mother of our Redeemer. He gave to the same church a golden chalice worth a hundred and fifty marks. He also gave to the aforesaid church two very precious hangings woven with silk and gold, the like of which, it was said, had never been seen in Valencia.[128] Everyone then celebrated Mass in that church with most sweet and agreeable and melodious songs of praise. Then with joyful hearts they praised our Redeemer the Lord Jesus Christ, to whom is due honour and glory with the Father and the Holy Spirit for ever and ever, amen.[129]

CHAPTER 74

It would take too long – and perhaps would tax the patience of readers – to narrate in order all the battles which Rodrigo and his companions fought and won, or to list all the lands and settlements which his strong right arm wasted and destroyed with the sword and other weapons. What our limited skill can do we have done: written of his deeds briefly and in a poor style, but always with the strictest regard for truth. While he lived in this world he always won a noble triumph over the enemies who fought him in battle. Never was he defeated by any man.

CHAPTER 75

Rodrigo died at Valencia in the month of July in the Era 1137 [= AD 1099].[130] After his death his sorrowing wife remained in Valencia with a great company of knights and footsoldiers. When the news of his death spread all the Saracens who lived across the seas mustered a considerable army and marched against Valencia. They laid siege to it on all sides and attacked the city for seven months.

127 *mezquitam*. It was common practice in Spain for Christian conquerors to reconsecrate mosques as churches.
128 He also gave endowments in landed property. The diploma recording this endowment has survived in its original form in the cathedral archive of Salamanca. The best edition of it is to be found in *RMP*, pp. 868–71; part of the document has been translated into English in Smith's *Christians and Moors*, no. 26, pp. 130–33.
129 Romans xvi.27; I Timothy i.17.
130 Later sources would date his death to 10 July.

CHAPTER 76

His wife, deprived of so great a husband, finding herself in her affliction so hard-pressed and unable to find the remedy of consolation in her unhappiness, sent the bishop of the city[131] to King Alfonso to ask him for pity's sake to help her. On receiving this appeal the king came swiftly to Valencia with his army. Rodrigo's unhappy wife received him with the greatest joy, and kissed his feet. She implored him to help her and all the Christians who were with her. But the king could find no one among his men who might hold the city and defend it from the Saracens; for it was far removed from his kingdom. So he returned to Castile, taking with him Rodrigo's wife with the body of her husband, and all the Christians who were then there with their household goods and riches.[132] When they had all left Valencia the king ordered the whole city to be burnt: then he led all these people to Toledo. The Saracens, who had fled the king's arrival and abandoned the siege, re-entered the city soon after the king's departure, although it was burnt, and resettled it and all its territories. They have never lost it since that day.

CHAPTER 77

Rodrigo's wife, accompanied by her husband's knights, bore his body to the monastery of San Pedro de Cardeña. There she gave it honourable burial, granting for the sake of his soul no small gifts to the monastery.[133]

131 Jerónimo, bishop of Valencia 1098–1102, subsequently bishop of Salamanca 1102–20. His transfer to Salamanca explains why the muniments of Valencia have survived in the Salamanca archives (above, n. 127). For a brief account of Jerónimo see Fletcher, *Quest for El Cid*, pp. 182–3.

132 1102, probably April: see Reilly, *Alfonso VI*, pp. 309–11.

133 No record of these has survived among the muniments of Cardeña. Doña Jimena, last traceable in 1113, is thought to have died in 1116. For a sketch of the posthumous history of the Cid and of the part played by the monks of Cardeña in cultivating his memory, see Fletcher, *Quest for El Cid*, ch. 12.

IV: *CHRONICA ADEFONSI IMPERATORIS*

Introduction to the *Chronica Adefonsi Imperatoris*

The *Chronica Adefonsi Imperatoris*, or Chronicle of the Emperor Alfonso, (henceforward *CAI*) is a panegyric in prose and verse devoted to the deeds of Alfonso VII of León–Castile (1126–57), from his accession to the throne in 1126 down to the campaign to conquer the port city of Almería in 1147.[1] To all appearances a contemporary (or near-contemporary) witness to the events it describes, the *CAI* furnishes the principal narrative account of the political and military affairs of the Leonese monarchy during the period in question. Despite its undoubted importance as a historical source, however, the Chronicle positively bristles with difficulties. For one thing, the text of the *CAI*, as it has come down to us, is far from satisfactory. The nine surviving manuscripts, all of which contain significant lacunae, are late paper copies of the sixteenth, seventeenth and eighteenth centuries. The three most important of them (Madrid, Biblioteca Nacional 1279, 1505 and 9237), upon which Antonio Maya Sánchez has based his recent edition, appear to have derived from a (now lost) glossed archetype of the fourteenth or fifteenth century, apparently written on parchment in 'letra gotica', held in the library of the cathedral of Toledo.[2] Textual difficulties aside, the knotty question of the authorship of the *CAI* remains unresolved, and we cannot even be sure of when or where it was composed.

1 *Chronica Adefonsi Imperatoris*, ed. A. Maya Sánchez, in *Chronica Hispana saeculi XII*, 109–248. This supersedes the earlier editions by P. de Sandoval, *Chronica del ínclito Emperador de España Don Alfonso VII deste nombre, rey de Castilla y León, hijo de Don Ramón de Borgoña y de Doña Hurraca, reyna propietaria de Castilla* (Madrid, 1600), 127–38, which included only the poetic colophon to the *CAI*; F. de Berganza, *Antigüedades de España*, II (Madrid, 1721), 590–624; E. Flórez (ed.), *Chronica Adefonsi Imperatoris*, ES 21 (Madrid, 1766), 320–409; A. Huici Miranda (ed.), *Las crónicas latinas de la Reconquista*, 2 vols (Valencia, 1913), II, 171–430; and L. Sánchez Belda (ed.), *Chronica Adefonsi Imperatoris* (Madrid, 1950). There is a Spanish translation of the chronicle by M. Pérez González, *Crónica del Emperador Alfonso VII* (León, 1997). The *CAI* was the object of an illuminating, yet sadly unpublished, study by G. West, *History as Celebration: Castilian and Hispano-Latin Epics and Histories, 1080–1210 AD* (Ph.D. thesis, University of London, 1975), ch. 4.

2 *CAI* (ed. Maya Sánchez), pp. 120–32.

The *CAI* is divided into two books. The first, which is subdivided into 95 chapters, is principally concerned with Alfonso VII's attempts to impose his authority over the kingdom after the death of his mother Queen Urraca in March 1126, and to re-establish the pre-eminence of León–Castile among the Christian realms of the peninsula after the political turmoil of his mother's reign. The narrative begins with a relatively comprehensive roll-call of the most powerful members of the lay élite of León and Castile who pledged their loyalty to the young king in 1126 (chs 1–8), before going on to describe the various rebellions that were subsequently launched against Alfonso VII's rule by important sections of the aristocracy (chs 18–23, 30–2, 43–6), and the campaigns that the king was forced to wage against his hostile neighbours in Aragon, Navarre and Portugal (chs 9–11, 13–17, 24–6, 73–91). In addition, there is coverage of such matters as the submission of the Muslim ruler of Rueda de Jalón, Sayf al-Dawla (chs 27–9), the raiding expedition that was led into al-Andalus by Alfonso VII and Count Rodrigo González in 1133 (chs 33–42), the crushing defeat suffered at Almoravid hands by Alfonso I of Aragon at Fraga in July 1134, and his death two months later (chs 49–61); the separation of the realms of Aragon and Navarre in 1134, the subsequent occupation of Nájera and Zaragoza by Leonese forces, and the submission of García Ramírez IV of Navarre, Ramiro II of Aragon, Count Alfonso Jordan of Toulouse, and other trans-Pyrenean magnates (chs 62–8); and the imperial coronation of Alfonso VII in León in May 1135 (chs 69–72). The book concludes with an elaborate description of the wedding of the emperor's illegitimate daughter Urraca and King García Ramírez IV of Navarre in León in June 1144 (chs 92–4), and the subsequent entry to the cloister of Alfonso VII's former concubine, Guntroda Pérez (ch. 95).

With the notable exception of the account of the submission of Sayf al-Dawla to the Leonese crown and of the raiding party that Alfonso VII led into al-Andalus in 1133, the attention of the first book of the *CAI* is focused squarely on the area north of the River Duero.[3] Book II, however, which is subdivided into 111 chapters, is given over to

3 It is possible that these episodes originally formed part of Book II and were later inserted into the first part of the chronicle. The dramatic style and rhythm of these sections, and the quantity and particular type of biblical phrases that they contain (for example, the adaptation of the Book of Judith in i, 35, which is repeated in ii, 36, 82), are closely in keeping with the narrative of the second book. Moreover, the account of the expedition of 1133 refers to the raid having avenged defeats which are subsequently described in the second book (i, 33, 42).

'the conflicts and battles which he [Alfonso VII], the nobles of Toledo and the commanders of Extremadura had with King 'Alī, with his son Tāshufīn, and with the other kings and princes of the Moabites and Hagarenes'. The chronicler details the bloody campaigns that were waged by Christian and Muslim armies from the death of Alfonso VI in 1109 down to the conquest of Córdoba by Alfonso VII in the spring of 1146. Particular attention is devoted to the raids on Toledo and the Tagus valley that were launched by Almoravid forces after 1109 (chs 1–8, 12–18), the various military expeditions that were led into Muslim territory by Alfonso VII (chs 36–9, 40–4, 51–63, 64–6, 81–2) and by the governors of Toledo, Count Rodrigo González and Rodrigo Fernández (chs 24–6, 31–4), the campaigns that were waged by the Galician warlord Muño Alfonso (chs 17, 49, 67–79, 84–90), and, finally, the preparations that were made for the Almería campaign (chs 107–8). In an important digression, there is also an account of the Muslim uprising that took place against Almoravid rule in 1144–6, the overthrow of the Almoravid empire in the Maghreb by the Almohads, and the first arrival of Almohad forces in the peninsula in 1146 (chs 92–105, 109).

At the end of Book Two, the chronicler, anxious, he tells us, to avoid boring his audience, launches into a poetic celebration, consisting of 385 and a half lines of rhythmic hexameters, of the campaign that was led by Alfonso VII and his allies to conquer Almería in 1147.[4] In the opening verses of the *Poem of Almería* (henceforward *PA*) the narrator sets out the theme of his work and refers to the crusading nature of the Almería expedition, before proceeding to paint a series of eulogistic portraits of eleven of the chief lay personages who accompanied the emperor on the expedition, and to briefly outline the preliminary military operations that were carried out in the region of the Upper Guadalquivir. The poem is then sadly interrupted in mid-line just as the bishop of Astorga gets up to harangue the emperor's troops prior to the final assault on Almería.[5]

The Latin of the *CAI* has been considered deficient by a number of commentators. Prudencio de Sandoval, writing in 1600, went so far as

4 *Prefatio de Almaria*, ed. J. Gil, in *Chronica Hispana saeculi XII*, 249–67. There is an excellent study of the poem by H. Salvador Martínez, *El 'Poema de Almería' y la épica románica* (Madrid, 1975). See also F. Castro Guisasola (ed. and trans.), *El Cantar de la conquista de Almería por Alfonso VII: un poema hispano-latino del siglo XII* (Almería, 1992).

5 On the reasons for the truncation of the *PA*, see Sánchez Belda, *Chronica*, p. xx; cf. Salvador Martínez, *'Poema de Almería'*, pp. 121–2, 126–8.

to describe the verse of the *PA* to be 'barbarous', and others since have been equally scathing.[6] But that is to judge the work by classical norms. Viewed in the cultural context of its times, the *CAI* is a far from aberrant work.[7] Besides, for all his supposed shortcomings as a literary stylist, our author was clearly a learned man. A glance at the notes to our translation of the prose part of the *CAI* will reveal the extent to which the chronicler drew inspiration from the Bible, and more particularly from the canonical and apocryphal books of the Old Testament Vulgate. Quite apart from the very large number of Biblical phrases that were incorporated wholesale into the narrative of the *CAI*, the influence of the Vulgate is everywhere conspicuous in the author's style, syntax and vocabulary.[8] With good reason the *CAI* has been dubbed 'a veritable biblical-medieval epic'.[9] Although it is conceivable that the author's account of the early years of the reign of Alfonso VII may have expanded upon on an earlier set of annals,[10] and although the influence of the Vulgate is more overt in the second book than the first, the stylistic similarities between the two parts of the prose chronicle are such that there can be little doubt that both are the product of the same pen.[11] Equally, far from consisting of a 'series of popular tales originally composed separately and only subsequently tacked together', as one historian has recently suggested, the second book of

6 Sandoval, *Chronica*, p. 127. Cf. N. Antonio, *Bibliotheca hispana vetus* (Rome, 1696), lib. 7, ch. 4, n. 77; Flórez (ed.), *Chronica Adefonsi Imperatoris*, pp. 318–19; Sánchez Alonso, *Historia de la historiografía*, pp. 123–4; Salvador Martínez, 'Poema de Almería', pp. 124–5.

7 Pérez González, *Crónica*, pp. 14–18. The metre of the Poem of Almería has been the object of a number of important studies by M. Martínez Pastor: see, for example, 'La rima en el "Poema de Almería"', *Cuadernos de Filología Clásica* 21 (1988), 73–95; 'Virtuosismos verbales en el *Poema de Almería*', *Epos* 4 (1988), 379–87; 'La métrica del "Poema de Almería": su carácter cuantitativo', *Cuadernos de Filología Clásica (Estudios Latinos)* 1 (1991), 159–93.

8 M. Pérez González, 'Influencias clásicas y bíblicas en la *Chronica Adefonsi Imperatoris*', in *I Congreso Nacional de Latín Medieval*, ed. M. Pérez González (León, 1995), 349–55, at pp. 351–4.

9 Salvador Martínez, 'Poema de Almería', p. 243.

10 A. Ubieto Arteta, 'Sugerencias sobre la *Chronica Adefonsi Imperatoris*', CHE 25–6 (1957), 317–26, at pp. 319–20. Cf. Salvador Martínez, 'Poema de Almería', pp. 184, 207.

11 Compare, for example, the account of Alfonso VII's triumphal entry into Zaragoza in 1134 (i, 65) with the description of the emperor's arrival in Toledo in 1139 (ii, 62); the various references to the singing of the *Te Deum laudamus* (i, 70; ii, 34, 59, 75); or the incorporation of quoted extracts of Bishop Pelayo's *Chronicon* or the Pelagian version of Sampiro (i, 61, 69, 72; ii, 7). There are also a number of explicit references from one book to the other (i, 47; ii, 34, 59, 75).

the *CAI*, conceived and composed in the style of a historical book of the Old Testament, is remarkably homogenous in style and inspiration.[12] Moreover, although, in keeping with its epic tone, the *PA* contains a small number of classical reminiscences, notably from the works of Virgil and Ovid, the poem appears to have been inspired chiefly by the Parallelistic verse of the Old Testament.[13] The chronicler also demonstrates a degree of acquaintance with peninsular works of historiography, notably the *Chronicon* of Bishop Pelayo of Oviedo and the Pelagian version of the *Chronicle* of Sampiro.

In an Iberian context, the *CAI* is a strikingly original piece of historiography. In marked contrast to most of the other Latin historical works produced in the north-west of the peninsula during the early Middle Ages, from the Asturian royal chronicles of the late ninth century to Rodrigo Jiménez de Rada's *De rebus Hispanie* of the mid-thirteenth, our chronicler did not hark back to the rebirth of the Visigothic monarchy in León; indeed, he had nothing whatsoever to say of the deeds of any of the royal ancestors of Alfonso VII.[14] Instead, the author of the *CAI* set himself a more limited objective: 'to describe the deeds of the Emperor Alfonso, just as I have learned and heard of them from those who witnessed them' (i, Preface). Unlike his near-contemporary, the author of the *Historia Silense*, our chronicler was less concerned with legitimacy and orthodoxy than with the all-consuming task of taking the fight to the Muslim Almoravids and their allies. Taking the Old Testament as his guide and inspiration (particularly in Book II of the prose chronicle), our author infused his heroic biography with a profound religious spirit. Alfonso VII, the 'terror of the Ishmaelites' (ii, 107), was portrayed not merely as an instrument of divine will, but as the leader of a chosen people, a latter-day Israelite king. Time and again, the chronicler emphasised the support lent by God towards Alfonso VII and his people (for example, i, 10, 17, 27; ii, 6) and the way in which, on account of their sins, the ambitions of the emperor's enemies (and even those of some of his supporters) were thwarted through divine arrangement (for example, i, 38, 46, 53, 55; ii, 7, 27–9, 90). It is made abundantly clear that the many campaigns which the Leonese monarch was forced to wage against the rebels in his own

12 Reilly, *King Alfonso VII*, p. 65 (cf. pp. 40, n. 76, 41, n. 80).
13 Pérez González, 'Influencias', 350–1; Salvador Martínez, 'Poema de Almería', pp. 210ff.
14 The one ruler with whom Alfonso VII is compared is the Emperor Charlemagne (*PA*, vv. 18–20).

kingdom, or against his Christian neighbours in Aragon, Navarre and Portugal, amounted to nothing less than a deflection from the true destiny God had prepared for him (ii, 19–20): to make war on 'that abominable people', as the Muslims of al-Andalus are dubbed (ii, 7).

At the very heart of the *CAI* lies a deepfelt sense of revenge (i, 33, 42). Central to the 'reconquest' ideal was the widely-articulated belief that the Christians were waging a campaign to reverse the wrongs that they had suffered at the hands of the Muslims in times past, and above all to restore to Christian hands the territories that had been lost.[15] Our chronicler takes particular delight in enumerating the many victories that were won over the Almoravids and their allies, the vast booty that was seized, the mosques and sacred Islamic texts that were burned, the prisoners that were taken, and the Muslims who were put to the sword (i, 36–7, 39–40; ii, 36, 72–9, 82, 92). The truncated *PA* continues in similar mood. In apocalyptic tones the author refers to 'the evil pestilence of the Moors, whom neither the ebb and flow of the sea nor their land protected... their life was wicked, and thus they were defeated. They did not recognize the Lord, and rightly perished. This people was rightly doomed.' (vv. 21–2, 24–6). Elsewhere, the final destruction of the Almoravids is heralded (v. 58); omens predict that 'the evil people was about to perish' (v. 164); and we are assured that once battle was joined the Christian troops would have no qualms about slaughtering their enemies (v. 355). In addition to the vein of hatred for the Muslims that runs throughout the whole poem, the *PA* is suffused with the spirit of crusade. We are told that the bishops of the kingdom summoned the faithful to battle, pardoning the sins of those who joined the expedition, and promising them the reward of both lives, as well as the prospect of earthly riches (vv. 38–45). The peoples of Spain yearned to make war on the Saracens, the poet tells us, as the trumpet of salvation rang out throughout all the regions of the world (v. 53); and when the bishop of Astorga got up to harangue the emperor's weary troops, he assured those present that the gates of Paradise were open to them (v. 382).

The author's decision to divide his account of the reign of Alfonso VII into two separate books, the latter devoted almost wholly to the military struggle against Islam, and against the Almoravids in particular, was therefore a deeply significant act. Warfare against the Muslims

15 See, in this context, McCluskey, 'Malleable Accounts', p. 219.

was presented as 'a distinctive and specially important kingly activity'.[16] But not just a kingly activity. For whereas previous chronicles had centred almost exclusively upon the deeds of the Leonese monarchy, the *CAI* also devotes considerable space to the military activities of the warrior aristocracy of the realm. With only a handful of exceptions, the nobles are presented as loyal and willing servants of the crown, eager to restore Alfonso VII's authority within his own kingdom, extend his power against his external foes, and, above all, take the fight to the Muslims. Thus, of the 111 chapters that make up Book II, very nearly a quarter are devoted to the exploits of Muño Alfonso. With the struggle against the Muslims in the peninsula now being viewed in the same light as the crusading campaigns being waged in the Holy Land, the lay magnates with their economic and military clout were recognised as key players if the campaigns of reconquest in al-Andalus were to be prosecuted successfully.[17]

As a historical record of its times the *CAI* is not without weakness. For one thing, it contains a number of factual errors: for example, the marriage of Alfonso VII to Berengaria of Barcelona (i, 12), the death of Alfonso I of Aragon (i, 58), the grant of Zaragoza to Ramón Berenguer IV of Barcelona (i, 67); the imperial coronation of Alfonso VII (i, 69), and the conquest of Coria (ii, 66) are all misdated; Alfonso VII was 21, not 19, at the time of his succession (i, 1); the see of Pamplona was occupied by Bishop Sancho, not Pedro, in 1128–9 (i, 15); and Viscount Gaston IV of Béarn lost his life in action near Valencia in 1130, not on the battlefield of Fraga (i, 57). Doubtless some of these errors, particularly those of a chronological nature, were the result of copyists' blunders, and the same may be true of the erroneous references to one Count Lope López (i, 82) and to Fernando Fernández de Hita (ii, 18). In other respects, the *CAI*'s coverage of events is occasionally found wanting: thus, its account of the wars

16 R. A. Fletcher, 'Reconquest and Crusade in Spain c. 1050–1150', *Transactions of the Royal Historical Society, 5th series*, 37 (1987), 31–47, at p. 41. It is worthy of note, however, that the chronicler was careful to distinguish between 'good' Muslims who were allies of the Leonese, notably Sayf al-Dawla of Rueda, and those who were the sworn enemies of the Christians, the Almoravids and their supporters: see further below, *CAI*, i, 27–9 and n. 83.

17 These matters are examined in further detail in S. Barton, 'From Tyrants to Soldiers of Christ: the nobility of twelfth-century León–Castile and the struggle against Islam', *Nottingham Medieval Studies*, (forthcoming). On the introduction of crusading ideology into the peninsula, see Fletcher, 'Reconquest and Crusade', 42–7; M. Bull, *Knightly piety and the lay response to the First Crusade: the Limousin and Gascony, c. 970–c. 1130* (Oxford, 1993), pp. 96–114.

waged by Alfonso VII in Portugal and Navarre is confused both as to
the chronology and sequence of the events it describes (i, 73–91);
and the positive 'spin' which the chronicler endeavours to put on
Alfonso VII's clashes with Alfonso I of Aragon in 1127–9 (i, 9–11, 13–
17), and with Afonso Henriques of Portugal in 1141 (i, 83–6) can be
shown from other sources to be less than wholly accurate. Elsewhere,
the large-scale incorporation of Old Testament phraseology by the
author often makes it difficult for us to distinguish straightforward
historical narrative from biblical pastiche (for example, i, 35; ii, 33, 84, 89).

These weaknesses notwithstanding, the importance and overall reliability
of the *CAI* as a historical source are beyond question. Not only do the
broad lines of its narrative concord with what can be reconstructed
from other narrative and documentary evidence, but there is a whole
wealth of incidental detail which can be shown to be accurate: it can,
for example, be demonstrated that Osorio Martínez *was* elevated to
comital rank soon after the aborted siege of Coria in 1138, as the
chronicler states (ii, 43), and that Pedro Alfonso achieved the same
rank early in 1148, shortly after his return from the Almería campaign (*PA*, v. 132); Bishop Pedro Domínguez was indeed killed during
the siege of Cordoba on 24 June 1146 (ii, 106); and far from amount-
ing to a conventional description which owes very little to actual
historical fact, as has been claimed, the catalogue of the lay magnates
who took part in the Almería campaign given in the *PA* can be shown
from documentary sources to be wholly accurate.[18]

The question of the authorship of the *CAI* has generated considerable,
yet inconclusive, scholarly debate. Various candidates have been put
forward (and subsequently rejected), including the secretary of Peter
the Venerable of Cluny, Pierre de Poitiers[19], Rodrigo Jiménez de Rada,
archbishop of Toledo (1209–47)[20], and Julián Pérez, the fictitious
creation of the seventeenth-century arch-forger Román de la Higuera.[21]
The dominant tendency among recent scholarship, however, has
been to attribute the work to Bishop Arnaldo of Astorga (1144–52),
who is mentioned both at the end of the prose section of the chronicle

18 Salvador Martínez, 'Poema de Almería', pp. 180–1; cf. Barton, *Aristocracy*, p. 178.

19 A. Ferrari, 'El Cluniacense Pedro de Poitiers y la *Chronica Adefonsi Imperatoris* y
   Poema de Almería', BRAH 153 (1963), 153–204. Ferrari's thesis has been ably
   demolished by Salvador Martínez, 'Poema de Almería', pp. 87–108.

20 F. Sota, *Chronica de los Príncipes de Asturias y Cantabria* (Madrid, 1681), p. 559. The
   attribution was rejected by Sánchez Belda, *Chronica*, pp. xvi–xvii.

21 *CAI* (ed. Maya Sánchez), p. 114.

(ii, 108) and at the end of its poetic colophon (vv. 374–86).[22] However, important doubts have recently been raised on that score. Peter Linehan has conjectured, rather, that the prose section of the *CAI* may in fact have been refashioned and interpolated by 'a patriotic Toledan', active during the latter part of the reign of Alfonso VIII of Castile (1158–1214), who was also responsible for tacking the poem about the Almería campaign onto the unfinished chronicle.[23]

The *CAI* itself provides us with only a handful of clues as to the author's background. First of all, given his providential view of history, his intimate knowledge of the Scriptures, and his frequent references to hymn-singing (for example, i, 70; ii, 34, 59, 75), we may safely assume that we are dealing with a cleric (a bishop, perhaps, given his extensive knowledge of Leonese court and military activities), and a cultured one at that. Second, it appears more than likely that our author was a contemporary, or at least a near-contemporary, to most of the events he described. True, as we have seen, the chronicler is guilty of a number of factual errors (not all of which may be ascribed to scribal blunders), and his recollection of events is sometimes hazy to say the least. Yet, although, in a verbal echo of the introduction to the Gospel of St Luke, the author declares that his account is based upon what he has learned and heard 'from those who witnessed them' (i, Preface), the detail and immediacy of many of the sections of the prose *CAI* – from the account of the aborted siege of Coria in 1138 (ii, 40–4) to the description of the nuptials of the Infanta Urraca with King García of Navarre in 1144 (i, 92–4) – strongly suggest that, if not necessarily an eye-witness, the chronicler was at least writing soon after the events he narrated. Similarly, the lengthy verse description of the preliminaries to the Almería campaign, and of the nobles who took part, gives the impression of having been penned by someone who had first-hand knowledge of the campaign, or who may even have accompanied the military expedition south. Then there are the opening lines of the *PA* itself to consider, in which the author declares: 'Sages have written of the wars of the kings of old, and we

22 The attribution first appears in J. Ferreras, *Synopsis histórica chronológica de España*, XVI (Madrid, 1775), appendix, p. 10. See also, Sánchez Belda, *Chronica*, pp. xvii–xxi; Ubieto Arteta, 'Sugerencias', 321–6; Salvador Martínez, 'Poema de Almería', pp. 109–22; A. Quintana Prieto, *El obispado de Astorga en el siglo XII* (Astorga, 1985), pp. 295–9; Pérez González, *Crónica*, pp. 24–5.

23 P. Linehan, review of *Chronica Hispana saeculi XII. Part I*, in *Journal of Theological Studies* 43 (1992), 731–7.

too must write of the famous battles of our Emperor, for they are anything but tedious. If it please the Emperor, let the writer be granted the greatest facilities so that he can recount the battles to come' (vv. 5–9). If we take these verses at their face value, the inference is clearly that Alfonso VII was still alive at the time of the poem's composition. We can therefore narrow down the date of the composition of the *CAI* to some time between the end of the Almería campaign in 1147 and the emperor's death in 1157. Moreover, the fact that the author omits to make any reference to the death of the Empress Berengaria in February 1149, has led Antonio Ubieto Arteta to conclude that the *CAI* must have been substantially completed by that date. [24]

There are other indications in the text which may tell us something about the background and attitudes of its author. On the one hand, the *CAI* displays clear Leonese sympathies. The chronicler knew and admired the royal city of León (i, 92–4; *PA*, vv. 79–99), expressed admiration and praise for some of the leading members of the Leonese aristocracy (i, 2, 16; ii, 18, 42–4; *PA*, vv. 100–13) and regarded with evident satisfaction the 'taming' of Castile by Alfonso VII (*PA*, vv. 150–7). Moreover, his references to the frontier region 'which is situated beyond the River Duero' (i, 5), and to the region of the Transierra (*trans Serram*) (ii, 1, 7, 13, 20, 25, 49, 50, 51), that is, the territory between the Sierra de Guadarrama and the River Tagus, appear to reflect the vantage point of somebody writing in the north of the kingdom. None the less, the author is sometimes rather less than well-informed about political and military events in the north of the peninsula. In particular, his uncertain knowledge of Castilian affairs, and his ambivalent attitude towards the Castilians in the *PA*, demonstrate that he could not possibly have been of Castilian extraction. By contrast, the chronicler was extremely well-acquainted with the topography of the city and region of Toledo (for example, ii, 3–4, 62–3, 74), and was remarkably knowledgeable about the feats of arms of the military leaders of that region.

It is possible that the author of the *CAI* was not a native of the Leonese kingdom at all. It has been conjectured that the chronicler may have been one of the many French clerics who entered the Iberian realms during the twelfth century, and that he perhaps served

24 Ubieto Arteta, 'Sugerencias', 325.

as a monk at the Cluniac abbey of Sahagún.[25] However, two considerations militate against such a suggestion. First, the incorporation into the *CAI* of a sizeable number of lexical items of Hispano-Arabic origin (*alcaydes, adalid, azecutis, azemelias,* etc.) including four (*algaras, alcaceres, celatas,* and the placename *Jerez,*) which the author explicitly refers to as being of *nostra lingua,* would appear to indicate a peninsular writer.[26] Second, if not overtly Francophobic in the manner of the author of the *Historia Silense,* the chronicler displays a clear ambivalence towards Alfonso VII's trans-Pyrenean allies (*PA,* vv. 337–60). On the other hand, his evident admiration for the Catalans Gaucelm de Ribas (ii, 35), Viscount Reverter of Barcelona (ii, 11, 101–3), Count Ponç de Cabrera (*PA,* vv. 176–98) and Count Ermengol VI of Urgel (*PA,* vv. 272–8), not to mention his relatively detailed knowledge of Mediterranean geography (ii, 9, 107), suggest that our author might well have been of Catalan origin. Perhaps, Antonio Ubieto Arteta has speculated, he was a cleric attached to the court of Count Ramón Berenguer III of Barcelona who took up residence in León at the time of marriage of the count's daughter Berengaria to Alfonso VII in 1127.[27]

These clues do not take us very far. More to the point, if our author *were* a Catalan churchman, how is it possible to reconcile his intimate knowledge of the Toledan frontier with his Leonese sympathies and viewpoint? At this point let us consider the figure of Bishop Arnaldo of Astorga, who has been linked by a number of scholars to the authorship of the *CAI.*[28] Several factors have encouraged such an identification: the bishop features at the end of both the prose chronicle and its poetic continuation; the Astorgan prelate was a regular visitor to the court of Alfonso VII (including the royal wedding celebrations of 1144) and was well-rewarded by the emperor for his loyal service; it was Arnaldo who in 1146 was dispatched as the Leonese monarch's special envoy to the counts of Barcelona and

25 Sánchez Belda, *Chronica,* pp. xix-xx. On the possible Sahagún connection, see Salvador Martínez, '*Poema de Almería*', pp. 109–22. On the monastery of Sahagún, see above *HS,* ch. 71, n. 86; Pelayo, *Chronicon,* p. 89, n. 99.

26 See the discussion in R. Wright, 'Twelfth-century Metalinguistics in the Iberian Peninsula (and the *Chronica Adefonsi Imperatoris*)', in *Early Ibero-Romance* (Newark, Delaware, 1994), 277–88, at pp. 282–6.

27 Ubieto Arteta, 'Sugerencias', 326. On the prominent role played by Catalan churchmen in the so-called 'Europeanization' of the Leonese church, see D. W. Lomax, 'Catalans in the Leonese Empire', *Bulletin of Hispanic Studies* 59 (1982), 191–7.

28 See above, n. 22.

Montpellier with the task of concerting an anti-Muslim coalition for the forthcoming attack on Almería; and charter evidence confirms that, just as the *PA* tells us, the bishop was present with Alfonso VII's army during the crusading campaign of 1147.[29] Unfortunately, the background of Bishop Arnaldo cannot be established with any certainty. His name, which is neither Leonese nor Castilian, suggests a French or a Catalan origin: Luis Sánchez Belda and H. Salvador Martínez plumped for the former;[30] Antonio Ubieto Arteta and Augusto Quintana Prieto for the latter.[31] Quintana Prieto went further, speculating that Arnaldo of Astorga was the same priest of the diocese of Gerona 'skilled in composing verse' who was active in 1088 and who must have travelled to León in the entourage of Queen Berengaria in 1127.[32] But this hypothesis may be challenged on numerous counts: Arnaldo was an extremely common name in a Catalan context and there is not a shred of evidence to demonstrate that the priest of Gerona and the bishop of Astorga were one and the same man; there is likewise no evidence that a priest of that name accompanied Berengaria of Barcelona to León in 1127; and even if he had done, and had subsequently been elevated to the see of Astorga, the priest of Gerona would presumably have been well into his eighties at the very least by the time of the Almería crusade.

Alternatively, and rather more plausibly one would suggest, there is the possibility that Bishop Arnaldo had served at the abbey of San Servando in Toledo prior to his election to the see of Astorga. The fortress-monastery at San Servando, which stood on the south bank of the Tagus, protecting the bridge that led to the Puerta de Alcántara, had been founded, or rather refounded, by King Alfonso VI, who on 11 March 1088 granted the monastery to the Holy See with the proviso that thereafter it be administered by the abbot of the Benedictine house of St Victor of Marseilles.[33] St Victor could boast over a dozen daughter-houses in Catalonia and it is likely that the earliest inmates of San Servando hailed from one or more of these

---

29 For a detailed study of the career of Bishop Arnaldo, see Quintana Prieto, *Obispado, siglo XII*, pp. 251–300.

30 See above, n. 25.

31 Ubieto Arteta, 'Sugerencias', 321–6; Quintana Prieto, *Obispado, siglo XII*, pp. 253–5.

32 Quintana Prieto, *Obispado, siglo XII*, pp. 253–5.

33 F. Fita, 'El monasterio toledano de San Servando en la segunda mitad del siglo XI: estudio crítico', *BRAH* 49 (1906), 280–331, at pp. 281–3. On the subsequent history of San Servando, see J. F. Rivera Recio, *La iglesia de Toledo en el siglo XII (1086–1208)*, II (Toledo, 1976), pp. 153–70.

institutions.[34] However, their tenure proved short-lived. In 1109 the monks were forced to flee the house when it was attacked and destroyed during the Almoravid siege of Toledo (ii, 2). Four years later, Queen Urraca restored the monastery and placed it under the authority of the church of Toledo, only for Alfonso VII to reaffirm the affiliation of San Servando to St Victor of Marseilles in 1129.[35] Between at least 1127 and 1143, the community of San Servando was ruled by its prior, Arnaldo, who was granted two generous endowments by Alfonso VII, in 1136 and 1143 respectively.[36] After 22 January 1143, however, Prior Arnaldo disappears from the record. His namesake, Arnaldo, bishop of Astorga, had been installed in that see by late February 1144, presumably at royal behest.[37] The chronology dovetails rather too neatly to be dismissed as mere coincidence; the most logical conclusion to be drawn is that the new incumbent of the Astorgan see was none other than Arnaldo of San Servando.

To sum up, although we cannot be sure who composed the *CAI* there is none the less a body of circumstantial evidence to attribute the work to Bishop Arnaldo of Astorga. If, as appears likely, the prelate had served previously as prior of the monastery of San Servando, he would have been resident in Toledo for nigh on two decades until his elevation to the see of Astorga in 1144, and would doubtless have been well-informed about military operations in the Tagus valley and beyond. After his transfer to Astorga, Bishop Arnaldo became a leading court figure who played an important diplomatic and military role in helping to bring the crusading plans of Alfonso VII to fruition, and who, given the ample rewards he received in return, had good reason to hold the emperor in particular esteem.[38] One can easily

34 A. M. Mundó, 'Monastic movements in the East Pyrenees', in *Cluniac Monasticism in the Central Middle Ages*, ed. N. Hunt (London, 1971), 98–122, at pp. 111–18. It is worthy of note that in a charter of San Servando issued in July 1148, some sixty years after its foundation, none of the monks who witnessed appear to have been of Leonese–Castilian birth, and one of them – the monk Carbonell – was definitely of Catalan origin: F. J. Hernández (ed.), *Los Cartularios de Toledo: catálogo documental* (Madrid, 1985), no. 62.

35 J. A. García Luján (ed.), *Privilegios reales de la catedral de Toledo (1086–1462)*, 2 vols (Toledo, 1982), II, no. 4; M. Guérard (ed.), *Cartulaire de l'abbaye de Saint-Victor de Marseille*, 2 vols (Paris, 1857), II, no. 830.

36 On the priorship of Arnaldo, see Hernández (ed.), *Los Cartularios*, nos 27, 31, 34, 37, 42, 44–5; Rivera Recio, *La iglesia*, II, pp. 162–4.

37 Quintana Prieto, *Obispado*, siglo XII, p. 255.

38 For examples of the largess granted by Alfonso VII to Bishop Arnaldo and the see of Astorga, see Quintana Prieto, *Obispado*, siglo XII, pp. 679–81.

imagine why such a bishop might have been prompted to pen a pane-gyric of the characteristics of the *CAI*.

We can take this hypothesis a stage further. If Arnaldo of San Servando/ Astorga *was* the author of the *CAI*, one is led to wonder where he would have been educated before taking over the priorship of San Servando, for given its turbulent early history and limited resources he is hardly likely to have acquired his book-learning at the Toledan monastery. Instead, the likelihood is that Arnaldo would have been recruited from one of St Victor's daughter-houses in Catalonia. Among these, by far the most prominent was the abbey of Ripoll. By the twelfth century Ripoll had already firmly established itself as one of the premier seats of learning in the Latin West. Home to a splendid library, the monastery had produced a distinguished school of writers working in such fields as mathematics, science and music.[39] But Ripoll also stood out among the monastic houses of the Iberian peninsula for both the quantity and quality of the poetry its monks composed.[40] When the author of the *PA* (vv. 233–4) made reference to those who sang of the deeds of El Cid, he may well have had in mind the *Carmen Campi Doctoris* (*c.* 1083), a Latin hymn of praise to Rodrigo Díaz displaying classical and ecclesiastical resonances, then held in the library of Ripoll.[41] This is pure speculation, of course. But if the monk, and later bishop, Arnaldo had served his education within the hallowed walls of Ripoll, it might go some way towards explaining why it was that the author of the *CAI*, when he came to narrate the crusade to Almería, had the technical ability and the cultural background to pen the ambitious and vibrant poetic celebration that he did.[42]

39 The classic guide remains R. Beer, 'Die Handschriften des Klosters Santa Maria de Ripoll', *Sitzungsberichte der Philosophisch–historiche Klasse der Kaiserlichen Akademie der Wissenschaften in Wien* 155 (1908), III. Abhandlung; 158 (1908), II. Abhandlung.

40 See L. Nicolau D'Olwer, 'L'escola poètica de Ripoll en els segles X–XIII', *Anuari del Institut d'Estudis Catalans* 6 (1915–20), 3–84.

41 A possibility raised by R. Wright, *Late Latin and Early Romance in Spain and Carolingian France* (Liverpool, 1982), p. 232; and Fletcher, *The Quest for El Cid*, p. 190. There is a detailed study of the *Carmen Campi Doctoris* by R. Wright, 'The first poem on the Cid – the *Carmen Campi Doctoris*', in *Papers of the Liverpool Latin Seminar*, II, ed. F. Cairns (Liverpool, 1979), 213–48; repr., with an updating postscript, in Wright, *Early Ibero-Romance*, pp. 221–64.

42 Nevertheless, Salvador Martínez emphasises the technical inferiority of the *PA* to the Ripoll compositions: '*Poema de Almería*', pp. 247, 266.

Chronica Adefonsi Imperatoris
(The Chronicle of the Emperor Alfonso)

HERE BEGINS THE CHRONICLE OF THE EMPEROR ALFONSO

PREFACE

Forasmuch as the record of past events, which is composed[1] by historians
and handed down to posterity in writing, makes the memory of kings,
emperors, counts, nobles and other heroes live anew, I have resolved
that the best thing I can do is to describe the deeds of the Emperor
Alfonso, just as I have learned and heard of them from those who
witnessed them. In particular those things which omnipotent God
worked through him and with him so that the salvation of the people
of Christ *in the midst of the earth*[2] might be achieved, starting with the
beginning of his reign, which commenced after the death of Queen
Urraca, the daughter of King Alfonso and Queen Constance[3], as will
become clear in what follows.[4]

BOOK ONE

1. It is to be noted, therefore, that Queen Urraca died on 15 March in
the Era 1164 [= AD 1126], after she had reigned for sixteen years,
eight months and seven days.[5] She was buried with honour in the city
of León alongside her ancestors in the royal pantheon[6]. Alfonso, her
son by Duke Raymond[7], by then a young man of 19 years old[8], who
with God's dispensation reigned on the day after his mother died, like

---

1 There is a lacuna at this point in most of the manuscripts, with the exception of
  MSS *A* (BN MS 1505) and *L* (BN MS 1279), which insert *semper* and *scripte*
  respectively; the latter is rendered here.

2 Psalm lxxiv.12.

3 See above, Pelayo, *Chronicon*, p. 87, nn. 80–1.

4 The Preface contains unmistakable echoes of Luke i.1–3.

5 All the manuscripts give the queen's death as occurring on *idus martii* (15 March),
  but this is probably the result of an earlier copyist's error. Other sources (including
  Urraca's own epitaph in León cathedral) state that she died on 8 March, that is,
  exactly sixteen years, eight months and seven days after her accession to the
  throne, just as the chronicler states: see Sánchez Belda, *Chronica*, pp. 4–5, n. 1.

6 A reminiscence of II Kings ix.28. The pantheon of the Leonese royal dynasty was
  housed in the monastery of San Isidoro de León. However, Urraca's father, Alfonso
  VI, chose to be buried in the abbey of Sahagún.

7 See above Pelayo, *Chronicon*, p. 87, n. 82.

8 In fact, the future Alfonso VII was probably born on 1 March 1105, so he would have
  just turned 21 on the death of his mother: see Sánchez Belda, *Chronica*, p. 5, n. 2.

a promise sent down from on high[9], came to the city of León from where the kingdom is governed, at the time of the blessed Jubilee Year,[10] led by the Lord. As the news of his imminent arrival was announced to the Leonese citizens, Bishop Diego,[11] together with all the clergy and people, set out to greet him with great joy as to their king, and in the church of Saint Mary on the appointed day they proclaimed him king, and they carried the king's banner in accordance with the proper custom.[12]

2. Then, after three days, Count Suero, a man who was firm in judgement and a seeker of truth, who held Astorga, Luna, Gordón with part of the Bierzo, together with Babia, Laciana and all the valley as far as the banks of the River Eo and as far as Cabruñana, came to him with his friends and relatives, namely his brother Alfonso and the latter's son, Pedro Alfonso, whom the king later made a count, together with Rodrigo Vermúdez, Rodrigo González, Pedro Rodríguez and Pedro Braoliz, and many others whose names it would take too long to mention.[13]

9 Luke xxiv.49.

10 The reference to a year of Jubilee has baffled many commentators. It clearly cannot refer to a 'Holy Year', during which the Pope grants a special Indulgence to the faithful on certain conditions, for that practice was not instituted until 1300 by Boniface VIII. Prior to that date, however, the term *iubileus* was used to refer to regularly recurring feasts in honour of a saint. The year 1126 may have been regarded as a Jubilee because it marked the fiftieth anniversary of the beginning of the cathedral and shrine of Santiago de Compostela, or else because the feast day of St James (25 July) fell on a Sunday: see B. Schimmelpfennig, 'Die Anfänge des Heiligen Jahres von Santiago de Compostela im Mittelalter', *JMH* 4 (1978), 285–303, at pp. 290–1; Flórez (ed.), *Chronica Adefonsi Imperatoris*, p. 316. Alternatively, the chronicler may simply have been referring to Lent: Huici Miranda, *Las crónicas latinas*, II, p. 172.

11 Diego, bishop of León (1112/13–1130).

12 The enthronement of Alfonso VII must have taken place soon after the death of Urraca. By the time Archbishop Diego Gelmírez of Santiago de Compostela arrived in León on Holy Saturday (10 April), the king had already left the city: *HC*, p. 384.

13 On Count Suero Vermúdez, see Barton, *Aristocracy*, pp. 300–1. As the chronicler indicates, the principal power-base of Count Suero lay in the mountainous districts in western Asturias and the extreme west and north of the province of León, although he also enjoyed property interests in Galicia, the Tierra de Campos and even as far south as Toro on the Duero. All the other nobles mentioned were prominent figures in the territories of León and the Asturias. On Alfonso Vermúdez, see J. de Salazar Acha, 'Una familia de la alta Edad Media: Los Velas y su realidad histórica', *Estudios Genealógicos y Heráldicos* 1 (1985), 19–64, at pp. 44–7. On Count Pedro Alfonso, see Barton, *Aristocracy*, pp. 273–4. On Rodrigo Vermúdez and Pedro Braoliz, see C. Estepa Díez, *Estructura social de la ciudad de León (siglos XI–XIII)* (León, 1977), pp. 283–4, 296. Pedro Rodríguez is perhaps the Asturian nobleman of that name who was associated with the monastery of Corias and who was a frequent visitor to the court of Urraca: Reilly, *Alfonso VII*, p. 16. The identity of the Rodrigo González mentioned by the chronicler is uncertain: see Sánchez Belda, *Chronica*, p. 252.

Moreover, the count of Toulouse, Alfonso Jordan, a relative of the king, who was the son of Count Raymond [IV] of Toulouse and the Infanta Elvira, the daughter of King Alfonso [VI], was already present with him.[14]

3. After many discussions, the king sent the two counts, Alfonso [Jordan] and Suero [Vermúdez], together with Bishop Diego, to those who were still in rebellion in the towers with the following message: 'I shall receive you in peace and you will be great in my kingdom if you hand over the towers to me without a fight.' But those who were in the towers, after they had sworn an oath many times that they would not give up the towers, asserted that *they would not have him to reign over them*,[15] for their hearts had placed their hopes[16] on the Castilians Count Pedro of Lara and his brother Count Rodrigo González, who preferred to be at war rather than at peace with their king.[17]

4. The next day, the king, with counts Alfonso and Suero and others who had joined him, together with the citizens of the same city, attacked the towers and captured them. However, by a prudent and necessary arrangement, he allowed those who had been captured in the towers to go free, a deed which greatly terrified the king's enemies. When they heard this, all the chief men of the territory of León, that is to say Rodrigo Martínez, his brother Osorio and Ramiro Froilaz, who were later made counts by him, and Count *** Ramírez[18], Pedro López and his brother Lope López, Count Gonzalo Peláez and Pedro Peláez de Valderas, came to him together, and in accordance with the king's

---

14 On the career of Alfonso Jordan, so-called because he was reputedly baptised in the river of that name, see E. Benito Ruano, 'Alfonso Jordan, Conde de Toulouse', in *Estudios sobre Alfonso VI y la reconquista de Toledo* (Toledo, 1987), 83–98; Sánchez Belda, *Chronica*, pp. 222–3. In 1125 the count had undertaken a pilgrimage to Santiago de Compostela, which might explain his presence with Alfonso VII in March of the following year. On the Infanta Elvira Alfonso, see above Pelayo, *Chronicon*, pp. 87–8 and n. 91.

15 Luke xix.14, 27.

16 There is an echo here of Susanna 35.

17 On the Castilian counts of Lara, Pedro and Rodrigo González, see J. González, *El reino de Castilla en la época de Alfonso VIII*, 3 vols (Madrid, 1960), I, pp. 265–8, 260–2; Barton, *Aristocracy*, pp. 280, 292–3. By the 'towers' of León the author was referring to the royal fortress of that city; during the twelfth century the castellan of León was customarily styled *tenens turres Legionis*. Estepa Díez, *Estructura social*, pp. 439–45.

18 All the manuscripts omit the first name of this nobleman. However, no count of León or Castile bore the patronymic Ramírez during the reign of Alfonso VII; it is clearly the result of a copyist's error.

wishes they made peace with him.[19] ***[20] Gonzalo Peláez, who was lord of the region of Asturias, [made peace with him and] was made a count by him; he was accompanied by the most distinguished among all the knights of Asturias and many [others who are not] named.[21]

5. Then the king went to Zamora and had a meeting at Ricobayo with Teresa, queen of the Portuguese, and with Count Fernando, and he made peace with them for a fixed period of time.[22] García Iñiguez, who held Cea, Diego Muñoz de Saldaña, Rodrigo Vélaz, count of Galicia, who held Sarria, Count Gutierre, the brother of Count Suero, who had made peace with the king in Galicia, together with the sons of Count Pedro Froilaz, among whom were Rodrigo, who was later made count by him, and also Velasco and García and Vermudo, who held great lordships[23] in Galicia, together with Count Gómez Núñez, Fernando Yáñez and Archbishop Diego of the see of Compostela, and many other bishops and abbots of Galicia, came before the king in Zamora and with humble devotion they placed themselves under his authority.[24] In the same manner, all the frontier region which is situated beyond the River Duero was placed under the king's authority by the hands of its magnates.

19 On the careers of the counts Gonzalo Peláez, Osorio Martínez, Pedro López, Ramiro Froilaz and Rodrigo Martínez, see Barton, *Aristocracy*, pp. 259, 271–2, 281, 288–9 and 294–5 respectively. On Lope López, see Sánchez Belda, *Chronica*, p. 240; Reilly, *Alfonso VII*, pp. 187–8. On Pedro Peláez de Valderas, see Sánchez Belda, *Chronica*, pp. 247–8. In 1126 Gonzalo Peláez had yet to be awarded the rank of count.

20 There is a lacuna at this point in all the manuscripts.

21 There are further lacunae here, with the exception of MS *A*, the renderings from which are placed within square brackets.

22 On Teresa of Portugal, see below i, 73. Ricobayo lies about 20 kilometres west of Zamora close to the modern border of Portugal. The Count Fernando referred to here is Count Fernando Pérez de Traba, Teresa's consort between *c.* 1120 and 1128, on whom see Barton, *Aristocracy*, pp. 241–2.

23 *honores*: see above, *HR*, p. 117, n. 62. Throughout my translation, *honor* is rendered as 'lordship'.

24 With the exception of García Iñiguez and Diego Muñoz, both of whom held tenancies on the borderlands between León and Castile, the nobles listed here comprised the secular élite of Galician society. The only absentee of any consequence was Count Muño Peláez, lord of Monterroso. On counts Gómez Núñez, Gutierre Vermúdez, Pedro Froilaz, Rodrigo Pérez and Rodrigo Vélaz, see Barton, *Aristocracy*, pp. 256, 262, 278–9, 297–8 and 299. On García Iñiguez and Diego Muñoz, see Sánchez Belda, *Chronica*, pp. 231–2, 227–8; Reilly, *Alfonso VII*, pp. 206–7. On Fernando Yánez, and García and Vermudo Pérez, see Sánchez Belda, *Chronica*, pp. 229–30, 232–3, 257; Barton, *Aristocracy*, pp. 36–7, 175–8, 316–17; Reilly, *Alfonso VII*, pp. 188–9. On the career of Archbishop Diego Gelmírez (1100–40), see Fletcher, *Saint James's Catapult*.

6. When the Castilian counts Pedro de Lara and his brother Rodrigo González, who dwelled in the land which is called Asturias de Santillana[25], and Jimeno Iñiguez who held Coyanza[26] in the region of León, saw that the powers of the king were growing day by day, they became very afraid and, whether they wanted to or not, they made their way to the king to speak with him of peace. And they made peace with him, although they did so deceitfully on account of the king of Aragon[27], whom they esteemed above all others.

7. The king of Aragon held Carrión, Castrojeriz, and other fortified castles in the region, the city of Burgos, together with Villafranca-Montes de Oca, Nájera, Belorado and other fortifications, and many moated and walled towns in the area, all of which he had seized from Queen Urraca through war and terror.[28] From these he violently attacked others, for he hated the Castilians, who supported the Leonese king and loved peace. Other Castilian magnates, apart from those named above, came to the king of León, even though the Aragonese king was attacking them, as has been described, and they made peace with him in their hearts. Among them were Rodrigo Gómez, who was later made count by him, and his brother Diego, Lope Díaz, who later received the title of count with a lordship, García Garcés, together with Gutierre Fernández, his brother Rodrigo, Pedro González and his brother Rodrigo de Villaescusa.[29]

8. However, *when* the citizens of Carrión and Burgos and those who lived in Villafranca, *saw that they had made themselves odious to* the king of León, who was their natural lord, *they sent*[30] messengers to him so that he might come quickly to recover their towns. After he had come and retaken them as he had promised, everyone submitted to him. But the castle of Burgos was held by an Aragonese knight named Sancho Arnaldi. Since he was unwilling to deliver the castle peacefully to the king, it was attacked by the Jews and Christians and he was wounded

25 Roughly conterminous with the modern province of Santander.
26 The modern Valencia de Don Juan, about 35 kilometres due south of the city of León.
27 Alfonso I 'the Battler' of Aragon (1104–34).
28 All the places named lay on the pilgrim road to Santiago de Compostela as it passed through Castile.
29 On counts Lope Díaz and Rodrigo Gómez, see Barton, *Aristocracy*, pp. 263, 291. On García Garcés, and Gutierre and Rodrigo Fernández, see Sánchez Belda, *Chronica*, pp. 232, 236–8, 251; González, *El reino de Castilla*, I, pp. 294–5, 321–4; Barton, *Aristocracy*, pp. 32–3; Reilly, *Alfonso VII*, pp. 186–7, 189–91.
30 I Chronicles xix.6.

by an arrow, as a result of which he died. Consequently, the castle which he held was captured and delivered to the king.[31] When he heard this, the king of Aragon became angry and troubled.

9. In the month of July in the Era 1165 [= AD 1127], the king of Aragon went to Castile to fortify Nájera, Castrojeriz and many other castles which were in the area. But it was of no use to him. For when he heard of this, Alfonso, king of León, quickly ordered the voices of the royal criers to ring out in Galicia and Asturias and throughout the whole of the land of León and Castile. When he had mustered a great army, he set out to confront him. They drew up their troops on either side between Castrojeriz and Hornillos at the place called Valle de Támara.[32] But Count Pedro de Lara, who stood in the vanguard of the king of León, did not wish to fight against the king of Aragon because his heart was with the latter and he had disagreements with the former.[33]

10. However, the king of Aragon realised that the Lord was with the king of León and he retreated so as not to have to fight with him and he returned to his camp. And when he realised that there was no way that he could return to his land without giving battle, he sent his chief men, namely Gaston of Béarn and Centulle of Bigorre[34], as ambassadors to the king of León to whom they said: 'Your uncle[35] the king

31 The castle of Burgos was captured on 30 April 1127, according to a charter issued by Alfonso VII on that day: L. Serrano, *El obispado de Burgos, y Castilla primitiva desde el siglo V al XIII*, 3 vols (Madrid, 1935), III, no. 87. As the chronicler indicates, Burgos, like many other urban centres on the pilgrim-road to Compostela, contained a sizeable Jewish community. The loyalty of the Jews of Burgos to the Leonese crown had similarly been demonstrated in 1113, at the height of the war with Alfonso I of Aragon: see *HC*, p. 138.

32 Hornillos del Camino lies about 18 kilometres due west of Burgos on the pilgrim road to Compostela. From Hornillos, Castrojeriz lies a similar distance to the south-west. On 31 July 1127 Alfonso I was at Isar, about 3 kilometres downstream from Hornillos: see below, n. 38.

33 *sermonem cum illo habebat*: on this interpretation of the chronicler's words see Pérez González, *Crónica*, p. 67, n. 23.

34 Viscount Gaston IV of Béarn and his half-brother Viscount Centulle II of Bigorre had taken part in the siege and capture of Zaragoza in 1118 and had been well rewarded by Alfonso I for their efforts, Gaston receiving the lordship of Zaragoza itself, and subsequently those of Huesca, Monreal de Ariza and Uncastillo, and Centulle that of Tarazona. When Gaston was subsequently killed in 1130, his lordships at Zaragoza and Uncastillo also passed to Centulle: see Ubieto Arteta, *Los 'Tenentes'*, pp. 202, 224; Bull, *Knightly piety*, pp. 99–103; Stalls, *Possessing the Land*, pp. 20–1, 124–9, 167–8.

35 Alfonso VII and Alfonso I of Aragon were related by common descent from Sancho III 'the Great' of Navarre: see Pérez González, *Crónica*, p. 67, n. 24.

of Aragon says to you: "Allow me to go peacefully to my land, and I *will not turn to the right hand nor to the left,*[36] but I will walk along the straight road, and I will swear to give to you all the castles and cities which I hold and which ought to serve you by hereditary right. And within forty days, I will give back to you all your kingdom, just as it was under your fathers, so that there may be peace and rectitude between you and me."'

11. When he heard this, the king of León *perceived that they spake deceitfully unto him*[37] and he did not wish to hear the words of the ambassadors. But having deliberated with his nobles, he acquiesced to the words of the supplicant. The king of Aragon swore with many great men of his court that everything would be carried out just as he had said earlier, and he was allowed to go to his land in peace.[38] But the king of Aragon broke his oath and plundered the areas he went through, and having lied he became a perjurer.

12. In the month of November in the Era 1166 [= AD 1128], Alfonso, the lord king of Léon, took as his wife, who travelled by sea,[39] the daughter of Ramón, count of Barcelona, whose name was Berengaria.[40] She was a very beautiful and extremely graceful young girl who loved chastity and truth and all God-fearing people. He married her at

36 Numbers xx.17, xxii.26; Deuteronomy v.32, xvii.11, xxviii.14; Joshua i.7; I Samuel vi.12; II Samuel ii.19; II Kings xxii.2; II Chronicles xxxiv.2; Proverbs iv.27; Isaiah ix.20, xxx.21.

37 I Maccabees xiii.17.

38 The agreement is referred to in a charter of Alfonso I, dated 31 July 1127, drawn up at Isar 'in illo rigo de Fornellos, ubi fuerunt factas illas iuras per illos conuenios quos fecimus ego predictus rex Adefonsus et rex Adefonsus de Castella': Lema Pueyo (ed.), *Colección diplomática*, no. 176. The precise terms of the treaty of Támara are glossed over by our chronicler, but a fourteenth-century Aragonese source, the *Crónica de San Juan de la Peña*, later claimed that the agreement provided that Alfonso I was to retain the territories from the Ebro up to near the city of Burgos and that he would renounce the imperial title which the kings of León claimed for their exclusive use. These matters are discussed in depth by R. Menéndez Pidal, 'Sobre un tratado de paz entre Alfonso el Batallador y Alfonso VII', *BRAH* 111 (1943), 115–31; and J. M. Lacarra, 'Alfonso el Batallador y las paces de Támara', *Estudios de Edad Media de la Corona de Aragón* 3 (1947–48), 461–73. Cf. the comments by Reilly, *Alfonso VII*, pp. 21–3.

39 This is not inconceivable if Alfonso I of Aragon had refused to allow the princess free passage across his territory.

40 Count Ramón Berenguer III of Barcelona (1097–1131). The nuptials between Alfonso VII and Berengaria were in fact celebrated in November 1127. The previous summer, one Pedro, archdeacon of the church of Barcelona, had travelled throughout Castile securing oaths of allegiance to Berengaria as queen of León–Castile from the leading magnates of the region: Reilly, *Alfonso VII*, pp. 19–20.

Saldaña and, by the grace of God, he fathered sons by her.[41] In everything that the king did he first consulted with his wife and with his sister the Infanta Sancha,[42] who possessed great and prudent judgement, and all their advice turned out favourably for the king and they acted with foresight in many matters. They were very God-fearing, builders of churches of God and monasteries of monks, protectors of orphans[43] and poor people, and lovers of all God-fearing people.

13. In the Era 1167 [= AD 1129], *when the year was expired*,[44] the king of Aragon, having again gathered a great number of knights, foot-soldiers and crosssbowmen, came to the frontier at Medinaceli, besieged Morón and began to attack the castles and towns that were in the area.[45] The inhabitants of Medinaceli and Morón, seeing that they were being overwhelmed, sent messengers to the king of León, saying: 'The king of Aragon is besieging us and wishes to subdue us, our wives and sons and all our property by violence. Come and free us from his hands and we will serve you surely.' When he heard this, the king replied to the messengers: 'Go and tell the inhabitants of Medinaceli and Morón: "*Be strong*, fight and be *of good courage*,[46] and I will come to your aid without delay and with God's help I will set you free."'

41 Berengaria bore Alfonso VII at least four sons and two daughters: Raimundo, Sancho (later king of Castile, 1157–8), Fernando (later king of León, 1157–88), García, Constanza and Sancha. A fifth son, Alfonso, may also have been born to the couple: Reilly, *Alfonso VII*, pp. 27–8, n. 38. The king's second wife, the Polish noblewoman, Rica, whom he married in 1152, bore two further children: Sancha and Fernando. In addition, the monarch had at least two illegitimate children: Urraca, the daughter of Guntroda Pérez; and another unnamed daughter whom he fathered by Countess Urraca Fernández, the widow of Count Rodrigo Martínez: see below i, 32, 91–2; M. Mañueco Villalobos and J. Zurita Nieto (eds), *Documentos de la Iglesia Colegial de Santa María la Mayor de Valladolid*, 3 vols (Valladolid, 1917–20), I, no. xxxv.

42 On the Infanta Sancha Raimúndez (d. 1159), García Calles, *Doña Sancha*; Reilly, *Alfonso VII*, pp. 139–41.

43 Among them Urraca Rodríguez, the orphaned daughter of Count Rodrigo González de Lara and the Infanta Sancha Alfonso, who was brought up in the household of the Infanta Sancha Raimúndez: L. Villar García (ed.), *Documentación medieval de la catedral de Segovia (1115–1300)* (Salamanca, 1990), no. 60.

44 II Chronicles xxxvi.10; I Chronicles xx.1; Leviticus xxv.30; Judges xi.40.

45 Medinaceli, in the valley of the Jalón near the border of the modern provinces of Guadalajara and Soria, was an important staging post on the line of communication that ran northwestwards from Toledo to the Ebro valley. Morón de Almazán lies about 25 kilometres further to the north. Reilly prefers to date these events to 1128, although he concedes that it is possible that some of the events narrated 'stretched well into 1129': Reilly, *Alfonso VII*, p. 26, n. 36.

46 Deuteronomy xxxi.6; Joshua i.18; I Samuel iv.9; I Chronicles xix.13, xxii.13, xxviii.20; II Chronicles xix.11, xxxii.7; Psalms xxvii 14; I Corinthians xvi.13.

14. Having mustered an army from the land of León and Galicia, and a few men from Castile, the king of León gathered together seven hundred brave knights and they assembled at Atienza.[47] But Count Pedro de Lara, his brother Count Rodrigo and their family and friends were unwilling to go to the aid of the king of León. Nevertheless, the king struck camp from Atienza and went to Santiuste and remained there.[48] The next day, having assembled his troops, he went from Santiuste to Morón. When the king of Aragon heard that the king of León was going to fight against him, he retreated from Morón and made his way to Almazán,[49] and he entered that town with all his host and began to fortify it with a great high wall. But the king of León, the day after he came to Morón, drew up his troops and stationed them before Almazán from dawn until dusk.

15. When the king of Aragon saw that those troops were few in number and that the men who were in them were brave and *girded* with *weapons of war*,[50] and he saw himself with many thousands of knights and foot-soldiers, he summoned his nobles and the leaders of the people and the bishops who were with him and asked them for advice as to what he ought to do. Then the bishop of Pamplona, whose name was Pedro,[51] said to the king: 'Lord, if you command me to do so, I shall speak.' And the king answered: 'Speak, sir.' And he said: 'Do you consider that army to be very small? It is not small, but large. For God is with it and God is its defender. He does not claim those things that do not belong to him, but those that are his. He loves peace, he seeks peace: for every lover of peace loves God. With God's help *it is no hard matter for many to be shut up in the hands of a few. For the victory of battle standeth not in the multitude of an host; but strength cometh from heaven.*[52] O King, remember the pact you made last year with the king of León: to give him Castrojeriz, Nájera and all the castles and towns which you took from his mother Queen Urraca, and so to live in peace with him. O King, do not fight with him! For if you fight with him, you will be defeated and killed, and all those who are with you.'

47 Atienza was a strongpoint about 35 kilometres west of Medinaceli.

48 Santiuste is situated about 14 kilometres south-east of Atienza and the same distance to the west of the cathedral city of Sigüenza.

49 Almazán, on the River Duero, about 35 kilometres north of Medinaceli, was another important strongpoint on the route towards the Ebro valley.

50 Deuteronomy i.41; I Chronicles xii.33, 37.

51 The chronicler is mistaken; in 1128–9 the incumbent of the see of Pamplona was Bishop Sancho de Larrosa (1122–42).

52 I Maccabees iii.18–19.

16. When they had heard the bishop's counsel, the king and all his nobles agreed with him, and he was unwilling to fight against the king of León. The latter, seeing that the king of Aragon did not wish to fight with him, sent messengers to him, namely Count Suero, who was a lover of peace and truth and was a faithful friend of the king, and Gonzalo Peláez, the leader of the Asturians, who said to him: 'Our king says this to you: you are aware of all the harm you have caused in Castile and throughout his kingdom, and you know how you swore an oath to him last year to give him the castles and towns which are in your power and ought to be in his. If you do this, there will be peace between you and him; and if you do not do so, fight with him, and to whom the Lord gives victory, let him have the kingdom in peace.'[53] The king replied to them: 'I will not fight with him, neither will I give him the castles nor the towns except *through a mighty hand.*'[54]

17. Then the king of León fortified Morón and Medinaceli and all the castles and towns that were in the area, and all their inhabitants took heart. The king returned to Castile and commanded the counts, nobles and knights that each of them should return home with joy. Everyone who heard that the king of Aragon with his multitude had been besieged by the king of León, glorified God saying: '*His mercy endureth for ever.*'[55] And all the neighbouring peoples who heard this began to fear the king and to obey him. The king of Aragon fortified Almazán and returned to his land, to the city of Jaca,[56] and from that day he never returned to Castile nor to the frontier region,[57] nor did he dare to set his face against the face of the king of León. *Now there was a* great *war* between the warriors of Castile, who supported the king of León, and the men who defended the cause of the king of Aragon. But those who followed the arms of the Leonese were always victorious. The palace of the king of Aragon *waxed weaker and weaker,* while the palace of the king of León, thanks to God, *waxed ever stronger* by the day.[58]

53 This is reminiscent of the words spoken by the messengers sent by Moses to the king of Edom: Numbers xx.14–16.

54 Numbers xx.20; Deuteronomy v.15, vi.21, vii.8, ix.26, xxvi.8; Judges iv.24.

55 See, for example, II Chronicles vii.3, 6; Psalm cvi.1, cvii.1, cxviii.1–4, 29, Jeremiah xxxiii.11; I Maccabees iv.24.

56 The city of Jaca, strategically situated just to south of the Somport pass across the central Pyrenees, was a seat of the kings of Aragon and an important staging-post on one of the two main routes taken by pilgrims to Compostela.

57 *Extremo*; in other words, the region south of the River Duero.

58 II Samuel iii.1. The CAI portrays the events of 1128/9 as a diplomatic triumph for Alfonso VII, when in reality his inability to bring Alfonso I to battle or to achieve the withdrawal of the Aragonese from Castrojeriz and Nájera, not to mention the

18. In the month of January in the Era 1168 [= AD 1130], the king of León went to the city of Palencia and captured Count Pedro de Lara and his son-in-law Count Bertran,[59] because they were opposed to his rule. As a result, Count Rodrigo, and their relatives and friends, immediately rebelled.[60] The king led the counts captive to León and kept them in prison there until they gave up all their castles and towns. After this he sent them away stripped of their lordships. Count Pedro de Lara wished to make war in Castile, but he was unable to, and he made his way to the king of Aragon, who was besieging Bayonne,[61] with the intention of bringing him back to Castile to wage war. But while he was there, the count of Toulouse, whose name was Alfonso Jordan, came to that city in order to defend it. When he became aware of this, Count Pedro challenged the count of Toulouse to *fight together*[62] and they both went out to do battle like two strong lions. Count Pedro was wounded by Count Alfonso's lance and falling from his horse he broke his arm and died a few days later.[63] But the count of Toulouse remained unhurt.

unwillingness of the counts of Lara to come to his aid, must have represented a considerable reverse: Reilly, *Alfonso VII*, p. 27. For his part, Alfonso I had more important fish to fry: in the latter part of 1128 he was engaged in the siege of the nearby Muslim town of Molina de Aragón, which fell to him in December.

59 Count Bertran of Risnel, cousin of Alfonso I of Aragon and half-brother of Alfonso Jordan of Toulouse, had played a leading role in the political affairs of León–Castile since the time of his arrival in the kingdom in 1113. His principal power-base was in the district of Carrión de los Condes, but from 1127 he held the governorship of the city of Burgos on behalf of Alfonso VII: Sánchez Belda, *Chronica*, p. 225; Reilly, *Urraca*, p. 195, 217, 285–6; Reilly, *Alfonso VII*, 165, 172, 205–6. The count's marriage to Elvira Pérez, the illegitimate daughter of Queen Urraca and Count Pedro González de Lara, may have been arranged by Alfonso VII himself: J. A. Fernández Flórez (ed.), *Colección diplomática del monasterio de Sahagún*, IV (1110–99) (León, 1991), no. 1360.

60 The rebellion of 1130 may have been prompted by the birth of a son, the Infante Raimundo, to Alfonso VII and Berengaria. The birth of the male heir and the subsequent confirmation of the legitimacy of his parents' marriage by the ecclesiastical authorities, at the council of Carrión in February 1130, may have decided Count Pedro González to take up arms to protect the rights to the throne of his own son, Fernando Pérez, who had been born of the count's liaison with Queen Urraca: see Reilly, *Alfonso VII*, pp. 29–33.

61 On the River Adour in south-west France. On the siege of Bayonne, see below ch. 50, n. 126.

62 There is an echo here of the account of the duel between David and Goliath in I Samuel xvii.10.

63 According to the *obituario* of Burgos cathedral, the count's death occurred on 16 October 1130: Serrano, *Obispado*, III, p. 390.

19. While this was going on, the king of León ordered Count Rodrigo Martínez and his brother Osorio to go to the land of León and besiege Pedro Díaz who was in rebellion in the castle of Valle with a great mass of knights and foot-soldiers.[64] They went and besieged that castle, but those who were inside hurled many insults at Count Rodrigo and his brother, and the count was unable to subdue them decisively. When he heard this, the king came quickly and ordered his servants to build mantelets, machines and many siege engines[65] around the walls of the castle. Those who were with the king shot many arrows and stones at those who were within and the walls were breached all the way round.

20. When Pedro Díaz saw that he was being utterly overwhelmed, he began to shout and call to the king: 'My lord king, I am the offender against you and I am guilty: I ask you by God, who assists you in everything, not to abandon me, nor my wife nor my children in the hands of Count Rodrigo, but instead to take your revenge on me according to your mercy.' When he heard this, the king was moved to pity, as usual, and he summoned him to his presence, together with Pelayo Froilaz[66] who was with him, and he sent them to his tent; and after a few days, he let them go free. But Pedro Díaz, left to wander in every direction without a king or protector, fell gravely ill and died poor and wretched.

21. Count Rodrigo, having taken charge of the other knights, put some of them in prison until they gave up all their possessions and he obliged others to serve him for many days without payment. But those who had insulted him he had yoked with oxen and made to plough, feed on grass, drink water in troughs and eat straw in a manger. And when he had stripped them of all their wealth, he allowed them to go away wretched and unhappy. When those who were in Coyanza, who supported Jimeno Iñiguez, saw this, they surrendered the town and the castle to the king.

22. After this, the king made his way to Castile and to Asturias de Santillana against Count Rodrigo [González] and against the other

---

64 On Pedro Díaz, see Estepa Díez, *Estructura*, pp. 259–60; Reilly, *Alfonso VII*, p. 193. The castle of Valle (modern Valle de Mansilla) lay about 20 kilometres to the east of the city of León.

65 *uineas et machinas et multa ingenia*. The *CAI* contains several revealing descriptions of contemporary siegecraft: see below, for example, ii, 41–2, 51, 64. Cf. R. Rogers, . *Latin siege warfare in the twelfth century* (Oxford, 1992), ch. 5.

66 On Pelayo Froilaz, see Barton, *Aristocracy*, pp. 73–80.

rebels. He captured their fortified castles, burnt up their estates and had their vineyards and trees cut down.[67] When the count saw that there was no way that he could escape from the king's clutches, either in castles, in mountains or in caves, he sent envoys to the king requesting he come to a meeting with him next to the River Pisuerga, with this condition: that each of them would go with only six knights. The king agreed to this and they immediately met and began to talk. But the king, hearing from the count what it was not permitted for him to hear, was greatly enraged and he seized the count by the neck and the two of them fell from their horses to the ground. When they saw this the count's knights abandoned him and fled shaken with terror.

23. The king seized the count, took him captive and kept him in prison until he surrendered to him all his lordships and castles. Then he sent him away empty handed and without honour.[68] But not long afterwards, the count came to the king, submitted to him and admitted his guilt against him. The king, as always, was most merciful and took pity on him, and granted him Toledo and great lordships along the frontier and in Castile.[69] And that count joined in many battles against the Saracens, killed and took prisoner many of them and seized great booty from their land.

24. In the month of May in the Era 1169 [= AD 1131], the king went to Castrojeriz. Inside the fortress was a mighty knight of the king of Aragon, Ariol Garcés,[70] with a large number of knights and foot-soldiers, who was waging war on a large area of Castile. The king surrounded the castle all the way round with a great wall and palisade, so that none of those who were inside the fortress could go in or out. They were seized by great hunger and thirst and they asked the king for a truce, and sent envoys to their lord, the king of Aragon, asking him to come and free them from the hands of the king of León. But the former did not dare to go nor to set foot in the land of the latter.

---

67 Judith ii.17 (Vulgate); cf. ii, 27 (Apocrypha). The campaign probably took place during the summer of 1130; on 26 August of that year Alfonso VII was in Asturias: Serrano, *Obispado*, III, no. 93.

68 The meaning of *honor* here is ambiguous, perhaps deliberately so.

69 These lordships included Segovia, which the count is reported as holding by 3 February 1133, Aguilar de Campoo and Castilla la Vieja: Barton, *Aristocracy*, pp. 292–3.

70 Ariol Garcés held the tenancy of Castrojeriz from at least October 1116 until its conquest by Alfonso VII in October 1131; his other lordships included that of Logroño in the Rioja between 1127 and 1130: Lema Pueyo (ed.), *Colección diplomática*, nos 75, 184, 231, 238; Ubieto Arteta, *Los 'Tenentes'*, p. 190.

25. When Ariol Garcés and those who were with him saw that they could not rely upon the king of Aragon, that many of them were dying of hunger and thirst, and that six months had already passed since they had been besieged, in the month of October, which is the sixth month after May, he asked the king *to be at one with* him and with his own men. The king *granted* it to them and *when he had put them out of thence*, he installed a garrison in that place.[71]

26. The other castles that were in the area, namely Herrera and Castrillo,[72] surrendered to the king and he drove the foreigners out of them and out of all Castile. *Salvation* and great peace *prospered* in all his kingdom,[73] and all the inhabitants began to build houses, plant vines and all kinds of trees, and to settle all the land which the king of Aragon had destroyed. There was great happiness throughout his kingdom such as there had not been up to that time since the death of his grandfather King Alfonso.

27. At that time there was a Saracen king in Rueda[74] called Zafadola.[75] He was of the most illustrious lineage of the kings of the Hagarenes.[76] All the deeds that had been performed by King Alfonso of León against the king of Aragon resounded in his ears: how our king had besieged him and how the king of Aragon had sworn to give him back his kingdom, had lied and had become a perjurer. When he heard this, King Zafadola summoned his children, wives, *alguaziles*,[77] *alcaides*[78]

71 The siege of Castrojeriz is directly compared to Simon Maccabeus's campaign against Jerusalem: I Maccabees xiii.50. The chronicler's chronology of events is corroborated by a charter of Alfonso VII issued at Castrojeriz on 28 September 1131: AHN, Códices, 1002B, fol. 5r.

72 The identity of these places is uncertain, but likely candidates are Herrera de Valdecañas, about 25 kilometres south of Castrojeriz, close to the road from Burgos to Palencia, and Castrillo de Murcia 10 kilometres to the north-east of Castrojeriz.

73 I Maccabees iii.6.

74 Rueda de Jalón, 35 kilometres west of Zaragoza.

75 Sayf al-Dawla, known to the Christians as Zafadola, was the son of the last of the Huddid rulers of Zaragoza before it was taken over by the Almoravids in 1110.

76 Our chronicler uses the term *Hagarenos*, that is, the descendants of Hagar, Abraham's Egyptian concubine and slave, to denote Muslims of Iberian extraction and to distinguish them from Alfonso VII's arch-enemies, the *Moabitas*, or Berber Almoravids. See also below, n. 83.

77 From the Arabic *al-wazīr*, 'minister, vizier'. In al-Andalus the *alguacil* was a civil governor with responsibility for the administration of a town and its territory; under the Christians the post of *alguacil* carried judicial functions.

78 From the Arabic *al-qā'id*, 'chief, general'. In al-Andalus the term was used to refer to a military commander; the Christians adopted the term to refer to the governor of a town or a castle.

and all his nobles, and he said to them: '*Do ye know* of all the deeds
that have been performed by King Alfonso of León against the king of
Aragon and against his rebels?' *And they said: 'We know.*'[79] And he said
to them: 'What shall we do? For how long shall we be besieged here?'
For indeed they were confined by fear of the Moabites, because the
Moabites had killed all the descendants of the kings of the Hagarenes
and had also taken their kingdom. King Zafadola was confined there
in Rueda together with some of his people, who had sought refuge
with him and were there with him, and he said to them: 'Listen to my
counsel: let us go to the king of León and let us make him king over
us, our lord and friend, for I know that he will rule over the land of
the Saracens, because God in heaven is his deliverer, and *God* on high
is his *help.*'[80] I know that with his assistance my children and I will
recover the other dominions that the Moabites plundered from me,
from my parents and from my people.'

28. When they had heard this, his nobles all said together: 'Great is
your counsel; your advice pleases all of *us well.*'[81] Meanwhile, Zafadola
sent his envoys to the king, saying: 'Send some of your nobles to me
with whom I may come to you in safety.' When he heard this, the
king rejoiced with great happiness and quickly sent to him Count
Rodrigo Martínez and Gutierre Fernández, who was one of the great
nobles of the king, on his behalf. They went to Zafadola in Rueda and
he received them with honour, gave them great gifts and went with
them to the king. Alfonso received him with honour, and made him sit
with him on the royal throne, and ordered that he be given quantities
of innumerable kinds of food. Seeing this, the nobles of King Zafadola
looked on with wonder and said to one other: '*Who is like unto* the king
of León *among the* kings?'[82]

29. After King Zafadola had seen the wisdom and riches of the king
of León and the great peace that there was in his palace and in all his
kingdom, he said to him: '*It was a true report that I heard* about you in
Rueda, *of thy wisdom* and of the mercy that is within you, and of the
peace that there is in your kingdom and of your riches. *Happy are thy
men, happy are these thy* nobles, both those who dwell with you and
those who are in your kingdom.' And Zafadola *gave the king* great gifts

79 Tobit vii.4.
80 Exodus xviii.4.
81 I Maccabees i.13.
82 Exodus xv.11; I Samuel xxvi.15; I Kings iii.13.

and very *precious stones.*[83] He and his sons made themselves knights of the king and promised to *serve* him *all the days of his life*, and he granted Rueda to him.[84] After he had accepted it, King Alfonso gave it to his son King Sancho of Castile. It was settled by the Christians and they began to invoke there the name of the Holy Trinity and the grace of the Holy Spirit; none of the inhabitants had ever known that the name of the Lord had been publicly invoked in Rueda until now. The king of León gave to King Zafadola castles and towns in the land of Toledo, in Extremadura and along the banks of the River Duero. And Zafadola came and lived in them and *served* the king *all the days of his life.*[85]

30. In the Era 1170 [= AD 1132] King Alfonso ordered his counts and nobles that on the appointed day they should gather in Atienza with their troops.[86] When they had already gathered, the king learned that the Asturian Count Gonzalo Peláez had held a meeting with his kinsman Rodrigo Gómez with the intention of rebelling. The king captured Count Rodrigo Gómez, stripped him of his lordship and sent him away.[87] Count Gonzalo fled, whereupon all his noble knights were captured there. The king pursued him into Asturias and ordered that all the captive knights be brought behind him under guard. He found Count Gonzalo in rebellion in Tudela and besieged him there. And the king's knights captured the castle of Gozón and other castles.[88]

83 This passage is strongly influenced by I Kings x.6–10 and II Chronicles ix.3–9. Here, Sayf al-Dawla is likened to the queen of Sheba acknowledging Solomon's virtues. It is striking that such biblical language should have been put into the mouths of 'good' Muslims, which suggests that the author of the *CAI* sometimes preferred to judge different Saracens in terms of their attitudes towards the Leonese, than to denounce Muslims as such.

84 I Kings iv.21.

85 *Ibid.* A substantially similar account of the submission of Sayf al-Dawla is given by the Muslim historian Ibn al-Kardabūs, *Historia de al-Andalus (Kitāb al-Iktifā')*, trans. F. Maíllo Salgado (Madrid, 1986), pp. 145–7. The surrender of Rueda to Alfonso VII probably took place some time after the fall of Castrojeriz in October 1131.

86 It is likely that from Atienza Alfonso VII planned to conduct a new campaign against the Aragonese, either north-east into the districts of Almazán or Soria, or east into that of Rueda de Jalón: Reilly, *Alfonso VII*, p. 38.

87 Count Rodrigo Gómez disappears from court records after 28 May 1132 and may not have been readmitted to the Leonese curia until February 1135. The charters of January 1133 which record his presence with Alfonso VII at Oña are far from reliable: M. Lucas Alvarez, *El reino de León en la Alta Edad Media. Vol. V: Las cancillerías reales (1109–1230)* (León, 1993), p. 128; cf. Reilly, *Alfonso VII*, p. 39, appendix, nos 158–62.

88 The castle of Tudela, by the River Nalón, lay about 10 kilometres south-west of the city of Oviedo; that of Gozón about 25 km to the north, on the Cantabrian coast. On the rebellion of Count Gonzalo Peláez, see Barton, *Aristocracy*, pp. 113–15; Reilly, *Alfonso VII*, pp. 38–42, 46, 58–9.

31. Seeing that the king had captured his knights, in whom he placed his trust, Count Gonzalo made the following agreement with him: they were to be bound by a peace treaty for a whole year; the king was not to wage war on him, nor was the count to plunder the land of the king nor wage war on him. Count Gonzalo gave Tudela and other castles to the king, but the count himself continued in rebellion in Proaza, Buanga and Alba de Quirós, which were very strong castles.[89]

32. While this was going on, the king took a concubine named Guntroda, the daughter of Pedro Díaz and María Ordóñez, who was very beautiful and belonged to the greatest family of the Asturians and Tinians.[90] He fathered by her a daughter called Urraca who was given to the king's sister, the Infanta Sancha, to be weaned and fed.[91]

33. In the seventh year of the reign of Alfonso, king of the Spaniards, son of Count Raymond and the most serene Queen Urraca, in the course of the Era 1171 [= AD 1133], the king, having deliberated with King Zafadola, summoned all the counts, chief men and commanders of his kingdom and *he communicated with them his secret counsel.*[92] He announced that his mind was wholly fixed upon the following: that he would invade the land of the Saracens in order to conquer them and to avenge himself on King Tāshufīn[93] and on the other kings of the Moabites, who had invaded the land of Toledo and had killed many leaders of the Christians, and had razed to the ground the castle of Aceca[94] and had put all the Christians they had found there to the sword. Moreover, Tello Fernández, their leader, along with other

---

89 The three strategic castles of Proaza, Buanga and Alba de Quirós, situated in the valley of the Trubia to the southwest of Oviedo, guarded the approaches to the mountain passes of La Mesa and Ventana which linked Asturias and León.

90 Tineo lies in the western district of Asturias de Oviedo. On Guntroda Pérez, see below i, 95 and n. 210.

91 Cf. above i, 12 and n. 43. In 1144 the Infanta Urraca Alfonso was married to King García Ramírez IV of Navarre: see below, i, 91–4. On the king's death in 1150, Urraca returned to León and three years later was awarded the tenancy of the territory of Asturias de Oviedo: see F. J. Fernández Conde, 'La reina Urraca "la Asturiana"', *Asturiensia Medievalia* 2 (1975), 65–94.

92 Judith ii.2.

93 Tāshufīn b. 'Alī, emir of the Almoravids (1143–45). In 1129 Tāshufīn was awarded the governorship of Granada and Almería by his father, the emir 'Alī b. Yūsuf b. Tāshufīn (1106–43), and in 1131 that of Cordoba, as a result of which he became the effective viceroy of the whole of al-Andalus, a position which he held until his recall to Morocco in 1138: Kennedy, *Muslim Spain and Portugal*, p. 186.

94 The castle of Aceca lay by the River Tagus, some 20 kilometres upstream from Toledo.

Christian prisoners, had been sent captive across the sea.[95] Everyone agreed with this pronouncement.

34. The entire army from the whole of his kingdom assembled in Toledo and pitched camp by the River Tagus. The king set out with Zafadola and his knights. He divided his forces into two, because there was not sufficient water for them to drink nor grass for the animals to graze on. The king and his army invaded the land of the Moabites through Puerto Rey, and the other army under Count Rodrigo González went through Puerto de Muradal.[96] For two weeks they marched through the wilderness, and the two armies met up near the Saracen castle of Gallello.[97] And from that day they found fodder for the animals and huge quantities of grain for themselves. *The multitude* of knights, foot-soldiers and archers *was without number and they covered the face of the earth like locusts.*[98]

35. From there, the king struck camp and began to advance across the plain of Córdoba, raiding to the left and right. He occupied all that land and plundered it, burning it as he went and taking many prisoners. Reaching the River Guadalquivir, he crossed it and moved away from the other bank, leaving Córdoba and Carmona[99] on his left and Seville, which the ancients called Hispalis, on the right. It was *in the time of wheat harvest,* so *he burnt up all their fields* and had all the vines, olive groves and fig trees cut down. *And dread of him fell upon all the inhabitants* of the land of the Moabites and Hagarenes.[100] Gripped by great fear, the Moabites and Hagarenes abandoned their towns and

---

95 Aceca fell to the Almoravids in the late summer of 1130. For a fuller description see below, ii.14. Tello Fernández hailed from the district of Saldaña, north of Carrión. In 1116 he held the castle of Torremormojón, about 20 kilometres east of Palencia: C. Monterde Albiac (ed.), *Diplomatario de la reina Urraca de Castilla y León (1109–1126)* (Zaragoza, 1996), no. 88.

96 Puerto de Muradal, better known as Despeñaperros, is the main pass across the Sierra Morena into Andalucía. The identity of Puerto Rey is less certain. Sánchez Belda suggested it lay in the vicinity of Despeñaperros, near the River Fresnedas: *Chronica*, p. 271. However, this is unlikely given the chronicler's assertion that the two armies marched for a fortnight before meeting up. Instead, it is conceivable that the force led by Alfonso VII marched south-west from Toledo and crossed the Montes de Toledo through the pass still known today as Puerto Rey, from where it could have continued south into the region of Córdoba.

97 The identity of Gallello is unknown.

98 The chronicler models his account on that of the campaigns waged by the Assyrian general Holofernes in Judith ii.19–20.

99 Carmona lies on the main route from Córdoba to Seville, about 25 kilometres to the north-east of the latter.

100 Judith ii.27–8 (cf. Vulgate, ii.17–18).

lesser castles, and shut themselves up in their strongest fortresses and defended cities. *They hid themselves* in the mountains, *in the mountain caves and in the clefts of the rock* and in the islands of the sea.[101]

36. Then the whole army encamped in the land of Seville and every day large companies of knights, known as *algaras*[102] in our language, sallied out of the camp and rode to the left and right. They plundered all the land of Seville, Córdoba and Carmona, burning the whole area, together with towns and castles, many of which were discovered to be deserted, for everyone had fled. They took captive countless men and women, just as they plundered horses and mares, camels and donkeys, as well as cattle, sheep and goats beyond reckoning. They took back to the camp huge quantities of grain, wine and oil. They destroyed all the mosques[103] they came upon and when they encountered any priests and doctors of their religion they put them to the sword. They also burned all the books of their religion in the mosques. In the course of their plundering, the knights travelled from the king's camp for a week after which they returned to it with the booty.

37. Afterwards, as plunder began to run short in the surrounding area, the king struck camp and went to a very rich city, which the ancients called Tuccis, Jerez[104] in our language. This he then plundered, demolished and destroyed. After that the king moved on and plundered the surrounding area and reached the fortress called Gallice,[105] which is on the coast.

38. But certain foolish knights, the sons of counts and magnates, and many others who were not in their *right mind*[106] and did not *walk after the king's counsel*,[107] heard that a nearby island was full of horses and cattle and other great riches. They crossed over to it filled with greed, but they were confronted by battle-lines of Moabites and Hagarenes drawn up, and these joined battle with them. In payment for their

101 See I Samuel xiii.6; Revelations vi.15; Judges xv.8; Isaiah ii.19, 21, vii.19; Jeremiah xvi.16, xlix.16.

102 From the Arabic *al-gāra*, 'a raiding party'. See also ii, 92.

103 Throughout the *CAI* mosques are referred to by the term *synagoge*: see also ii, 36, 93, 106.

104 Jerez de la Frontera, about 20 kilometres to the north-east of Cadiz. In fact, the town known as *Tucci* to the Romans was not Jerez at all, but the town of Martos near Jaén: Wright, 'Twelfth-century Metalinguistics', p. 283.

105 Modern Cadiz.

106 Mark v.15; Luke viii.35.

107 II Chronicles xxii.5.

sins, the Christians were defeated and the sons of the counts and magnates and many others perished by the sword. Others fled back to the camp and recounted to the army all that had happened to them. Finally, then, the whole army began to fear the king, and to obey him, and thenceforth no knight dared to go out from among the tents without the royal command.

39. The king stayed there for many days. All the raiding parties returned in great triumph, bringing with them many thousands of Saracen prisoners, together with a huge numbers of camels, horses, mares, oxen, cows, rams, sheep, goats and nanny-goats, which were from the royal estates,[108] and many other kinds of wealth.

40. Afterwards, the king struck camp and made his way to Seville, crossing the River Guadalquivir. A great mass of Moabites and Hagarenes, which had gathered there with their battle-lines drawn up close to the city walls, was soon cut off by a few armed Christians. All the lands around Seville were raided: they burnt up their crops and houses, destroyed the vineyards, fig trees and olive trees, and cut down many royal orchards, which were on both sides of the river.[109] The Moabites did not capture anybody, but instead received the ultimate penalty due to prisoners.

41. When the princes of the Hagarenes saw this, they secretly sent messengers to King Zafadola, saying: 'Speak to the king of the Christians and, with his aid, free us from the hands of the Moabites. We will give to the king of León royal tributes larger than those our forefathers gave to his, and with you we will serve him free from fear, and you and your sons will reign over us.' On hearing this, King Zafadola, having deliberated with the king and with his loyal counsellers, replied to the messengers: 'Go, and tell my brothers the princes of the Hagarenes: "Take some strong castles and some strong towers within the cities, wage war in all parts, and the king of León and I will swiftly come to your aid".'

42. Then the king struck camp, crossed the Puerto de Amarela Pass and went to his city Talavera.[110] And having accomplished these

---

108 *que erant regum et reginarum:* literally 'which were of the kings and queens'.

109 See Judith ii.27 (cf. Vulgate, ii.17).

110 The precise location of the Amarela pass is unknown to us. However, like Puerto Rey, it is likely to have led across the western reaches of the Montes de Toledo. A possibility would be modern Puerto de San Vicente, from where Talavera, 40 kilometres away on the Tagus, can be easily reached.

things, *every one* returned *to his house*[111] with great joy and in triumph, praising and blessing God, who had granted the king and his followers punishment and revenge for Tello Fernández and his comrades, who had perished at Aceca, and for Gutierre Armíldez, the governor of Toledo, and for the other commanders whom the Moabites had slain together with other Christian knights in the land of Toledo.[112]

43. After a few days had passed, the king, mindful that Count Gonzalo remained in rebellion, went to Asturias de Oviedo. He asked Count Gonzalo for his castles, namely Buanga, Proaza and Alba de Quirós, in which he remained in rebellion. But the count refused to give him the castles and, if this was not enough, he also did battle with him in Proaza and killed the horse on which the king was mounted and many others. The king, seeing that Count Gonzalo was set on evil,[113] left Count Suero, his nephew Pedro Alfonso and all the Asturians to face him. The king went away to Castile.

44. Count Suero besieged Buanga and Pedro Alfonso Alba de Quirós, while Count Gonzalo remained in Proaza. They hemmed them in vigorously on all sides, set ambushes in the area around the castles, on the roads and on the mountain paths, and whomsoever they came across they sent away having cut off their hands or feet. This went on for many days. Nevertheless, Count Gonzalo remained in rebellion against the king for nearly two years.

45. Seeing that he was being completely overwhelmed, Count Gonzalo made a pact with Count Suero, Pedro Alfonso and Bishop Arias of León.[114] He went with them to the king, threw himself at the king's feet and admitted his guilt. The king received him peacefully and spoke fine words to him, for as the holy author says: *'The king's heart is in the hand of the Lord, as the rivers of water.'*[115] The count stayed at the king's palace in great honour for many days; afterwards he asked the king with many entreaties for Luna.[116] So the king summoned his sister the Infanta Sancha, his wife Berengaria and other counsellors, whom he knew were prudent in such matters. Having taken

111 II Samuel vi.19, xx.22.
112 On the demise of Gutierre Armíldez, see below ii, 15–16.
113 *intentus esset ad malum*, an echo of Genesis vi.5.
114 Arias, bishop of León (1130–35).
115 Proverbs xxi.1; cf. Pérez de Urbel, *Sampiro*, p. 316.
116 The castle of Luna, by the River Orbigo, was situated in the far north-west of the territory of León.

counsel with them, he received Proaza, Buanga and Alba de Quirós from the count, and ordered that he be given what he had asked for, namely Luna. This was done so that he would not rebel again, just as he had rebelled against Queen Urraca who had previously granted him a lordship.

46. Afterwards, having made peace with the king twice, Count Gonzalo lied and rebelled. Finally, Pedro Alfonso, together with some of the king's knights, captured Count Gonzalo, and Pedro Alfonso sent him in chains to the castle of Aguilar.[117] They held him until the king ordered him to be freed, and commanded him that on an appointed day he should leave his land. The count, obeying the king, whether he wanted to or not, went to Portugal to King Afonso, who was a relative of the king's, the son of Queen Teresa and Count Henry, with the intention that from there he could wage war by sea on Asturias and Galicia.[118] But God, *that seeth all things*,[119] did not wish to arrange matters in this way. For his part, the king of Portugal received him with great honour and promised him great fiefs, for he trusted that he would make war on Asturias and Galicia. But by God's disposition, the count was seized by a fever and died a foreigner in a foreign land. Nevertheless, his knights bore away his corpse and buried him in Oviedo.[120]

47. In the Era 1172 [= AD 1134], in the month of October, while all these things were going on, Count Rodrigo González realised that the

---

117 This may refer either to Aguilar, about 10 kilometres south-east of Oviedo, or else to the castle of Aguilar de Esla to the north-east of the city of León. The chronology of the Asturian rebellion, which in the *CAI* is vague to say the least, may be tentatively reconstructed as follows: having first rebelled in 1132, Count Gonzalo was readmitted to the Leonese court in the spring of 1135. However, the count disappears from court records after June 1135 and in July Alfonso VII confiscated his lands and granted them to Count Rodrigo Martínez and Count Rodrigo González de Lara. In December, according to the dating clause to an Asturian charter, Count Gonzalo was once more in revolt in the castle of Buanga. The following spring, king and magnate were seemingly reconciled again, and Count Gonzalo remained on the court scene until the autumn of 1136. His final rebellion and capture probably occurred shortly afterwards: details in Barton, *Aristocracy*, p. 114–15.

118 Count Gonzalo Peláez is almost certainly the *Gundisaluus comes* who may be sighted at the court of Afonso I of Portugal in October 1137: R. de Azevedo (ed.), *Documentos medievais portugueses: documentos régios*, I (Lisbon, 1958), pp. 197–8.

119 II Maccabees ix.5 (Vulgate), xii.22, xv.2.

120 According to an *obituario* compiled in Oviedo cathedral, the count's death occurred in March 1138: M. E. García García, 'El conde asturiano Gonzalo Peláez', *Asturiensia Medievalia* 2 (1975), 39–64, p. 64.

king's *countenance had changed*[121] for the worse, and he surrendered Toledo and the towns and fortresses which he held to the king. When the king had received them, he granted them straightaway to Rodrigo Fernández and made him *alcaide* of Toledo. The latter joined in many battles in the land of the Moabites and the Hagarenes. The battles which Count Rodrigo González and Rodrigo Fernández waged with the kings of the Moabites and Hagarenes were extremely hard-fought, but they are not described in this book.

48. After Count Rodrigo González had kissed the king's hand and said farewell to his family and friends, *he took a far journey*[122] to Jerusalem where he joined in many battles with the Saracens. He built a very strong castle at Toron opposite Ascalon, fortified it greatly with knights, foot-soldiers and provisions, and entrusted it to the knights of the Temple.[123] Afterwards the count crossed the Adriatic Sea and came to Spain, but he did not meet the king, nor was he received in Castile on the estates of his family; instead he stayed with Count Ramón of Barcelona and with García, king of Pamplona.[124] Then he went to Avengania,[125] the prince of the Saracens of Valencia, and stayed with him for several days. But the Saracens gave him a potion and he caught leprosy. When the count realised that his body had changed, he went again to Jerusalem and stayed there until the day of his death.

121 Daniel vii.28.

122 Matthew xxi.33; Mark xii.1, xiii.34; Luke xv.13. The clear inference is that the count travelled as a *peregrinus*, or pilgrim, to Jerusalem.

123 The castle near Ascalon the chronicler refers to is that of Toron des Chevaliers, on which see D. Pringle, *Secular buildings in the Crusader Kingdom of Jerusalem* (Cambridge, 1997), pp. 64–5.

124 Ramón Berenguer IV of Barcelona (1131–62); García IV Ramírez of Navarre (1134–50). Count Rodrigo's movements during these years can be followed only sketchily. Between at least 1139 and December 1141 he held the lordships of Huesca and Jaca in the central Pyrenees; he can be traced on Castilian soil on 8 February 1141, when he made a grant of property to the monks of Arlanza; two years later he had taken up residence in the Catalan county of Urgel: he is probably the *comes Roricus* who witnessed the will that was drawn up by his brother-in-law, Ermengol VI of Urgel, on 24 March 1143: see Ubieto Arteta, *Los 'Tenentes'*, p. 271; Barton, *Aristocracy*, p. 116, n. 80.

125 Yaḥyā b. Ghānīya was a leading figure among the Almoravid ruling élite of al-Andalus. Having first held the governorship of Murcia, in 1133 he was appointed to that of Valencia, and the following year commanded the Muslim army which defeated Alfonso I of Aragon at Fraga: Kennedy, *Muslim Spain and Portugal*, pp. 186–7, 189–92, 203–4. See also below, i, 48, 51, 53; ii, 52, 53, 80, 94 (and n. 189), 99, 100 and 105.

49. Setting to one side the previous order of our narrative, so that we
may make a brief digression concerning the events that relate to the
subject, we shall undertake the history of the king of Aragon, so that
we may speak of his death and of what he did after he returned from
Morón and Almazán.

50. At that time, while the king of León waged war against his rebels,
and against Count Pedro de Lara and his brother Count Rodrigo, who
had joined them, and against other unfaithful men, so that he might
capture them in battle, the king of Aragon mustered a great army of
knights and foot-soldiers. Leaving his land, he made his way to the
borders of Gascony and besieged the town of Bayonne, which is situated next to the River Garonne. He stayed there for many days and
devastated all the land in the area. He built catapults, machines and
many siege engines, and he attacked that town but was unable to take
it.[126] Afterwards he returned to his land without honour.

51. He mustered a great army from his land and from Gascony.
Having taken counsel with the nobles of his region, he gathered some
very brave and powerful men to strengthen his forces, among whom
were the bishop of Lescar, whose name was Guy, and Bishop Dodo of
Jaca, the bishop of San Vicente de Roda, the abbot of San Victorián,
Gaston of Béarn and Centulle of Bigorre, other brave French troops
and many foreigners.[127] He moved his army and went to the great city
of Zaragoza and to the other towns and castles that he had captured
from the Saracens. Then he struck camp and invaded the land of the
Moabites, and besieged a very strong town called Fraga.[128] All the
land of Valencia, Murcia and Granada was plundered and his raiding
parties invaded the land of Almería, made great slaughter and took
many prisoners and burned all that land. But Avengania, a Saracen of
the tribe of the Moabites and the supreme leader of Valencia and

126 Bayonne lies on the River Adour, not the Garonne. The siege of Bayonne, which
    lasted from at least 26 October 1130 until October 1131, may have been
    undertaken in support of Alfonso I's ally, Count Alfonso Jordan of Toulouse, who
    in 1130 was at war with Duke William IX of Aquitaine: Lema Pueyo (ed.),
    Colección diplomática, nos 232, 242; Reilly, *The Contest*, pp. 170–1.

127 The figures named may be identified as Guy, bishop of Lescar (1115–41), a friend
    and ally of Archbishop Diego Gelmírez of Santiago de Compostela, whom he is
    known to have visited in 1121 and 1138; Arnal Dodo, bishop of Huesca and Jaca
    (1130–34); Pedro Guillem, bishop of Roda (1126–34); and Durando, abbot of San
    Victorián de Sobrarbe (1125–34). On Gaston of Béarn and Centulle of Bigorre, see
    above, n. 34.

128 Fraga is situated on the banks of the Cinca, about 25 kilometres south-west of
    Lérida.

Murcia, gathered together many Moabites and Hagarenes and went
to Fraga to fight with the king of Aragon. Avengania was defeated
twice and, as he fled from the battlefield, left great spoils to the
Christians.

52. The king of Aragon always took with him on campaign a casket
made of pure gold, decorated with precious stones on the inside and
outside. Inside there was a cross made of the salvation-giving wood,
venerable among relics, on which our Lord Jesus Christ, the son of
God, was hanged in order to redeem us. The king had stolen it during
the time of war from the house of the martyr saints Facundus and
Primitivus, which is in the land of León, near the River Cea.[129] He also
had other ivory caskets covered with gold, silver and precious stones,
full of the relics of Saint Mary and of the cross, and of apostles,
martyrs, confessors, virgins, patriarchs and prophets. They were kept
in the tents where the chapel was, which always stood next to the
king's tent.[130] The priests, deacons and a great many of the clergy
watched over and looked after them daily, and they always offered the
sacrifice to the Lord God over them.

53. The Moabites and Hagarenes, who were inside Fraga, wished to
surrender the town to the king so that he might let them go in peace.
However, he did not wish to receive it because God *had hardened his
heart*[131] in order that all the harm that he had inflicted upon the
Christians in the land of León and Castile should fall upon himself and
upon his own people, just as it later did. For he wished to capture the
town and swore by a royal oath that all the Saracen nobles were to
suffer the capital sentence, also that their wives and sons were to be
taken captive, and that they were to be stripped of all their wealth
without mercy.[132] Finally, the Saracen Avengania gathered an army of

129 That is, the Cluniac monastery of Sahagún near León. The bejewelled *lignum
     crucis*, to which the chronicler refers here, had been given to Alfonso VI by the
     Emperor Alexius I Comnenus of Byzantium (1081–1118) in 1101, and
     subsequently placed upon the altar of the abbey church of Sahagún; the cross had
     then been appropriated by Alfonso I of Aragon in 1112: A. Ubieto Arteta (ed.),
     Crónicas anónimas de Sahagún (Zaragoza, 1987), pp. 17–18, 52.
130 The Norman monastic chronicler Orderic Vitalis also makes mention of these
     relics: Orderic Vitalis, *The Ecclesiastical History*, ed. and trans. M. Chibnall, 6 vols
     (Oxford, 1969–80), VI, p. 410.
131 See, for example, Exodus ix.12, x.20, 27, xi.10, xiv.8.
132 A similar version of events is provided by Orderic Vitalis, who also reports that
     the previous year, after the capture of nearby Mequinenza, the Muslim inhabitants
     were beheaded by the soldiers of Alfonso I of Aragon: Orderic Vitalis, *The
     Ecclesiastical History*, VI, pp. 410–16.

Moabites and Arabs from overseas, and the kings of Córdoba, Seville, Granada, Valencia and Lérida, and all the peoples who were on this side of the sea. And after Avengania had sent ambassadors to them, countless thousands of horsemen, foot-soldiers and archers came to Fraga. But in payment of his sins, all this was concealed from the king, whom God did not wish to help, but to confound.

54. One day at dawn, on 17 July, when the king's sentries, who guarded the camp by night and day, looked up, they saw that innumerable vast formations of Saracens were advancing. Running into the camp they reported this to the king. The king commanded the archbishops, nobles, knights and foot-soldiers to remain in the camp ready and armed to defend themselves and the camp. But many of the Aragonese nobles and many other knights had already left the camp by order of the king and were in Aragon with the intention of returning to the camp once they had prepared all the necessary things. These men were not at the battle.

55. Then, through the agency of divine vengeance, the troops of the Moabites and Hagarenes came and surrounded the camp and began to fight. They hurled many spears, arrows, darts and stones at them, and killed many men-at-arms and animals. When they saw this, the bishops, clergy and all the Christian people began to beseech Lord God to deliver them from the hands of the Saracens and not to remember the sins of the king, nor those of his relations, nor those of them who were with him, but to chastise them gently. But, in payment for their sins, their prayers were not heard before God, because the Archangel Gabriel, the most important messenger of God, did not carry them before the judgement-seat of Christ; nor was Michael, the leader of the celestial army, sent by God to help them in battle.

56. When the nobles and all the men-at-arms and bishops saw that they could not continue the battle in the camp, they sallied forth onto the battlefield towards them and the battle grew greatly worse. Then, while they fought, troops of pagans who had been in hiding came up from the rear and began to attack the camp, and they razed it to the ground. They seized the golden casket in which was the cross of the salvation-giving wood, and the other caskets already mentioned. They stormed the royal chapel and pulled the king's tents to the ground and captured the bishop of Lescar, the priests, deacons and all the clergy, and all the people who were in the camp, as well as the members of the royal household. In the battle died Bishop Dodo of Jaca, the bishop of San Vicente de Roda, and the abbot of San Victorián.

57. These are the leaders of the army [who died]: Garsión of
Gabescán, Bertrán of Laon, Fortunel of Fol, Ogier of Miramont,
Raimundo of Talar, Calvete of Sua, Quio***[133], Gastón of Béarn,
Centulle of Bigorre and Almaric of Narbonne.[134] Many French troops
and many foreigners and all the nobles and knights of the Aragonese
also died bravely. And seven hundred brave foot-soldiers of the king,
who protected him when he went on campaign, all fell together in the
same place.

58. Finally, the king fled with ten knights (one of whom was García
Ramírez[135]), he passed through Zaragoza and made his way to the
monastery called San Juan de la Peña in Aragon.[136] He went inside,
ordered the doors to be closed and on account of his great sorrow *he
laid him down upon his bed.*[137] After a few days, *grieved at his heart,*[138] he
died in the same monastery and was buried with his forefathers in the
royal pantheon. After him, or before, there was no one equal to him
among the former kings of the Aragonese, nor as strong, nor as
prudent, nor as warlike as he. But he had made no arrangements for
his estate or for his kingdom, because he left no offspring.[139] He died
on 25 August in the Era 1172 [= AD 1134].[140]

133 There is a lacuna at this point in all the manuscripts.

134 In fact, Viscount Gaston of Béarn had been killed in action against the governor
of Valencia four years earlier: Kennedy, *Muslim Spain and Portugal,* p. 186.

135 On García Ramírez, see below n. 149. The size of Alfonso's escort is corroborated
by Orderic Vitalis, *The Ecclesiastical History,* VI, p. 416. Shortly after his defeat at
Fraga, the king issued a charter expressing gratitude to those who had gained
control of his frightened horse in the battle: Lema Pueyo (ed.), *Colección
diplomática,* no. 280.

136 In fact, after his defeat at Fraga the Aragonese king fled north to Sariñena, about
45 kilometres south-west of Huesca, where he remained until his death; he was
subsequently buried at the monastery of Montearagón: Lema Pueyo (ed.),
Colección diplomática, no. 284.

137 1 Maccabees i.5; vi.8.

138 Genesis vi.6.

139 Although Alfonso I died childless, it is not quite true to say that he had made no
provision for the succession. By the terms of the will he had drawn up during the
siege of Bayonne in October 1131, he divided his kingdom between three military
orders, the Templars, the Hospitallers and the Order of the Holy Sepulchre, and
he confirmed these provisions at Sariñena, on 4 September 1134, shortly before
his death. However, as the chronicler makes clear below, the terms of the will
were never carried out. For a detailed discussion of these matters, see E. Lourie,
'The Will of Alfonso I, *el Batallador,* King of Aragón and Navarre: a reassessment',
Speculum 50 (1975), 635–51; A. J. Forey, 'The Will of Alfonso I of Aragon and
Navarre', *Durham University Journal* 73 (1980), 59–65.

140 The chronicler is mistaken; the king died on 7 September 1134.

59. The bishop of Lescar was taken as a prisoner to Valencia. They subjected him to immense torture so that he might renounce Him who was hung on a cross for us and his baptism, so as to circumcise him in accordance with their laws. After this, he gave hostages on his behalf, paid three thousand gold *morabetinos* and returned to his see in Lescar.[141]

60. When the Christians who lived in the fortified castles and towns beyond Zaragoza saw that the king had died, they fled for fear of the Saracens and shut themselves up in Zaragoza. The Saracens came and took possession of the towns that had been abandoned by the Christians and made them ready for occupation.[142] All the inhabitants of Zaragoza and of all the towns wept, particularly those of the castles which King Alfonso had captured from the Saracens by the sword and handed over to be settled by the Christians, and they said: 'Great Defender, whom have you left to defend us? The kingdom which you with your royal power seized from the hands of the Saracens will now be invaded by the Moabites and we will be taken captive without anyone to defend us.'

61. Then the Aragonese, both *nobles and commoners, citizens* and foreigners, gathered together in groups. *They tore out their hair and rent their clothes, and the women scratched their faces,* and with great weeping they cried to heaven:[143] 'Oh king! *How are you fallen, that made us safe!*[144] On account of the weight of our sins the wrath of God fell upon us so that we would lose the liberator of the Christians. Now the impious Saracens and our enemies will invade us.'

62. So the noble and commoner knights[145] of all the land of Aragon, the bishops and abbots and all the people gathered together in the

141 The *morabetino* or *maravedí* was the gold dinar minted by the Almoravid rulers of North Africa and al-Andalus, and by their Almohad successors, but widely used in Christian Spain too. Bishop Guy had secured his release by 26 December 1134, when he joined the court of Alfonso VII at Zaragoza: Lacarra, 'Documentos', no. 86. On this and other accounts of the captivity of the bishop of Lescar, see P. Carter, 'The historical context of William of Malmesbury's Miracles of the Virgin Mary', in *The Writing of History in the Middle Ages. Essays presented to Richard William Southern*, eds R. H. C. Davis and J. M. Wallace-Hadrill (Oxford, 1981), 127–65, at pp. 154–8.

142 On the Almoravid territorial gains, see J. M. Lacarra, 'La Reconquista y repoblación del valle del Ebro', in *La Reconquista española y la repoblación del País* (Zaragoza, 1951), 39–83, at pp. 60–1.

143 This appears to be closely based upon Bishop Pelayo's account of the death of Alfonso VI of León: see above, Pelayo, *Chronicon*, p. 88.

144 I Maccabees ix.21; II Samuel i.19, 25.

145 *nobiles et ignobiles milites*: see above, Pelayo, *Chronicon*, p. 88, n. 97.

royal city of Jaca. They chose as their king a certain monk called
Ramiro, who was the king's brother, and they gave him as his wife a
sister of the count of Poitou.[146] This *sin was very great before the Lord*,[147]
but the Aragonese, having lost their dear lord, did this so that
children of royal descent should be raised up.[148] However, the Pamplonans and Navarrese gathered in the city of Pamplona and chose as
their king García Ramírez, the man who had fled from the battle of
Fraga with King Alfonso.[149] King Ramiro *went in unto his wife, who
conceived and gave birth*[150] to a daughter whereupon, having consulted
with his nobles, he immediately betrothed her to Count [Ramón]
Berenguer [IV] of Barcelona. He gave the kingdom to the count and
admitted that he was a sinner before God and did penance.[151]

63. After this, the king of León, having learned of the situation
regarding the kings, went to Nájera and they received him there; and
not only there, but in all the towns and castles which should have
been under the authority of the king of León. King García came unto
his presence and promised to serve him for the rest of his life, and he
was made a knight of the king of León, who gave him gifts and a
lordship.[152] When the king of León heard that the nobles of Aragon,

146 Ramiro II, king of Aragon (1134–37), had previously served as a monk of the
    abbey of San Pedro el Viejo in Huesca; his bride Agnes of Poitou was the daughter
    of William IX of Aquitaine. In the immediate aftermath of the debacle at Fraga,
    Ramiro had been nominated to the see of Roda, following the death in battle of the
    incumbent Bishop Pedro Guillem; however, within four days of the death of
    Alfonso I he had been installed as king of Aragon: Lema Pueyo (ed.), *Colección
    diplomática*, no. 281; A. Ubieto Arteta (ed.), *Documentos de Ramiro II de Aragón*
    (Zaragoza, 1988), no. 12. Ramiro's marriage to Agnes of Poitou took place in Jaca
    on 13 November 1135.

147 I Samuel ii.17.

148 There are echoes here of Genesis xxxviii.8; Deuteronomy xxv.5; II Samuel vii.12;
    I Chronicles xvii.11; Matthew xxii.24; Luke xx.28.

149 García Ramírez IV of Navarre (1134–50) was a great-great-grandson of Sancho
    Garcés *el Mayor* of Navarre (1000–35), albeit through an illegitimate line. At the
    time of the death of Alfonso I he held the lordships of Monzón and Tudela, among
    others: Ubieto Arteta, *Los 'Tenentes'*, p. 223. He had established himself as 'king of
    the Pamplonans' before the end of 1134.

150 Genesis xxx.5, iv.17, xvi.4; Exodus ii.1; II Samuel xii.24.

151 Petronila, daughter of Ramiro II and Queen Agnes, was born in the summer of
    1136 and betrothed to Ramón Berenguer IV of Barcelona in August 1137. The
    following November, Ramiro II designated his future son-in-law regent for
    Aragon on the understanding that any offspring of the couple would be heir to the
    combined realms of Aragon and Barcelona. This political settlement achieved,
    Ramiro retired to the cloister.

152 The meeting between Alfonso VII and García Ramírez IV in Nájera probably took
    place in November 1134. The Leonese king recognized García as the legitimate

King Ramiro and all the people were in great terror and dread, he said to his nobles: 'Let us go to Aragon and take pity on our brother King Ramiro, and let us offer him advice and assistance.'

64. When King Ramiro, together with all the noble magnates of his palace, the bishops, the abbots and all the people, heard that the king of León was coming come to their land, they went out to greet him. They received him with great honour and served him. The king of León *spake* many fine and *peacable words unto them*,[153] and he promised that he would help them *with all his heart and with all his mind*.[154] King Ramiro, having consulted with the bishops and with all the nobles of his kingdom, gave Zaragoza to the king of León, so that it would always remain under his dominion and that of his sons.[155] And the kings made their way there together in order that it might be delivered to the emperor.

65. When all the people heard that the king of León was coming to Zaragoza, all the nobles of the city and all the people went out to greet him with drums, *harps, psalteries and all kinds of musick*,[156] singing and calling out:'*Blessed is he that cometh*, blessed is he and the kingdom of his forefathers, blessed is the kingdom of León, and blessed is your mercy and your patience.'[157] And they led him into the city.

66. Afterwards, the bishop of Zaragoza[158] went into the city square with a great procession of clergy and monks. He greeted the king of León and they went with him into the church of Saint Mary singing and calling out: '*Fear God, and keep his commandments*',[159] and so on. Finally, having been blessed by the bishop, as is the custom of kings,

---

ruler of Navarre, in return for which he recovered the Rioja and the other territories on the west bank of the Ebro that his mother Urraca had lost to Alfonso I of Aragon. The following May, having briefly allied himself with Ramiro II of Aragon, the Navarrese monarch renewed his oath of loyalty: see H. Grassotti, 'Homenaje de García Ramírez a Alfonso VII', *CHE* 37-8 (1963), 318–29; Reilly, *Alfonso VII*, pp. 46–9.

153 I Maccabees i.30, vii.15, x.3; Exodus xviii.7; Judges xviii.15.

154 Mark xii.30; Matthew xxii.37; Luke x.27.

155 Alfonso VII entered Zaragoza in December 1134. Under the terms of his settlement with Ramiro II, the Leonese king not only gained the lordship of that city and its territory, but the lands around Almazán and Soria too.

156 Daniel iii.5, 7, 10, 15.

157 There are echoes here of Psalm cxviii.26; Matthew xxi.9, xxiii.39; Mark xi.10; Luke xiii.35, xix.38.

158 García de Majones, bishop of Zaragoza (1130–36).

159 Ecclesiastes xii.13. Cf. below ii, 63.

they accompanied him to the royal palace and gave him abundant tribute. The king stayed in Zaragoza for several days and stationed a large garrison of knights and foot-soldiers there to guard the city. After this, at the king's command, having received the blessing of the bishop and of all the people, they returned to Castile praising and blessing God, who gives peace to those who trust in him.

67. In the same year as these things happened, the king's brother-in-law, Count Ramón of Barcelona, and his relative, Count Alfonso of Toulouse, came before the king of León and they promised to obey him in all matters. They were made his knights, after they had touched the king's right hand to confirm their loyalty.[160] The king gave Zaragoza as a lordship to the count of Barcelona,[161] as is the custom of the king of León, and he gave to the count of Toulouse, in addition to a lordship, a very fine gold cup of thirty marks in weight, many horses and numerous other gifts.

68. In addition, all the nobles who dwelled in the whole of Gascony and throughout all that land as far as the River Rhône, and William [VI] of Montpellier, came of one accord to the king and they received from him silver and gold, many varied and precious gifts, and many horses. They all submitted to him and obeyed him in all things. Many sons of the counts of France, of dukes and nobles, and many Poitevins, came before him and received from him weapons and many other gifts. *And the border of* the kingdom of Alfonso, king of León, was from the great Ocean Sea, that is, from Padrón de Santiago, *unto* the River Rhône.[162]

69. After this, in the Era 1173 [= AD 1135] the king *appointed* the second of June, Pentecost Sunday,[163] *as the date to hold a council in the* royal city of León, with the archbishops, *bishops*, abbots, counts, nobles,

---

160 This was a typical gesture of homage in the twelfth century. See J. Le Goff, 'Le rituel symbolique de la vassalité', in Le Goff, *Pour un autre Moyen Âge* (Paris, 1977), 349–420.

161 The chronicler is mistaken. In September 1135 Alfonso VII ceded Zaragoza to García Ramírez of Navarre who did homage for it; in August of the following year the emperor returned the city to Ramiro II of Aragon. The grant to the count of Barcelona occurred towards the end of 1137, that is, shortly after Ramiro II appointed his future son-in-law as regent for Aragon: see Reilly, *Alfonso VII*, p. 51, 54–5, 61, n. 33.

162 A passage inspired by Genesis x.19; Joshua xiii.23, xvi.5, xix.10. Padrón, on the Atlantic coast, about 20 kilometres south-west of the city of Santiago de Compostela, was the reputed landing point of the disciples of St James when they bore the apostle's body by sea to Spain.

163 In 1135 Pentecost Sunday fell on 26 May.

governors and judges *who were in his kingdom. On the appointed day, the king arrived with his wife* Queen Berengaria, his sister the Infanta Sancha, and with them King García of Pamplona; and, just as the king had commanded, they all gathered in León. There also arrived a great throng of monks and clergy, together with countless common folk, *to know, to hear* or to speak *the divine word.*[164]

70. On the first day of the council,[165] all the nobles and commoners gathered with the king in the church of Saint Mary, and there they discussed those things which the mercy of our Lord Jesus Christ suggested to them, and those which are proper for the salvation of the souls of all the faithful. On the second day, on which the arrival of the Holy Spirit to the Apostles is celebrated, having taken divine counsel, the archbishops, bishops, abbots, all the nobles and commoners and all the people assembled again in the church of Saint Mary, together with King García and the king's sister, to proclaim the king emperor, because King García, King Zafadola of the Saracens, Count Ramón of Barcelona, Count Alfonso of Toulouse and many counts and magnates from Gascony and France obeyed him in all things. Having dressed the king in a fine cloak woven with wonderful skill,[166] they placed on his head a crown of pure gold and precious stones, and after having placed a sceptre in his hands, King García held him by the right arm and Bishop Arias of León by the left, and together with the bishops and abbots they led him before the altar of Saint Mary, singing the '*Te Deum laudamus*' until the end, and calling out: 'Long live the Emperor Alfonso!' Having given him the blessing, they held Mass according to the custom of feast days.[167] Afterwards each of them returned to their tents. The emperor ordered a great banquet to be

---

164 This chapter is closely based upon the spurious account of the council of Oviedo allegedly convoked by King Alfonso III of Asturias (866–910) which was interpolated into Sampiro's *Chronicle* by Bishop Pelayo of Oviedo: see Pérez de Urbel, *Sampiro*, pp. 289–91. The witness-lists to the charters drawn up during and immediately after the council of León reveal the names of some and the great and the good who attended: the Infanta Sancha, King García of Navarre, the archbishop of Toledo, thirteen bishops and five archdeacons, eight counts and at least another eleven lay magnates. Archbishop Diego of Santiago de Compostela also appears to have been present, although some doubts have been expressed on that score: Fletcher, *St James's Catapult*, p. 274, n. 34. Those from outside the kingdom who attended included Bishop Guy of Lescar, Bishop García of Zaragoza, Bishop Miguel of Tarazona and Count Ermengol VI of Urgel.

165 That is, Saturday, 25 May 1135.

166 A recollection of I Kings vii.17 .

167 On the coronation of Alfonso VII, see Linehan, *History and the Historians*, pp. 235ff.

held in the royal palace, and the counts, nobles and governors *served at the* royal *tables.*[168] The emperor also ordered large sums of money to be given to the bishops and abbots, and to everyone else, and great gifts of clothing and food to be given to the poor.

71. On the third day, the emperor and the others, as they were accustomed to do, gathered again in the royal palace and dealt with those matters *which concerned the salvation of the whole of the kingdom of Spain.*[169] The emperor bestowed customs and laws upon all his kingdom, just as they had been in the time of his grandfather King Alfonso; he commanded that all the estates and serfs which had been lost without trial or justice be restored to all the churches; he commanded that the villages and lands which had been destroyed during wartime be repopulated, and that vines and all kinds of trees be planted; and he commanded all the judges to eradicate severely vice in those men who were discovered to be acting contrary to justice and to the decrees of kings, nobles, authorities and judges. They, for their part, judged justly, hanging some from the gallows, leaving others to have their hands or feet cut off, not sparing the wealthy nor the highborn any more than the poor, but distinguishing everything according to the level of guilt. Moreover, the emperor ordered that witches were in no way to be tolerated, just as the Lord said to Moses 'Thou shalt not suffer a witch to live'.[170] And in the sight of everyone some of these *workers of iniquity*[171] were captured and hanged from the gallows.

72. The emperor commanded the governors of Toledo and all the inhabitants from the whole frontier to form armies continually, to make war on the infidel Saracens every year and not to spare their cities or fortresses, but to claim them all for God and Christian law. *These things having been accomplished, once the council had dissolved they all returned joyfully to their homes*[172] singing and blessing the emperor and calling out: 'Blessed are you and blessed is the kingdom of your forefathers and blessed is God on high, who made the heaven and the

168 Acts vi.2. The celebrations were not confined to feasting. On 26 May 1135, Alfonso VII granted the village of Varea near Logroño to one Ramiro Garcés in recognition of the fact that the latter had held the monarch's shield during the coronation ceremony, and had bravely killed a bull during the subsequent festivities: I. Rodríguez de Lama (ed.), *Colección diplomática de la Rioja: Documentos, 923–1168*, II (2nd edn., Logroño, 1992), no. 107.

169 Pérez de Urbel, *Sampiro*, pp. 304–5.

170 Exodus xxii.18.

171 A reminiscence of I Maccabees iii.6; Luke xiii.27.

172 Pérez de Urbel, *Sampiro*, p. 305.

earth, the sea and all the things that are in them, because He has visited us and shown us the mercy which He promised to those who have faith in Him.'[173]

73. However, when one year of the aforementioned treaty had passed by peacefully, King García of Navarre and all his warriors rose up against the lord emperor. King Afonso of the Portuguese, the son of Count Henry and Queen Teresa, likewise rebelled at the same time.[174] Teresa was the daughter of King Alfonso [VI], but was born not of a legitimate wife but of a concubine, though one greatly loved by the king, called Jimena Muñoz.[175] Because of his love and honour [for Teresa], the king gave her in marriage to Count Henry and gave her a magnificent dowry by granting her the land of Portugal to hold by hereditary right. When Count Henry died, the Portuguese proclaimed her queen, and when she died, they proclaimed her son king, as indeed he later was, in honour of her name.[176]

74. These two kings, as has been said above, waged war on the emperor at the same time and each of them launched a campaign from their own region: King García in Castile and the king of Portugal in Galicia. The king of Portugal marched to Galicia and captured the city of Tuy[177] and other castles. Count Gómez Núñez, who held many castles and the territory of Toroño,[178] and Count Rodrigo Pérez the Hairy, who held castles in Limia[179] and a lordship from the emperor, deceived their lord the emperor and gave their castles and lordships to the king of Portugal.[180] If this was not enough for them, they also waged war to their own cost, all of which caused the counts difficulties during all of the rest of the days of their lives.

173 This is redolent with biblical phraseology: see, for example, I Samuel xxv.32; II Samuel xviii.28; Judith xiii.17–18; Mark xi.10.

174 Afonso I Henriques of Portugal (1128–85). The attacks against Alfonso VII were probably launched in the spring of 1137, while the emperor was campaigning in the upper Guadalquivir valley: Reilly, *Alfonso VII*, pp. 57–8.

175 *non de legitima [uxore], sed de concubina*, following MS *A*. On Jimena Muñoz, see above Pelayo, *Chronicon*, pp. 87–8, n. 90.

176 On Count Henry of Burgundy, see above Pelayo, *Chronicon*, p. 88, n. 93. On the emergence of an independent realm of Portugal, see Reilly, *The Contest*, pp. 141–3, 200–4.

177 Tuy lies in the lower valley of the Miño on the modern frontier between Spain and Portugal.

178 Roughly conterminous with the diocese of Tuy.

179 The territory of Limia lies to the south of the modern province of Orense.

180 On counts Gómez Núñez and Rodrigo Pérez, see i, 5 (and n. 24), 77, 87.

75. At that time there was in Limia a noble named Fernando Yáñez,[181] who was a brave knight and a faithful friend of the emperor. He held the castle of Allariz[182] and many others. For this reason, he and his sons, brothers and friends bravely waged war against the king of Portugal. And although they were exhausted by the war against the king, they did not lose their honour but attained the greatest glory. Already in times past the aforementioned king of Portugal had gone to Galicia on many occasions and had been expelled from there by Count Fernando Pérez, Rodrigo Vélaz and the other magnates of Galicia, and had returned to his land without honour.[183] He came to Limia again and built a castle at Celmes.[184] He reinforced it with noble knights and the bravest foot-soldiers from his palace, and despatched to it large supplies of bread, meat, wine and water, and returned to his land of Portugal.

76. When the emperor heard this, having gathered a great army from Galicia and León and many knights, he went quickly to Limia and besieged the castle of Celmes. After a few days had passed, he stormed it and captured there a large number of noble knights from the palace of the king of Portugal, and he kept them under guard for many days. This caused unbearable sadness in the palace of the king of Portugal, *because it had not befallen him as he looked for.*[185]

77. Having fortified the castle, the emperor was delighted that all Limia had returned to him and he went back to the land of León. This happened before he was proclaimed emperor, but after he was proclaimed emperor, as we said earlier, Count Gómez Núñez and Count Rodrigo, who was called the Hairy, rebelled in Galicia and surrendered their lordships and castles to the king of Portugal, who fortified them and returned to his land.

78. Again, having mustered his army, the king of Portugal went to Limia. On hearing this, Count Fernando Pérez, Count Rodrigo Vélaz and other of the emperor's nobles in Galicia, having all assembled with their knights at the same time, set out against the king and they encountered him at the place called Cernesa. Once they had drawn up

---

181 On Fernando Yáñez, see i, 5, 81; ii, 100; *PA*, vv. 199–216.

182 Allariz lies about 15 kilometres south of the city of Orense.

183 On Fernando Pérez and Rodrigo Vélaz, see i, 5 (and nn. 22 and 24), 78; *PA* vv. 74–8.

184 The castle at Celmes was erected near Ginzo de Limia, south of Orense.

185 I Maccabees vi.8. The chronology of the account of the Portuguese wars provided by the chronicler is unclear to say the least; however, it is likely that the Celmes campaign took place in the spring of 1134: Reilly, *Alfonso VII*, pp. 42–3.

their troops, they began to fight and, in payment for their sins, the counts took to flight and were vanquished. Count Rodrigo Vélaz was captured in the battle by some of the king's knights, but he was immediately freed by two of his armour bearers, who carried out an ingenious plan, and he fled with them.[186]

79. After this victory, the king immediately returned to the land of Portugal to relieve those who were in the castle of Erena. He had built the castle opposite another, Santarém, which the Moors held, in order to wage war on Santarém, Lisbon, Sintra and the other castles of the Saracens which are in the surrounding area.[187]

80. At that same time the Moabites and Hagarenes went to the castle of Erena and they took it by storm. All the Christian warriors, over 250 of them, and some of the king's magnates, perished there by the sword, which caused great sadness and alarm in the household of the king of Portugal.[188]

81. While all this was going on, the emperor waged war in the land of King García. He captured his fortified castles and Count Ladrón[189] of Navarre, the most noble of all the magnates of the household of King García. He destroyed, plundered and burned his land and had the vines and trees cut down. Count Ladrón of Navarre, having sworn an oath to the emperor, served him for many years. However, after peace had been made between the emperor and Count Ladrón of Navarre, there was war for several years between King García and the

186 The location of Cernesa is unknown, although probably lay in the disputed border territory of Limia. The date of the campaign described here is impossible to establish with any certainty; see, however, Sánchez Belda, *Chronica*, pp. xlii–xliii. It is striking that our chronicler has nothing to say of the emperor's response to the Portuguese invasion of 1137. According to the *Historia Compostellana*, when Alfonso VII heard of the invasion he journeyed west from Zamora to Tuy in only three days with a small escort of knights and swiftly forced the Portuguese to come to terms: *HC*, p. 520. The peace treaty between the emperor and Afonso I of Portugal was agreed at Tuy on 4 July 1137: Fernández Flórez (ed.), *Colección diplomática*, IV, no. 1263.

187 Afonso I had begun to build the castle of Erena, better known as Leiria, about 70 kilometres south-west of Coimbra, in December 1135: see E. Flórez (ed.), *Chronicon Lusitanum*, ES 14 (Madrid, 1758), p. 409. Santarém lies on the Tagus, about 80 kilometres upstream from Lisbon and nearby Sintra.

188 Leiria fell to the Almoravids in 1140: Flórez (ed.), *Chronicon Lusitanum*, pp. 410–11.

189 The Navarrese campaign took place in October 1137. Count Ladrón Iñiguez, whose principal power-base lay in the Basque territories of Alava and Guipúzcoa, was an effectively independent magnate whose loyalties shifted between the Leonese and Navarrese courts according to the political exigencies of the time. He was a frequent visitor to the court of Alfonso VII between 1136 and 1140, and again between 1151 and 1157: see Reilly, *Alfonso VII*, pp. 164–5, 181–2.

emperor. But the power of King García against the emperor was small or non-existent. Meanwhile, in Portugal, Fernando Yáñez, the lord of Limia, together with others faithful to the emperor, made war on the king daily, with whom he did battle and fought bravely. The king himself was wounded by a spear that was bravely hurled by one of Fernando Yáñez's foot-soldiers, and he suffered for many days until he was cured by doctors. In this war Fernando captured some of the king's nobles and released them once he had stripped them of great wealth.[190]

82. It came to pass that after all these things had happened, the emperor ordered the counts of Castile, namely Rodrigo Gómez and Lope López, and the magnate Gutierre Fernández and other magnates, to be ready to make war on King García daily.[191] The emperor himself, having mustered a great army in the land of León, went to Portugal, captured many fortified castles, and destroyed and plundered a large amount of territory. For his part, the king of Portugal, having gathered his army, went to do battle with a few who had foolishly gone away from the emperor's army. After he had encountered Count Ramiro [Froilaz], who was attacking his land, they both joined battle and Count Ramiro was defeated and captured by the king.[192]

83. Afterwards, the emperor encamped outside the castle of Peña de la Reina, in the place called Portela de Vez.[193] The king of Portugal pitched his tents opposite the emperor's camp in a place that was higher and more rugged, *and there was a valley between them.*[194] Then, without the emperor's command, many nobles and knights, and the king's knights, left their camp and joined battle with one another, and many were captured on both sides as they fell from their horses to the ground.

84. Observing this battle, the high born among the Portuguese said to their king: 'Lord king, it is neither good nor useful to us to be at war with the emperor, nor will we constantly be able to withstand *so great a multitude and so strong.*[195] Tomorrow will not be like today for

190 Again, the chronology of these events is impossible to establish.

191 On the nobles mentioned, see i, 4, 7 and nn. 19 and 29. Lope López of Carrion never held comital rank; the chronicler perhaps had in mind Count Lope Díaz, the emperor's right-hand man in the Rioja, on whom see i, 7 and n. 29.

192 The campaign took place in the summer of 1141. On Count Ramiro Froilaz, see i, 4 (and n. 19), 86; *PA*, vv. 100–13.

193 Near modern Arcos de Valdevez to the north of the River Limia.

194 I Samuel xvii.3.

195 I Maccabees iii.17.

us. If there had been peace between us, all our brothers who perished
at the hands of the Saracens in the castle of Erena would not have
died. You must ensure that the Moabites and Hagarenes do not by
any chance come again against our towns and castles which are
beyond the River Duero, and cause even worse damage than they
caused before. You must command some of us, therefore, to go to ask
the emperor to make peace with us. Let us give him all his castles
which we hold, and let him return to us those which his knights
captured from us. For it is better for us to have peace than war.'

85. When he had heard his nobles' counsel, the king was pleased and
sent some of the chief men of his household as messengers to the
emperor to inform him of the discussions concerning peace between
the kings. The emperor heard them and was pleased by them. After
this, the king's messengers received a pledge from the nobles that
there would be a truce between them until the said peace was either
fulfilled or, which God would not permit, was broken. Then, finally,
the emperor's nobles went to the king's camp and likewise received a
pledge from the king's nobles in the same manner as had been given
to them.

86. The next day, the emperor's counts met with the king's nobles
and made peace between the emperor and the king, not absolutely for
ever, but for a few years. And they swore that they would establish it
more strongly on another occasion, so long as there was peace, if both
parties saw fit. All the castles which the king of Portugal had
captured in Galicia were returned to the emperor's deputies, and
likewise those of the king, which the emperor's knights had captured
from him in the war, were returned to him. Then Count Ramiro was
released and all the knights who had been captured on both sides
were set free.[196]

87. There was peace between them for many years, which, because it
was good for the Christians, was deemed to be advantageous. The
king expelled Count Rodrigo and Count Gómez Núñez from his
presence, because they had provoked discord between the emperor
and the king. Realising his guilt, Count Gómez Núñez was ashamed

196 If we are to believe the Portuguese version of events, the action at Valdevez may
   have been far more of a reverse than our chronicler is willing to admit. The
   Chronicon Lusitanum reports not only that a number of other Leonese magnates,
   including Ponç de Cabrera, Rodrigo Fernández, Vermudo Pérez and the
   emperor's half-brother, Fernando Pérez de Lara, were captured in battle, but that
   it was the emperor himself who was forced to seek terms: Flórez (ed.), *Chronicon
   Lusitanum*, p. 411.

and fled across the Pyrenean mountains, whether he wanted to or not, because there was no place for him to live, and he became a monk in the monastery of Cluny.[197] The emperor, moved by pity for Count Rodrigo, ordered him to eat bread in his presence in his palace and to be given payments of gold and silver just like one of his nobles who served him.[198]

88. The emperor decided to go to Santiago to pray, and after he had done as he had vowed he returned to the land of León and Castile. Then he went to Pamplona, in the land of King García and, having pitched camp on the plain of Pamplona, he sent raiding parties throughout the territory of King García. They set fire to much of the land, cut down vines and trees, and returned to the emperor at the camp carrying with them a great booty of oxen, cows, horses, mares and vast riches.

89. While this was going on, King García, having mustered his troops, confronted a large army from Aragon and Barcelona under Count Ramón of Barcelona. He joined battle with them, and King García was the victor on the battlefield and he captured their spoils. But while the victors divided the spoils among themselves, the emperor arrived suddenly with only thirty knights. Seeing the emperor's banners, King García and all his entourage fled, leaving all the booty in the camp and the emperor pursued the fugitives as far as their city of Pamplona.[199]

90. After this, the emperor and all his camp returned to his town of Nájera with great triumph and joy. Afterwards he went to Castile and ordered that royal proclamations should ring out throughout all the

197 The count's close relations with the Cluniacs dated from 26 July 1126 when, with his brother Fernando, he had granted the monks the monastery of Budiño near Tuy: A. Bruel (ed.), *Recueil des chartes de l'abbaye de Cluny*, 6 vols (Paris, 1876–1903), V, no. 3993.

198 The reconciliation between Alfonso VII and Count Rodrigo Pérez may not have been as immediate as the chronicler suggests. The evidence of the diplomas issued by the emperor indicates that apart from a brief spell in 1146–8, when the count can be traced at court, the Galician continued to maintain close links with Afonso I of Portugal and did not rejoin the Leonese curia on a regular basis until 1152: Barton, *Aristocracy*, p. 130 and n. 147.

199 The events described probably took place in the autumn of 1141. Alfonso VII may be traced at Nájera on 3 November of that year, and another charter of the same month records that it had been drawn up in the year that both the emperor and the count of Barcelona had gone with their armies to Pamplona: A. Ubieto Arteta (ed.), *Cartularios (I, II, y III) de Santo Domingo de la Calzada* (Zaragoza, 1978), no. 12; A. Durán Gudiol (ed.), *Colección diplomática de la catedral de Huesca*, 2 vols (Zaragoza, 1965), I, no. 157; cf. Reilly, *Alfonso VII*, p. 72.

land of León and Castile, so that in the middle of the month of May all
the knights and foot-soldiers would gather once again in Nájera to
make war on King García. When King García realised that there was
no way he could avoid war with the emperor, he was greatly saddened
and summoning his own counsellors he said to them: 'Ponder what
decision we may take, because once again the emperor, having made
peace with the king of Portugal, wishes *to come against us to destroy
us*[200] and our land, either by battle or by siege.' In the end, being unable
to come to any decision as to what they ought to do, Count Alfonso
Jordan of Toulouse,[201] who was going on a pilgrimage along the royal
road to Santiago in order to pray, turned up unexpectedly and on seeing him the king, and those who were with him, rejoiced with great
happiness.

91. Having come to a decision, Count Alfonso and other nobles of the
king went to meet the emperor. First of all, they made peace between
the emperor and the king with the following agreement: King García
would serve the emperor without deceit for all the days of both their
lives. When this had been done, the count of Toulouse and the king's
nobles asked the emperor to give King García his daughter, the
Infanta Urraca, whom he had fathered by Guntroda, the daughter of
Pedro Asturiano.[202] When they heard this, all the magnates of the
emperor's palace, together with Count Alfonso, advised the emperor
to confirm King García as his son-in-law, once he had granted him his
daughter, the aforementioned lady, as his wife. The emperor heeded
their advice and was inwardly pleased and he promised to give her to
the king. As a result, they appointed 24 June[203] as a suitable date to
hold the nuptials in the city of León.

92. Having dispatched messengers, the emperor commanded his own
knights, and all the counts, nobles and governors who were in all his
kingdom, that each of them should come prepared for the royal
nuptials with their escort of noble knights. This news was pleasing to
all, but especially to the Asturians and Tineans who, just as the
emperor had ordered, competed to come to the nuptials unsurpassably
prepared. The emperor arrived with his wife the Empress Berengaria
and a very great crowd of nobles, counts, governors and knights of
Castile. King García also arrived with a not inconsiderable troop of

200 I Maccabees iii.20.
201 See above, i, 2–4 and n. 14.
202 See above, i, 32, 95.
203 The Feast of St John the Baptist.

knights, prepared and adorned as befits a king who is betrothed in marriage. The most serene Infanta Sancha entered León through the Puerta Cauriense[204] with her niece the Infanta Urraca, King García's bride, with a great mass of noble knights, clerics, women and girls, whom the nobles of all of Spain had begotten.

93. The Infanta Sancha installed the marriage bed in the royal palace in San Pelayo,[205] and around the marriage bed there was a great crowd of minstrels, women and girls who sang with organs, flutes, *harps, psalteries and all kinds of musick.*[206] Moreover, the emperor and King García sat on the royal throne in an elevated position in front of the doors of the emperor's palace, while the bishops, abbots, counts, nobles and governors were on seats around them. Some of the nobles – among the most illustrious, indeed, in Spain – in the custom of the country spurred on their horses to gallop and they hurled their lances at a construction made of planks to demonstrate both their own skill and the strength of their horses. Others, with their spear at the ready, killed bulls which had been provoked to anger by barking dogs. Finally, in the middle of an open space they placed a pig among some blind men, who would win it if they could kill it; but in trying to kill the pig they often harmed each other, which caused great laughter among all the spectators.[207] So there was great joy in that city and they praised God, who always brought good fortune to them in everything. These nuptials were held in the month of July in the Era 1182 [= AD 1144].[208]

94. The emperor gave valuable gifts of silver and gold, horses and mules and many other riches to his daughter and to his son-in-law, King García. He blessed them and he allowed them to return to their

204 The Puerta Cauriense, one of the main gateways into León, was situated to the west of the city towards the banks of the River Bernesga.

205 The palace of San Pelayo was situated next to the church of San Isidoro.

206 Daniel iii.5, 7, 10, 15.

207 Entertainments of this kind appear to have been popular at weddings and other festivities. *The Poem of the Cid c.* 1207, for example, records that on the occasion of the wedding of the Cid's daughters to the Infantes de Carrión the Cid had seven plank turrets set up, which were all knocked down before the assembled company went in to the wedding banquet: I. Michael (ed.), *The Poem of the Cid* (Manchester, 1975), vv. 2249–50. On the popularity of bull-fighting in this period, see above n. 168.

208 All the MSS indicate that the nuptials were celebrated *in mense iulio*. However, not only does the chronicler himself earlier give the wedding date as 24 June, but two charters issued by the emperor on 30 June 1144 indicate that the marriage had taken place by that date: AHN, Clero, 518/15; 1481/6–9.

land with honour. For her part, the Infanta Sancha gave her niece many gold and silver dishes, and mules and she-mules loaded with royal riches. King García and his men set out from León amid great glory and he had in his retinue Count Rodrigo Gómez, Gutierre Fernández and many other Castilian nobles, who accompanied the king and his wife as far as their city of Pamplona.[209] King García held a magnificent royal banquet for the Castilians who were with him and for all the knights and nobles of his kingdom, and they celebrated the royal nuptials for many days. The king gave the counts and nobles of Castile great gifts and each one of them returned to his land.

95. The mother of the aforementioned queen, King García's wife, whom above we called Guntroda, after she had seen the thing that she wished for above all else, the immense honour of her daughter who, having been made queen, had been doubly honoured by her marriage to a king, having fulfilled her wordly desires, longed for heaven with all her might. Now, offering herself to God, she so clung to his service that, having become a nun in the city of Oviedo and joined with others in the church of Saint Mary,[210] the mother of God, whom she had divined to be the author and mediator of her joy, she pleased God by praising him unceasingly by day and night. And exerting herself at this task and with pious longing, bedewing the floor of the church with the fountain of her tears through her prayers, she awaited the glorious end of her life.

HERE ENDS THE FIRST BOOK

---

209 On Gutierre Fernández, see above i, 7, 28, 82; ii, 50; *PA*, vv. 279–85. On Count Rodrigo Gómez, see i, 7, 30, 82.

210 Guntroda Pérez granted a charter of endowment to the convent of Santa María de Vega in Oviedo on 13 October 1153, although it is perfectly possible that she entered the cloister well before that date. The nunnery was affiliated to the French house of Fontevrault and was ruled by Guntroda Pérez until her death in 1186: Barton, *Aristocracy*, pp. 202–3.

BOOK TWO

HERE BEGINS BOOK TWO OF THE HISTORY OF THE EMPEROR ALFONSO. OF THE
CONFLICTS AND BATTLES WHICH HE, THE NOBLES OF TOLEDO AND THE
COMMANDERS OF EXTREMADURA HAD WITH KING ʿALĪ, WITH HIS SON
TĀSHUFĪN, AND WITH THE OTHER KINGS AND PRINCES OF THE MOABITES AND
HAGARENES.

1. Departing from the natural order of things, let us come to deal
with the wars which in times past were particularly hard-fought for
the Christians. After the death of King Alfonso [VI], father of Queen
Urraca, who was the mother of the Emperor Alfonso [VII], King ʿAlī,
who was the most powerful among the Saracens, and who as king of
Marrakesh ruled over the Moabites, and on this side of the sea over
the Hagarenes far and wide, and over many other islands and peoples
of the sea, like a serpent thirsting in the summer heat, raised his head
and, as if he would triumph everywhere after the death of such a great
man, summoned all the princes, commanders and soldiers of the
Moabites, together with a great army of Arab mercenaries, and many
thousands of horsemen, crossbowmen and great companies of foot-
soldiers, as numerous *as the sand which is upon the sea shore.*[1] Having
received advice from his experts, he gathered an army and crossed the
sea with his son Tāshufīn and went to Seville. He commanded all the
kings, princes and commanders of the Moabites, who ruled over the
Hagarenes, that each of them, having assembled an army of horsemen,
crossbowmen and foot-soldiers according to his ability, should bring
scaling-ladders, siege-towers and great engines of iron and wood in
order to attack both the city of Toledo, towards which he was hasten-
ing, and the other castles and towns which are in the Transierra.[2]

2. He struck camp from Seville and in a few days reached Córdoba
and there he was joined by all the peoples who were in the land of the

1 A common biblical metaphor: see, for example, Joshua xi.4; I Samuel xiii.5; and
Judges vii.12.

2 The term *trans Serram* (literally 'beyond the Sierra') is used by our chronicler to
designate the territory that lies between the Sierra de Guadarrama and the River
Tagus. The chronology of this campaign is not altogether clear. The Christian
Anales Toledanos refer to two distinct campaigns waged by ʿAlī: the first, in 1109,
which saw the fall of Talavera on 16 August; the second, the following year, during
which Toledo was unsuccessfully besieged: E. Flórez (ed.), *Anales Toledanos, ES 23*
(Madrid, 1767), 381–423, at pp. 403, 387. However, the impression given by the
majority of the Muslim sources is that ʿAlī crossed to Spain in the summer of 1109
and that the assault on Toledo followed immediately after the fall of Talavera: J.
Bosch Vilá, *Los Almorávides* (Tetuán, 1956; repr. Granada, 1990), pp. 184–5; cf.
González, *Repoblación*, I, pp. 100–1 and n. 1.

Hagarenes. They struck camp from Córdoba and advanced through the land of Alvar Fáñez,[3] capturing castles and towns, some of which they destroyed, others which they fortified. Then they reached Toledo and destroyed San Servando[1] and Aceca. Then, approaching the city itself, they set up siege engines in strategic places and for a long time they attacked the city with arrows, stones, spears, darts and fire. But in the city was the valiant leader of the Christians, Alvar Fáñez, together with a great number of knights, archers, foot-soldiers and strong young men, who, stationed on the tops of the city walls and above the towers and gates, bravely fought against the Saracens. Many thousands of Saracens fell there, as a result of which they were forced by the valour of the Christians to flee far from the towers of the city, so that they were no longer able to harm the city nor those who were on top of the walls.

3. Seeing this, King 'Alī commanded his foot-soldiers to bring up large quantities of firewood from the vineyards and woods, and to place it secretly by night at the foot of the very strong tower situated at the head of the bridge[5] opposite San Servando. Then at midnight the Saracens began to shoot crossbow bolts and arrows with flaming tar at the wood so as to burn down the tower; but the Christians who were inside poured a large amount of vinegar onto the wood and the fire went out. At the same time, inside the city with Alvar there were a large number of old men wise in counsel and able to foresee what was likely to happen, whom King Alfonso [VI] had left there to look after the city until there should arise a king of his own lineage who might free it from war with the Saracens.

4. Seeing this, King 'Alī was inflamed with great rage and the next day at daybreak he ordered his army commanders to form up great battle-lines of *assecuti*[6] foot-soldiers with all their siege engines, then

3 Alvar Fáñez was a prominent figure on the Iberian political scene between *c.* 1080 and his death in 1114. Although later poetic legend, in particular the *Poema de mio Cid*, would portray him as the trusty lieutenant of the Cid during the latter's long periods of exile, there is no evidence that the historical Alvar Fáñez ever became estranged from the Leonese court. His main base of operations lay on the middle and upper Tagus, and he enjoyed almost viceregal authority in Toledo between 1109 and his death in Segovia in 1114. The association of Alvar Fáñez with the Cid is first made in the *Poem of Almería*: see below, *PA*, vv. 222–43.

4 On the monastic fortress of San Servando, see above pp. 159–60.

5 That is, the Puente de Alcántara, which links San Servando to Toledo.

6 The term *assecuti*, which derives from the Arabic *al-saca*, meaning 'rearguard', probably refers to the crack troops who made up the military escort which accompanied the Almoravid emir or his generals into battle.

others of the Hagarenes, and behind them yet others of the Moabites and Arabs, bringing their engines to strategic places at the foot of the city walls. *They set* by the Puerta de Almaquera[7] and on all sides numerous *artillery with engines and instruments to cast fire and stones, and pieces to cast darts and slings,*[8] mantelets, battering rams with which to undermine the city walls, and scaling-ladders to place against the towers.

5. *Whereupon* the Christians *also made engines against their engines, and held them battle*[9] for seven days without inflicting any harm upon the city. On the seventh day, at sunset, the Christian warriors bravely sallied forth out of the city through its gates and, as the *assecuti* and Hagarenes had fled, they set fire to all the siege towers which those who had fled had left behind, and to all the siege engines with which King 'Alī and his commanders had intended to undermine the city walls. And with God's help, the city remained unharmed.[10]

6. While these battles were going on, the archbishop of the church of Toledo, Bernard,[11] together with the clergy, monks, old men, women and poor, prostrated on the floor of the church of Saint Mary, prayed *all with one consent* to Lord God and to Saint Mary that the sins of the kings and of their people should not be remembered, that they themselves should not be handed over into captivity or to the sword, *nor their children for a prey, and their wives for a spoil,* and their city *to destruction,* and the holy law of God *to profanation and reproach* and contempt.[12] And Lord God on high heard their prayers and took pity on His people, and sent the Archangel Michael to guard the city of Toledo, strengthen its walls so that they would not be broken down, comfort the spirits of the warriors and defend the lives of the Christians. This could not have happened had not God protected them, for as David says: '*Except the Lord keep the city, the watchman waketh but in vain.*'[13]

7. King 'Alī, seeing that the *battle went sore against*[14] the Saracens and

---

7 The Puerta de Almaquera, which still stands to this day, was situated in the northern perimeter wall of the city.

8 I Maccabees vi.51.

9 I Maccabees vi.52.

10 The *Anales Toledanos I* record that the siege lasted for nine days: Flórez (ed.), *Anales Toledanos*, p. 387.

11 Bernard of Sédirac, archbishop of Toledo (1086–1124).

12 Judith iv.12; ix.4.

13 Psalm cxxvii.1.

14 I Samuel xxxi.3.

that his commanders and countless men were dying, withdrew from the city with all his army and went to all the towns and castles which are in the Transierra and attacked them. In payment for their sins, he destroyed the walls of Madrid, Talavera,[15] Olmos and Canales, and many others, he took many prisoners and carried out great slaughter and plunder. But the very strong towers of the aforementioned towns, which in our language are called *alcaceres*,[16] were not captured and many survivors among the Christians remained in them.[17] Guadalajara[18] and other towns and castles remained unharmed and their walls were not breached, because *the heavenly King, remembering His customary piety, wrought vengeance on* the Saracens. Indeed, that abominable people *began to fall away ceaselessly by sudden death and by the sword* of the Christians, *and to come closer to annihilation*.[19]

8. Seeing this, King 'Alī returned in haste to his city of Córdoba and while he was there he summoned his son Tāshufīn and said to him: 'Take for yourself all the kingdoms of the Hagarenes and reign over all the kings, princes and commanders that there are from the Mediterranean sea as far as Toledo, the city of the Christians, and as far as Santarém, and on the other side as far as Zaragoza, and after that as far as Barcelona. First and foremost, my son, I command you to *cause* Toledo *to fall by the sword*,[20] and afterwards their other towns and castles as far as the River Duero, because the people of Toledo have scorned me and made ready for war against me. Also, send across the sea any of the Christian warriors, slaves, boys, virtuous women and girls whom you capture'. After this, King 'Alī made his way to Seville and afterwards he crossed the sea to his city of Marrakesh, in the land of the Moabites. He took with him to Marrakesh all the Christian prisoners whom he had captured and all the prisoners, both men and women, that he had been able to find in the land of the Hagarenes.

15 According to Muslim sources, Talavera was stormed on 14 August 1109; the Christian *Anales Toledanos II* assign the event to 16 August: see González, *Repoblación*, I, p. 102 n. 9; Flórez (ed.), *Anales Toledanos*, p. 403.

16 From the Arabic *al-qaṣr*, 'fortress'.

17 A similar observation was made by the Muslim historian Ibn al-Kardabūs, *Historia*, p. 142.

18 Guadalajara, about 110 kilometres north-east of Toledo, was an important strong-point on the route that led to Zaragoza and the Ebro valley.

19 Cf. Pelayo, *Chronicon*, p. 79.

20 Jeremiah xix.7.

9. In King 'Alī's household there was a certain nobleman called Ali-
menon,[21] an intrepid and expert sailor, who held the command of all
the men of this trade in his country. Realising that the time was ripe,
and having procured a very large number of ships, he crossed the
Ocean Sea to attack Galicia, then sailed through the English Channel
and across the Mediterranean to attack the area of Ascalon and the
regions of Constantinople, Sicily, the town of Bari and other coastal
towns, the region of Barcelona, and all the kingdoms of the Franks,
attacking and devastating, massacring and slaughtering the Christians.[22]
Those whom he captured at each of the towns and castles he led to
the court of his lord, King 'Alī, and there were a great number of
Christians of noble and common birth, and of both sexes, men and
women, at the court of the king.

10. But at that time God granted His grace to the prisoners who were
in the royal court of their lord, King 'Alī, and moved His *heart
toward*[23] them in order to favour the Christians. 'Alī regarded them
above all of the men of his own eastern people, for he made some of
them chamberlains of his private apartments, and others captains of
one thousand soldiers, five hundred soldiers and one hundred soldiers,
who stood at the forefront of the army of his kingdom.[24] He furnished
them with gold and silver, cities and strongly-fortified castles, with
which they could have reinforcement in order to make war on the
Muzmutos and the king of the Assyrians, called Abdelnomen, who
attacked his territories without interruption.[25]

21 This is Muḥammad b. Maymūn, who was appointed commander of the Almoravid
    fleet in 1116. For details of his career, see A. Huici Miranda, *Historia musulmana de
    Valencia y su región*, 3 vols (Valencia, 1969–70), III, pp. 116–22.

22 For a graphic description of the havoc wrought on the coast of Galicia by such
    seaborne attacks and on the steps taken by the Christians to defend themselves, see
    HC, pp. 174–6, 262–4.

23 An echo of II Samuel xiv.1.

24 This fanciful description of the military hierarchy of the Almohad army appears to
    have been inspired by Exodus xviii.21; Deuteronomy i.15. However, the presence
    of Christian troops in the ranks of the Almoravid army is amply confirmed by other
    sources: see J. Alemany, 'Milicias cristianas al servicio de los sultanes musulmanes
    del Almagreb', in *Homenaje a D. Francisco Codera* (Zaragoza, 1904), 133–69.

25 By *Muzmutos* our chronicler is referring to the Berber Maṣmūda tribes of the Atlas
    Mountains who formed the bedrock of support for the Almohad movement
    founded by Ibn Tūmart *c.*1120. *Abdelnomen* refers to Ibn Tūmart's successor, 'Abd
    al-Mu'min (1130–63), the first caliph of the Almohads, who, from his base at
    Tīnmal in the Atlas Mountains, engaged in a bitter struggle for ascendancy with
    the Ṣanhāja Almoravids which was to culminate in the fall of the capital Marrakesh
    to his forces on 24 March 1147. Between 1147 and 1172 the whole of al-Andalus
    was brought under Almohad authority: for details, see A. Huici Miranda, *Historia*

11. Among King 'Alī's prisoners was *an honourable counsellor*[26] from Barcelona named Reverter, *and that man was* just and *perfect, and one that feared God*.[27] The king placed him in charge of the captive Christian knights and the barbarians so that he would be the commander in all his wars, for he had never been defeated in battle. And for this reason, throughout all the days of King 'Alī's life, all the king's wars were conducted by him and through his counsel. But King 'Alī grew old and *was gathered to his fathers*[28] in great old age; and his son King Tāshufīn reigned in his stead and favoured the Christians during all the days of his life, just as his father King 'Alī had done.

12. WHEN OREJA WAS CAPTURED BY THE KINGS OF THE MOABITES
It came to pass in the days of Queen Urraca that the king of Seville, the king of Córdoba and the other kings and princes of the Moabites who were in the land of the Hagarenes, having mustered a great number of horsemen, foot-soldiers and crossbowmen, came to the land of Toledo and took the castle of Oreja by storm; and they carried out a great slaughter of the Christians and took others prisoner.[29] They captured another castle, which is called Zorita,[30] fortified it

---

política del imperio Almohade, 2 vols (Tetuán, 1956–57); M. J. Viguera Molíns, *Los reinos de taifas y las invasiones magrebíes (Al-Andalus del XI al XIII)* (Madrid, 1992), pp. 203 ff.; Kennedy, *Muslim Spain and Portugal*, pp. 196ff.; cf. below, ii, 101–5. By referring to 'Abd al-Mumin as *rex Asiriorum* the chronicler appears to be comparing the Almohad caliph with King Nebuchadnezzar of the Assyrians.

26 A reminiscence of Mark xv.43.

27 Job i.1; i.8; ii.3. Reverter was the son of Gelabert Udalard of the viscomital house of Barcelona, which, having emerged as a leading family among the Catalan aristocracy in the late tenth century, suffered a precipitous decline in its fortunes during the twelfth: see Bensch, *Barcelona and its rulers*, pp. 128–35. There are some brief notes on his career in I. Frank, 'Reverter, vicomte de Barcelone (vers 1130–1145)', *Boletín de la Real Academia de Buenas Letras de Barcelona* 26 (1954–56), 195–204; S. Sobrequés i Vidal, *Els Barons de Catalunya* (Barcelona, 1957), pp. 31–2; Huici Miranda, *Historia política*, I, pp. 117–20, 123–6, 128–9, 131–2. Our chronicler's knowledge of and admiration for Reverter may say something about his own origins and loyalties: see above, p. 158, and below, ii, 101–5.

28 I Maccabees ii.69; The History of the Destruction of Bel and the Dragon i; Acts xiii.36. 'Alī b. Yūsuf died in 1143.

29 The castle of Oreja lay on the banks of the Tagus, about 50 kilometres upstream from Toledo. Oreja was conquered by the Almoravids in the summer of 1113: González, *Repoblación*, I, p. 103–4.

30 Zorita de los Canes, also on the Tagus, lies about 40 kilometres south-east of Guadalajara. The conquest of Zorita is not reported by any other source – Muslim or Christian – and a royal charter issued by Queen Urraca on 15 February 1114, which is confirmed by *Albar Fannez de Zorita*, suggests that at that date the fortress remained in Christian hands: Monterde Albiac (ed.), *Diplomatario*, pp. 118–19.

strongly with horsemen, foot-soldiers, supplies and many weapons and crossbows, and then they returned to their land.

13. At that same time, some evil men, who said that they were Christians but were not, surrendered Coria[31] to the Saracens, who also captured another castle in Extremadura called Albalate.[32] They fortified Coria and Albalate with a great number of horsemen and foot-soldiers, who daily waged war throughout all Extremadura as far as the River Duero. Those who were in Oreja attacked Toledo and the other towns which are in the Transierra every day, carrying out many massacres and seizing numerous spoils.[33]

14. After some years, King Tāshufīn, having gathered all his army, went again to Toledo; but his arrival did not escape the attention of the Christians and they fortified the city. King Tāshufīn and all his army crossed the River Tagus and they made their way to the castle called Aceca, which had been settled again by Tello Fernández, a commander from Saldaña, and by other Christians.[34] They attacked that place from midnight until sunset, the castle was stormed and captured, and they razed it to the ground. All the Christians, around three hundred warriors, perished by the sword. Tello Fernández, their leader, was taken prisoner along with many other captives. They took him with them to the great city of Córdoba, and from Córdoba he was sent across the sea to the palace of King 'Alī, and he never again returned to *the land of his nativity*.[35]

15. In those days there was in Calatrava[36] a commander called

31 Coria lies to the north of the modern province of Cáceres. On the campaigns led by Alfonso VII to conquer the city, see below ii, 40–4, 64–6.

32 The castle of Albalate lay close by the Tagus about 75 kilometres east of Coria.

33 Muslim and Christian sources refer to a number of Muslim attacks on Toledo and its territory in 1114: Ibn al-Kardabūs, *Historia*, p. 147; Flórez (ed.), *Anales Toledanos*, pp. 387, 403–4.

34 See above, i, 33 and nn. 94–5

35 Genesis xi.28; xxiv.7; xxxi.13; Jeremiah xlvi.16; Ezekiel xxi.30; xxix.14. Aceca was captured in the summer of 1130. The version of events provided by our chronicler is broadly corroborated by the *Anales Toledanos II*, which date the campaign to 1128, although it gives the number of casualties as 180 men. The same source states that after Aceca had fallen, the Almoravids went on to capture nearby Bargas, where fifty men were put to the sword, and to launch an attack on San Servando, outside Toledo, where a further twenty knights were killed: Flórez (ed.), *Anales Toledanos*, p. 404.

36 Calatrava, in the modern province of Ciudad Real, was an important fortress town dominating one of the main routes that led across La Mancha from Toledo to Andalucía.

Farax,[37] the *adalid*[38] of the tribe of the Hagarenes; and there was in San Esteban[39] another who was called 'Alī,[40] of the tribe of the Moabites. These two nobles waged a mighty war and caused great slaughter in the land of Toledo. They gathered together all the horsemen of the Moabites and Hagarenes who were in Oreja, and in all the towns and castles as far as the River Guadalquivir. When they had assembled, they made their way stealthily by night to the outskirts of the towns of the Toledans and in a hidden place they set ambushes, which in our language are called *celatas*.[41] This escaped the attention of Gutierre Armíldez,[42] the *alcaide*[43] of Toledo, who was in Alamín.[44]

16. Early in the morning the next day, a few Moabite horsemen went out into the countryside, rounded up a few oxen and then made as if to flee. Gutierre Armíldez pursued them with forty knights and they came to the place where the ambush had been prepared. Seeing this, the soldiers who were lying hidden in ambush suddenly emerged and fought with Gutierre Armíldez and with his knights. The fighting intensified greatly and Gutierre Armíldez was killed in the battle and the majority of the knights who were with him were slain.[45]

17. A knight of Toledo, whose name was Muño Alfonso,[46] who had been born in Galicia and was the governor of Mora,[47] was also captured together with some other Christian knights in the aforementioned battle. He was taken to Córdoba and they imprisoned him and tortured him with hunger and thirst. But after many days he ransomed

37 On this personage, see below ii, 35, 83, 85, 88, 95. On 9 January 1147, shortly after the conquest of Calatrava, Alfonso VII would grant to the see of Segovia *omen hereditatem Pharagii Adalil, quam in Calatrava et in ceteris villis et locis terre maurorum habuit*: Villar García (ed.), *Documentación*, pp. 86–7.

38 From the Arabic *ad-dalīl*, 'guide, military commander'.

39 This has been identified as San Esteban del Puerto, near Iznatoraf, in the modern province of Jaén: Sánchez Belda, *Chronica*, p. 272.

40 He later held the fortress of Oreja: see below ii, 51, 57–60.

41 Deriving from the Latin *celare*, 'to hide, conceal, keep secret'.

42 Gutierre Armíldez was a prominent figure in the territory of Toledo: see Hernández (ed.), *Cartularios*, nos. 25, 28–9; L. Serrano, *Los Armíldez de Toledo y el monasterio de Tórtoles* (Madrid, 1933), p. 9.

43 See above, i, 27 n. 78.

44 The castle of Alamín was situated near Escalona, on the route that led across the Sierra de Gredos from Toledo to Avila.

45 This action took place in 1131: Flórez (ed.), *Anales Toledanos*, p. 404.

46 The family origins of Muño Alfonso are unknown. On his subsequent activities, see below ii, 46, 48–9, 67–79, 81, 83–91.

47 Mora lies about 30 kilometres south-east of Toledo.

himself with gold and much silver, mules, horses and many weapons; and having ransomed himself he made his way to Toledo and then to his castle of Mora. This man later waged many campaigns in the land of the Moabites and Hagarenes and he slew famous kings and commanders, as is written in this book.

18. The aforementioned Saracen commanders again went to the towns of Toledo and fought with two brothers, Domingo Alvárez and Diego Alvárez, who were the governors of Escalona, and with many Christian knights from the other towns.[48] In payment for their sins, the Christians were defeated and the governors of Escalona together with many Christians perished by the sword.[49] On another occasion, they slew Rodrigo González,[50] a brave knight from the land of León who had gone to Toledo with some other knights to help the Christians. And again they fought with Fernando Fernández, the governor of Hita, and he, having been defeated, perished and many others with him.[51]

19. At the same time as the aforementioned battles took place, the sword and flame of King Alfonso of Aragon subdued all of Castile and a great part of the land of León, and the *aliens*[52] were in Castrojeriz, in Herrera, in Castrillo, in the castle of Burgos, in San Esteban de Gormaz,[53]

---

48 On Escalona, see above, n. 44. *Didacus Alvarez de Escalona* features among the witnesses to the will that was drawn up on behalf of one Vermudo Pérez some time between 1123 and 1131: Hernández (ed.), *Cartularios*, no. 31. The *fuero*, or charter of privileges, which was purportedly granted to Escalona by the Alvarez brothers on 4 January 1130 is a far from reliable text: T. Muñoz y Romero (ed.), *Colección de fueros municipales y cartas pueblas* (Madrid, 1847), pp. 485–9; Reilly, *Alfonso VII*, p. 29 n. 41.

49 This may refer to the heavy defeat which Christian forces are recorded to have suffered at *Massatrigo*, near Calatrava, in July 1132: Flórez (ed.), *Anales Toledanos*, p. 338; González, *Repoblación*, I, p. 138.

50 Perhaps the noble of the same name who submitted to Alfonso VII on the king's accession to the throne in March 1126: see above, i.2.

51 Hita lies about 25 kilometres north-east of Guadalajara. The chronicler almost certainly had in mind Fernando Garcés de Hita, *alcaide* of Medinaceli and Guadalajara in 1107, who was granted Hita and nearby Uceda by Queen Urraca in 1119, and who remained a dominant figure in that region until his death *c*. 1125: Hernández (ed.), *Cartularios*, no. 14; Reilly, *Urraca*, pp. 221–2, 299. On the family background of Fernando Garcés, see J. de Salazar Acha, 'El linaje castellano de Castro en el siglo XII: consideraciones e hipótesis sobre su orígen', *Anales de la Real Academia Matritense de Heráldica y Genealogía* 1 (1991), 33–68. On his son, Martín Fernández de Hita, see below ii, 48, n. 105.

52 An echo of I Maccabees iii.45.

53 San Esteban de Gormaz is situated on the banks of the River Duero, about 50 kilometres east of Soria.

in Villafranca, in Belorado, in Grañón,⁵⁺ in Nájera and in many other
castles, against which the emperor and his followers waged war daily.
The emperor was not helped with all his heart by Count Pedro of
Lara, nor by his brother Count Rodrigo González, nor by Count
Gonzalo Peláez of Oviedo. Pedro Díaz was in rebellion in Valle and
Jimeno Iñiguez in Coyanza and on their *tongues* was *mischief and
vanity*.⁵⁵ They were negotiating with King Alfonso of Aragon, and for
this reason they met a bad end, as has been written above.

20. When the war with the king of Aragon had finished, there arose
another war in Castile with King García of Pamplona and with King
Afonso of Portugal, who attacked Galicia as we have described above.
On account of these wars the emperor did not campaign in the land of
the Saracens, and for this reason the Saracens prevailed over the land of
the Christians. The strength of the Saracens and their great power continued until the Emperor Alfonso went to Jerez, and until he captured
Oreja and Coria.⁵⁶ But although the Saracens waged mighty wars, it
was always the custom of the Christians who lived in the Transierra
and in all Extremadura every year to gather themselves frequently
into formations, which sometimes were of one thousand, two thousand,
five thousand or ten thousand knights, more or less. They would go
into the land of the Moabites and Hagarenes, carry out great slaughter,
take many Saracens prisoner, seize great booty, start many fires, and
kill many kings and commanders of the Moabites and Hagarenes, and
waging war they would destroy castles and villages. They inflicted
more harm than that which they received from the Saracens.⁵⁷

21. King Tāshufīn, King Azuel⁵⁸ of Córdoba and King Avenceta⁵⁹ of
Seville, and the other princes and commanders of the Moabites and
Hagarenes, gathered an army as numerous *as the sand which is upon the*

54 Grañón lies roughly half-way between Logroño and Burgos, close by the pilgrim-
   road to Compostela.

55 Psalm x.7; x.14; xc.10; Jeremiah xx.18.

56 On the Jerez campaign of 1133, see above i, 33–42; on the capture of Oreja and
   Coria, see below ii, 50–61, 64–6.

57 The best guide to the activities and organisation of the militia forces of the frontier
   territories is J. F. Powers, *A Society Organized for War: the Iberian Municipal Militias
   in the Central Middle Ages, 1000–1284* (Berkeley, 1988).

58 This is Al-Zubayr b. 'Amr al-Lamtūnī, who played a decisive role in the Almoravid
   victory at Fraga in July 1134. See below, ii, 46, 52, 65, 67, 69, 72, 88.

59 The identity of this figure has not been established with any certainty. On his
   activities, see below, ii, 46, 52, 65, 67, 69–71, 88. The chronicler refers to these
   personages as *reges*, 'kings', but they were of course provincial governors acting at
   the behest of the Almoravid emir.

sea shore,[60] and they planned to go suddenly against the towns of Toledo, to destroy them and to win great fame for themselves. Having left Córdoba, after a few days they came to the plain of Lucena[61] and they pitched camp there.

22. While they were there, it came to pass that on the same day one thousand hand-picked and powerfully armed knights from Avila and Segovia, together with a great number of foot-soldiers, were making their way along the road which leads to the countryside of Córdoba. As they went, they learned that King Tāshufīn and his camp were in the plain of Lucena; and they called out in prayer to the God of heaven and earth, to Saint Mary and to Saint James so that they would help and defend them. Having taken divine counsel, they pitched their tents in the place where they were and, after they had divided the foot-soldiers into two equal parts, they left half of them in their tents to guard their baggage. However, the armed and well-equipped knights and the other half of the foot-soldiers marched from midday without stopping and at about the fourth hour of the night they suddenly attacked the tents of King Tāshufīn and caused great confusion in the camp.[62]

23. However, a great multitude of Moabites and Hagarenes rushed to arms and began to fight, and the battle grew greatly worse. A large number of the Saracens died and the rest fled this way and that. King Tāshufīn himself was wounded in the thigh by lances and he fled having mounted a saddleless horse. Then the Christians seized their tents, the royal standards, mules, camels, gold, silver and great wealth, and they went back to their own tents. Afterwards they returned to Extremadura, each one of them to their own towns, praising and blessing God. But King Tāshufīn returned in shame to Córdoba, was attended to by doctors and after many days he was cured of his wounds. However, he remained lame for the rest of his life.

24. After the death of Gutierre Armíldez, the commander of the army of Toledo, which has been described above, Count Rodrigo González *obtained* the emperor's *kindness*[63] and the emperor appointed him commander of the army of Toledo and lord of all Extremadura.[64] The

60 Cf. ii, 1, n. 1.

61 This may refer to Luciana, by the River Guadiana, near Calatrava: González, *Repoblación*, I, p. 140, n. 27.

62 The date of the battle of *Lucena* has not been established.

63 Esther ii.9; cf. Genesis vi.8; xxxix.4; Ruth ii.13.

64 See above, i, 23.

count, having mustered a great army from Castile and Extremadura, as well as knights and foot-soldiers from Toledo, and from the other towns which are under the authority of Toledo, advanced into the land of Seville and destroyed all that region, carried out many massacres and started many fires, and had all the fruit trees cut down.[65] He took countless men, women and children prisoner and captured immense spoils from them, gold and silver, abundant precious garments, and countless numbers of horses, mares, asses, oxen and cows, and all the beasts of the field.

25. Seeing this, the king of Seville[66] mustered many thousands of Moabites, Arabs and Hagarenes from the islands of the sea and from the coastal areas, neighbours, friends, and many princes and commanders, and he set out to find the count's camp. But this did not escape the count's notice and he *removed* his army *out of their tents, and stood over against* the Saracens, the foot-soldiers of the Christians *being divided into two troops, and their slingers and archers* with them; *and they that marched in the foreward were all mighty men.*[67] Then came the company of knights from Avila against the troops of the Arabs, and next was the company from Segovia against the troops of the Moabites and the Hagarenes. The count stood in the rearguard of the army from Toledo, the Transierra and Castile, so that he might lend aid to the helpless and consolation to the wounded.

26. Once the battle had begun, the Saracens cried out and appealed to Mohammed with bronze trumpets, drums and voices. For their part, the Christians cried out with all their hearts to Lord God, the Blessed Mary and Saint James so that they would take pity on them and forget the sins of their kings, their own and those of their relatives. And *many were slain on both parts.* Finally, the count *perceived that the strength of* the *army* was with the king of Seville, *he took with him* to the battle *all the hardy men,* and the king of Seville fell in the battle and died, and many princes and commanders with him; all the battle lines of the pagans were obliterated and they fled. The count *pursued them*

65 The campaign took place in the summer of 1132. Muslim sources reveal that the count and his forces concentrated their attention on the territory of El Aljarafe, to the west of the city of Seville: A. Huici Miranda, 'Contribución al estudio de la dinastía almorávide: el gobierno de Tasfīn ben 'Alī ben Yūsuf en el Andalus', in *Études d'orientalisme dédiées à la mémoire de Lévi-Provençal,* II (Paris, 1962), 605–21, at pp. 611–12.

66 This was Abū Ḥafṣ 'Umar b. al-Ḥājj al-Lamtūnī, known as Wamagūz, who had been appointed to the post in 1130: Huici, 'Contribución', pp. 611–2 and n. 34.

67 I Maccabees ix.11.

unto the gates of Seville, seized their spoils and booty and began the return to his camp.[68]

27. At the same time, the nobles of Salamanca invaded the land of Badajoz,[69] saying to one another, when they saw that the count wished to go to the land of Seville: 'Let us also go to the land of Badajoz, *let us also get us a name*[70] and let us not surrender the prestige of our glory to any noble or commander.' Having mustered a great army, they *went forth by the way that leadeth to*[71] Badajoz. They devastated all that region and caused many massacres and fires, took many men, women and children captive, took all their chattels, and abundant riches of gold and silver. On top of this, they seized great wealth, horses, mules, camels, asses, oxen, cows, and all the beasts of the field.[72]

28. While this was happening, King Tāshufīn gathered an army as numerous *as the sand which is upon the sea shore*[73] in order to fight with Count Rodrigo. But when he learned from a Saracen who had fled from Count Rodrigo's camp that the king of Seville had died with his nobles, he feared to go against him. He also learned from the same Saracen that the Christian camp was in the region of Badajoz, so he pursued them and set up his camp opposite the Christian one. But he did not join battle with them that day because nightfall was approaching. Seeing this, the Christians killed all the Saracen prisoners, both men and women, in case, if they obtained weapons, they would throw their camp into confusion. King Tāshufīn ordered his interpreters to ask the Christians who was the commander or chief of their army. The Christians answered them: 'We are all commanders and chiefs of our lives.' When he had heard this, King Tāshufīn realised that they were foolish and senseless, he was filled with great joy and said to those who were nearby: 'You should know that their God has abandoned these foolish men.' Many of the nobles of Salamanca, seeing what was going to happen, left the camp and fled. In the morning, once battle had begun, the Christians took to flight and all the knights and foot-soldiers were

---

68 The passage is heavily influenced by I Maccabees ix.14–17; v.21. According to Ibn 'Idhārī, the battle took place on 1 June 1132 at Azareda, on the Guadalquivir, to the north-east of Seville: Huici, 'Contribución', pp. 612–13. This is confirmed by the *Anales Toledanos I:* Flórez (ed.), *Anales Toledanos*, p. 388.

69 That is, the southern half of the modern region of Extremadura. The town of Badajoz lies on the Guadiana close by the frontier with Portugal.

70 I Maccabees v.57; iii.14; II Samuel vii.9; viii.13.

71 I Maccabees ix.2; v.24.

72 This is reminiscent of Numbers xxxi.9; Joshua vii.24.

73 Cf. ii, 1, n. 1.

killed; only a few of them survived and they fled on horseback. The defences of the camp were captured and *a great slaughter among the*[74] Christians was brought about. King Tāshufīn, taking all the spoils of the Christians, returned victoriously to his city of Córdoba.[75]

29. But this disaster was not enough for the men of Salamanca, for in that same year and in those that followed the same thing happened to them three times, because they trusted in their strength and not in Lord God, and for this reason they perished wretchedly.[76] After this, they did penance for their sins, they called out to the Lord and gave tithes and first-fruits to God. And God heard them and gave them skill and courage with which to wage war. With Count Ponç,[77] and with other of the emperor's commanders, they always went to the land of the Moabites and Hagarenes, they fought many battles, won victory and took great booty from their land. And the city of Salamanca became great and famous through its knights and foot-soldiers and very wealthy.

30. However, Count Rodrigo [González] returned to Toledo with all his army without any difficulty, praising and blessing the Lord, *who saveth them that trust in him.*[78] The other battles that Count Rodrigo fought with the kings of the Moabites and Hagarenes, and the slaughter which he carried out, are not described in this book. Once these things had been achieved, Count Rodrigo became a pilgrim and went across the sea to Jerusalem to pray, as we have written above.[79]

31. Finally, the emperor gave Toledo and many towns and castles in Extremadura and Castile to Rodrigo Fernández,[80] and he appointed

74 I Samuel iv.17.

75 The chronicler gives the impression that this action took place at the same time as Count Rodrigo González's expedition to Seville. However, not only do the Muslim sources make no mention of such a campaign, but they record that in the late spring of 1132 Tāshufīn and the governor of Córdoba suffered an important defeat at Christian hands near the Portuguese town of Evora. The disastrous Badajoz campaign which is described here appears to have taken place in March 1134: Huici, 'Contribución', pp. 613, 616.

76 Two of the military failures alluded to may have occurred in October 1134 and June 1136: Huici, 'Contribución', pp. 616–18.

77 On Count Ponç de Cabrera: see below ii.96; *PA*, vv. 176–98. For details of his career, see S. Barton, 'Two Catalan magnates in the courts of the kings of León–Castile: the careers of Ponce de Cabrera and Ponce de Minerva re-examined', *JMH* 18 (1992), 233–66; Barton, *Aristocracy*, pp. 284–5.

78 Susanna, 60.

79 See above i, 48.

80 On whom, see i, 7, 47 and n. 29; ii, 34, 36, 50, 60.

him commander of the army of Toledo. Mustering the army of Toledo
and Castile, both knights and foot-soldiers, he went to the land of the
Moabites and Hagarenes and carried out many massacres, started
many fires and took many prisoners. He captured much gold and silver,
precious garments, and all the beasts of the field, *and every place
whereon the soles of their feet* trod remained devastated.[81]

32. Hearing this news, King Tāshufīn *was angry, and gathered together
all his friends, and the captains of his army, and those that had charge of the
horse. There came also unto him from other kingdoms, and from isles of the
sea, bands of hired soldiers,*[82] from the other side of the sea, great troops
of horsemen of the Arabs and Moabites, and there were countless
horsemen, crossbowmen and foot-soldiers. He resolved suddenly to
destroy the camp of the Christians and he went out to meet them at a
place called Almonte.[83]

33. When he saw them, the commander of Toledo said to the Christians: '*Fear ye not their multitude, neither be ye afraid of their assault.
Remember how* the lord king Alfonso and *our fathers* by waging war
captured Toledo and all the kingdom as far as the River Duero. *Now
therefore let us cry unto heaven, if peradventure* our God *will have mercy
upon us,* and may God *destroy* them *before our face this day.'*[84] When the
battle-lines of horsemen, foot-soldiers and crossbowmen had been
drawn up on both sides, they joined battle and it pleased God that
many thousands of Saracens were killed. King Tāshufīn was defeated
and he fled from that battlefield with all his army. The Christians *got
much gold, and silver, and* horses, mules, camels *and great riches. After
this they went home* to Toledo *and sang a song of thanksgiving, and praised
the Lord in heaven: because it is good, because his mercy endureth for ever.*[85]

34. Again, for a second time, Rodrigo Fernández, the commander of
Toledo, having gathered an army, went to the land of the Moabites
and Hagarenes. Their kings went out to meet him at a place called
Serpa,[86] and the commander of Toledo was the victor, captured great

81 Deuteronomy xi.24; Joshua i.3.
82 I Maccabees vi.28–9; iii.27.
83 Its location is unknown. The chronicler may be referring to the River Almonte
   near Cáceres, or perhaps to Almonacid to the south-east of Toledo.
84 The speech is modelled chiefly upon that attributed to Judas Maccabeus before he
   did battle with Gorgias: I Maccabees iv.8–10; iii.22.
85 I Maccabees iv.23–4.
86 This probably refers to the locality of the same name in the modern Portuguese
   province of Beja.

spoils from the Saracens, and returned to Extremadura with great joy. And again, for a third time, the commander of Toledo, having gathered his army, went into the land of his enemies and inflicted great slaughter, and killed many Moabites and Hagarenes. Whereupon their kings, having mustered a great number of horsemen and foot-soldiers, went to meet him at a place called Silves and, once battle had commenced, the Moabites and Hagarenes took to flight, many thousands of them were killed, and the rest fled in all directions.[87] The commander of Toledo was the victor of the field, the Christians captured great spoils of theirs and they returned to Toledo with great joy and gladness singing 'Te Deum laudamus, te Dominum confitemur' until the end.

35. At that time there was a knight in Extremadura, a warlike man called Gaucelm de Ribas.[88] He was very wealthy in gold, silver, bread and wine, and in all the riches of this world. This knight went to the emperor and asked him to instruct him to rebuild the castle of Aceca, and the emperor agreed. So Gaucelm went to Aceca with his sons, his wife, his sons-in-law and their wives, together with the commander of Toledo and a large army. They pitched their camp at the foot of the castle which had been destroyed by King Tāshufīn when he carried off Tello Fernández from there, and they builded up the castle with high walls and strong towers round about, lest the Moabites and Hagarenes should come and tread it down, as they had done before. The same knight set there with him many warlike knights and well-armed foot-soldiers to keep it, and as the guardian of Toledo he also fortified it with every kind of food, that the people of Toledo might have a defence against Oreja, where there were many Moabites and Hagarenes who waged a great war in the land of Toledo and in all Extremadura.[89] They fought a great battle with Farax, the adalid of Calatrava, and with those who were in Oreja, often conquering and fleeing in turn.

---

87 The victory at Silves in southern Portugal, took place in 1142, according to an entry in the *Anales Toledanos I*, which also claims that Rodrigo Fernández seized over ten thousand prisoners: Flórez (ed.), *Anales Toledanos*, p. 388.

88 Given his Christian name, Gaucelm de Ribas was probably of Catalan extraction. On 27 October 1136, Alfonso VII granted him rights to half of the rents owed in the district of the castle of Calatalifa; on 12 May of the following year Gaucelm witnessed a charter issued by the emperor in favour of the see of Toledo: Villar García (ed.), *Documentación*, pp. 65–6; Hernández (ed.), *Cartularios*, no. 38. *Ribas* may conceivably be Rivas de Jarama near Madrid.

89 The passage is inspired by I Maccabees iv.60–1. The reconstruction of Aceca had taken place by 1138; in that year the knight confirmed a charter of Archbishop Raymond of Toledo as *Goscelmus de Acecha*: Hernández (ed.), *Cartularios*, no. 39.

36. In the month of May in the Era 1176 [= AD 1138], the Emperor
Alfonso took with him Rodrigo Fernández, the commander of the
army of Toledo, who was renowned in warfare, Count Rodrigo[90] from
the land of León, and other men and nobles from his household,
together with a great army from Extremadura, and after they had set
off he pitched camp by the River Guadalquivir. Many raiding parties
travelled far away for many days and plundered all the land of Jaén,
Baeza, Ubeda, Andújar and many other towns.[91] They set fire to all
the villages they found, destroyed their mosques and consigned to the
flames the books of the law of Mohammed. They put to the sword all
the doctors of that law that they encountered. They had the vines,
olive groves, fig trees and all the other trees cut down,[92] *and every place
whereon the soles of their feet* trod remained devastated.[93] After many
days they returned to the emperor at the camp, bringing with them a
large number of men, women and children captive, gifts of gold and
silver, precious garments, all their riches and chattels, together with
large numbers of stallions, mares, oxen, cows, sheep and goats.[94]

37. While this was happening, part of the army of Extremadura
crossed the River Guadalquivir without the emperor's command or
that of his nobles, and invaded the land of the Saracens. They took
great plunder and started many fires, and returned to the same place
where they had previously crossed the river; but through their slug-
gishness and the abundance of the riches that they had captured, they
did not cross the river and stayed there. At midnight there was a
great downpour of rain and the water rose greatly. The next morning,
that people was unable to cross the river either by swimming or by
any other means.[95]

38. The emperor, forseeing what was going to happen, went far away
with his own army so as not to witness the death of his people. At
around the third hour of the day, that multitude, lifting their gaze,
saw great companies of horsemen and foot-soldiers of the Moabites

90 This almost certainly refers to Count Rodrigo Martínez.

91 All the towns mentioned lay in the region of the Upper Guadalquivir.

92 Judith ii.27–8 (cf. Vulgate ii.17–18).

93 Deuteronomy xi.24; Joshua i.3.

94 Muslim sources date this campaign to 1137. However, what we know of Alfonso
     VII's itinerary during that year renders that unlikely: Huici, 'Contribución', p. 619;
     Reilly, *Alfonso VII*, pp. 344–6.

95 Heavy rainfall and flooding are also said to have hindered the progress of the
     raiding party that Alfonso VII dispatched into the region of the Upper Guadal-
     quivir: Huici, 'Contribución', p. 619.

and Hagarenes drawn up, coming to destroy them. Seized with terror, their courage and skill in warfare deserted them, and they shouted to the commander of Toledo and to Count Rodrigo to have pity on them. The nobles answered them: 'You can see that *between us and you there is a great gulf fixed;* for neither can you pass over to us, nor can we pass over to you.'[96] Again the nobles said: '*Confess your faults one to another, and pray,*[97] and partake of the consecrated bread which you have with you, and God will have mercy upon your souls.'

39. Then the Christians, well provided in faith and weapons, killed all the Saracen captives, men, women and children, whom they had taken prisoner, as well as the animals which they had with them. Then the Saracens attacked them without delay and all the Christians were slain, and none of them survived except for one Christian knight, who flung himself into the water and emerged on the other side of the river among the Christians. All the Christians and Saracens who saw this miracle were astonished. The Saracens went away, taking with them many heads of the Christians and their spoils. After things had turned out in this manner, the counts struck camp and went to the emperor and recounted to him everything that had happened; the emperor was saddened and he returned to Toledo and everyone else went back to their own land.

40. In July of the same year, the emperor summoned Count Rodrigo of León, his own household troops, and the men of Salamanca, and he set off to conquer Coria, and set ambushes far from its walls.[98] Then he sent raiding parties around Coria to seize the men, women and all the beasts of the field, which they did. Seeing this, the Moabites and Hagarenes bravely sallied forth out of the town gates in order to pursue the Christians; the latter pretended to flee in terror, wishing to draw them far from the town. When they passed the places where the Christians were hidden, the emperor appeared on the field, and those who were lying in ambush came out and killed all the Moabites and Hagarenes and their commanders, and not one of them remained.

41. Seeing this, those who had remained inside the town blocked the gates with a big, strong wall. Then the emperor ordered camps to be set up around the town and he sent messengers throughout all the land of Extremadura and the land of León, so that all the knights and

96 Inspired by Luke xvi.26.

97 James v.16.

98 This entire chapter is inspired by Judges xx.29–33; Joshua viii.13–16. Again, the chronicler is referring to Count Rodrigo Martínez.

foot-soldiers would go to the siege of the town; and he who did not go would offend the emperor and his house would be confiscated. The town was besieged in such a way that no Saracen could go in or out, because the Christian commanders and nobles built very high wooden towers, which rose up above the walls, and siege engines and mantelets with which to assault the town.

42. One day, before sunrise, the emperor summoned the counts, nobles and commanders, and ordered them to draw up the siege towers to assault the town at daybreak. He himself went to the mountain with his hunters to kill deer, wild boar and bears. When day broke, they began to assault the town, and Count Rodrigo Martínez climbed up one of the wooden towers which he had built, and with him went many knights, archers and slingers. Then a certain Saracen shot an arrow by chance towards the siege tower which the count had climbed. Alas! in payment for the count's sins, the arrow struck through the framework of the siege tower; the shaft lodged in the frame, but the iron head was separated from the wood and, penetrating his helmet and hauberk, it struck the count's neck and wounded him.

43. However, as soon as the count realised that he had been hit, he hastily took hold of the arrowhead in his hand and drew it from the wound, from which blood immediately began to flow; and neither the skill of sorcerers nor doctors could staunch it that day. Finally he said to those around him: 'Take off my armour, for I am gravely wounded.' They removed his armour straightaway and carried him to his tent, and for the whole day they devoted themselves with the utmost diligence to curing the wound, until at sunset all hope in medicine was lost at the same time as his life. As soon as this became known in the camps, there was great wailing and lamentation beyond reckoning by all men. Hearing this, as he returned from the mountain and discovered its cause from those whom he asked, the emperor came to the camps and, summoning his nobles, in the presence of all of them made the dead man's brother, Osorio, count in his place.[99]

44. The following day, the emperor, seeing himself overwhelmed by many misfortunes and yielding to circumstance, withdrew from the besieged town and all his nobles went away with him at the same time. He travelled in safety to Salamanca, and the others returned to

99 The chronicler's claim that Osorio Martínez was elevated to comital rank soon after the siege of Coria is supported by documentary evidence: Barton, *Aristocracy*, p. 271, n. 4.

their homes. However, Count Osorio, who had recently been made a count, as has been described, and his own escort of knights and that part of the dead man's which had joined him, having taken the body of Count Rodrigo, made their way to León with great lamentation which grew from town to town; and they *buried him* with every honour *in the sepulchre of his fathers*, next to the church of Saint Mary where the episcopal seat is to be found.[100]

45. After this, King Tāshufīn went across the sea to the city of Marrakesh, to the palace of his father King 'Alī, and he took with him many Christians who are called Mozarabs, who had lived in the land of the Hagarenes since ancient times.[101] He also took with him all the prisoners whom he had found in all the land that was under his authority, and he settled them with other Christian captives in towns and castles facing those people who are called Muzmutos,[102] who were attacking the whole of the land of the Moabites.

46. After a few years, King Azuel of Córdoba, King Avenceta of Seville and other kings and princes, having gathered a great multitude of horsemen and foot-soldiers who were in the land of the Hagarenes, came again to the towns of Toledo. They caused great slaughter and much harm in Escalona and Alamín, and they captured the castle of Mora through the negligence of Muño Alfonso.[103] I say it was through negligence because he had not strengthened it with men and provisions as he should have done; and for this reason it was captured by the Saracens, and they fortified it with strong warriors and supplies.

47. When they came to the land of Toledo or to its towns, the armies of the Moabites and Hagarenes did not tarry there in combat for any

100 I Maccabees ix.19. The pantheon of Rodrigo Martínez and his kin may have been situated in the monastery of San Pedro de los Huertos, close by León cathedral, which the count's parents, Count Martín Flaínez and Countess Sancha Fernández, had received from the royal infantas Urraca and Elvira Fernández in 1099: P. Martínez Sopena, 'El conde Rodrigo y los suyos: herencia y expectativa del poder entre los siglos X y XII', in *Relaciones de poder, de producción y parentesco en la Edad Media y Moderna*, ed. R. Pastor (Madrid, 1990), 51–84, at p. 52, n. 3.

101 Mozarab, from the Arabic *musta'rib*, meaning 'Arabized', was a term used to denote Christians who lived under Muslim rule in al-Andalus. Tāshufīn b. 'Alī left the peninsula in January 1138 and reached Marrakesh the following March: Huici, 'Contribución', p. 619.

102 See above, ii, 10 and n. 25.

103 Escalona was stormed by Almoravid forces under the command of Tāshufīn b. 'Alī in December 1136: González, *Repoblación*, I, p. 139 and n. 25; Huici, 'Contribución', p. 619. According to Ibn 'Idhārī, the castle of Mora was captured in 533 AH (9 September 1138 to 28 August 1139): González, *Repoblación*, I, p. 143.

more than a single day and night, and they immediately returned to their own land for fear of the emperor and of the warriors who lived in Avila, Segovia and in all Extremadura; and for this reason they returned home without giving battle.

48. When the emperor heard that Mora had been captured, he went there and built a better and stronger castle facing it called Peña Negra.[104] He garrisoned it with knights, warlike foot-soldiers and provisions, and entrusted it to the care of a nobleman whose name was Martín Fernández,[105] who daily attacked those who were in Mora until the emperor captured it.[106] However, after the Saracens had captured Mora, Muño Alfonso was ashamed and for many days he did not dare to appear before the emperor. Instead he placed himself in great danger, and with his friends, the warriors of Toledo, Guadalajara, Talavera, Madrid, Avila, Segovia and other towns, he did not cease to make war daily in the land of the Moabites and Hagarenes. He inflicted great slaughter, fires and pillage, he fought with many of the princes and commanders of the Moabites and Hagarenes, and he vanquished and slew them, and captured their spoils.

49. Seeing that Muño Alfonso was a warlike man, the emperor summoned him to his presence, granted him his favour and appointed him second-in-command,[107] that is to say the deputy *alcaide* of Toledo, and he commanded all the knights and foot-soldiers who lived in all the towns and castles in the Transierra to obey him. Similarly, all the warriors of the whole of Extremadura obeyed him, on account of his honesty and his military expertise displayed in the many battles which they fought with him in the land of the Saracens. But the Moabites and Hagarenes who lived in Oreja caused great harm to Toledo and to all its towns.

104 The remains of the castle of Peña Negra can still be seen today; for a rough sketch of the ground-plan, see J. Porres Martín-Cleto, *Los Anales Toledanos I y II* (Toledo, 1993), p. 118.

105 Martín Fernández, son of Fernando Garcés de Hita, came to play a leading role in the campaigns waged by Alfonso VII in al-Andalus and was rewarded with tenancies in Calahorra and Peñafiel: see below ii, 81, 84–6, 96; *PA*, vv. 256–71; Reilly, *Alfonso VII*, pp. 191.

106 Somewhat surprisingly, our chronicler omits to mention that Mora was recaptured by the Christians in April 1144: Flórez (ed.), *Anales Toledanos*, p. 389.

107 *secundum principem*. In other words, Muño Alfonso was to be second in command to the acting governor, Rodrigo Fernández de Castro.

50. WHEN THE EMPEROR COMMANDED THE GOVERNOR OF TOLEDO, RODRIGO
FERNANDEZ, AND HIS BROTHER, GUTIERRE, TO BESIEGE OREJA

In the thirteenth year of the rule of the Emperor Alfonso, the emperor
himself, seeing that *the Lord had given him rest round about from all his
enemies,*[108] having deliberated with his own counsellors, commanded
two of his nobles, namely Gutierre Fernández and his brother
Rodrigo Fernández, who was the most important among the *alcaides*
of Toledo, that each of them with their own escort of knights, and
with all the knights and foot-soldiers who were in Toledo and in all
the towns which are in the Transierra, together with all the
inhabitants of the whole of Extremadura, should besiege the castle of
Oreja. And it was besieged in the month of April.[109]

51. Afterwards, the emperor, having mustered an army of knights
from all Galicia, from the land of León and from Castile, together
with a large troop of infantry, went to Oreja and surrounded the
castle with great fortifications.[110] But inside the fortifications of the
castle was the aforementioned commander 'Alī, that murderer of the
Christians and of the commanders who had been slain in the Transierra, and with him was a large company of foot-soldiers, crossbowmen and horsemen of the Moabites and Hagarenes. The castle was
very strong and was well fortified with all kinds of weapons and
crossbows. Nevertheless, the emperor ordered his engineers to build
siege towers and many engines with which to attack the castle, he
ordered sentries to be placed along the riverbank in order that he
might destroy them by thirst, and he ordered a mantelet to be erected
at the place where the Saracens secretly drew water.[111]

52. On hearing this, King Azuel of Córdoba, King Avenceta of Seville
and Avengania, the military commander of Valencia,[112] were saddened
and greatly troubled, and they summoned the other kings, princes
and commanders, and all the horsemen and foot-soldiers who were in

108 II Samuel vii.1; vii.11.

109 A Muslim source records that the siege of Oreja began in Ramadan 533 AH, that
is, May 1139: Huici Miranda, *Historia musulmana de Valencia*, III, p. 97.

110 These siege works are referred to in a charter of Alfonso VII, drawn up on 25 July
1139 and issued *in illo castello novo quod fecit imperator predictus iuxta Aureliam
quando eam tenebat obsessam*: M. Romaní Martínez (ed.), *Colección diplomática do
mosteiro cisterciense de Sta María de Oseira (Ourense) (1025–1310)*, I (Santiago de
Compostela, 1989), no. 16.

111 The phrase is inspired by Judith vii.9 (Vulgate).

112 On *Avengania*, see above i, 48, n. 125.

the whole of the land of the Hagarenes, and a great number from the islands of the sea. Another great army of Moabites and Arabs, sent by King Tāshufīn of Marrakesh, came to their aid and they were joined by very large companies of foot-soldiers, who are called *azecuti*,[113] who followed the great caravans of camels loaded with flour and with *all food that is eaten*.[114] There were almost thirty thousand horsemen, and the number of foot-soldiers and crossbowmen was beyond reckoning.

53. Striking camp from Córdoba, they made their way along the royal road which leads to Toledo and they reached the wells of Algodor,[115] pitched camp there, and laid many hidden ambushes. With them was King Avengania of Valencia with all his army, and they commanded them and said: 'If the emperor comes to join battle with us, go up to his camp by the other side, put all the warriors to the sword, set the camp on fire and reinforce the castle with horsemen, foot-soldiers, arms and *all food which is eaten*,[116] which we have on our camels, and with water. Then follow us to where you know we shall be. We shall go to Toledo and there we shall await the emperor to give battle.'

54. However, the emperor's spies came to him at the camp and reported to him in the presence of all his magnates, nobles and commanders the decisions and actions of the Saracens.[117] Having taken divine counsel that they should not go out to fight the Saracens, but wait for them in their camps, for the castle would be lost***.[118] The immense army of the Moabites and Hagarenes went to Toledo and attacked San Servando, but its high towers were not damaged. They did, however, destroy a watchtower which stood opposite San Servando and four Christian souls perished in it; and many of them went to Aceca but they did not do any harm there.

55. Afterwards they began to destroy the vineyards and orchards, but in the city was the Empress Berengaria with a great troop of knights, crossbowmen and foot-soldiers, who stationed themselves on the gates, towers and walls of the city and defended it. On seeing this, the empress sent messengers to the kings of the Moabites to say to them: 'This the empress, the wife of the emperor, says to you: "Can you not

113 See above, ii, 4, n. 6.

114 Genesis vi.21.

115 This probably refers to a location near the River Algodor, south of Mora.

116 Genesis vi.21

117 There are echoes here of Genesis xlii.29.

118 There is a lacuna in all the manuscripts at this point, with the exception of MS *A*, which inserts *perderent.*

see that you are attacking me, a woman, and that this is dishonourable for you? If you wish to fight, go to Oreja and fight the emperor, who is waiting for you with his battle-lines armed and prepared.'" On hearing this, the kings, princes and commanders, and the whole army raised their eyes and saw the empress seated on the royal throne in a fitting place at the top of a very high tower, which in our language is called an *alcázar*, dressed as befitted the wife of an emperor, and round her was a great crowd of virtuous women singing to drums, harps, cymbals and psalteries. When the kings, princes, commanders and the whole army saw her, they were amazed and overcome by shame; they hung their heads in the presence of the empress and went away, and thenceforth they caused no further harm. They withdrew the ambushes which they had laid and returned to their land without honour or victory.

56. Meanwhile, the emperor ordered sentries to be placed along the riverbank, so that the Saracens could not draw water and he might destroy them by thirst; and they erected a mantelet at the place where they secretly drew water.[119] But the Moors[120] sallied out of the castle and set fire to it, because they found it unguarded. However, *they also of* the castle *were kept so strait, that they could neither come forth, nor go out, wherefore they were in great distress for want of victuals, and a great number of them perished through famine*[121] and thirst because the water tanks that were inside were emptied and they could not obtain water by any means. Then the emperor's engineers drew up siege engines and catapults against the castle and they began to destroy the towers.

57. Seeing this, 'Alī, having taken counsel with his followers, sent messengers to the emperor saying: '*Make a covenant with us* and *give us* one month's *respite, that we may* again *send messengers* across the sea *unto* our king, Tāshufīn, and to the whole of the land of the Hagarenes. *And then, if there be no man to save us, we will come out to thee* and give you the castle, on condition that you let us go in peace with all that is ours to our city of Calatrava.' The emperor replied to them: 'I will make a truce with you on this condition: you will hand over to me fifteen noble hostages from among your followers, excepting 'Alī; *and then, if there be no man to save* you, you will surrender the castle to me; all the crossbows, weapons and all the royal wealth are to remain there, but you may take your personal possessions with you; moreover,

119 Cf. ii, 51 and n. 111.

120 This is one of the few occasions in the prose chronicle where the chronicler employs the term *Mauri* to refer to the Muslims.

121 Our chronicler takes as his inspiration the Biblical account of the siege of Jerusalem by Simon Maccabeus: I Maccabees xiii.49.

all the Christian captives who are in your prison shall be fed from my
own table by my servants and they are also to remain behind with
me.'[122] 'Alī and his followers reluctantly agreed to these words, he
handed over the hostages and they were sent under guard to Toledo,
and he promised on oath to comply with all the conditions which have
been written down above; and the emperor was satisfied by this.

58. Then messengers travelled across the sea to the palace of King
Tāshufīn, who ruled in place of his father 'Alī, and they *told him*
everything that the kings who were in the land of the Hagarenes had
done and everything that *had happened* at the castle. *When he heard
thereof,* he, his princes, commanders and all his household were *con-
founded,* for events were not turning out as they had wished.[123] The
messengers, finding no comfort at the palace of King Tāshufīn, nor
any decision from the kings who were in the land of the Hagarenes,
returned to Oreja and, on behalf of King Tāshufīn and the others, informed 'Alī and those who were with him, that they should not harbour
any hope and that they should surrender the castle to the emperor.

59. And so, on the last day of the month, early in the morning, the
castle was surrendered and the towers were filled with Christian
knights, and the royal standards were raised above a high tower.
Those who held the standards shouted out loud and proclaimed:
'Long live Alfonso, emperor of León and Toledo!' Hearing and seeing
this, the bishops, all the clergy and everyone who were in the camps
raised their hands to heaven and sang *'Te Deum laudamus, te Dominum
confitemur'*, and so on.

60. 'Alī and those who were with him went out of the castle, taking
with them their own possessions and leaving behind in the hands of
the Christians the Christian captives and all the royal wealth. They
came before the emperor, who received them peacefully, and they
stayed with him at the camp for a few days and their hostages were
returned to them. After this, he let them go away to Calatrava and
Rodrigo Fernández went with them in order to protect them, because
the Toledans wished to kill them.[124]

122 This account of the negotiations is modelled upon I Samuel xi.1–3.

123 The passage echoes the reaction of Lisias to the defeat of Gorgias by Judas
   Maccabeus: I Maccabees iv.26–7.

124 One is tempted to conclude from this episode that there was precious little enthusiasm among the frontier militia forces for the chivalrous code practised towards
   a vanquished foe by the emperor and his magnates; cf. below ii, 98; J. Gillingham,
   'Conquering the barbarians: war and chivalry in twelfth-century Britain', *Haskins
   Society Journal* 4 (1993), 67–84.

61. The castle was besieged by the Emperor Alfonso in the month of April and captured in the month of October in the Era 1177 [= AD 1139], and *the reproach was put away*[125] and with it the greatest war that had been waged in the land of Toledo and in the whole of Extremadura.[126] Afterwards, the emperor ordered the castle to be reinforced with a garrison of knights and foot-soldiers, crossbows, engines and all kinds of weapons, and water and *all food which is eaten*.[127] All the army, and the nobles and commanders returned to their own homes singing and praising God, because a great victory had been won *into the hand of*[128] his servant, the Emperor Alfonso.

62. After this, the emperor resolved to go to Toledo. When all the people heard that the emperor was coming to Toledo, all the nobles among the Christians, Saracens and Jews and all the people of the city went far out of the city to greet him with drums, *harps, psalteries and all kinds of musick*,[129] each one of them in their own language praising and glorifying God, who brought success to every one of the emperor's deeds, and calling out: '*Blessed is he that cometh in the name of the Lord*, blessed are you, your wife and your children and the kingdom of your forefathers, and blessed is your mercy and your patience.'[130] And they led him into the city through the Puerta de Alcántara.[131]

63. Inside, Archbishop Raymond[132] of the church of Toledo went into the city square with a great procession of clergy and monks. He greeted

125 I Maccabees iv.58.

126 The *Anales Toledanos I* consign the conquest of Oreja to September 1139: Flórez (ed), *Anales Toledanos*, p. 388. However, the evidence of the emperor's own diplomas indicates that the castle probably fell to his forces some time between 18 and 26 October of that year: Reilly, *Alfonso VII*, p. 66. On 27 October, the Infanta Sancha made a grant to the abbey of Sahagún *eo anno et mense quo capta est Aurelia*: Fernández Flórez (ed.), *Colección diplomática*, pp. 165–6.

127 Genesis vi.21.

128 Judges xv.18.

129 Daniel iii.5, 7, 10, 15.

130 Cf. Psalm cxviii.26; Matthew xxi.9, xxiii.39; Mark xi.10; Luke xiii.35, xix.38. The passage bears numerous similarities with that which describes Alfonso VII's entry into Zaragoza in 1134: see above, i, 65.

131 The Puerta de Alcántara was the gateway into the city that stood at the end of the bridge across the Tagus opposite the castle of San Servando. Alfonso VII had reached Toledo by 26 October 1139 when he made a grant of property to one Miguel Pérez: C. de Ayala Martínez (ed.), *Libro de privilegios de la Orden de San Juan de Jerusalén en Castilla y León (siglos XII–XV)* (Madrid, 1995), no. 39. On 3 November, while still in Toledo, the emperor put in train the resettlement of Oreja by granting it a *fuero*, or charter of rights and obligations: A. García Gallo, 'Los fueros de Toledo', *AHDE* 45 (1975), 341–488, at pp. 469–71.

132 Raymond of Sauvetot, archbishop of Toledo (1124–52).

the emperor, and they went with him into the church of Saint Mary singing and calling out: *'Fear God, and keep his commandments'*,[133] and so on. When he had given the blessing, the archbishop withdrew, and the emperor was received in the *alcázar* and the royal palace, and he stayed there for several days. Afterwards he went to the towns of Toledo and its castles, *destroying the ungodly out of them, and all the workers of iniquity* who were in the whole of Extremadura *were troubled.* And *salvation,* mercy, peace and virtue *prospered in his hand* and all those who were in his entire kingdom were *glad with his acts.*[134]

64. After Oreja had been captured, when a period of two years and six months had passed by, the emperor approached Coria. He surrounded it with camps and ordered his engineers to build a wooden tower, which rose up above all the town walls, and siege engines, catapults and mantelets, with which they began to undermine the town walls and to destroy the towers. Then, seized with great terror, the Moabites and Hagarenes who were inside the town blocked all the gates with a big, strong wall and *were kept so strait, that they could neither come forth, nor go* out.[135] Finally, a mighty famine overcame the town and many of the Hagarenes died of hunger.

65. When the Moabites saw that they were being completely over-whelmed, they asked the emperor for a solemn pledge of peace, as follows: that they might seek someone who would free them for up to a period of thirty days; but if not, they were to surrender the town peacefully with all its prisoners and royal revenues. When they heard this, the emperor and all his counsellors agreed. And so, having sent messengers to their king, Tāshufīn, who ruled in place of his father 'Alī, to the palace of King Avenceta, and to the palace of King Azuel, they reported to them everything that had happened to them, and what kind of pact they had made with the emperor of León. King Tāshufīn and the kings, lacking the power to liberate them or their city, with great lamentation ordered them to surrender the town, to save their lives and to comply with everything that they had agreed with the emperor. And it was done thus without delay.

---

133 Ecclesiastes xii.13; cf. above, i, 66.

134 The passage is heavily influenced by I Maccabees iii.6–8. The chronicler's statement that Alfonso VII left Toledo to visit the towns and castles in the vicinity can be partially corroborated: on 15 November 1139 the emperor and his entourage may be traced at nearby Maqueda: P. Rassow (ed.), 'Die Urkunden Kaiser Alfons VII. von Spanien', *Archiv für Urkundenforschung* 11 (1930), 66–137, no. 16.

135 I Maccabees xiii.49; cf. above ii, 56.

66. After the town had been surrendered to the emperor, it was cleansed of the *uncleaness* of the barbarian people and of the pollution of Mohammed, and having removed all the filth of the pagans of that town and of their temple,[136] they dedicated a church in honour of Saint Mary forever virgin and all the saints, and they ordained there as bishop a religious man named Navarro,[137] given that in antiquity it had been an episcopal see in the time of Archbishop Ildefonsus[138] and King Reccared,[139] when all that land belonged to the Christians from the Mediterranean as far as the Ocean Sea.[140] The city of Coria was captured in the Era 1181 [= AD 1143], in the month of June.[141] After the emperor, with God's help, had enriched himself with such triumph and victory, he returned honourably and peacefully with all his army to his city of Salamanca, praising God whose *mercy endureth for ever.*[142]

67. WHEN THE TERRIFIED MOABITES ABANDONED THE CASTLE OF ALBALATE

When the Moabites and Hagarenes who were in Albalate saw that Coria had been captured, they were greatly frightened and they left and abandoned the castle. The Christians from Avila and Salamanca went there and razed it to the ground. The next year, a very valiant man, Muño Alfonso, of whom as *alcaide* of Toledo we have spoken above, chose nine hundred of the bravest knights from Toledo and from the other towns of the Toledans, and from Avila and Segovia,

136 The passage is inspired by the description of the aftermath of the fall of Gaza to Simon Maccabeus: I Maccabees xiii.47–48.

137 Navarro, bishop of Coria (1142–51), and later bishop of Salamanca (1151–58/9).

138 St Ildefonsus, bishop of Toledo (657–67), was a distinguished scholar and a leading luminary of the Visigothic Church.

139 Reccared I, king of the Visigoths (586–601), who, by renouncing the Arian heresy and adopting the Catholic faith, helped bring about the religious unity of the peninsula.

140 Alfonso VII endowed the church of Coria on 30 August 1142: J. L. Martín Martín (ed.), *Documentación medieval de la iglesia catedral de Coria* (Salamanca, 1989), no. 1. This grant notwithstanding, the see remained impoverished throughout the twelfth century: Fletcher, *Episcopate*, pp. 32–4.

141 In fact, Coria fell some time in June 1142, although the city was still under siege on 6 June when the emperor made a grant to the see of Zamora: Zamora, Archivo de la Catedral, *Tumbo Negro*, fols 12v–13r. Given that the chronicler indicates at the beginning of chapter 64 that Coria was besieged two years and six months after the fall of Oreja, the chronological lapse here may be safely laid at the door of a subsequent copyist.

142 See, for example, II Chronicles vii.3, 6; Psalm cvi.1, cvii.1, cxviii.1–4, 29, Jeremiah xxxiii.11; I Maccabees iv.24. The emperor and his army had reached Salamanca by 28 July 1142: A. Barrios García, *La catedral de Avila en la Edad Media* (Avila, 1973), pp. 99–100.

and one thousand hand-picked foot-soldiers and, as was his custom, made his way with them to the middle of the countryside around Córdoba and fixed his tents there. He seized gold, silver and great riches, took many prisoners, and carried out great slaughter throughout all the countryside around Córdoba. A certain Saracen prisoner escaped and fled, and made his way to King Azuel of Córdoba and to King Avenceta of Seville, who had met together and were seeking a plan on how to make war in the land of the Christians, and how to advance on Toledo; but they could not find a suitable plan. Suddenly the aforementioned Saracen, who had fled from the Christians, arrived, and in their presence reported to them everything that the Christians had done in their land.

68. Hearing this, with great haste they immediately ordered cries and proclamations to ring out throughout all the countryside of Córdoba, Carmona and Seville, and drums and trumpets to resound in the towns, castles and villages. They were joined by many thousands of horsemen, foot-soldiers and crossbowmen, and they pursued the Christians up the well-worn road along which the latter had returned. Muño Alfonso, looking far into the distance, saw that behind him, advancing this way and that, there were numerous companies of Moabite and Hagarene horsemen assembled, with the royal standards raised, and very many battle-lines of foot-soldiers, crossbowmen, *azecuti*[143] and Hagarenes.

69. Seeing this, Muño Alfonso realised that they were King Azuel of Córdoba and King Avenceta of Seville, and he said to his comrades: 'I can see that behind us the kings of the Moabites are advancing with great companies of horsemen and foot-soldiers. Let us now hurry and go to the scrubland at Montiel,[144] and let us wait for them there with our battle-lines drawn up.' They went to that place, pitched their tents there, and everyone, on bended knee, called to the Lord in prayer, saying: 'O Jesus of Nazareth, who was hung on the cross for us and who shed your blood for us, behold the Moabites and Hagarenes, your enemies and ours, are gathered against us to destroy us. Take pity on us and rescue us. O mighty Virgin of Virgins, intercede for us before your son, our Lord Jesus Christ, and if you deliver us, we will faithfully give to your church in Toledo the tithes of all that you have given or will give to us. Saint James, apostle of Christ, defend us in

143 See above, ii, 4, n. 6.
144 Presumably the territory known as Campo de Montiel, which straddles the borders of the modern provinces of Ciudad Real and Albacete.

battle so that we may not perish by the terrible judgement of the Saracens.'[145]

70. Having said these things, Muño Alfonso prepared two very strong companies of knights against the Saracens, and again Muño said: 'O sons of the Christians of God, *be of good courage,*[146] and let us fight boldly and valiantly against King Avenceta of Seville, who is the strongest of all the Saracens; for if Avenceta were defeated or killed, they would all be vanquished. See to it that none of you die fleeing, *for it is better for us to die in battle*[147] in one place than to scatter this way and that.' Again he said: 'Remember, my comrades, that on another occasion I and sixty-two knights who were with me, some of whom are present and others who have remained in our towns, fought with King Tāshufīn, with all the army of Córdoba, and with many thousands of horsemen and foot-soldiers on the field which they call Almodóvar de Tendas.[148] And the Lord delivered them into our hands, and they were defeated; King Tāshufīn fled and his princes, commanders, and many hundreds of horsemen and foot-soldiers died, while the rest fled. None of us was killed, except for a single knight, and we captured innumerable spoils from them and returned to our towns in peace.' Again he said: 'It is as easy for God *for many to be shut up in the hands of a few,*[149] as a few in the hands of many. Now, *nevertheless, as the will of God is in heaven, so let him do.*'[150] Then they shared in the sacrifices of the Mass of the priests whom they had with them.

71. Then the armies of Moabites and Hagarenes arrived, their royal standards aloft, and they arranged in battle-order their numerous and very strong troops against the Christian troops. King Avenceta, seeing that the Christian ranks were very small and that there was no nobleman's standard among them, except for that of Muño Alfonso, the *alcaide* of Toledo, said to those around him: 'O foolish Christians, sons of dogs, you have come to lose your heads!' But once the battle

---

145 On the emergence of St James, *Santiago Matamoros,* as the patron saint of the Christian armies in their struggle against Islam, see Fletcher, *Saint James's Catapult,* pp. 65–77, 296–7.

146 Deuteronomy xxxi.6; Joshua i.18; I Samuel iv.9; I Chronicles xix.13, xxii.13, xxviii.20; II Chronicles xix.11, xxxii.7; Psalms xxvii.14; I Corinthians xvi.13. Cf. I, 13.

147 I Maccabees iii.59.

148 In all likelihood this refers to modern Almodóvar del Campo, to the south of Calatrava.

149 I Maccabees iii.18; cf. i, 15.

150 I Maccabees iii.60.

had begun, King Avenceta was immediately struck down by two
knights of Toledo (one was called Pedro Alguacil and the other
Roberto de Mongomariz),[151] he died, and his head was cut off.[152]

72. Seeing this, therefore, King Azuel and the other princes and
commanders, together with all the Moabite and Hagarene horsemen
and all the foot-soldiers, immediately took to flight, and fled this way
and that along the mountain tracks, and hid themselves in rock caves.
Muño Alfonso and the other Christians pursued them, and as he fled
King Azuel was brought to the ground by Muño Alfonso's lance, and
his head was cut off. Many princes and commanders of the Moabites
and Hagarenes died, together with many thousands of horsemen, and
foot-soldiers whose number is beyond reckoning. Many commanders,
princes and noble horsemen were captured, and very many foot-
soldiers were taken prisoner, as many as each one of the Christians,
according to their might, could lead away.

73. They seized much silver and gold, the royal standards, precious
garments, excellent weapons, hauberks, helmets, shields, fine horses
with their saddles, mules, she-mules and camels loaded with great
riches. They hung the heads of the kings from the top of the spears
upon which were the royal standards, and on each of the lances they
hung the heads of the commanders and princes. Muño Alfonso
ordered the kings' bodies to be wrapped in fine silk materials, he
placed them in a green field, and left Saracens with them, who were to
guard over them until they were taken away from there. *After this they
went home* to the camp *and sang a song of thanksgiving and praised the
Lord, because his mercy endureth for ever.*[153]

74. When the next day arrived, Muño Alfonso and his comrades
struck camp, and went to Toledo, and entered the city through the
Puerta de Alcántara. The royal standards went before them held high,
with the kings' heads on the tops of the lances, next the noble
horsemen prisoners in chains, and afterwards the Saracen people with
their hands tied behind their backs. They were followed by the

---

151 Pedro Alguacil and Roberto de Montgomariz can be traced in contemporary
    documents: see Sánchez Belda, *Chronica*, pp. 245–6, 255. The two knights sub-
    sequently took part in the unsuccessful siege of Córdoba in May 1150: Hernández
    (ed.), *Cartularios*, no. 74.
152 The taking of heads as grisly battle trophies was common practice on either side
    of the frontier; some Christian *fueros* offered a reward of 5 or 10 *morabetinos* to
    anyone who brought back the head of a Muslim commander: Powers, *A society
    organized for war*, pp. 176–7; see also below ii, 72, 88.
153 I Maccabees iv.24.

Christian foot-soldiers, who brought the kings' horses and the mules and she-mules of the commanders, nobles and horsemen, with their magnificent saddles worked in gold and silver; and afterwards mules and she-mules, which are called *azemilas*,[154] and camels burdened with weapons and all kinds of spoils.

75. They came thus before the doors of the church of Saint Mary, where the Empress Berengaria, the emperor's wife, was waiting with Archbishop Raymond of Toledo, all the clergy, all the knights of the city and all the people, who had come to see the marvel and the victory. And after they had seen the heads of the kings of the Saracens on the tops of the lances upon which the royal standards were raised, they were all astonished, and they entered the church of Saint Mary singing and intoning with great joy 'Te Deum laudamus, te Dominum confitemur', until the end. Having given the blessing, the archbishop and everyone else went to their homes.

76. The next day, early in the morning, the Empress Berengaria and Muño Alfonso and his companions sent messengers to the emperor, who was in Segovia, saying: 'Your wife, the empress, and Muño Alfonso, whom you appointed *alcaide* of Toledo, say this to the lord emperor: "Be not slothful in coming to us, nor make any delay, but come to your palace in Toledo, and there you will see many marvels and the victory which the Lord has offered to you and to all your kingdom."' Hearing this, the emperor was filled with great joy and quickly made his way to Toledo.[155]

77. When Muño Alfonso and his victorious comrades heard that the emperor was coming to Toledo, they went far out of the city to greet him. Before them went the royal standards, with the kings' heads hanging from the tops of the lances and the heads of the commanders and nobles hanging in the same way; the Saracen horsemen prisoners in chains, and afterwards the Hagarene people with their hands tied behind their backs; the kings' horses, the mules and she-mules of the princes and horsemen, and all kinds of weapons; and the *azemilas* and the camels burdened with numerous spoils. After the emperor had seen all these things and the heads of the kings hanging from the tops of the lances upon which were the royal standards, he was astonished and, giving great thanks to the Lord God, he said: 'Blessed be *Lord God, Creator of all things, who art fearful and strong, and righteous, and*

---

154 From the Arabic *az-zemila*, 'beast of burden'.

155 The emperor had reached Toledo by 21 April 1143: J. Guallart and M. P. R. Laguzzi, 'Algunos documentos reales leoneses', *CHE* 2 (1944), 363–81, at pp. 367–8.

merciful, and the only and gracious King, the only giver of all things, the only just, almighty and everlasting, who delivered you from the sword of these kings, and from the clutches of the Saracens, and who always delivers me and his followers *from all trouble.'*[156]

78. After these things had happened, they went into the royal palaces in the city. Once everyone had first given tithes to God and to the church of Saint Mary, they afterwards gave the fifth part to the emperor, as is the custom among kings,[157] and also the royal standards, the kings' horses, the she-mules and many other gifts, and they set aside from the common booty valuable gifts which they sent to Santiago de Compostela.[158] Muño Alfonso and his comrades divided up the rest among themselves, according to their custom.[159]

79. Muño Alfonso ordered the heads of the kings and the other heads of the princes and commanders to be *hanged upon the tower* of Toledo, so that there would be a *manifest sign of the help of the Lord* to all Christians, Moabites and Hagarenes.[160] But after a few days, the empress, moved by great pity, commanded the kings' heads to be taken down and ordered Jewish and Saracen doctors to anoint them with myrrh and aloes, to wrap them in the finest materials, and to place them in caskets worked in gold and silver. Afterwards, the empress sent them with honour to Córdoba to the queens who were the kings' wives. This victory was given by God in the Era 1181 [= AD 1143] in the month of March.[161]

80. When it was heard in the palace of King Tāshufīn that the kings who ruled in the land of the Hagarenes had died, that king was saddened and *troubled, and all* his kingdom *with him,* and *when he had gathered*[162] all the chief men of the Christians whom he had with him,

156 II Maccabees i.24–25.

157 The *quinto,* or one-fifth tax on booty, derived from the Muslim practice of granting to Allāh the same proportion of the spoils gained in Holy War: Powers, *A society organized for war,* pp. 163, 167, 173–4.

158 These were doubtless to be placed at the shrine of St James in Compostela Cathedral.

159 On the rules governing the division of spoils, see Powers, *A society organized for war,* pp. 162–87.

160 II Maccabees xv.35.

161 The *Anales Toledanos I* date this battle to 1 March 1143 and record that it took place by the *Rio que dicen Adoro,* which may refer either to the Azuer near Montiel, or else to the Algodor near Mora: Flórez (ed.), *Anales Toledanos,* p. 389; Sánchez Belda, *Chronica,* p. 242; González, *Repoblación,* I, p. 146, n. 25.

162 Matthew ii.3–4. The passage is inspired by the account of King Herod's reaction on hearing of the birth of Christ.

and of the Moabites and the Arabs, that is to say his own counsellors, he said to them: *'What counsel give ye?*[163] What am I to do with the land of the Hagarenes, which is without a king?' They all answered as one and said: 'Behold your faithful friend Avengania[164] is present. There is no one better than him either here or there.' So Tāshufīn granted him the governorship of Córdoba, Carmona, Seville and Granada, and all the land of the Hagarenes, and said to him: 'Take gold and silver in abundance from my treasuries, go to the land of the Christians, and avenge our brother kings who have been slain. Your sword should not spare any of their regions, and you will subjugate every fortified town and castle to me and to you.'[165]

81. In the same year as Muño Alfonso waged the aforementioned wars, the emperor mustered large companies of knights, foot-soldiers and crossbowmen, and they pitched camp in Toledo by the River Tagus. Finally, the emperor summoned two of his commanders, namely Muño Alfonso, the *alcaide* of Toledo, and Martín Fernández, the *alcaide* of Hita and other towns, and he said to them:*'Take ye the charge of this people*[166] and land, and defend yourselves in the fortress of Peña Negra, known as the Christian Rock, and look out that the Moabites and Hagarenes do not come and fortify the castle of Mora.'

82. The emperor and all his army invaded the region of Córdoba. It was *in the time of wheat harvest, and* he *burnt up all their fields,* and had the fruit trees, vines, olive groves and fig trees cut down;[167] he set fire to all the land of Córdoba, Carmona and Seville and all that land was burned and nothing remained, except the fortified towns and castles. And he carried out great slaughter, took very many prisoners and abundant booty.

83. But at the time that the emperor was in the land of Córdoba, the *adalid* Farax, who was the commander of Calatrava, and all the princes and commanders of the Moabites and Hagarenes who were in all the towns and fortresses as far as the River Guadalquivir, met together and resolved that they would go to the land of Toledo, fortify the castle of Mora, and set ambushes for Muño Alfonso and kill him; the latter was in the castle of Peña Negra.

163 I Kings xii.9.

164 See above, i, 48, n. 125.

165 These instructions echo those issued by Nebuchadnezzar to Holofernes: Judith ii.6 (Vulgate).

166 I Maccabees v.19.

167 Judith ii.27 (cf. Vulgate, ii.17–18).

84. It so happened that on the first day of the month of August the aforementioned Muño, the *alcaide* of Toledo, departed from that castle before daybreak with forty knights of Toledo, having left his comrade Martín Fernández there to guard over it. Muño Alfonso and his comrades climbed a mountain facing Calatrava in order to see or hear whatever was going on. And while the knights of the *alcaide* of Toledo marched this way and that, *they found* a Saracen who was hiding in a cave *and*, having seized him, *brought him* before the *alcaide* of Toledo. *And* Muño Alfonso *said unto him: 'To whom belongest thou? and whence art thou?* And where are you going?' *And he said* to him: *'I am a young* Hagarene *man, servant to* Farax, the *adalid* of Calatrava, and my master has sent me to spy on you.'[168] Muño Alfonso said to him: 'Where is the *adalid* Farax?' And he replied to him: 'Behold, behind my back I am being followed by a great multitude of horsemen and foot-soldiers, bringing with them camels, mules, horses, and asses burdened with flour and *all food which is eaten*,[169] so that the castle of Mora may be fortified. Behind this multitude is the *adalid* Farax with a very great multitude of Moabites and Hagarenes, horsemen, foot-soldiers and crossbowmen, about four thousand in number. They have come to kill you, and those who are with you, if they can find you in any place.' The words were still on his lips when lo and behold the first company of Saracens arrived unexpectedly. Muño Alfonso and his comrades joined battle with them, the Saracens were immediately defeated and fled, many of them were slain, and the others fled this way and that leaving great spoils on the battlefield.

85. After this, Muño Alfonso returned to Peña Negra and told Martín Fernández everything that he had done that day, and that the *adalid* Farax was coming with a great army to fight with them. Having taken counsel, they ate some bread and wine. Afterwards, Muño Alfonso, Martín Fernández and all the knights who were with them, having prepared their troops, went out to meet the Saracens and they came upon the pagan army drawn up by the wells of Algodor.[170] When battle began, many perished by the sword on either side, Martín Fernández was wounded, and the Saracens marched away from the Christians, and the Christians from the Saracens, and a great space remained between the battle-lines of the Saracens and the Christians.

168 Here, our chronicler draws inspiration from the account of the chance encounter between the troops of David and an Egyptian slave shortly before the victory of the former over the Amalekites: I Samuel xxx.11–13.
169 Genesis vi.21
170 See above ii, 53, n. 115

86. Muño Alfonso, realising that *time* did not *serve him*,[171] said to Martín Fernández: 'Don Martín, leave me and go with all your knights to Peña Negra and guard it carefully in case the Moabites and the Hagarenes on the other side should come and take the castle first, which would cause great uncertainty in the household of our lord the emperor. My comrades and I will fight with them; *as the will of God is in heaven, so let him do.*'[172] So Martín Fernández and all his knights went back to the castle to guard it. For his part, Muño Alfonso said to his step-son, his wife's son, whom he had knighted on Easter Day that year: 'Go to Toledo, to your mother's house, and take care of her and of my sons, your brothers. May God not wish for your mother to be bereaved of you and me in a single day.' Then that knight said to him: 'I will not go, but will die with you.' Then Muño Alfonso struck him furiously with a spear-shaft, and he went reluctantly to Toledo crying and lamenting.

87. At that moment, the Moabites and Hagarenes attacked Muño Alfonso and his comrades, and *many were slain on both parts.*[173] When Muño Alfonso saw that he and his companions were being completely overwhelmed, they climbed a crag which is called Peña del Ciervo,[174] *and the archers hit him*; and Muño the Toledan *was sore wounded of the archers*[175] and died. All the knights who were with him died around him, and the majority of the nobles of the Moabites and Hagarenes died.

88. The *adalid* Farax arrived and cut off his head, his right arm, shoulder and hand, and his right foot and leg, and he *stripped off his armour* and wrapped his mutilated body in clean linen. They cut off many of the Christian knights' heads and sent Muño Alfonso's head to Córdoba, to the palace of the wife of Azuel, and [then] to Seville, to the palace of King Avenceta, and afterwards across the sea to the palace of King Tāshufīn, *to publish it* throughout all the land of the Moabites and Hagarenes. *They fastened* Muño Alfonso's arm and foot and the heads of the other knights to a high tower which stands in Calatrava.[176]

---

171 I Maccabees xii.1.

172 I Maccabees iii.60.

173 I Maccabees ix.17.

174 The location of this place, called *Penna Cervi* by the chronicler, is unknown.

175 I Samuel xxxi.3.

176 With the exception of the phrase *truncum corpus eius inuoluit* ('he wrapped his mutilated body'), which is a reminiscence of Judith xiii.10 (Vulgate), this passage is inspired by the account of the treatment of Saul's body by the Philistines: I Samuel xxxi.9–10.

89. *And when the inhabitants of* Toledo *heard of that which* the Saracens *had done,* they went and *took the body* of Muño Alfonso *and the bodies of his* comrades, and *buried them* in the cemetery of Saint Mary in Toledo.[177] For many days Muño Alfonso's wife with her friends and the other widows would go to the tomb of Muño Alfonso and would lament *with this lamentation* and say: 'O Muño Alfonso we are *distressed for thee.* Just as a woman loves her only husband, so the city of Toledo loved you. Your *shield* was never deflected in battle and your spear *turned not back;* your *sword returned not empty. Tell not* the death of Muño Alfonso in Córdoba and in Seville, *publish it not* in the palace of King Tāshufīn, *lest the daughters of the* Moabites *rejoice, lest the daughters of the* Hagarenes *triumph* and the daughters of the Toledans be saddened.'[178]

90. Muño Alfonso, of whom as *alcaide* of Toledo we have already spoken of sufficiently, died, and all the warriors who were with him, on account of the great sin that he committed against God. That is to say, he killed his own daughter, whom he had by his lawful wife, because she had been having a love affair with a young man. And he did not feel pity for his daughter, in the same way as the Lord was merciful in all the battles which he waged, nor was he mindful of the woman caught in adultery, whom the scribes and Pharisees brought before the Lord and wished to stone to death, to whom the Lord said: *'He that is without sin among you, let him first cast a stone at her.'*[179] Muño Alfonso grieved for this sin during all the days of his life and he wished to go on a pilgrimage to Jerusalem. However, Archbishop Raymond of the church of Toledo, and the other bishops and clergy, beseeched by the emperor that he should not go on pilgrimage, ordered him by way of penance to make war continuously on the Saracens, just as he did until he was slain by them.[180]

91. While this was going on, the emperor, having traversed all the land of Córdoba, Carmona and Seville, returned with great victory, and as he approached Talavera he pitched camp on the plain near the River Tagus. The knights of the town and its stewards came to him

177 I Samuel xxxi.11–13.

178 The lament is modelled upon that which David pronounced on learning of the death of Saul and Jonathan: II Samuel i.17–27.

179 John viii.7.

180 The belief that warfare might have a spiritual and penitential value if it were directed against the enemies of Christendom took root in the Iberian peninsula during the first half of the twelfth century: Fletcher, 'Reconquest and Crusade', 42–6; Barton, *Aristocracy*, pp. 155–6, and 'From Tyrants to Soldiers of Christ', (forthcoming).

and from them he learned of what had happened to Muño Alfonso, and he was greatly saddened. The counts, nobles and commanders, seeing the great sadness on the emperor's face, came to him together and stood round him, and said to him: 'Lord emperor, there are many who are similar and better to Muño Alfonso in your kingdom. The good fortune which men attributed to Muño Alfonso was, is, and will be yours for all the days of your life, for God granted it to you.' Hearing this, the emperor pondered their words and, after having kept silent for nearly half an hour, he replied to them: 'Each of you, return to your homes and next year all of you, all the army of Galicia, León and Castile, and all the knights and foot-soldiers of the whole of Extremadura join me in Toledo in the middle of the month of September.' Hearing this, they returned to their homes.

92. *When the year was expired*,[181] that is, in the month of September in the Era 1182 [= AD 1144], all the emperor's counts, nobles and commanders, each one of them with their own escort of knights, the royal household militia, and all the *alcaides*, knights and foot-soldiers of the whole of Extremadura went to Toledo. After this, the emperor moved his army and sent large raiding parties[182] before him into all the region of Córdoba, Carmona, Seville and Granada. They destroyed all the land of Baeza and Ubeda and all the countryside of Córdoba and Seville. They reached the border with Almería and destroyed all the vines, olive groves and fig trees. They cut down and set alight all the orchards, set fire to their towns, villages and hamlets, and sent up in flames many of their castles. They took their men, women and children captive, and seized a great booty of horses, mares, camels, mules, asses, oxen, cows and every kind of beast, gold and silver, all the valuables which were in their homes and all their possessions: whatever they could lay their hands on. They carried all of the above to the emperor at the camp in the land of Granada. All the kingdom of the Hagarenes from Almería to Calatrava was destroyed, and there remained but a few very strong cities and castles. After this, the emperor and all his army returned to Toledo carrying with them abundant riches, together with a great victory and peace.[183]

181 II Chronicles xxxvi.10; cf. I Chronicles xx.1; Leviticus xxv.30; Judges xi.40.

182 *algaras*: see above i, 36, n. 102.

183 The emperor had reached Toledo by October 1144: Villar García (ed.), *Documentación*, no. 36. The following month, Alfonso's charters record their issue *in reditu fossati quod fecerat eo tempore predictus imperator in terra Cordube et Granate*: A. Barrios García (ed.), *Documentación medieval de la catedral de Avila* (Salamanca, 1981), no. 5; cf. Ayala Martínez (ed.), *Libro de privilegios*, no. 51.

93. Then, when the princes, commanders and all the Hagarene people saw *that miseries were multiplied, and that* the emperor and his *forces did encamp themselves in their borders*[184] every year, and that the armies of Toledo, Segovia, Avila, Salamanca and the other towns destroyed their land daily, they gathered in the squares, in the porticos of the towns, and in the mosques and they said: 'What can we do, since we shall not be able to withstand war with the emperor and his commanders?' Some of them replied saying: 'The Moabites *eat the fat of the land,*[185] they take away our possessions and our gold and silver from us, and they oppress our wives and children. Let us fight against them, therefore, let us kill them and cast off their lordship, for *we have no part* in King Tāshufīn's palace *neither have we inheritance in the* sons of 'Alī and of his father Yūsuf'.[186] Others said: 'First of all, let us make a peace agreement with the emperor of León and Toledo, and let us give him royal tribute, just as our fathers gave it to his fathers.' This seemed good in their eyes and they agreed to make ready for war against the men of Marrakesh. Then, returning to their mosques, they prayed, asking their pseudo-prophet Mohammed for mercy, so that he might help them in their undertakings and actions. Sending messengers, they called upon King Zafadola and all the lineage of the kings of the Hagarenes to come and make war on the Moabites.

94. In the month of October in the Era 1183 [= AD 1145], the commander Mohammed, who was of royal lineage, killed all the Moabites who were in Mértola and within all its borders.[187] Afterwards, those who were in Valencia, Murcia, Lérida, Tortosa, and many other castles were killed in battle by the Hagarenes. At that time King Zafadola and all the citizens of Córdoba, Jaén, Ubeda, Baeza, Andújar, Seville, Granada, Almería, and that region which is near the Mediterranean Sea as far as Toledo, all joined in war against the Moabites, and against their leader Avengania, and many thousands of Moabites and Hagarenes were killed. The Hagarenes were victorious, and drove Avengania out of Córdoba and all the Moabites out of many other towns and castles. Having been expelled, Avengania took up position in the high towers of Córdoba, which in our language is called the *alcázar*, in Almodóvar, Montoro, Carmona and Seville. All the Moabites who escaped the

---

184 I Maccabees iii.42.

185 Genesis xlv.18.

186 II Samuel xx.1; I Kings xii.16; II Chronicles x.16.

187 Muḥammad ibn Yaḥyā al-Salṭīsī, known as Ibn al-Qābila, seized Mértola, by the Guadiana in southern Portugal, on 12 August 1144: Bosch Vilá, *Los Almorávides*, pp. 287–8 and n. 6.

sword of the Hagarenes fled to him and *were* a great *stay unto* him.[188] Nevertheless, there was great slaughter and confusion in all the land of the Hagarenes, such as there had not been since the day in which the Hagarenes crossed the Mediterranean to first take that land.[189]

95. At that time there was in Córdoba a certain priest of the law of Mohammed, of the lineage of the Hagarenes, and his name was Abenfandi, and he was richer than all the men who dwelled in Córdoba.[190] He summoned before him the *adalid* of Calatrava, Farax, all the nobles of Córdoba, and his relatives and friends, and *he communicated with them his secret counsel:*[191] they would kill King Zafadola and he would reign in his place. This plan did not escape the attention of King Zafadola, and he summoned all his faithful Christian knights and foot-soldiers, whom he had in his retinue, and he left Córdoba with them, together with the *adalid* Farax. King Zafadola said to the *adalid* Farax: 'Since you wished to betray me, I will make sure that you are unable to do so.' And turning to the Christians he said: 'Attack him and kill him'; and they killed him there and then.

96. *Taking occasion*[192] thereby, Abenfandi and the Cordobans wished to kill King Zafadola, and they pursued him. But the latter went to Jaén and then to Granada, and joined in many battles with the Moabites, and captured their towns and castles; Abenfandi was appointed governor of Córdoba.[193] Then King Zafadola sent messengers to the

188 I Maccabees ii.43.

189 The principal rebellions against Almoravid rule unfolded between 1144 and 1147. In the spring of 1147 Almohad troops crossed from North Africa and began to secure the allegiance of the Andalusian towns. Ibn Ghānīya, the *Avengania* of the Chronicle, was driven out of Seville, Córdoba and other places in 1148 and, having come to terms with the invader, was finally forced to retire to Granada, where he died in January 1149. For details, see F. Codera, *Decadencia y desaparición de los Almorávides en España* (Zaragoza, 1899); Bosch Vila, *Los Almorávides*, pp. 285–95; Viguera Molíns, *Los reinos de taifas*, pp. 189–201, 217–20; Kennedy, *Muslim Spain and Portugal*, pp. 189–95.

190 Ibn Hamdīn had served as *qāḍī*, or judge, in Córdoba since 1134/35. Early in 1145 he had received an oath of allegiance from the citizens and had assumed the duties of governor; but soon after he had been deposed by Sayf al-Dawla (Zafadola): Bosch Vilá, *Los Almorávides*, pp. 288–89.

191 Judith ii.2.

192 Romans vii.8, 11.

193 Ibn Hamdīn was reappointed governor of Córdoba on 1 March 1145: Bosch Vilá, *Los Almorávides*, p. 289. The *CAI's* version of events is supported by the *Anales Toledanos I:* Flórez (ed.), *Anales Toledanos*, p. 389. Zafadola remained in Granada until he was ousted by Almoravid forces in the late summer of 1145 and was forced to withdraw, first to Jaén, and finally to Murcia in January 1146: Bosch Vilá, *Los Almorávides*, pp. 290–1; Kennedy, *Muslim Spain and Portugal*, p. 194.

244 THE WORLD OF EL CID

emperor saying: 'The land of Ubeda and Baeza and their castles do not wish to obey me, nor render tribute to you.' Hearing this, the emperor summoned the counts Manrique,[194] Ermengol[195] and Ponç, together with Martín Fernández, and he said to them: 'Go and subdue for me, and for King Zafadola, Baeza, Ubeda and Jaén and all the rebels; and may your sword not spare any of them.'

97. Going away with a great army, they destroyed all that rebellious land and seized abundant booty and many prisoners. When the citizens of that region saw that they were being completely overwhelmed, they sent an embassy to King Zafadola saying: 'Come, deliver us from the hands of the Christians, and we will serve you surely.' He immediately came with a great army and, having left it facing the Christians, went in peace to their camp and said to the counts: 'Surrender to me the prisoners and the booty that you have taken, and I will go with you to the emperor, and I will do whatever the emperor may command me.' The counts replied to him: 'Far be it from us, for you sent messengers to the emperor saying: "The men of Ubeda and Baeza are rebels against me and you. Send an army now to destroy them and their land." And just as you and the emperor commanded, so we have done.' Zafadola replied to them saying: 'If you do not give up all the prisoners and booty to me, I will take up arms and fight against you.' The counts replied to him: 'Now is the time and the opportunity.' Straightaway, having drawn up their troops, they joined battle and the conflict intensified greatly.[196]

98. Finally, the Hagarenes took to flight and were defeated, and King Zafadola was captured in the battle by the counts' knights. While they held him to take him to the tents, the knights who are called *pardos*[197]

194 Count Manrique Pérez was the son of Count Pedro González de Lara: see González, *El reino de Castilla*, I, pp. 271–4; Barton, *Aristocracy*, pp. 264–5. See also below, *PA*, vv. 318–332.

195 Ermengol VI of the Catalan county of Urgel was a prominent figure on the Leonese–Castilian scene between 1134 and his death twenty years later. For details of his career, see S. Barton, 'The count, the bishop and the abbot: Armengol VI of Urgel and the abbey of Valladolid', *English Historical Review* 111 (1996), 85–103, at pp. 89–93; Barton, *Aristocracy*, pp. 231–2. See also below, *PA*, vv. 272–8.

196 The battle took place near Chinchilla, in the modern province of Albacete, on 5 February 1146: Huici Miranda, *Historia musulmana de Valencia*, III, pp. 112–13.

197 By *pardos* (probably so-called because of the brown colour of their garments) the chronicler is referring to the *caballeros villanos*, knights of non-noble birth, who comprised the mainstay of the militia forces of the frontier towns, and enjoyed some noble privileges by virtue of their military service: Ubieto Arteta (ed.), *Crónicas anónimas*, pp. 41, 44; R. Pastor, *Resistencias y luchas campesinas en la época del crecimiento y consolidación de la formación feudal: Castilla y León, siglos X–XIII*, (2nd edn, Madrid, 1990), pp. 125–6.

arrived and when they recognized him they killed him. Seeing this, the counts were greatly saddened, and they sent messengers to the emperor, who was in the royal city of León. The messengers told him all about the battle, but after they had told him 'Your friend King Zafadola has died' the emperor, greatly saddened, said: *'I am guiltless from the blood of* my friend Zafadola.'[198] And all the Christians and Saracens from Arabia, which is next to the River Jordan, as far as the Ocean Sea knew that the emperor was never party to the death of King Zafadola.

99. Afterwards, Abenfandi, the governor of Córdoba, could not sustain the war against Avengania and the Moabites, so he and his friends fled to Andújar, and the citizens of that town received him.[199] However, Avengania pursued him and besieged Andújar, and built siege towers, catapults and many siege engines, and began to fight bravely against Abenfandi and against those who were with him in the town. When Abenfandi saw that he was being completely overwhelmed, he sent messengers to the emperor saying: 'Behold, Avengania and all his army have besieged me. Take pity on me according to your mercy, and free me and my friends, and I will serve you surely.'

100. After he had heard the words of Abenfandi's messengers, the emperor summoned to his presence Fernando Yáñez, a faithful friend and lord of Limia, who had helped the emperor in Limia against King Afonso of Portugal, and he said to him: 'Take whichever and however many of my knights that you wish, and go to Andújar. You and Abenfandi are to hold the city until I make my way there.' Fernando immediately set off with a great number of knights, and they entered Andújar; and Abenfandi and the citizens of that town were greatly overjoyed when they saw this. Fernando Yáñez and the Christians who were with him, and Abenfandi and his men, joined in many battles with Avengania, even outside the city, and many men perished on either side.

101. While these wars were being waged in the land of the Hagarenes, Reverter, the leader of the captive Christian people, who were on the other side of the sea in the palace of King Tāshufīn, died.[200] And

---

198 II Samuel iii.28; Susanna, 46; Acts xx.26.

199 Ibn Ḥamdīn was expelled from Córdoba by Ibn Ghānīya in January 1146 and fled to Badajoz before transferring his base of operations to Andújar, about 70 kilometres upstream from Córdoba: Bosch Vilá, *Los Almorávides*, p. 291–2.

200 On Reverter, see above ii, 11 and n. 27. Reverter was killed doing battle with the Almohads, probably in 1144: see Bosch Vilá, *Los Almorávides*, pp. 259–60 and n. 10.

all the captive Christian people, scattering dust and mud over themselves, mourned and cried: 'O Reverter, our leader, shield and armour, why do you abandon us and leave us desolate?[201] Now the Muzmutos will invade and kill us, as well as our wives and children.' And King Tāshufīn and all his palace grieved for Reverter.

102. When the king of the Assyrians, whose name was Abdelnomen,[202] who ruled in the Claros Montes,[203] in Mount Colobrar[204] and in Bugia,[205] over the peoples called the Muzmutos, and over many other nations, heard that Reverter, the leader of the captive Christian people, who made war on him daily, had died, he was filled with great joy. He immediately approached the borders of the territory of King Tāshufīn with over one hundred thousand horsemen; the number of crossbowmen and foot-soldiers was beyond reckoning. He captured strongly fortified towns and castles, killed many nobles and commanders of the Christians, Moabites and Arabs, carried out innumerable massacres of men, women and children, and burnt all the land wherever he passed through. After this, the king of the Muzmutos set out to go to the city of Marrakesh.

103. *When* King Tāshufīn *heard* about the aforementioned wars, he was seized with great fear and *he was troubled and all* his territory *with him. And when he had gathered*[206] all the nobles and commanders of the Christians, who were next in rank to Reverter, the princes and commanders of the Moabites and Arabs, the magistrates of the people, and all the army of his kingdom, he went out to confront the king of the Muzmutos in battle; and they fought for several days. Finally, King Tāshufīn was defeated, and he fled and entered a castle. However, the king of the Muzmutos pursued him and besieged him in the castle, and with crossbows and arrows he cast a very fierce fire, which is called tar, towards the tower where King Tāshufīn was staying. And it set fire to that tower, and King Tāshufīn was burned in it and many nobles of the Christians, Moabites and Arabs, and countless thousands of horsemen and foot-soldiers were burned with him and perished.[207]

201 Cf. the lament for the death of Alfonso VI in Pelayo, *Chronicon,* p. 88.

202 See above, ii, 10, n. 25.

203 The Atlas Mountains.

204 The location of *mons Colobrar* is unknown.

205 Modern Bejaia (Bougie) on the coast of Algeria.

206 Matthew ii.3–4; cf. above ii, 80.

207 Muslim sources, which unsurprisingly provide a far fuller account of the demise of the Almoravid empire, indicate that Tāshufīn met his death on 23 March 1145 as he tried to escape the Almohad siege of Oran: Bosch Vilá, *Los Almorávides,* pp. 262–4.

104. *So was there a great* confusion in the palace of King 'Alī, *the like whereof was not since the time that* the Moabites began to reign across the sea.[208] Once King Tāshufīn had died, the king of the Muzmutos took many castles by storm, took over all the fortifications and destroyed many very well-fortified and wealthy cities.[209] He arrived at the city of Marrakesh and attacked the city; he carried out many massacres there and captured the high towers and fortified them with brave warriors who were to wage war in the city. All those who resisted whom they could capture were cast into the flames with their wives and children.[210]

105. *And when* Avengania and all the Moabites, who were with him in the land of the Hagarenes, *heard that* King Tāshufīn *was dead* and with him many princes and commanders of all peoples, their *hands* and hearts *were feeble,*[211] but the Hagarenes were overjoyed. The emperor's household was not saddened by the death of King Tāshufīn, rather ***[212]

106. *** of John the Baptist, in the place where a mosque to Satan had previously been built.[213] The bishop of Burgos perished in that siege, while the emperor still remained there, on the aforementioned nativity of Saint John ***.[214]

208 I Maccabees ix.27; Exodus ix.18.

209 Cf. Judith ii.12–16 (Vulgate).

210 Marrakesh fell to the Almohads on 24 March 1147; for a description of the siege and its aftermath, see Bosch Vilá, *Los Almorávides*, pp. 277–80.

211 II Samuel iv.1; Genesis xlix.24; Joshua v.1; II Chronicles xv.7; Jeremiah vi.24.

212 There is a sizeable lacuna in all the MSS at this point; MS *A* indicates that two entire folios are missing. The chronicler presumably went on to give some account of the campaign that led to the occupation of Córdoba by Alfonso VII in May 1146; the final lines of that account survive in ch. 106.

213 Having forced Ibn Ghānīya to raise the siege of Andújar, Alfonso VII and Ibn Ḥamdīn pursued him to Córdoba and overran most of the city, with the exception of the citadel, which remained in the hands of Ibn Ghānīya. A Muslim source states that the emperor's forces entered Córdoba on 24 May 1146, and this is confirmed by the emperor's own chancery: a diploma of 23 May 1147 would record that it had been drawn up *in fine anni quo prenominatus ipse rex acquisiuit Cordubam*: Bosch Vilá, *Los Almorávides*, p. 292; García Larragueta (ed.), *Colección*, no. 158. It may have been the news that an Almohad army had landed in southern Spain that prompted the emperor to come to terms with Ibn Ghānīya, whom he recognized as ruler of Córdoba, on condition that the latter became his vassal; for his part, Ibn Ḥamdīn eventually found refuge in Málaga, where he died in November 1151. The vassalage of Ibn Ghānīya and the conversion of the great mosque of Córdoba into a Christian church, which the *CAI* may be referring to here, is mentioned in the charter issued by Alfonso VII in Toledo on 19 August 1146, *post reditum fossati, quo prenominatus principem Maurorum Abinganiam sibi uassallum fecit, et quandam partem Cordube depredauit cum mesquita maiori*: Rassow, 'Die Urkunden', no. 27.

214 Pedro Domínguez, bishop of Burgos (1139–46). The *Obituario* of Burgos cathedral confirms that the bishop's death occurred on 24 June 1146: Serrano, *Obispado*, III,

107. None the less, one must not cease to praise and honour God, who watching over his slaves everywhere, crushes the enemies of his law and reduces them to nothing. Thus, while the emperor of León, the terror of the Ishmaelites, was still at the siege of the aforementioned city, some noble and eloquent envoys of the Genoese came to him urging him *** so that with his sign ***[215] to destroy Almería, a base of sea pirates.[216] The pirates, traversing many seas, would sometimes go ashore suddenly in the land of Bari, the land of Ascalon and the region of Constantinople, Sicily and Barcelona; at others in the region of Genoa, or in Pisa, France, Portugal, Galicia or Asturias, and they would flee carrying Christian captives in their ships as booty. Since this is engraved upon the memory by dint of frequent repetition,[217] finally, so that it does not appear that we are holding up the narrative by confusing it with words, having received from the emperor thirty thousand *morabetinos*, [the Genoese] promised to appear with many ships loaded with men, weapons, siege-engines and money, and both they and the emperor fixed the first of August as the deadline for their arrival.[218]

p. 383. The chronicler's comment that the prelate died *in illa obsidione* might suggest that siege operations, designed to flush out Ibn Ghānīya and his supporters from the city *alcázar*, were still in progress a month after Alfonso VII entered Córdoba. There is a further lacuna in the MSS here.

215 The text is corrupt at this point.

216 The Genoese had already attacked Almería in the summer of 1146, but had had to abandon the siege because of the onset of winter. The motives for the campaign attributed to the Genoese by the author of the *CAI* are echoed by Caffaro, *De captione Almerie et Tortuose*, ed. A. Ubieto Arteta (Valencia, 1973), pp. 17–18, 21. There were also important commercial advantages to be derived from the conquest of the city: see B. Garí, 'Why Almería? An Islamic port in the compass of Genoa', *JMH* 18 (1992), 211–31.

217 A Classical reminiscence: see, for example, Quintilian, *Institutiones Oratoriae*, 1, 1, 31.

218 Alfonso VII reached formal agreement with the Genoese in September 1146. Under the terms of the treaty, the emperor undertook to subsidize the Genose war-effort to the tune of 20,000 gold *morabetinos* (not 30,000, as the chronicler states) and grant the Genoese one third of all the land and property they both might conquer in Almería; moreover, Genoese merchants were promised safe-conduct throughout León–Castile and exemption from tolls. Both parties agreed that their forces would be ready to go into action in May 1147. A subsequent treaty between Count Ramón Berenguer IV of Barcelona and the Genoese provided for a joint assault on Tortosa on the Ebro once Almería had fallen: C. Imperiale di Sant' Angelo (ed.), *Codice diplomatico della Repubblica di Genova*, I (Rome, 1936), nos 166–69.

108. Moreover, the emperor sent Bishop Arnaldo of Astorga[219] as an envoy to the count of Barcelona, and to William, lord of Montpellier, so that, for the redemption of their souls, they would all be present at the same time on the first of August to destroy the aforementioned nest of pirates. Receiving these words with great joy, they promised that they would be present with the Genoese.[220]

109. In the same year that God secured the aforementioned victory at Córdoba, the people who are commonly known as the Muzmutos came from Africa, crossed the Mediterranean Sea and, displaying great skill, waging war they first took Seville and other fortified towns and fortresses in the surrounding area and further afield. They settled in them and killed their nobles, the Christians who are called Mozarabs, and the Jews, who had been there since ancient times, and they seized their wives, houses and riches.[221]

110. At this time, many thousands of Christian knights and foot-soldiers, together with their bishop and a large part of the clergy who had belonged to the household of King 'Alī and that of his son Tāshufīn, crossed the sea and came to Toledo.[222]

111. Now, however, going on to greater deeds by way of verse, so that we may avoid weariness by the variety of poetry, we have decided to describe in the following manner which commanders of the Franks and Spanish came to the siege which had been agreed beforehand.

---

219 On Arnaldo, bishop of Astorga (1144–52), see the introduction to this text, pp. 158–61.

220 The chronicler's statement that the princes of Barcelona and Montpellier were invited to take part in the Almería campaign *pro suarum animarum redemptione* strongly suggests that the expedition was underpinned by a burgeoning crusading enthusiasm. Although no papal bull concerning Almería has survived, Pope Eugenius III (1145–53) is known to have taken a close interest in Iberian affairs. Besides, the salvatory character of the campaign is also referred to by the *Poem of Almería* and by Caffaro, who states that 'the Genoese were instructed and summoned by God through the Apostolic See and made an oath to raise an army against the Saracens of Almería': see G. Constable, 'The Second Crusade as seen by Contemporaries', *Traditio* 9 (1953), 213–79, at pp. 227–31, 257–60; Caffaro, *De captione*, p. 21.

221 On the Almohad campaigns alluded to here, see Viguera Molíns, *Los reinos de taifas*, pp. 217–20.

222 The bishop in question may have been one Miguel, whose poignant colophon to an Arabic translation of the Gospels was completed in the city of Fez in 1137 'in the eleventh year after the removal of the Andalusi Christians to this place (may God restore them to their homeland!)': R. Fletcher, *Moorish Spain* (London, 1992), pp. 112–13.

The Poem of Almeria

Holy king, valiant king, with whom rests the final judgement of death,
give us peace and provide us with a fluent style, so that, singing
eloquently and copiously of your wonderful deeds, I may describe the
glorious wars of honourable men. /[5] Sages have written of the
wars of the kings of old, and we too must write of the famous battles
of our Emperor, for they are anything but tedious. If it please the
Emperor, let the writer be granted the greatest facilities so that he
can recount the battles that are to come. /[10] The right hand of the
labourer awaits the merciful gifts of the Thunderer,[1] and constantly
seeks the reward of the warrior. Therefore, I shall set out the theme
that I have chosen: the campaign undertaken in Almería, for it was
then that the tribe of the pagan people was defeated.

The leaders of the Hispanic and Frankish peoples arrived together; /
[15] by land and sea they seek to do battle with the Moors. The
commander of them all was the king of the Toledan Empire, Alfonso,
who holds the title of Emperor, continuing the deeds of Charlemagne,[2]
with whom he is rightly compared. They were equal in courage, and
in the power of their weapons, /[20] equal was the glory of the campaigns which they waged. There stood as witness the evil pestilence
of the Moors, whom neither the surging sea nor their own land
protected. They cannot submerge themselves in the deep nor raise
themselves upwards into the clouds above,[3] for their life was wicked,
and thus they were defeated. /[25] They did not recognize the Lord,
and rightly perished. This people was rightly doomed: they worship
Baal, but Baal does not set them free.[4] This barbarous people was
deadly unto itself. The month of Adar[5] proclaims the battles that are

---

1 *Tonans*, the Classical epithet of Jupiter, which later came to be associated with the
  Christian deity.

2 Charlemagne, king of the Franks (768–814) and Emperor of the West (800–14).

3 *Nec possunt iusum mergi uel ad ethera sursum*: a reminiscence of Proverbs viii.28.

4 Baal was a Semitic fertility and agricultural deity whose worship was denounced
  by the Hebrew prophet Elijah: I Kings xviii.19–40. Here, Baal is associated with
  the Muslim Allāh.

5 All the MSS give *adorat menses*, corrected by the poem's editor, J. Gil, to *Adar at
  mensis: Prefatio de Almaria*, p. 256. Adar was the twelfth month of the Hebrew
  calendar, during which King Ahasuerus (probably to be identified with Xerxes I of
  the Persians) is said to have commanded that all the Jews who were in his kingdom
  were to be exterminated; later, the king countermanded this order and directed
  that on the thirteenth day of Adar the Jews were to be allowed to avenge themselves on their enemies: Esther iii.13, viii.12–13.

to come. /[30] The evil that had been wrought earlier was not allowed to go unpunished. The divine sword destroyed young and old alike in wars, not sparing the children in turn. The rest of the people are put to the sword like sheep;[6] not even the children who are discovered save themselves. /[35] The terrible divine wrath falls upon them.

Now, however, so that we are not troubled by a lengthy hold-up or a greater delay, we must return to the main part of the work we have begun.

All the bishops of [the kingdoms of] Toledo and León, unsheathing the divine and material sword, /[40] exhort the adults and urge on the young so that all may go bravely and surely to battle. They pardon sins and raise their voices to heaven, pledging to all the reward of this life and the next.[7] They promise prizes of silver and, with victory, /[45] they assure them once more that they will have all the gold which the Moors possess. Such was the clamour and the pious ardour of the bishops, at times promising at others crying out loud, that the young could scarcely be restrained by their mothers. *As the hart* beset by dogs in the woods /[50] *panteth after the water brooks*[8] as it leaves the mountains all around, so the Spanish people, yearning to do battle with the Saracens, do not sleep by day or by night. The trumpet of salvation[9] rings out throughout all the regions of the world. The name of cruel Almería is well known to all: /[55] there is nothing as sweet; it is a name that will resound for generations. It is the nourishment of the young, the florid gift of the old, the guide of the poor, the pious light of the young men, the law of the bishops, the final destruction of the Moabites, the good fortune of the Franks, the terrible death of the Moors. /[60] Conflict is peace for the Franks, but for the Moors it is a most famous scourge. For the Spanish it is a blessing; in short, it is the custom of its warriors. The reward is a share of the silver, a share of the gold. A long rest is torment, while the glory of waging war is life itself.

It is the month of May, the Galicians advance forward /[65] having first received the blessing of St James.[10] Like the stars in the sky, so a thousand spears shine forth and a thousand shields gleam; the weapons

6 *Cetera gens gladiis ceduntur moris bidentis:* an echo of Virgil, *Aeneid,* v, 96.

7 These verses provide a clear indication of the crusading nature of the Almería campaign. See above, *CAI,* ii, 108 and n. 220.

8 The verse is inspired by Psalm xlii.1.

9 This is another clear crusading metaphor.

10 See above, *CAI,* ii, 69 and n. 145; ii, 78 and n. 158.

have been skilfully honed. The people are ready for war, for all remain helmeted. The clang of iron and the neighing of the horses /[70] thunder in the mountains and dry up the springs on every side. With the grazing, the flowering fields lose their covering, the moonlight grows pale through the clouds of dust, and the brightness of the sky is darkened by the gleam of the weapons. This troop is guided by the valiant Count Fernando[11] /[75] restraining with royal diligence the privileges of the Galicians. He was sustained by the guardianship of the Emperor's son.[12] If you saw the latter, you would think that he was already king: he shines with royal as well as with countly glory.

After these men, the flower of the knights of the city of León, /[80] standards held high, rush forward like a lion. León occupies the summit of the whole of the Hispanic kingdom, with royal diligence she investigates the privileges of the king. The laws of the fatherland are interpreted according to her judgement; with her assistance fierce wars are waged. /[85] As the lion exceeds other animals in reputation, so León surpasses all the other cities in honour. Since ancient times this law held: the first battles belong to her. Her ensigns, which protect against all ill fortune, are to be found among the standards and weapons of the Emperor; /[90] they cover themselves with gold whenever they are carried off to battle. The troop of the Moors prostrates itself in their sight and, seized with terror, is unable to stand firm against them in such a confined space. As the wolf pursues the sheep, and the wave of the sea presses back the lion,[13] so this light crushes the fleeing[14] Ishmaelites.[15] /[95] Having first taken counsel in the court of St Mary, and having been granted the forgiveness of

---

11 The presence of Count Fernando Pérez on the Almería campaign is confirmed by the charter issued by Alfonso VII at Baeza on 25 November 1147 *quando ... imperator redibat de Almaria, quam tunc cum auxilio Ianuensium ceperat et iuri christianorum submiserat*: Fernández Flórez (ed.), *Colección diplomática*, IV, no. 1294.

12 That is, the future Fernando II of León (1157–88).

13 *Vt lupus urget oues, maris ut premit unda leones*: a reminiscence of Ovid, *Metamorphoses*, i, 304.

14 *vitatos*. Alternatively, it has been speculated (not altogether convincingly) that the verse may originally have read *vittatos*, that is, that the Muslims wore ribbons around their heads: Gil (ed), *Prefatio de Almaria*, p. 258; Pérez González, *Crónica*, p. 134 n. 183.

15 *Ismaelitas*: literally the descendants of Ishmael, the son of Abraham and his concubine and slave Hagar. Muslim belief holds that the followers of Islam are descended from Ishmael, hence its use here.

their sins according to the manner of their ancestors,[16] that blazing sword advances with standards unfurled, and its resolute courage occupies the whole earth. The pasture is grazed, the straw is ground ceaselessly.[17]

/[100] They are followed by Count Ramiro,[18] admirable among his class, prudent and affable, concerned for the salvation of León. Distinguished in appearance, born of royal lineage,[19] he is beloved by Christ for overseeing the administration of the law. At all hours he carries out the commands of the Emperor, /[105] whom he serves willingly with watchful care. He was the flower of flowers, fortified with the strength of the good, skilled in arms, full of charm, powerful of counsel, famous for his just rule, he surpasses all the bishops in the retinue of kings /[110] and he excels his equals when judging the limits of the law. What else can I say? His rights surpass all others. No one would be slow to serve such a count. With such a great count León seeks out the fiercest battles.

Meanwhile, the indefatigable Asturian is not the last to rush forth. / [115] This people is detestful or loathsome to no one. Land or sea may never overcome her. Endowed with resolute strength, she does not fear the cups of death. Of handsome appearance, she scorns the final resting-place. Ready to wage war and no less skilled in hunting, /[120] she explores the mountains and recognises the water brooks one by one. She is as disdainful of the waves of the sea, as she is of the clods of the earth. She is overcome by no man, overcoming whatever

16 This probably refers to a ceremony in which the Leonese troops and their weapons were blessed in the cathedral of St Mary in León prior to their departure on campaign. On the form such a ceremony might have taken, see C. Sánchez Albornoz, *Una ciudad de la España cristiana hace mil años* (10th edn., Madrid, 1984), pp. 91–110; cf. M. McCormick, *Eternal victory. Triumphal rulership in late antiquity, Byzantium, and the early medieval West* (Cambridge, 1987), pp. 308–11.

17 It is possible that the author had in mind the action of a threshing sledge grinding the straw into bits: cf. Fletcher, *Saint James's Catapult*, p. 7, n. 17.

18 We do not know for sure whether Count Ramiro Froilaz took part in the assault on Almería; however, the count may be traced with the emperor's army at Calatrava between 9 and 11 June 1147, en route to the south: M. Recuero Astray, M. González Vázquez and P. Romero Portilla (eds), *Documentos Medievales del Reino de Galicia: Alfonso VII (1116–1157)* (Santiago de Compostela, 1998), no. 114; J. Carro García, 'El privilegio de Alfonso VII al monasterio de Antealtares', *Cuadernos de Estudios Gallegos* 7 (1952), 145–57, at pp. 148–55.

19 Presumably a reference to Count Ramiro's mother, Estefanía Sánchez, who was the daughter of the Infante Sancho Garcés of the royal house of Navarre. The countess was referred to as *ex regali sanguine et prosapie horta* in the grant made to her and to her consort Count Froila Díaz by Count Henry of Portugal on 1 March 1112: Azevedo (ed.), *Documentos medievais portugueses*, I, no. 28.

obstacles present themselves. This people, beseeching at all times the help of St Saviour,[20] abandons the swollen waves at the gallop /[125] and joins up with other comrades with their ranks drawn up. Their leader was the illustrious Pedro Alfonso.[21] He was not yet a count, but by his merits he was already the equal of all. He is harsh to no man, he stands out among all by his virtue. He is illustrious for his integrity, and surpasses his equals in honesty. /[130] He is as handsome as Absalom and as strong as Samson and, well versed in good customs, he possesses the wisdom of Solomon. On his return he was made count: if his deeds were those of a count, he obtained [the title] on account of his great merits.[22] Enriched with this honour, he is respected by the Emperor among his peers, /[135] he is distinguished on account of his royal wife, the pious María: she was born of a count, with good reason she will be made a countess; thus she will be the everlasting jewel of her people for centuries to come.[23]

Behind them there advance the thousand spears of Castile, famous and powerful citizens through long centuries. /[140] Their camps shine like the stars in the sky and blaze with gold. They use silver dishes: there is no poverty, only great wealth, among them. There is no beggar, weakling or laggard among them: all are strong and firm in battle, /[145] there is a great abundance of meat and wine in their camps, and a generous supply of wheat is freely doled out to whomever asks for it. The flashes from their weapons are as many as the stars, and their many steeds are protected by iron or cloth. Their speech sounds out like a trumpet accompanied by a drum.[24] /[150]

---

20 St Saviour (San Salvador) was the patron of the cathedral church of Oviedo, whose celebrated *Arca Santa* housed a remarkable collection of relics: see above Pelayo, *Chronicon*, pp. 70-1; Suárez Beltrán, 'Los origenes', 37–55.

21 Pedro Alfonso witnessed the charter issued by Alfonso VII at Baeza on 25 November 1147 as the emperor's army returned from Almería: see above, n. 11.

22 The poet is well-informed; Pedro Alfonso was first styled count in a charter of Alfonso VII of 1 March 1148: J. L. Martín Martín, L. M. Villar García, F. Marcos Rodríguez and M. Sánchez Rodríguez (eds), *Documentos de los archivos catedralicio y diocesano de Salamanca (siglos XII–XIII)* (Salamanca, 1977), no. 14.

23 María Froilaz, sister of Count Ramiro Froilaz, was the daughter of Count Froila Díaz and Countess Estefanía Sánchez of Navarre; see above, n. 19.

24 Although the majority of the MSS give *tympanotriba* ('effeminate'), this is probably a scribal misreading of *tympanotuba*. 'With these words', Roger Wright has written, 'the author was referring to their tone of voice; to the proud spirit of independence of the Castilians with respect to the Leonese king, which made them speak in a loud and confident manner': Wright, 'Twelfth-century Metalinguistics', p. 286.

They are very proud and exceptionally wealthy.[25] The men of Castile were rebellious down the ages. Noble Castile, eager for terrible wars, could scarcely bring herself to bow her neck to any king.[26] She lived untamed while the light of heaven shone. /[155] But now the Emperor's good fortune has tamed her for good. He alone has tamed Castile like a she-donkey,[27] placing the new covenant of the law upon her untamed neck. However, remaining unyielding in her strength, mighty Castile marches on to close combat, /[160] with her banners unfurled. Terror rises up in the Ishmaelites who, as it later came to pass, were destroyed by the sword.

Innumerable, unconquerable and without concern, Extremadura, forseeing everything that was to happen, boldly joins them, for it knew by means of auguries that the evil people was about to perish, /[165] having seen so many signs.[28] If anybody knew the number of the stars that there are in the sky or the waves in the storm-tossed sea, the raindrops or the blades of grass in the fields, he would be able to count this people. Drinking large amounts of wine, strengthened with abundant bread, /[170] it is able to bear the burden, it despises the heat of summer. This people covers the earth like a plague of locusts. The sky and sea do not suffice to sate them. They break the mountains asunder, they dry up the springs one by one. When they rise up together they blot out the lights in the heavens; /[175] a wild people, a valiant people, they do not fear the cups of death. This army is commanded by Count Ponç,[29] the noble lance. He had the strength of Samson, the sword of Gideon, he was the equal of Jonathan, as illustrious as Joshua,[30] he

25 The reputation of Castile as a land of plenty is also evinced in the twelfth-century pilgrim's guide to Santiago de Compostela: see J. Vielliard (ed.), *Le guide du pèlerin de Saint-Jacques de Compostelle* (Paris, 1963), pp. 32–3.

26 This is presumably a reference to the fact that for much of the tenth century Castile, under its counts Fernán González (*c.* 931–70), García Fernández (970–95) and Sancho Garcés (995–1017), had been able to detach itself from Leonese overlordship, and to maintain itself as a virtually independent principality.

27 From the unflattering comparison one may safely conclude that the poet was not of Castilian extraction! See above, p. 157.

28 The importance reportedly attached to omens by the people of the Extremadura does not appear to have been unique. Rodrigo Díaz de Vivar was accused by Count Berenguer Ramón of Barcelona of trusting more in the auguries of birds than in God: see above, *HR*, p. 124 and n. 79. On similar beliefs in early twelfth-century Galicia, see *HC*, p. 89.

29 The presence of the Catalan magnate Count Ponç de Cabrera on the Almería campaign is amply confirmed by documentary sources: see Barton, *Aristocracy*, p. 178.

30 *Iesu Nave.* 'Joshua', which is rendered 'Jesus' in Greek, was traditionally referred to as 'the son of Nave': Ecclesiasticus xlvi.1.

was the leader of his people like the valiant Hector. /[180] Generous and truthful like the invincible Ajax, he yields to no man and he never retreats in battle. He does not turn his back, he never flees to the rearguard; forgetting his wife or his love while he fights: he scorns kisses while battle is being waged, /[185] he scorns the table, he rejoices while he wounds with the sword. When he brandishes his lance, the evil people falls prostrate exhausted. Never mournfully does he endure the heat of battle. His right hand wounds resolutely, his voice rings out, the enemy is overthrown. When he dispenses counsel, he possesses the wisdom of Solomon. /[190] He swaps swords for pitchforks and while he counts the months,[31] he himself prepares the food, it is he who pours out wine to the weary knights, while he removes his rough helmet. He is the ruin of the Moors, Almería was later a witness to that. Count Ponç would rather be exiled /[195] than give up wielding the sword in wartime. By virtue of such service, he always pleases the Emperor: he grows rich through the king's favour on account of the victorious campaigns and rules over all the kingdoms with supreme valour.[32]

All these men are joined by Fernando Yáñez.[33] /[200] Renowned in military prowess, he was never defeated in war. The king of Portugal feared to be vanquished by him when he saw him resplendent on the battlefield waging war;[34] for wherever he looked or went, he terrified all, at the same time as he overcame all of them with his sword. / [205] Not one of those whom he has wounded with his lance in close combat remains in the saddle. Often did he defeat the Moors in fierce battles, and he did not doubt to attack many of them with only a few men, for all those who know who he is flee from Fernando. His numerous offspring also take part in the long campaign, /[210] for his wife bore him many sons, who follow faithfully in their father's footsteps and maim the Hagarenes with their swords. A father who can unleash such swords may feel untroubled. He was followed by all Limia mobilised for war. He is glad to bring together many peoples from the

---

31 *numerandoque menses*: the sense, perhaps, is that outside the campaigning season Count Ponç was counting the months until he would go into action once more.

32 For an idea of the lavish rewards that Count Ponç gleaned from his service to Alfonso VII, see Barton, 'Two Catalan magnates', 241–2, 244–5, 247–8.

33 The presence of Fernando Yáñez on the Almería expedition may be confirmed by Alfonso VII's charter of 25 November 1147: see above, n. 11.

34 On the military reverses suffered by Afonso I of Portugal at the hands of Fernando Yáñez, see above, *CAI*, i, 75, 81.

frontier region,[35] /[215] and the king is delighted to receive so many knights, and receives such a great man into his entourage with splendour. Here comes Alvaro, the son of the noble Rodrigo.[36] He brought death upon many and held Toledo;[37] the father is glorified in the son, and the son on his own account. /[220] The former was truly brave, but the glory of the son was no less. The son is illustrious through his father, but even more so through his grandfather. Known to all is his grandfather, Alvar,[38] the fortress of uprightness, the city of goodness, although there was none that was more implacable towards his enemies.[39] Thus, I have heard it said that Alvar Fáñez /[225] conquered the Ishmaelite peoples and that neither their towns nor their fortified castles could resist. He broke their strength, thus did that brave man press down upon them. I confess the truth without reservation: if Alvar had been the third man after Oliver in the time of Roland, /[230] the Hagarene people would have been subjected to the Frankish yoke and his dear comrades would not have been overcome by death.[40] There was no better lance under the clear sky. That Rodrigo, often called My Cid, of whom it is sung that he was never vanquished by his enemies, /[235] who subdued the Moors, and also subdued our counts,[41] himself used to praise him [Alvar Fáñez] and

35 This may be a reference to the frontier lordships which Fernando Yáñez had earlier been awarded in Maqueda and Talavera: Barton, *Aristocracy*, p. 37; Reilly, *Alfonso VII*, pp. 188–9.

36 The poet is almost certainly referring to Alvaro Rodríguez, son of the Galician magnate Count Rodrigo Vélaz, whose principal power-base lay in the districts of Montenegro and Lugo in eastern Galicia, just as the poet indicates below: Barton, *The Aristocracy*, p. 230. Although we cannot be sure whether Alvaro was present at the siege of Almería, he may be traced with the emperor's army at Andújar on 17 July 1147: Recuero Astray *et al.* (eds), *Documentos*, no. 116.

37 There is no evidence that Alvaro Rodríguez ever held the governorship of Toledo.

38 Alvaro Rodríguez was descended from Alvar Fáñez through his mother, Urraca Alvarez: Salazar Acha, 'Una familia', p. 53.

39 I have followed the reading given in the MSS: *Cognitus omnibus est avus Alvarus, arx probitatis, Nec minus hostibus extitit impius urbs bonitatis.* On the difficulties presented by these verses, see Gil (ed.), *Prefatio de Almaria*, p. 262; cf. Sánchez Belda, *Chronica*, p. 178 and n. 111; Pérez González, *Crónica*, p. 138, n. 203.

40 The verse demonstrates that our poet was well-acquainted with the legend of Roland, although whether via a Castilian translation of the vernacular *Chanson de Roland*, or via a Latin epic poem on the same subject, has been a matter for lengthy but inconclusive debate: see Salvador Martínez, *El 'Poema de Almería'*, pp. 267–344.

41 *comites domuit quoque nostros.* Ramón Menéndez Pidal believed this was a reference to Count García Ordóñez and Count Berenguer Ramón II of Barcelona, both of whom suffered humiliation in battle at the hands of the Cid: R. Menéndez Pidal (ed.), *Cantar de Mio Cid*, 3 vols (3rd edn., Madrid, 1954), I, p. 23. By contrast, Antonio

used to consider himself of lesser reputation. But I proclaim the truth which the passage of time will not alter: My Cid was the first, and Alvar the second. Valencia wept at the death of her friend Rodrigo, / [240] the servants of Christ could not delay it any longer. O Alvar! the tears of the young men whom you raised with such care and whom you knighted[42] mourn you and honour you with their tears. By supporting the great in battle you gave heart to the young.[43] Descended from such great and so noble ancestors, /[245] behold Alvaro flies into a rage, for he truly hates the Moors. Navia[44] sends troops, Montenegro also provides many and the land of Lugo lends protection with the sword. Horsemen are not lacking, for, being rich, it provided many. Equipped for everything, having prepared their supplies with care, /[250] they mount their mules, and riderless horses go ahead too, led by squires carrying shields on their shoulders. Now they drew near to the camp and saw the smoke.[45] The king saw

Ubieto Arteta argued that it was unlikely that our poet, who was perhaps of Catalan extraction, would have referred to these magnates, one a Castilian and the other a Catalan, as *comites nostri*, and suggested that he was referring to Berenguer Ramón II of Barcelona and his nephew and successor Count Ramón Berenguer III: Ubieto Arteta, 'Sugerencias', 322–3. However, there is no evidence that the Cid ever defeated Ramón Berenguer III in battle, although the latter is reported to have lifted the siege of Oropesa in 1098 on hearing that the Cid was coming to fight him. Instead, one might speculate either that the *comites nostri* our poet had in mind were the various Catalan princes, among them the counts of Ampurdán, Cerdaña and Besalú, who, with Count Berenguer Ramón II of Barcelona, were routed by the Cid at Almenar in 1082, or else, as Salvador Martínez suggested, that the poet's tribute to the Cid was simply an *elogio genérico* applicable to all the Christian counts who suffered at the hands of the *Campeador*: HR, chs 14–16, 70; Salvador Martínez, El 'Poema de Almería', p. 395, n. 67.

42 *Quos bene nutristi, quibus et pius arma dedisti.*

43 The above verses, in which Alvar Fáñez is associated with the Cid, have given rise to considerable debate among scholars. The reference to *Ipse Rodericus, Mio Cidi sepe uocatus, De quo cantatur quod ab hostibus haud superatur* clearly indicates that our poet was aware of the existence of a contemporary poem (or even poems) on the Cid, but whether he had in mind a vernacular work, perhaps a precursor of the celebrated early thirteenth-century *Poema de mio Cid*, or a Latin composition, such as the *Carmen Campi Doctoris*, we simply do not know: Salvador Martínez, El 'Poema de Almería', pp. 345–95; J. J. Duggan, The 'Cantar de mio Cid': Poetic Creation in its Economic and Social Contexts (Cambridge, 1989), pp. 128–9; Fletcher, The Quest for El Cid, pp. 189–90. Cf. above, p. 161.

44 According to Sánchez Belda, this is probably the village of Navia de Suarna in the modern province of Lugo: Chronica, p. 269. It is not inconceivable, however, that our poet was referring to the coastal settlement of Navia in the western Asturias, where Alvaro Rodríguez held lordships in nearby Ribadeo and Suarón: Barton, Aristocracy, p. 230, nn. 7 and 9.

45 *Iamque propinquabant castris fumosque uidebant:* a reminiscence of Virgil, Aeneid, ix, 371.

that a cloud of dust covered all the ground, he ordered his escort to mount /[255] and finally receives these warriors with splendour.

Martín, the son of Fernando,[46] orders the weapons to be taken out of the houses: he will inflict great blows upon the Moors. Thus does Hita rejoice, for he is her lord. He is white of face, ample of body and limb, /[260] he is handsome, strong and upright, he has charge of the army. When his voice thunders out the Moors flee in fright. It was he who armed handsome youths with gleaming weapons, the camp of Martín resounds with its youthful throng. The latter despise death, and in so doing they also make themselves brave, /[265] they enjoy themselves more in war than one friend does with another. With their banners raised they enter the king's tent urging the leaders to war: 'Why are you here, laggards?' After uttering such words, which they swear not to be false, they all dismount, and together they seek out the king together with his court /[270] and on bended knee they say to him 'Greetings, good king'. Finally they take up position in the fresh meadows.

I do not wish the illustrious Count Ermengol[47] to be forgotten. He shines like a star among the allied troops, he is respected by Saracens and Christians alike. /[275] If I may say so, he may be compared to anyone, except to kings. Having taken up arms, as is his custom, trusting in God's power, he came with a great escort to the battle, in which he slays many with his sword.

Gutierre Fernández[48] did not arrive late for the campaign, /[280] for he has been entrusted with the tutorship of a king. He is Sancho, the son of our Emperor, who as soon as he was born was entrusted to him to be brought up.[49] He brings him up with care, for he wishes him to surpass all others. Gutierre shares in the greatest honours. /[285] He makes his way into battle advancing in formation.

46 Martín Fernández may be traced with Alfonso VII's army at Calatrava on 4 June 1147, but disappears from the record thereafter: Fletcher, 'Diplomatic and the Cid', 332–3.

47 Ermengol VI of Urgel confirmed the charter issued by Alfonso VII at Baeza on 18 August 1147, shortly before the advance on Almería; the count's presence at the siege is referred to by the Genoese historian Caffaro, who claimed that the count and King García Ramírez IV of Navarre were sent by Alfonso VII to negotiate with the defenders of Almería, from whom they received 100,000 *morabetinos* in return for a promise that the emperor would withdraw: Rodríguez de Lama (ed.), *Colección diplomática*, II, no. 146; Caffaro, *De captione Almerie et Tortuose*, p. 27.

48 Gutierre Fernández may be traced at the court of Alfonso VII throughout 1147: Barton, *The Aristocracy*, p. 178.

49 That is, the future Sancho III of Castile (1157–58).

The beloved son-in-law of the Emperor, García by name, having slackened the reins, also hastens to war carrying the royal standards.[50] All Pamplona joins with Alava, and Navarre shone with the sword. / [290] Supported by these regions, the son of Ramiro, although he was later related to the king,[51] delights securely in the battle. Rejoicing at his arrival, all Hispania receives him like a lord, for they know that he is dear to the king: he is no different from any other kings, he is even their equal in the whirl of his lance.

/[295] With such reinforcements the king's camp is filled. Strengthened with such and so many columns, Hispania, her banners unfurled, takes possession of the outskirts of Andújar. Andújar was the first to taste the wine of suffering, when she was besieged by command of the majestic Emperor. /[300] This fortress is demolished, just as that of Almería is destroyed.[52] She cries out to Baal, but Baal is deaf to her; he refuses to give help, for he is unable to lend it. Thus, for three months their harvests are lost everywhere, they lose all that their labour had produced. /[305] Their strength having been exhausted, their provisions all consumed, and having given hostages, they seek a truce. Unable to survive, they surrender themselves and their property to the king. The noble castle of Baños[53] also surrenders. Illustrious Bariona,[54] the crown having been reluctantly spurned,[55] /[310] surrenders to the invincible standards of the Emperor. Another noble town, which

50 The presence of García Ramírez IV, king of Navarre, on the Almería campaign is confirmed by documentary and narrative sources alike: Rodríguez de Lama (ed.), *Colección diplomática*, II, no. 146; Caffaro, *De captione Almerie et Tortuose*, p. 27. Once the Almería campaign had concluded, the Navarrese monarch accompanied Alfonso VII to Toledo where, on 25 and 29 December 1147, he witnessed the emperor's charters as *Ego rex Garsias Pampilone qui tunc ueneram in auxilio imperatoris ad rapiendam Almariam*: Recuero Astray *et al.* (eds), *Documentos*, no. 117; Hernández (ed.), *Cartularios*, no. 59 (where dated 28 December).

51 The statement is puzzling given that García Ramírez had married into the Leonese royal house three years before the Almería campaign began: see above, *CAI*, i, 91–4. It is just possible that the poet is referring to the subsequent betrothal of the emperor's eldest son, Sancho, to the king of Navarre's daughter, Blanca, which probably took place some time during 1150: Reilly, *Alfonso VII*, p. 110.

52 Andújar had been besieged by 17 July 1147: see above, n. 36.

53 This is probably Baños de la Encina, near La Carolina in the modern province of Jaén.

54 *Bariona* cannot be identified with any certainty; Gil suggests Bailén, about 20 kilometres east of Andújar: *Prefatio de Almaria*, p. 265.

55 If *spreta* (rather than *scripta*) is the more plausible reading, the sense might be that the inhabitants of Bariona had not wanted to oppose Alfonso VII, but were forced to by their leaders: see Gil (ed.), *Prefatio de Almaria*, p. 265. Either way, the meaning of the verse remains obscure.

bears the name of Baeza, seeing so many banners, shaken with great trembling, once it has laid to one side its former pride, lowers its neck and gladly surrenders, since it cannot rebel.[56] /[315] The other castles of the Moors which are in the vicinity, plead for their lives as a reward, while they surrender everything. Once this has been granted, they revive their exhausted bodies.

Count Manrique, a sincere friend of Christ, valiant in warfare, is placed in charge of all these towns.[57] /[320] He was liked by all, just as he was liked by the Emperor, so that he shone among Saracens and Christians alike. Illustrious in reputation and beloved by all, bountiful and generous, he was niggardly to no man. He was skilled in arms, he possessed the mind of a sage, /[325] he delighted in battle and was a master of the science of war. He took after his father in everything that he did. His father was Count Pedro of Lara,[58] who ruled his own land for many years. The son also follows in all his father's footsteps. /[330] Still in the flower of youth, but enriched with honour and respected by the Emperor as is his nature, he was the upholder of the law, the worst scourge of the Moors.

When all that we have described had been completed and fulfilled, when the time of the campaign had expired, /[335] the citizens return in victory to the walls of their fathers, in the manner of their ancestors, except for a few who are retained through the king's foresight.[59]

56 Baeza had been conquered by 18 August 1147, when Alfonso VII made a grant of property to the Navarrese knight Rodrigo de Azagra in recognition of his sterling service during the capture of the town: Rodríguez de Lama (ed.), *Colección diplomática*, II, no. 146.

57 The presence of Count Manrique Pérez de Lara in the entourage of Alfonso VII during the Almería campaign can be amply confirmed by documentary sources: Barton, *Aristocracy*, p. 178. As the poet indicates, the count was awarded the lordship of Baeza immediately after the conquest of the town, being styled *dominans in Toleto and Baecia* in the emperor's charter of 18 August 1147: see above, n. 56.

58 See above, *CAI*, i, 3, 6, 9, 14, 18, 50; ii, 19.

59 The poet's statement that Alfonso VII allowed many of his troops to return home after the fall of Baeza is confirmed by Caffaro, who records that the emperor disbanded his army and retained only 400 knights and 1000 foot-soldiers: Caffaro, *De captione Almerie et Tortuose*, pp. 23–4. It is likely that those who were allowed to return north in August 1147 were members of the municipal militias whose term of service was limited, perhaps to a maximum of three months: Powers, *A Society Organized for War*, pp. 116–18; cf. Reilly, *Alfonso VII*, pp. 98–9. Later chroniclers, however, regarded the withdrawal of these troops as an act of treachery: see, for example, Lucas of Tuy, *Chronicon Mundi*, ed. A. Schottus, *Hispania illustrata*, IV (Frankfurt, 1608), 1–116, at p. 104; Rodrigo Jiménez de Rada, *Historia*, p. 232. The army that continued south to Almería was presumably made up of the members of the emperor's own military household, such as the Leonese knight García Pérez,

It was the first of August when the distinguished, though bitter for many, messengers of the Franks arrive by sea, and, having greeted the Emperor in their manner, /⌈340⌉ the messengers speak as follows: 'O Glory of the entire kingdom, illustrious honour, the brilliant youth of the Franks loyally salutes you with sails unfurled, and awaits you on the seashore with their armed knights. Your brother-in-law Ramón, just as he promised, /⌈345⌉ is marching furiously towards the enemy,[60] and the people of Pisa are arriving at the same time as those of Genoa.[61] Count William of Montpellier, great among his class, is following them in his great and powerful ship.[62] They are very well armed, prepared for fierce battles, /⌈350⌉ they are mindful of the agreement: now finally reaching port, they also bring hard stones against the Moors. A thousand ships they command,[63] loaded with decorated weapons and delicious foods. They say that you are late,[64] they will fight for the plundered gold once battle commences, /⌈355⌉ and they will certainly slay your enemies with pleasure. The admirable troop does not require anyone's help, if it is supported by your present glory.'

When they had spoken such words thus, the messengers fell silent. The Emperor's mind smiles as he hears such things, /⌈360⌉ but the brave cohorts become restless at such words. Each man, weeping, speaks in this way to his dear comrade:[65] 'Until now in all places wars

---

who was subsequently rewarded for his service at Almería, the great nobles and bishops of the realm, and their knights. For the grant to García Pérez, see above, n. 11.

60 Ramón Berenguer IV was reportedly accompanied to Almería by a contingent of 53 knights: Caffaro, *De captione Almerie et Tortuose*, p. 24. The count had departed for Almería by 7 September 1147, according to a charter of that date drawn up *anno quo comes Barchinonensis et princeps Aragonie ivit cum Ieuensibus usque ad Almariam*: Durán Gudiol (ed.), *Colección diplomática*, I, no. 181.

61 The presence of Pisan troops at Almería is not recorded by Caffaro, or indeed any other source.

62 The previous year, Alfonso VII had sent Bishop Arnaldo of Astorga to William VI of Montpellier and had received an undertaking from the count that he would take part in the Almería campaign: see above, *CAI*, ii, 108.

63 This is something of an exaggeration: the Genoese fleet comprised 63 galleys and 163 other ships, according to Caffaro: *De captione Almerie et Tortuose*, p. 22.

64 A similar complaint is voiced by Caffaro, who records that the messengers who visited Alfonso VII at Baeza were led by the Genoese general Otto di Bonovillano: Caffaro, *De captione Almerie et Tortuose*, pp. 23–4. Under the terms of the treaty of September 1146, both sides had agreed to besiege Almería the following May; the *CAI* records, however, that Alfonso VII and the Genoese agreed to begin the siege at the beginning of August: see above, ii, 107 and n. 218.

65 *Proximus ad socium lacrimans sic fatur amicum*: an echo of Virgil, *Aeneid*, vi, 1.

have mingled with other wars. These tidings have pleased the king, but they are bitter to us. The enemy is everywhere like posts on the roadside; /[365] the road is too long and sowed with many spines. No food or drink remains in the saddlebags, the warlike sword pursues us on all sides. O the gleam of coveted silver, the flash of a talent, would that you had not been placed on our left side![66] /[370] For a little gold we will be cut down by the sword on the battlefield, our wives will surely please other husbands, and the children will weep when others take over our beds, and the birds of the sky tear our flesh apart.'

Among the bishops who are present /[375] is the prelate of Astorga,[67] whose glorious sword shines brightly, who, seeing this, comforts the cohorts more than his fellows, and addresses the troops who were already on the point of collapse. With shouts and with his right hand he achieves a great silence. 'May the glory of heaven sing unto [the Lord] on high', he said. /[380] 'And may there be peace on earth to the people who serve the Lord. Now it is necessary that each one confesses fully and fairly, and is aware that the sweet doors of paradise are open to him. Have faith in God, I beseech you, for He is truly the God of gods and also the Lord of all lords, /[385] who alone has gladly performed miracles for us. And the heavens show...'[68]

66 For the ancients the left hand was associated with theft and avarice: Pérez González, *Crónica*, p. 143, n. 227.

67 Arnaldo, bishop of Astorga, may be traced with Alfonso VII's army at Andújar on 17 July 1147, but he does not appear in the witness-lists to any of the subsequent charters issued by the emperor that year: see above, n. 36.

68 All the MSS break off at this point. Given that the poem cuts off in the middle of a verse, it is highly unlikely that the rest of the poem has been lost due to the mutilation of the archetype MS. One can only conclude that, for whatever reason, our poet was unable to continue with his work: Sánchez Belda, *Chronica*, pp. xx–xxi; Salvador Martínez, *El 'Poema de Almería'*, p. 127.

BIBLIOGRAPHY

For a comprehensive bibliographical guide to Hispano-Latin historical writing in the Iberian peninsula between the eighth and twelfth centuries, see M. Huete Fudio, *La historiografía latina medieval en la Península Ibérica (siglos VIII–XII): fuentes y bibliografía* (Madrid, 1997).

Primary sources

'Abd Allāh, *The Tibyān. Memoirs of 'Abd Allāh b. Buluggīn, last Zirid amir of Granada*, trans. A. T. Tibi (Leiden, 1986).

Adémar of Chabannes, *Chronique*, ed. J. Chavanon (Paris, 1897).

Ayala Martínez, C. de (ed.), *Libro de privilegios de la Orden de San Juan de Jerusalén en Castilla y León (siglos XII–XV)* (Madrid, 1995).

Azevedo, R. de (ed.), *Documentos medievais portugueses: documentos régios*, I (Lisbon, 1958).

Barrios García, A. (ed.), *Documentación medieval de la catedral de Avila* (Salamanca, 1981).

Berganza, F. de (ed.), *Antigüedades de España*, 2 vols (Madrid, 1721), II.

Blanco Lozano, P. (ed.), *Colección diplomática de Fernando I (1037–1065)* (León, 1987).

Bruel, A. (ed.), *Recueil des chartes de l'abbaye de Cluny*, 6 vols (Paris, 1876–1903).

Caffaro, *De captione Almerie et Tortuose*, ed. A. Ubieto Arteta (Valencia, 1973).

Casariego, J. E. (trans.), *Crónicas de los reinos de Asturias y León* (León, 1985).

Caspar, E. (ed.), *Gregorii VII Registrum* (Berlin, 1920–23; repr. 1955).

Castro Guisasola, F. (ed. and trans.), *El Cantar de la conquista de Almería por Alfonso VII: un poema hispano-latino del siglo XII* (Almería, 1992).

Durán Gudiol, A. (ed.), *Colección diplomática de la catedral de Huesca*, 2 vols (Zaragoza, 1965).

Erdmann, C. (ed.), *Papsturkunden in Portugal* (Göttingen, 1927).

Falque Rey, E. (trans.), 'Traducción de la "Historia Roderici"', *Boletín de la Institución Fernán González* 62 (1983), 339–75.

— (ed.), *Historia Compostellana*, CCCM 70 (Turnhout, 1988).

— (ed.), *Historia Roderici vel Gesta Roderici Campidocti*, in *Chronica Hispana saeculi XII*, Part I, CCCM 71 (Turnhout, 1990), 1–98.

— (trans.), *Historia Compostelana* (Madrid, 1994).

Falque Rey, E., J. Gil, and A. Maya (eds), *Chronica Hispana saeculi XII*, Part I, CCCM 71 (Turnhout, 1990).

Fear, A. T. (trans.), *Lives of the Visigothic Fathers*, Translated Texts for Historians, vol. 26 (Liverpool, 1997).

Fernández Flórez, J. A. (ed.), *Colección diplomática del monasterio de Sahagún (857–1300)*, IV (1110–1199) (León, 1991).

Flórez, E. (ed.), *Chronicon Lusitanum*, in *ES* 14 (Madrid, 1758), 402–19.

— *Chronicon Compostellanum*, in *ES* 20 (Madrid, 1765), 608–13.

— *Chronicon Iriense*, in *ES* 20 (Madrid, 1765), 598–608.

— *Chronica Adefonsi Imperatoris*, in *ES* 21 (Madrid, 1766), 320–409.

— *Annales Complutenses*, in *ES* 23 (Madrid, 1767), 310–14.

— *Anales Toledanos*, in *ES* 23 (Madrid, 1767), 381–423.

Floriano Cumbreño, A. (ed.), *Colección diplomática del monasterio de Belmonte* (Oviedo, 1960).

García Larragueta, S. (ed.), *Colección de documentos de la catedral de Oviedo* (Oviedo, 1962).

García Luján, J. A. (ed.), *Privilegios reales de la catedral de Toledo (1086–1462)*, 2 vols (Toledo, 1982).

Gil, J. (ed.), *Prefatio de Almaria*, in *Chronica Hispana saeculi XII*, Part I, CCCM 71 (Turnhout, 1990), 249–67.

Gómez Moreno, M. (trans.), *Introducción a la Historia Silense con versión castellana de la misma y de la Crónica de Sampiro* (Madrid, 1921).

Gregory the Great, *Dialogorum Liber.* A. de Vogüé (ed.), *Grégoire le Grand, Dialogues*, Sources Chrétiennes, vol. 260 (Paris, 1979).

— *Homiliae in Evangelia, PL* 76.

Guérard, M. (ed.), *Cartulaire de l'abbaye de Saint-Victor de Marseille*, 2 vols (Paris, 1857).

Hernández, F. J. (ed.), *Los Cartularios de Toledo: catálogo documental* (Madrid, 1985).

Huici Miranda, A. (ed.), *Las crónicas latinas de la Reconquista*, 2 vols (Valencia, 1913).

Ibn al-Kardabūs, *Historia de al-Andalus (Kitāb al-Iktifā')*, trans. F. Maíllo Salgado (Madrid, 1986).

Ibn 'Idhārī, *La caída del Califato de Córdoba y los reyes de Taifas (al-Bayān al-Mugrib)*, trans. F. Maíllo Salgado (Salamanca, 1993).

Imperiale di Sant'Angelo, C. (ed.), *Codice diplomatico della Repubblica di Genova*, I (Rome, 1936).

Inventario General de Manuscritos de la Biblioteca Nacional, IV (Madrid, 1958).

Jaffé, P., S. Loewenfeld *et al.* (eds), *Regesta Pontificum Romanorum ad annum 1198*, 2 vols (Leipzig, 1885).

Lacarra, J. M. (ed.), 'Documentos para el estudio de la reconquista y repoblación del valle del Ebro', *Estudios de Edad Media de la Corona de Aragón 2* (1946), 169–574.

Lema Pueyo, J. A. (ed.), *Colección diplomática de Alfonso I de Aragón y Pamplona (1104–1134)* (San Sebastián, 1990).

Lucas Alvarez, M., *El reino de León en la alta Edad Media*, vol. V: *Las cancillerías reales (1109–1230)* (León, 1993).

Lucas of Tuy, *Chronicon Mundi*, ed. A. Schottus, *Hispania illustrata*, IV (Frankfurt, 1608), 1–116.

Mañueco Villalobos, M. and J. Zurita Nieto (eds), *Documentos de la Iglesia Colegial de Santa María la Mayor de Valladolid*, 3 vols (Valladolid, 1917–20).

Martín López, M. E. (ed.), *Patrimonio cultural de San Isidoro de León I/1: Documentos de los siglos X–XIII. Colección diplomática* (León, 1995).

Martín Martín, J. L. (ed.), *Documentación medieval de la iglesia catedral de Coria* (Salamanca, 1989).

Martín Martín, J. L., L. M. Villar García, F. Marcos Rodríguez and M. Sánchez Rodríguez (eds), *Documentos de los archivos catedralicio y diocesano de Salamanca (siglos XII–XIII)* (Salamanca, 1977).

Maya Sánchez, A. (ed.), *Chronica Adefonsi Imperatoris*, in *Chronica Hispana saeculi XII*, Part I, CCCM 71 (Turnhout, 1990), 109–248.

Melville, C. and A. Ubaydli (ed. and trans.), *Christians and Moors in Spain, vol. III, Arabic sources (711–1501)* (Warminster, 1992).

Menéndez Pidal, R. (ed.), *Cantar de Mio Cid*, 3 vols (3rd edn., Madrid, 1954–6).

Michael, I. (ed.), *The Poem of the Cid* (Manchester, 1975).

Migne, J.-P., (ed.), *Patrologia cursus completus. Series Latina*, 217 vols (Paris, 1844–64).

Monterde Albiac, C. (ed.), *Diplomatario de la reina Urraca de Castilla y León (1109–1126)* (Zaragoza, 1996).

Muñoz y Romero, T. (ed.), *Colección de fueros municipales y cartas pueblas* (Madrid, 1847).

Núñez Contreras, L. (ed.), 'Colección diplomática de Vermudo III, rey de León', *Historia. Instituciones. Documentos* 4 (1977), 381–514.

Orderic Vitalis, *The Ecclesiastical History*, ed. and trans. M. Chibnall, 6 vols (Oxford, 1969–80).

Pelayo of Oviedo, *Crónica del obispo Don Pelayo*, ed. B. Sánchez Alonso (Madrid, 1924).

Pérez Celada, J. A. (ed.), *Documentación del monasterio de San Zoilo de Carrión* (Burgos, 1986).

Pérez González, M. (trans.), *Crónica del Emperador Alfonso VII* (León, 1997).

Pérez de Urbel, J. and A. González Ruiz-Zorrilla (eds), *Historia Silense. Edición crítica e introducción* (Madrid, 1959).

Rassow, P. (ed.), 'Die Urkunden Kaiser Alfons VII. von Spanien', *Archiv für Urkundenforschung* 11 (1930), 66–137.

Recuero Astray, M., M. González Vázquez and P. Romero Portilla (eds), *Documentos medievales del Reino de Galicia: Alfonso VII (1116–1157)* (Santiago de Compostela, 1998).

Rodrigo Jiménez de Rada, *Historia de rebus Hispanie sive Historia Gothica*, ed. J. Fernández Valverde, CCCM 72 (Turnholt, 1987).

Rodríguez de Lama, I. (ed.), *Colección diplomática de la Rioja: Documentos, 923–1168*, II (2nd edn., Logroño, 1992).

Romaní Martínez, M. (ed.), *Colección diplomática do mosteiro cisterciense de Sta María de Oseira (Ourense) (1025–1310)*, I (Santiago de Compostela, 1989).

Ruiz Asencio, J. M. (ed.), *Colección documental del Archivo de la Catedral de León (775–1230)*, vol. III (986–1031) (León, 1987); vol. IV (1032–1109) (León, 1990).

Sánchez Belda, L. (ed.), *Chronica Adefonsi Imperatoris* (Madrid, 1950).

Sandoval, P. de, *Chronica del ínclito Emperador de España Don Alfonso VII deste nombre, rey de Castilla y León, hijo de Don Ramón de Borgoña y de Doña Hurraca, reyna propietaria de Castilla* (Madrid, 1600).

Santos Coco, F. (ed.), *Historia Silense* (Madrid, 1921).

Smith, C. (ed. and trans.), *Christians and Moors in Spain, vol. I: AD 711–1150* (Warminster, 1988).

— Ubieto Arteta, A. (ed.), *Colección diplomática de Pedro I de Aragón y Navarra* (Zaragoza, 1951).

— (ed.), *Crónica Najerense* (Valencia, 1966).

— (ed.), *Cartularios (I, II y III) de Santo Domingo de la Calzada* (Zaragoza, 1978).

— (ed.), *Crónicas anónimas de Sahagún* (Zaragoza, 1987).

— (ed.), *Documentos de Ramiro II de Aragón* (Zaragoza, 1988).

Valcarcel, V. (ed.), *La 'Vita Dominici Silensis' de Grimaldo* (Logroño, 1982).

Vielliard, J. (ed.), *Le guide du pèlerin de Saint-Jacques de Compostelle* (Paris, 1963).

Villar García, L. (ed.), *Documentación medieval de la catedral de Segovia (1115–1300)* (Salamanca, 1990).

Wolf, K. B. (trans.), *Conquerors and Chroniclers of Early Medieval Spain*, Translated Texts for Historians, vol. 9 (Liverpool, 1990).

Wright, R. (ed. and trans.), 'The first poem on the Cid – the *Carmen Campi Doctoris*', in *Papers of the Liverpool Latin Seminar*, II, ed. F. Cairns (Liverpool, 1979), 213–48; repr., with an updating postscript, in Wright, *Early Ibero-Romance*, pp. 221–64.

Secondary works

Alemany, J., 'Milicias cristianas al servicio de los sultanes musulmanes del Almagreb', in *Homenaje a D. Francisco Codera* (Zaragoza, 1904), 133–69.

Antonio, N., *Bibliotheca hispana vetus* (Rome, 1696).

Barrios García, A., *La catedral de Avila en la Edad Media* (Avila, 1973).

Bartlett, R., *Trial by Fire and Water. The Medieval Judicial Ordeal* (Oxford, 1986).

Barton, S., 'Two Catalan magnates in the courts of the kings of León–Castile: the careers of Ponce de Cabrera and Ponce de Minerva re-examined', *JMH* 18 (1992), 233–66.

— 'The count, the bishop and the abbot: Armengol VI of Urgel and the abbey of Valladolid', *English Historical Review* 111 (1996), 85–103.

— *The Aristocracy in Twelfth-century León and Castile* (Cambridge, 1997).

— 'From Tyrants to Soldiers of Christ: the nobility of twelfth-century León–Castile and the struggle against Islam', *Nottingham Medieval Studies* (forthcoming).

— 'Spain in the Eleventh Century', in *The New Cambridge Medieval History*, IV, eds D. Luscombe and J. Riley-Smith (forthcoming).

Beer, R., 'Die Handschriften des Klosters Santa Maria de Ripoll', *Sitzungsberichte der Philosophisch–historiche Klasse der Kaiserlichen Akademie der Wissenschaften in Wien* 155 (1908), III, Abhandlung; 158 (1908), II. Abhandlung.

Benito Ruano, E., 'Alfonso Jordan, Conde de Toulouse', in *Estudios sobre Alfonso VI y la reconquista de Toledo* (Toledo, 1987), 83–98.

Bensch, S. B., *Barcelona and its Rulers 1096–1291* (Cambridge, 1995).

Bishko, C. J., 'The Liturgical Context of Fernando I's last days according to the so-called *Historia Silense*', *Hispania Sacra* 17–18 (1964–5), 47–59; reprinted in Bishko, *Spanish and Portuguese Monastic History 600–1300* (London, 1984), no. VII.

— 'Fernando I y los orígenes de la alianza castellana–leonesa con Cluny', *CHE* 47–8 (1968), 31–135, and 49–50 (1969), 50–116; English translation in Bishko, *Studies in Medieval Spanish Frontier History* (London, 1980), no. II.

Bisson, T. N., *The Medieval Crown of Aragon. A Short History* (Oxford, 1986).

Blázquez y Delgado Aguilera, A., 'Elogio de Don Pelayo, obispo de Oviedo y historiador de España', *Memorias de la Real Academia de la Historia* 12 (1910), 439–92.

268 BIBLIOGRAPHY

Bonnassie, P., *La Catalogne du milieu du Xe à la fin du XIe siècle: croissance et mutations d'une société*, 2 vols (Toulouse, 1975–76).

Bosch Vilá, J., *Los Almorávides* (Tetuán, 1956; repr. Granada, 1990).

— *Albarracín Musulmán* (Teruel, 1959).

Bull, M., *Knightly piety and and the lay response to the First Crusade: the Limousin and Gascony, c. 970–c.1130* (Oxford, 1993).

Caldwell, S. H., 'Urraca of Zamora and San Isidoro de León: fulfilment of a legacy', *Woman's Art Journal* 7 (1986), 19–25.

Calleja Puerta, M., 'Una genealogía leonesa del siglo XII: la descendencia de Vermudo II en la obra cronística de Pelayo de Oviedo', in *La nobleza peninsular en la Edad Media* (León, 1999), 527–39.

Canal Sánchez-Pagín, J. M., 'La Infanta Doña Elvira, hija de Alfonso VI y de Gimena Muñoz, a la luz de los diplomas', *Archivos Leoneses* 33 (1979), 271–87.

— '¿Crónica Silense o Crónica Domnis Sanctis?', *CHE* 63/64 (1980), 94–103.

— 'Jimena Muñoz, amiga de Alfonso VI', *Anuario de Estudios Medievales* 21 (1991), 11–40.

Carro García, J., 'El privilegio de Alfonso VII al monasterio de Anteltares', *Cuadernos de Estudios Gallegos* 7 (1952), 145–57.

Carter, P., 'The historical context of William of Malmesbury's Miracles of the Virgin Mary', in *The Writing of History in the Middle Ages. Essays presented to Richard William Southern*, eds R. H. C. Davis and J. M. Wallace-Hadrill (Oxford, 1981), 127–65.

Codera, F., *Decadencia y desaparición de los Almorávides en España* (Zaragoza, 1899).

Collins, R., *The Basques* (Oxford, 1986).

— *Early Medieval Spain. Unity in Diversity 400–1000* (2nd edn., London, 1995).

— *Spain. An Oxford Archaeological Guide* (Oxford, 1998).

Constable, G., 'The Second Crusade as seen by Contemporaries', *Traditio* 9 (1953), 213–79.

Cowdrey, H. E. J., *Pope Gregory VII 1073–1085* (Oxford, 1998).

David, P., *Etudes historiques sur la Galice et le Portugal du VIe au XIIe siècle* (Paris, 1947).

Deyermond, A. D., *Epic Poetry and the Clergy: Studies on the 'Mocedades de Rodrigo'* (London, 1969).

Díaz y Díaz, M. C., 'Isidoro en la edad media hispana', in *Isidoriana* (León, 1961), 345–87; repr. in Díaz y Díaz, *De Isidoro al siglo XII. Ocho estudios sobre la vida literaria peninsular* (Barcelona, 1976), 141–201.

Duggan, J. J., *The 'Cantar de mio Cid': Poetic Creation in its Economic and Social Contexts* (Cambridge, 1989).

Durán Gudiol, A., *La Iglesia de Aragón durante los reinados de Sancho Ramírez y Pedro I* (Rome, 1962).

Escalona, R., *Historia del Real Monasterio de Sahagún* (Madrid, 1782).

Estepa Díez, C., *Estructura social de la ciudad de León (siglos X–XIII)* (León, 1977).

Falque Rey, E., 'Cartas entre el Conde Berenguer de Barcelona y Rodrigo Díaz de Vivar', *Habis* 12 (1981), 123–37.

Fernández Conde, F. J., *El Libro de los Testamentos de la catedral de Oviedo* (Rome, 1971).

— 'La obra del obispo ovetense D. Pelayo en la historiografía española', *Boletín del Instituto de Estudios Asturianos* 25 (1971), 249–91.

— 'La reina Urraca "la Asturiana"', *Asturiensia Medievalia* 2 (1975), 65–94.

Fernández del Pozo, J. M., 'Alfonso V, rey de León', in *León y su historia: miscelánea histórica* 5 (León, 1984), 9–262.

Ferrari, A., 'El Cluniacense Pedro de Poitiers y la *Chronica Adefonsi Imperatoris* y *Poema de Almería*', *BRAH* 153 (1963), 153–204.

Ferreras, J., *Synopsis histórica chronológica de España*, XVI (Madrid, 1775).

Fita, F., 'El monasterio toledano de San Servando en la segunda mitad del siglo XI: estudio crítico', *BRAH* 49 (1906), 280–331.

Fletcher, R., 'Diplomatic and the Cid revisited: the seals and mandates of Alfonso VII', *JMH* 2 (1976), 305–38.

— *The Episcopate in the Kingdom of León in the twelfth century* (Oxford, 1978).

— *Saint James's Catapult. The Life and Times of Diego Gelmírez of Santiago de Compostela* (Oxford, 1984).

— 'Reconquest and Crusade in Spain *c*. 1050–1150', *Transactions of the Royal Historical Society*, 5th series, 37 (1987), 31–47.

— *The Quest for El Cid* (London, 1989).

— *Moorish Spain* (London, 1992).

— 'The Early Middle Ages', in *Spain: a History*, ed. R. Carr (Oxford, 2000), 48–68.

— 'A Twelfth-Century View of the Spanish Past', in *The Medieval State. Essays presented to James Campbell*, eds J. R. Maddicott and D. M. Palliser (London: 2000), pp. 147–61.

Flórez, E., M. Risco *et al.*, *España Sagrada*, 51 vols (Madrid, 1747–1879).

Forey, A. J., 'The Will of Alfonso I of Aragon and Navarre', *Durham University Journal* 73 (1980), 59–65.

Frank, I., 'Reverter, vicomte de Barcelone (vers 1130–1145)', *Boletín de la Real Academia de Buenas Letras de Barcelona* 26 (1954–56), 195–204.

French, P., *Younghusband* (London, 1994).

García Calles, L., *Doña Sancha, hermana del Emperador* (Barcelona and León, 1972).

García Gallo, A., 'El Concilio de Coyanza: contribución al estudio del Derecho Canónico español en la Alta Edad Media', *AHDE* 20 (1950), 275–633.

— 'Los fueros de Toledo', *AHDE* 45 (1975), 341–488.

García García, M. E., 'El conde asturiano Gonzalo Peláez', *Asturiensia Medievalia* 2 (1975), 39–64.

García Gómez, E. and R. Menéndez Pidal, 'El conde mozárabe Sisnando Davídez y la política de Alfonso VI con los Taifas', *Al-Andalus* 12 (1947), 27–41.

García González, J., 'Traición y alevosía en la alta edad media', *AHDE* 32 (1962), 323–45.

Garí, B., 'Why Almería? An Islamic port in the compass of Genoa', *JMH* 18 (1992), 211–31.

Gillingham, J., 'Conquering the barbarians: war and chivalry in twelfth-century Britain', *Haskins Society Journal* 4 (1993), 67–84.

Gómez Moreno, M., *Introducción a la Historia Silense* (Madrid, 1921).

González, J., *El reino de Castilla en la época de Alfonso VIII*, 3 vols (Madrid, 1960).

— *Repoblación de Castilla la Nueva*, 2 vols (Madrid, 1975–76).

Grassotti, H., 'Homenaje de García Ramírez a Alfonso VII', *CHE* 37–8 (1963), 318–29.

Guallart, J. and M. P. R. Laguzzi,, 'Algunos documentos reales leoneses', *CHE* 2 (1944), 363–81.

Huici Miranda, A., *Historia política del imperio Almohade*, 2 vols (Tetuán, 1956–57).

— 'Contribución al estudio de la dinastía almorávide: el gobierno de Tasfīn ben 'Alī ben Yūsuf en el Andalus', in *Études d'orientalisme dédiées à la mémoire de Lévi-Provençal*, II (Paris, 1962), 605–21.

— *Historia musulmana de Valencia y su región*, 3 vols (Valencia, 1969–70).

Kennedy, H., *Muslim Spain and Portugal: a political history of al-Andalus* (London, 1996).

Lacarra, J. M., 'Alfonso el Batallador y las paces de Támara', *Estudios de Edad Media de la Corona de Aragón* 3 (1947–48), 461–73.

— 'La Reconquista y repoblación del valle del Ebro', in *La Reconquista española y la repoblación del País* (Zaragoza, 1951), 39–83.

— 'Dos tratados de paz y alianza entre Sancho el de Peñalén y Moctadir de Zaragoza (1069 y 1073)', in *Homenaje a Johannes Vincke*, I (Madrid, 1962), 121–34; repr. in Lacarra, *Colonización, parias, repoblación y otros estudios* (Zaragoza, 1981).

Le Goff, J., 'Le rituel symbolique de la vassalité', in Le Goff, *Pour un autre Moyen Âge* (Paris, 1977), 349–420.

Le Jan, R., *Famille et pouvoir dans le monde franc (VIIe–Xe siècle)* (Paris, 1995).

Linehan, P., 'Religion, nationalism and national identity in medieval Spain and Portugal', in *Religion and National Identity*, ed. S. Mews, *Studies in Church History* 18 (Oxford, 1982), 161–99.

— Review of *Chronica Hispana saeculi XII. Part I*, in *Journal of Theological Studies* 43 (1992), 731–7.

— *History and the Historians of Medieval Spain* (Oxford, 1993).

Lomax, D. W., 'La fecha de la *Crónica Najerense*', *Anuario de Estudios Medievales* 9 (1974–9), 405–6.

— *The Reconquest of Spain* (London, 1978).

— 'Catalans in the Leonese Empire', *Bulletin of Hispanic Studies* 59 (1982), 191–7.

Lourie, E., 'The Will of Alfonso I, el Batallador, King of Aragón and Navarre: a reassessment', *Speculum* 50 (1975), 635–51.

McCluskey, R., 'Malleable Accounts: Views of the Past in Twelfth-century Iberia', in *The Perception of the Past in Twelfth-century Europe*, ed. P. Magdalino (London, 1992), 211–25.

— 'The early history of San Isidoro de León (X–XII c.)', *Nottingham Medieval Studies* 38 (1994), 35–59.

McCormick, M., *Eternal Victory. Triumphal rulership in late antiquity, Byzantium, and the early medieval West* (Cambridge, 1987).

MacKay, A., *Spain in the Middle Ages: from Frontier to Empire 1000–1500* (London, 1977).

Mansilla, D., 'La supuesta metropolí de Oviedo', *Hispania Sacra* 8 (1955), 259–74.

Martínez, M. G., 'Regesta de Don Pelayo, obispo de Oviedo', *Boletín del Instituto de Estudios Asturianos* 18 (1964), 211–48.

Martínez Pastor, M., 'La rima en el "Poema de Almería"', *Cuadernos de Filología Clásica* 21 (1988), 73–95.

— 'Virtuosismos verbales en el *Poema de Almería*', *Epos* 4 (1988), 379–87.

— 'La métrica del "Poema de Almería": su carácter cuantitativo', *Cuadernos de Filología Clásica (Estudios Latinos)* 1 (1991), 159–93.

Martínez Sopena, P., 'El conde Rodrigo y los suyos: herencia y expectativa del poder entre los siglos X y XII', in *Relaciones de poder, de producción y parentesco en la Edad Media y Moderna*, ed. R. Pastor (Madrid, 1990), 51–84.

Menéndez Pidal, R., 'Sobre un tratado de paz entre Alfonso el Batallador y Alfonso VII', *BRAH* 111 (1943), 115–31.

— *La España del Cid*, 2 vols (7th edn., Madrid, 1969).

Mundó, A. M., 'Monastic movements in the East Pyrenees', in *Cluniac Monasticism in the Central Middle Ages*, ed. N. Hunt (London, 1971), 98–122.

Nicolau D'Olwer, L., 'L'escola poètica de Ripoll en els segles X–XIII', *Anuari del Institut d'Estudis Catalans* 6 (1915–20), 3–84.

Niermeyer, J. F., *Mediae Latinitatis Lexicon Minus* (Leiden, 1976).

Otero, A., 'La Mejora', *AHDE* 33 (1963), 5–131.

Pastor, R., *Resistencias y luchas campesinas en la época del crecimiento y consolidación de la formación feudal: Castilla y León, siglos X–XIII* (2nd edn., Madrid, 1990).

Pérez González, M., 'Influencias clásicas y bíblicas en la Chronica Adefonsi Imperatoris', in *I Congreso Nacional de Latín Medieval*, ed. M. Pérez González (León, 1995), 349–55.

Pérez Prendes, J. M., 'La potestad legislativa en el reino de León. Notas sobre el Fuero de León, el Concilio de Coyanza y las Cortes de León de 1188', in *El reino de León en la alta Edad Media. I: Cortes, Concilios y Fueros* (León, 1988), 497–545.

Pérez de Urbel, J., *Sampiro, su crónica y la monarquía leonesa en el siglo X* (Madrid, 1952).

Porres Martín-Cleto, J., *Los Anales Toledanos I y II* (Toledo, 1993).

Powell, B., *Epic and Chronicle: the 'Poema de Mio Cid' and the 'Crónica de Veinte Reyes'* (London, 1983).

Powers, J. F., *A Society Organized for War: the Iberian Municipal Militias in the Central Middle Ages, 1000–1284* (Berkeley, 1988).

Pringle, D., *Secular buildings in the Crusader Kingdom of Jerusalem* (Cambridge, 1997).

Quintana Prieto, A., *El obispado de Astorga en los siglos IX y X* (Astorga, 1968).

— *El obispado de Astorga en el siglo XII* (Astorga, 1985).

Reilly, B. F., 'On getting to be a bishop in León–Castile: the "Emperor" Alfonso VII and the Post-Gregorian Church', *Studies in Medieval and Renaissance History* 1 (1978), 37–68.

— *The Kingdom of León–Castilla under Queen Urraca, 1109–1126* (Princeton, 1982).

— (ed.) *Santiago, Saint-Denis, and Saint Peter: The Reception of the Roman Liturgy in León–Castile in 1080* (New York, 1985).

— *The Kingdom of León–Castilla under King Alfonso VI, 1065–1109* (Princeton, 1988).

— *The Contest of Christian and Muslim Spain, 1031–1157* (Oxford, 1992).

— *The Kingdom of León–Castilla under King Alfonso VII, 1126–1157* (Philadelphia, 1998).

Reuter, T., 'Die Unsicherheit auf den Strassen im europäischen Früh- und Hochmittelalter: Täter, Opfer und ihre mittelalterlichen und modernen Betrachter', in *Träger und Instrumentarien des Friedens im Hohen und Späten Mittelalter*, ed. J. Fried, Vorträge und Forschungen XLIII (Sigmaringen, 1996), 169–202.

Rivera Recio, J. F., *La iglesia de Toledo en el siglo XII (1086–1208)*, 2 vols (Toledo, 1966–76).

Rogers, R., *Latin siege warfare in the twelfth century* (Oxford, 1992).

Ruiz Asencio, J. M., 'Rebeliones leonesas contra Vermudo II', *Archivos Leoneses* 23 (1969), 215–41.

Salazar Acha, J. de, 'Una familia de la alta Edad Media: Los Velas y su realidad histórica', *Estudios Genealógicos y Heráldicos* 1 (1985), 19–64.

— 'El linaje castellano de Castro en el siglo XII: consideraciones e hipótesis sobre su orígen', *Anales de la Real Academia Matritense de Heráldica y Genealogía* 1 (1991), 33–68.

— 'Contribución al estudio del reinado de Alfonso VI de Castilla: algunas aclaraciones sobre su política matrimonial', *Anales de la Real Academia Matritense de Heráldica y Genealogía* 2 (1992–93), 299–343.

Salvador Martínez, H., El *'Poema de Almería' y la épica románica* (Madrid, 1975).

Sánchez-Albornoz, C., 'El anónimo continuador de Alfonso III', in Sánchez-Albornoz, *Investigaciones sobre historiografía hispana medieval (siglos VIII al XII)* (Buenos Aires, 1967), 217–23.

— 'Sobre el autor de la llamada Historia Silense', in Sánchez-Albornoz, *Investigaciones sobre historiografía hispana medieval (siglos VIII al XII)* (Buenos Aires, 1967), 224–34.

— *Una ciudad de la España cristiana hace mil años* (10th edn., Madrid, 1984).

Sánchez Alonso, B., *Historia de la historiografía española* (Madrid, 1947).

Sánchez Candeira, A., 'La reina Velasquita de León y su descendencia', *Hispania* 10 (1950), 449–505.

Schimmelpfennig, B., 'Die Anfänge des Heiligen Jahres von Santiago de Compostela im Mittelalter', *JMH* 4 (1978), 285–303.

Serrano, L., *Los Armíldez de Toledo y el monasterio de Tórtoles* (Madrid, 1933).

— *El obispado de Burgos, y Castilla primitiva desde el siglo V al XIII*, 3 vols (Madrid, 1935).

Smith, C., *The Making of the 'Poema de Mio Cid'* (Cambridge, 1983).

— 'A conjecture about the authorship of the *Historia Roderici*', *Journal of Hispanic Research* 2 (1993–4), 175–81.

Sobrequés i Vidal, S., *Els Barons de Catalunya* (Barcelona, 1957).

— *Els Grans Comtes de Barcelona* (2nd edn., Barcelona, 1970).

Sota, F., *Chronica de los Príncipes de Asturias y Cantabria* (Madrid, 1681).

Stafford, P., 'Queens, Nunneries and Reforming Churchmen: Gender, Religious Status and Reform in Tenth- and Eleventh-Century England', *Past and Present* 163 (1999), 3–35.

Stalls, C., *Possessing the Land. Aragon's Expansion into Islam's Ebro Frontier under Alfonso the Battler 1104–1134* (Leiden, 1995).

Suárez Beltrán, S., 'Los origenes y la expansión del culto a las reliquias de San Salvador de Oviedo', in J. I. Ruiz de la Peña Solar (ed.), *Las peregrinaciones a Santiago de Compostela y San Salvador de Oviedo en la Edad Media* (Oviedo, 1993), 37–55.

— *The Art of Medieval Spain AD 500–1200* (Metropolitan Museum of Art, New York, 1993).

Turk, A., *El Reino de Zaragoza en el siglo XI de Cristo (V de la Hégira)* (Madrid, 1978).

Ubieto Arteta, A., 'Sugerencias sobre la "Chronica Adefonsi Imperatoris"', *CHE* 25–6 (1957), 317–26.

— 'La "Historia Roderici" y su fecha de redacción', *Saitabi* 11 (1961), 241–6; repr. in Ubieto Arteta, El *'Cantar de Mio Cid' y algunos problemas históricos* (Valencia, 1973), 170–7.

— *Los 'Tenentes' en Aragón y Navarra en los siglos XI y XII* (Valencia, 1973).

Vázquez de Parga, L., *La División de Wamba* (Madrid, 1943).

Vázquez de Parga, L., J. M. Lacarra and J. Uría Ríu, *Las peregrinaciones a Santiago de Compostela*, 3 vols (Madrid, 1948–49).

Viguera Molíns, M. J., *Los reinos de taifas y las invasiones magrebíes (Al-Andalus del XI al XIII)* (Madrid, 1992).

Villar García, L. M., *La Extremadura castellano–leonesa: guerreros, clérigos y campesinos (711–1252)* (Valladolid, 1986).

West, G., 'La "Traslación del cuerpo de San Isidoro" como fuente de la Historia llamada Silense', *Hispania Sacra* 27 (1974), 365–71.

— *History as Celebration: Castilian and Hispano-Latin Epics and Histories, 1080–1210 AD* (London Ph.D., 1975).

— 'Hero or Saint? Hagiographic elements in the life of the Cid', *Journal of Hispanic Philology* 7 (1983), 87–105.

Williams, J. W., 'San Isidoro in León: Evidence for a New History', *The Art Bulletin* 55 (1973), 170–84.

— 'Generationes Abrahae: Reconquest Iconography in León', *Gesta* 16 (1977), 3–14.

— 'León: the Iconography of the Capital', in *Cultures of Power. Lordship, Status and Process in Twelfth-century Europe*, ed. T. N. Bisson (Philadelphia, 1995), 231–58.

Wreglesworth, J., *The Chronicle of Alfonso III and its significance for the Historiography of the Asturian Kingdom, 718–910 AD* (Leeds D.Phil., 1995).

Wright, R., *Late Latin and Early Romance in Spain and Carolingian France* (Liverpool, 1982).

— 'Twelfth-century Metalinguistics in the Iberian Peninsula (and the *Chronica Adefonsi Imperatoris*)', in *Early Ibero-Romance* (Newark, Delaware, 1994), 277–88.

INDEX

Notes: (i) Homonyms are listed thus: clerical personnel precede lay; kings, queens, princes and princesses, ordered chronologically, precede other lay persons; remaining lay persons are likewise ordered chronologically. (ii) Individual natives of the Christian kingdoms of Spain are listed by given name, not patronymic: 'Rodrigo Díaz', not 'Díaz, Rodrigo'. (iii) An asterisk indicates that the person is to be found on the genealogical table on page xiii. (iv) 'n' after a page reference indicates a note number on that page.

Printed in the United States
207376BV00004B/11/A

9 780719 052262